Advance praise for *A Continuous Struggle*:

"I've been waiting for years for a biography of Martin Sostre worthy of its subject. This is it. Garrett Felber tells an engrossing story of a complex and committed man who dedicated his life to the struggle for liberation of the oppressed with depth and revolutionary love. A new generation will now get to know someone whose contributions have made all our lives more possible. *A Continuous Struggle* will be a mainstay on my shelf and my book recommendations." **—Mariame Kaba**

"Now that Garrett Felber has given us such a deeply researched and compelling biography of Martin Sostre, Sostre's pivotal and far-reaching contributions to the movement against prisons and the broader abolitionist movement can no longer be ignored. This book is more than a biography of a single individual—it charts the collective work that guides us today." **—Angela Y. Davis**

"*A Continuous Struggle* is urgent reading for organizers everywhere. Martin Sostre's project-oriented revolutionary vision gifts us with insights. Garrett Felber vividly shows how Sostre understood the consciousness-expanding power of frequently modest 'objective examples.' As a result, the man's life and this book encourage us to notice the many unsung people who work towards a new society in militantly practical ways." **—Ruth Wilson Gilmore**

"A rigorous examination of Sostre's revolutionary life that offers vital lessons for those seeking to carry on the struggle." **—Orisanmi Burton**

"The radical, indeed revolutionary life of Martin Sostre, a Black Puerto Rican political prisoner, is a remarkable one. He entered prison thinking himself nonpolitical, but learned, through hard-fought struggles and experience, that every time we wrestle with the State (Leviathan) we are engaged with politics. . . . His bio tells the tale of a man who transformed when faced with new challenges, becoming more radical with each transformation. Those students of the '60s, the Black nationalist and the prisoners' rights movement would do well by reading his work." **—Mumia Abu-Jamal**

A Continuous Struggle

A Continuous Struggle

The Revolutionary Life of Martin Sostre

Garrett Felber

Foreword by Robin D. G. Kelley

A Continuous Struggle: The Revolutionary Life of Martin Sostre

ISBN 9781849355902
E-ISBN 9781849355919
Library of Congress Number: 2024949073

AK Press
370 Ryan Avenue #100
Chico, CA 95973
United States
www.akpress.org

AK Press
33 Tower St.
Edinburgh EH6 7BN
Scotland
www.akuk.com

Cover design by Zachary Dean Norman
Printed in the USA on acid-free paper

Contents

Foreword

"I'm not going to submit."
—MARTIN SOSTRE, FROM THE DOCUMENTARY FILM *FRAME-UP!* (1974)

I recently encountered someone wearing a T-shirt that read "More Malcolm Than Martin." To call it a conversation starter is an understatement; this was a provocation. Younger people are more inclined to share the sentiment, whereas students of the long Black freedom movement cite the late King's critique of war and capitalism as evidence of his radical turn. Invariably, "More Malcolm Than Martin" is the sort of pithy slogan that leads down the rabbit hole to tired old debates over the virtues of violence versus nonviolence based on an overly simplistic understanding of Malcolm X and Martin Luther King Jr. Garrett Felber's magnificent book compels us to ask a different question—one guaranteed to shift the conversation in a more productive direction: Which Martin?

A Continuous Struggle: The Revolutionary Life of Martin Sostre brings to light the other radical "Martin" whose impact on postwar liberation movements is immeasurable. A contemporary of King and Malcolm, Martin Ramírez Sostre was arguably more revolutionary than both men. His ought to be a household name in the US, especially for students of social movements and budding abolitionists. This Harlem-born, working-class

Black Puerto Rican with a tenth-grade education had earned a reputation as an outstanding jailhouse lawyer before the other Martin delivered his 1963 "I Have a Dream" speech at the March on Washington. While serving a twelve-year prison sentence in New York, Sostre successfully argued for the right of imprisoned Black Muslims to have access to the Holy Qur'an, and that prison conditions and the punitive treatment meted out to Muslims violated the fourteenth amendment. Upon his release in 1964, Sostre settled in Buffalo, opened *three* radical bookstores that became hubs of Black political activity, and in the wake of the city's 1967 rebellion was arrested on manufactured drug charges and sentenced to forty years in prison.

Alongside Huey Newton, George Jackson, and Angela Davis, Sostre soon became one of the most famous political prisoners in the country. Amnesty International and the writers' group PEN America took up his case, as well as notable celebrities such as Joan Baez, Jean-Paul Sartre, Dr. Benjamin Spock, Jean Genet, Dick Gregory, and Allen Ginsberg. In 1970, just months before Bantam Books released George Jackson's prison letters, *Soledad Brother*, McGraw-Hill published *The Crime of Martin Sostre* by Vincent Copeland, a white veteran labor organizer, Trotskyist, and cofounder of the Workers World Party. *Frame-Up!*, a short documentary on Sostre's case by Pacific Street Films, circulated widely and played a major role in building an international campaign that ultimately pressured New York governor Hugh Carey to grant him clemency in 1975.

A little over a decade after his release, Sostre began to fade from public consciousness, although he never fully retreated from public view or from his commitment to, in his words, "liberation from oppression, in all its manifestations."[1] He spent more than two decades organizing for tenant and housing rights, teaching and creating safe space for Black and Brown youth, and fighting to free political prisoners. Yet, when he died in 2015, no major news outlet carried his obituary.[2] Thanks to a new generation of activist-intellectuals drawn to abolition and Black anarchism, we have seen renewed interest in Sostre spawned by Mariame Kaba, Lorenzo Kom'boa Ervin, Ashanti Alston, Zoé Samudzi, William C. Anderson, and, above all, Felber himself.

A Continuous Struggle is more than a biography; it is a political and intellectual history of a woefully understudied Black revolutionary tradition told through the trials, tribulations, and thought of Martin Sostre. Felber portrays him as an original thinker who moved astutely from Black

nationalism to Marxism to anarchism, working through a broad range of ideologies and analyses that defy any easy categorization. We learn that Sostre was a man of words *and* action. He left no memoir, very few of his speeches were recorded and archived, and his written body of work consists of voluminous correspondence, legal briefs, interviews, and a few important articles. Essays such as "The New Prisoner" and "Martin Luther King Was a Lawbreaker," published in the 1970s, still offer resonant insights for today in arguing for the power and efficacy of militant civil disobedience, and the indivisibility of prison rebellions from liberation struggles in the so-called free world.

Renowned for his eloquence and sharp wit, Sostre nevertheless believed actions spoke louder than words. And he was a man of bold actions. For Buffalo's Black community, his Afro-Asian Bookshop functioned more as a community center, a gathering space for youth (especially after Sostre added a turntable, loudspeakers, and a few crates of hip records), and an informal school for political education. The Afro-Asian Bookshop resembled Lewis Michaux's African National Memorial Bookstore and Una Mulzac's Liberation Bookstore, both in Harlem. In other words, Sostre was not an entrepreneur but, above all, an organizer. The state knew it and thought that locking him up would silence him—a devastating miscalculation. He simply organized inside, becoming one of the most effective prison organizers in history. In 1968, while incarcerated at Green Haven Prison, he was held for thirteen months in solitary confinement for "practicing law without a license" because he was using his considerable skills to help fellow prisoners. In August 1969, he was transferred to Wallkill State Prison, where he led efforts to organize a prisoners' labor union. Three years later, he was sent to Auburn State Prison, where he organized a strike of workers in the license plate shop and was put in solitary for refusing to shave his beard. He was transferred yet again in December 1972 to Clinton Correctional Facility and held in solitary for refusing to shave his beard and submit to rectal exams, for which the guards beat and raped him nearly a dozen times.

Sostre's story is central to understanding the genealogy of the modern abolition movement and its direct links to the eighteenth- and nineteenth-century anti-slavery movement. Radical Black abolition is rooted not in pacifism or sentimentality but in the rebellions of the enslaved, including mutinies on the floating dungeons used to transport captured Africans across the Atlantic. In other words, abolition was a

militant and military response to what John Brown called "a most barbarous, unprovoked, and unjustifiable war of one portion of its citizens upon another portion."[3] Anthropologist Orisanmi Burton brilliantly captures the continuum in his assertion that prisons are "sites of counter-war, a term that reflects the fact that captive rebels were responding to an antagonism they did not initiate."[4] For this reason, Sostre and his comrades who had been locked up for political activity—Dr. Mutulu Shakur, Herman Bell, Albert Woodfox, Russell "Maroon" Shoatz, Romaine "Chip" Fitzgerald, Abdullah Majid, Jalil Muntaqim, Sundiata Acoli, Jamil al-Amin (formerly H. Rap Brown), Veronza Bowers, Patrice Lumumba Ford, Robert "Seth" Hayes, Ruchell "Cinque" Magee, Hugo Pinell, Ed Poindexter, Kamau Sadiki, Sekou Odinga, Mumia Abu-Jamal, and others—referred to themselves as "captives" and "prisoners of war." Sostre minced no words when he spoke about the liberation struggle—both inside and outside of prison—as nothing less than "revolutionary war." "A distinction must be made between reformists and revolutionaries," he wrote. "Reformists seek merely to *reform* through legal means, and not overthrow the existing fascist system. That's why they panic when the people exercise their right to armed self-defense against the genocidal violence of the fascist ruling class. Revolutionaries seek the *complete overthrow* of the fascist system by all means necessary including armed struggle."[5]

Felber also contributes to the genealogy of Black anarchism by documenting Sostre's complicated break with the Workers World Party, his halting disillusionment with aspects of Marxism-Leninism, and his critical embrace of Black nationalism and anarchism. Lorenzo Kom'boa Ervin, author of the landmark text *Anarchism and the Black Revolution* (1979), credits Sostre with introducing him to anarchism while the two were briefly incarcerated together. Although several years passed before Kom'boa could fully process the lessons Sostre had imparted to him, the timing of their meeting is significant. Less than a year later, the Tombs, Rikers Island, and other New York City jails became the site of a wave of rebellions that set the stage for the Attica uprising in September 1971. The organization of Attica under prisoner control adopted many anarchist principles of decentralized leadership, deliberative democracy, and mutual care.

Yet, while Sostre became a committed anarchist, he was never a "purist." Rather, he was something of a pragmatist. For example, while he sought to abolish the state, he believed it was possible, even necessary,

to engage the state without legitimizing it. He found in the criminal legal system a usable tool to create political space as well as a forum to draw attention to the utter bankruptcy of liberalism and the courts. Above all, he understood anarchist practice in terms of building community spaces to educate and guide young people, to provide for the people's basic needs, and to create liberated territory through local control. As Felber points out, his efforts to transform abandoned buildings in the postindustrial cities of Passaic and Paterson, New Jersey, into a community center, a day care, and low-rent housing during the 1980s and '90s were modeled after "the Black Panther Party's Survival Programs and Fannie Lou Hamer's Freedom Farm Cooperative," not to mention his own Afro-Asian Bookshops.

Martin Sostre was neither a saint, a guru, nor a god. He made mistakes, sometimes exercised poor judgment, and could be unforgiving—especially toward those closest to him. He was, however, a revolutionary and thus a human being dedicated to transforming the world to liberate humanity from all forms of oppression, and transforming humanity to change the world. By critically and honestly reconstructing Sostre's life and the world that made him, Garrett Felber has given us a precious gift. A revolutionary life is not a perfect life, but it is a life in motion—a continuous struggle. There are many lessons here, some compelling us to rethink the past, others forcing us to rethink the future we're trying to build and how we get there. But if Martin Sostre's life teaches us anything, it is that change comes from movements, from people's struggles, and that struggle must be collective, bold, and perpetual. To create an egalitarian society requires new political identities, new forms of community, new modes of belonging. No charismatic figure will lead us there. Only the people in motion, refusing to submit, willing to put their bodies on the line. In a phrase, we need "More Martin than Martin and Malcolm."

Robin D. G. Kelley
Los Angeles, Juneteenth 2024

Introduction: "An Original Black Political Ideology"

On June 28, 1975, Martin Sostre wrote a letter to a new supporter, a college student in nearby Potsdam, New York. "Though I've been imprisoned 8 years, I am fully aware of the apathy, aimlessness, racism, sexism, factionalism, nationalism and other divisive tendencies prevalent among the people," he told her. "These are our greatest obstacles to constructing the egalitarian society based on maximum human freedom, spirituality, and love." Sostre was fifty-two years old and had decades remaining on his 31–41-year sentence. His legal appeal had recently been denied despite the state's key witness recanting his story and testifying in federal court that he had framed Sostre and his codefendant, Geraldine Robinson. Meanwhile, Sostre had been assaulted almost a dozen times by prison guards for his refusal to submit to rectal "examinations" when leaving or returning to his solitary confinement cell. Earlier that June, he was charged and convicted of assault for his resistance. Yet he wrote the student optimistically that "conditions have never been as favorable for my release." He explained that to bring about this egalitarian society, "not only must we provide the example by personal conduct, but organize structures or bases that are prototypes of the society we want to build. Without living objective examples to expand the consciousness of the people and to which they can relate, no new society will replace the present exploitative one."[1] Sostre's letter succinctly laid forth, in plain language, a political vision that was decades in the making. It was what he called "an original Black political ideology."[2]

Central to Sostre's political vision was his internationalism. Born to Puerto Rican migrant parents and raised in Harlem during the Great Depression, he was exposed to a range of radical political traditions through street corner orators, Spanish-speaking social clubs, and Black nationalist bookstores. Sostre's awareness of Puerto Rico's long anticolonial struggle was deepened in jail, where he was politicized by the revolutionary lawyer and nationalist Julio Pinto Gandía. During his incarceration from 1952 to 1964, Sostre joined the Nation of Islam, which identified with the burgeoning anticolonial movements that met at the 1955 "Afro-Asian Conference" in Bandung, Indonesia. Sostre adopted a "universal perspective of our war of liberation," emphasizing the shared domination and struggle for self-determination of Black Americans, Africans, Asians, and others across the globe.[3] "By forcing the enemy to fight an internal war of liberation in his own nerve center," he wrote, "we neutralize his entire strategic defense system which is designed to guard his external economic interests against the progressive peoples of the world."[4]

When he was released from prison in 1964, Sostre opened a revolutionary bookstore in Buffalo whose name exemplified this anticolonial solidarity—the Afro-Asian Bookshop. The bookstore was one of the few that carried radical antiwar literature, and people came from the surrounding region to purchase the quotations of Chairman Mao Tse-tung, the autobiography of Ho Chi Minh, and the speeches of Fidel Castro and Pedro Albizu Campos. Sostre was framed and scapegoated for the Buffalo rebellion of 1967, and called himself a "Black Viet Cong" during his trial at the height of the Vietnam War. In the 1970s, he described the struggle of Palestinians as "a war of national liberation and independence against imperialism, colonialism, and racism of the Israeli State supported by the United States."[5] And in the 1980s, he educated teenagers about South African apartheid and revolutionary movements in Latin America, triumphantly flying a Sandinista flag from a window of the day care center he cofounded in New Jersey.

Sostre's internationalism led him to the straightforward conclusion that liberation requires multiple, escalating strategies—culminating in armed struggle. "The irrefutable truth is that a liberation struggle is revolutionary war," he wrote. "Revolutionary war is a complicated process of mass struggle, armed and unarmed, peaceful and violent, legal and clandestine, economic and political, where all forms of struggle are developed harmoniously around the axis of armed struggle."[6] Writing to his

compatriot and fellow prisoner of war, Lolita Lebrón, Sostre expressed his frustration that while the "revolution needs organizers, writers, reporters, distributors of our newspapers and literature, paste-up posters, propagandists, fund contributors, pickets, actors, speakers . . . the military arm is too short in comparison with the political arm."[7] Sostre's emphasis on the necessity of armed struggle was clearest in his support for political prisoner exchanges, arguing in several essays that captured agents of the US be held hostage and exchanged for imprisoned revolutionaries.

Sostre's political philosophy centered two anarchist principles dedicated to action. The first of these was propaganda of the deed—the idea that a single action could serve as a catalyst for mass revolutionary struggle. "A dynamic deed . . . really mobilizes people," he said. Revolutionary struggle, according to Italian anarchist Errico Malatesta, "consists more of deeds than words."[8] While this strategy has often been associated with assassinations and bombings, one of the first theorizers of the term, the Italian revolutionary Carlo Pisacane, captured the way Sostre approached it: "Ideas spring from deeds and not the other way around."[9] Actions were not simply to prove the effectiveness of an idea, but to test them through experimentation. "This is what anarchism thrives on," he said. "On deeds instead of words, on action instead of inaction."[10] Sostre defined his anarchist practice explicitly through this concept, describing it as "the explicit and dynamic personal code of conscience which I follow even in prison."[11]

The second was a belief in prefiguration—the commitment to putting our politics into practice and building the future that we imagine, both within our movements and in our material world. Sostre captured this succinctly: "If we do it right, it will end up right."[12] Beginning with the establishment of revolutionary bookstores in Buffalo, Sostre recognized the need for structures that could serve as living examples of the new society being forged. "We're going to have to show something tangible in order to get people to come to our side," he said.[13] In the mid-1970s, he reorganized his defense campaign from a centralized group in Buffalo to a network of autonomous committees that would serve as revolutionary bases for future-oriented, multidimensional struggle. Sostre considered this prefigurative act his first experiment in anarchist organizing. His work from the 1980s through the early 2000s with his comrade Sandy Shevack in New Jersey embodied this idea. They mentored and employed over one hundred young people from impoverished neighborhoods while transforming abandoned buildings into a community center, affordable

housing, and a day care. When the New World Day Care Center opened in the early 1990s, Sostre told a journalist: "You can't get any more concrete than this."[14] His emphasis on action is reflected in the scarcity of essays where he theorized these practices. Despite being one of the forebears of Black anarchism, he left few writings dedicated to outlining his view of anarchism.[15] Instead, his richest theorizations came amid struggle and are embedded in his letters to comrades, with whom he corresponded as frequently as possible despite the prison's rules banning contact with those outside. When he was not incarcerated, he preferred to engage in face-to-face dialogue.

Sostre's theory of revolutionary struggle began and ended with the individual person. Just as he saw prisoners' rights as human rights, and the prison and social control by the state as differing forms of confinement, he was also able to think about resistance at the scale of the earth, the people, the body, and the spirit. His understanding of oppression was as vast as the state, while his notions of freedom were conceived at the scale of the individual. "The struggle for liberation," he argued, "ultimately boils down to the individual exertion of his or her faculties to the fullest extent." We can see this embodied in his resistance to state-sanctioned sexual assaults in prison, which he regarded as a one-person version of the people's war waged by the National Liberation Front in Vietnam. Sostre's theorizing of freedom from society's most repressive spaces led him to see liberation as small, principled acts of defiance that opposed larger, interwoven systems of coercion and control. Resistance against wide-ranging forms of oppression would expose contradictions and draw retaliatory violence, thereby catalyzing ever-broadening dissent. These collective forms of resistance, however, were unsuccessful if they left the individuals unfree. "I don't care what ideology you have, it isn't good if it doesn't afford a person, first, personal freedom on its most basic personal individual level," he explained. "That is my concept of the struggle or the war of liberation. It's not to replace one State by another, it's to liberate the individual."[16] Sostre believed that revolution was a worldwide collective struggle that began with actions at the personal level, was based on solidarity and voluntary cooperation, and ended with the emancipation of every individual.

Sostre was a revolutionary thinker, organizer, and community educator who envisioned personal freedom and collective liberation from conditions of oppression and captivity. With clarity of purpose, Sostre

sought to create an egalitarian society free from coercion and domination in which all peoples would enjoy the world in common. His internationalism nurtured his understanding of white supremacy, capitalism, militarism, sexism, and colonialism as interlocking global systems of power. Sostre regarded the prison as a concentrated manifestation of the repressive state. Dismantling both, he believed, was necessary to bring this new world into being. No one better represented the political transformation of criminalized people during the mid-century Black freedom struggle.

At the height of his prominence, Sostre was a well-known political prisoner among both revolutionaries and reformers.[17] Yet relatively few today are aware of his life and work. Sostre is a key progenitor of contemporary Black anarchism and abolitionism, and his life and legacy deserve to be better known. In many cases, the reasons for Sostre's omission from historical accounts are precisely why he remains so important. He offered an analysis of United States that is fundamentally incompatible with the redemptive national fables so often told in our history books. At the same time, his extended isolation in prison separated him from many comrades, and his incisive and unrelenting critiques of fixed ideologies spared few of the organizations with whom he worked. His constant political evolution makes it impossible to freeze him in a particular moment, and the wide range of strategies and fronts on which he fought do not fit neatly into accounts of single-issue struggles. At various points in his life, Sostre identified as a Black nationalist, Marxist-Leninist, and revolutionary anarchist. There is never a point when his thinking was fixed or static. Instead, he moved through these periods of struggle by learning from—and identifying briefly with—movements or groups, assessing the contradictions that emerged, and transitioning to a new phase that built upon the lessons from the last. These shifts were a direct result of his experimentation with different actions against the state, and he repeatedly reevaluated and refined his strategy to meet each new set of conditions.

Sostre was a dialectical thinker who denounced dogma but adhered to steadfast principles. Reflecting a central characteristic of the Black radical tradition, he harnessed what got him closer to freedom and dispensed with what did not. Unlike many of his radical counterparts, who sought to identify and mobilize a particular "revolutionary class," Sostre saw all spaces within an oppressive society as possible sites of resistance. During his long life, he was a jailhouse lawyer, yogi, bookseller, educator, anti-rape activist, tenant organizer, and youth mentor. "Since oppression

is multi-dimensional does not common-sense dictate that resistance to it be multidimensional; with each level of oppression challenged by a commensurate level of revolutionary resistance?" he asked rhetorically.[18]

While many of his contemporaries were assassinated, murdered, or exiled, Sostre managed to withstand the state's efforts to kill him while remaining defiant and principled: "I will never sell out the Black struggle for liberation," he declared, "nor can the enemy break my revolutionary spirit."[19] In some ways, Sostre defied the narrow expectations projected onto revolutionary Black men. After his release from prison in 1976, he lived a long and relatively quiet life with his wife Liz, and two children, Mark and Vinny. His life exposes the one-dimensionality of popular portrayals of Black revolutionaries. For Sostre, a life of continuous struggle meant an ongoing commitment to revolutionary principles with consistent action to create the world—and himself—anew. Revolution did not happen in a specific place, or through a particular strategy and set of tactics; it was everywhere, in our actions every day. His dynamic thinking and ever-shifting strategies demonstrate the nature of revolutionary struggle: it can never be captured and extinguished by state repression, because it lives in the bodies and minds of the oppressed, shifting in form and energy, emerging again elsewhere in space and time. On August 12, 2015, Martin Sostre passed away at the age of ninety-two. In accordance with his wishes, his family did not publicly announce his death. Four years later, the *New York Times* eulogized him belatedly as a "pioneering fighter for prisoners' rights."[20]

I briefly corresponded with Sostre during the final years of his life. In 2013, he wrote his last letter to me. Included were a handful of original primary sources: "The enclosed documents contain more information than I could possibly convey to you via email or phone." One was a revolutionary Black newsletter he produced from prison in 1971, with a hand-drawn masthead and Black liberation flag in the corner with a black star. "The red surrounding the star is the blood shed by Black people since their enslavement," he explained.[21] The newsletter outlined the key objectives for a revolutionary Black vanguard that would engage in guerilla warfare to free liberated territories and ultimately form a Black socialist nation. Another document was a newspaper article from over twenty years

later, featuring a photo of Sostre and Shevack seated with children at a day care graduation. In the article, Sostre is quoted: "People dream. Sandy and I objectified our dream."[22] Part of what struck me was his reluctance to narrate his life and his preference to let his actions speak for him. I came to understand this gesture as I learned more about Sostre. He once wrote Lolita Lebrón that "the best way to say is to do."[23]

Sostre's emphasis on deeds attracted him to anarchism. Often defined using its Greek etymology, anarchism translates roughly as "without rulers" or "government of no one." Although it is many things at once, anarchism is not as it is popularly misrepresented—violent, chaotic, nihilistic, and disordered. As historian Andy Cornell writes, "Anarchism is characterized by its simultaneous advocacy of social equality and personal freedom."[24] It is also, as journalist Eric Laursen points out, "the only theoretical approach that fully recognizes the connection between capitalism and the state and completely denies the assertion that there is no alternative to either."[25] Anarchism's focus on individual sovereignty, resistance, and the necessity of action especially appealed to Sostre, as did its rejection of the state in any form. He was also drawn to anarchists' understanding of (re)education as a fundamental precondition for all revolutionary organizing. Sostre believed that anarchism unleashed natural creative forces, latent within people but too often disciplined by mass movements and organizational hierarchies, as well as stifled by the larger society. "Anarchism is the spontaneity of the people," he said.[26]

Sostre came to anarchism through statist ideologies such as Black nationalism and Marxism-Leninism. His interest was piqued at a particular historical juncture in the late 1960s and early 1970s—what Cornell calls the "threshold in the history of U.S. anarchism." Works by Emma Goldman, Peter Kropotkin, and Mikhail Bakunin were being republished after a long nadir in US-based anarchism.[27] Sostre entered this world of almost entirely white nineteenth-century thinkers by way of the Black radical tradition. "I am reluctant to categorize myself as an anarchist," he wrote in 1972, explaining that while it was congruent with his philosophy of direct action against the state to seize liberated territories, the "objective of this struggle is to establish a 'Black nation'—which negates anarchism."[28] Like others before him and since, Sostre questioned the relevance of anarchism to the history and conditions of Black people. The following year, he nevertheless described himself as a "revolutionary anarchist"—"since the word 'revolutionary' is *in*," he explained. He was

one of the first anarchists to define the ideology principally through its meaning to Black liberation. Frustrated with the hierarchy and dogma of Marxist-Leninist groups on the predominantly white left and the limitations of Black nationalism coming out of Black Power, he forged a new path. As writer and activist William C. Anderson points out, Black anarchism emerged from within "Black movements as opposed to simply being an effort to diversify or revise classical anarchism. . . . It is Black-centered, specific to Black people and our unique conditions."[29]

Martin Sostre's contributions have slowly gained recognition since his death. Although journalists, criminologists, and legal historians have characterized him narrowly as a jailhouse lawyer or prison reformer, Black anarchism is his equally important legacy, which he transmitted through the direct and indirect mentorship of other imprisoned Black revolutionaries. Prominent among them is Lorenzo Kom'boa Ervin, whose influential *Anarchism and the Black Revolution* was first published inside a federal prison in 1979. Many of the questions animating Ervin's revolutionary pamphlet grew out of a chance encounter with Sostre while both were incarcerated at Manhattan's Federal House of Detention in the fall of 1969. "I would not be an anarchist today if I had not met Martin Sostre," Ervin reflected over fifty years later.[30]

Ashanti Alston, another comrade who was a former Black Panther and part of the Black Liberation Army, compared Sostre's influence on the East Coast to George Jackson's in California.[31] Alston wrote that while "searching for some good anarchist shit from the '60s to hold up and show 'proof' that the anarchists were better on the position of Nationalism than the Marxists and Leninists, I found hardly anything!"[32] He came across Sostre's writings in pamphlets and underground newspapers, describing them as crucial to his own political growth. "I did not need the traditional canon on anarchism," Alston said. "I needed to hear it from some Black folks who I had a lot of respect for."[33] Although Sostre is often named as a central forbearer of Black anarchism, his life and ideas have remained in the "bits and pieces," as Alston put it.[34] Moreover, Sostre's anarchism should not be seen as an end. Throughout his life, he aligned himself with ideologies only as shorthand descriptors for his own personal code of conscience, never as containers for them. He argued that the state was defenseless against widespread principles and spontaneous action, which it feared more than "all other ideologies combined." He believed that, when unleashed, a people's uprising would bring about the overthrow of

capitalism and generate a society "based on complete spiritual and individual freedom."[35]

Sostre demanded that we expand our sense of what is possible. In his ideas and actions, he demonstrated alternative ways to struggle and to live. What does it mean that the person most responsible for the legal reforms of prisons in the United States did not believe the system was reformable? Although he trailblazed a legal path, Sostre reminded that "you have to break the law to get justice."[36] The success of freedom struggles is often misjudged by assessing their ability to refigure the very structures they sought to abolish. Rather than measuring Sostre's significance in legal reforms, we might consider how he changed the lives of those who struggled alongside him and the questions they asked, as well as the possibilities we can now imagine. As literary scholar Saidiya Hartman puts it, "What shape might the radical imagination assume when the state is no longer the horizon of possibility or the telos of struggle?"[37]

Many, including Sostre, have asked whether liberation is possible under a state formation and concluded it is not.[38] While I hope this book will help others struggling through that question for themselves, Sostre's life offers lessons beyond it. Reflections on *when* and *how* to confront the state may be more productive in advancing our understandings of collective liberation and individual freedom. One of the central premises of Sostre's organizing was that engaging the state does not necessarily mean legitimizing it. He believed that legal victories could create meaningful room for revolutionary prisoners to maneuver. He also used the courts as a political arena to publicly expose the inconsistencies and contradictions of the criminal legal system. He even invoked the American Revolution in defense of revolutionary violence, writing after the Attica uprising that "hostage-taking is to us as legitimate a means of struggle as was your seizure of agents of the Crown during the American Revolutionary War, and the seizure of British tea during the Boston Tea Party. We, and not our oppressors, are the sole deciders of what means to employ in our liberation struggle."[39] The point was not to position the formation of the United States as just but to reveal the hypocrisy of the state's assertion of a monopoly on violence.

Abolitionist geographer Ruth Wilson Gilmore makes a crucial point about the oft-quoted Audre Lorde line that "the master's tools will never dismantle the master's house." It is the master's *possession* of the tools, she insists, drawing our attention to the apostrophe in Lorde's phrase, which

is central to oppression, not the tools in and of themselves.[40] The creative adaptation of state-regulated tools of violence to undermine their effectiveness and demonstrate their true intent, as Sostre repeatedly demonstrated, is a necessary part of resisting and overthrowing the state. In a sense, this too was prefiguration: refashioning what *is* into what *will be*. Martin Sostre gives us the language to go beyond the binary form of the "state question" to a more nuanced discussion of how to constantly reposition ourselves and our struggles vis-à-vis the state. When do we make demands upon it? How do we do so while still rejecting its legitimacy? How do we bring out its contradictions without reproducing identities and relations mandated and mediated by it? At stake is not the question of whether a state can deliver justice, but constant analysis and debate of our relation to it until it is successfully overthrown.

After Sostre passed, I met his family for lunch. Unprompted, his wife Liz turned to me and said that he would never want a biography written about him. Years later, she clarified: "He wanted to make sure that his biography would be a weapon or an organizing tool" and that readers "would intuit from it a lifestyle committed to revolution and change."[41] I have taken that challenge seriously. This book is meant to be not merely a history of a revolutionary organizer, but a revolutionary organizers' toolkit. It is not interested in heroes and villains, or in innocence and guilt, much less settling scores. As anarchist researcher Charlie Allison notes, "Every heroic pedestal has a weak base."[42] This is not because we choose the wrong heroes but because creating them is itself a counterrevolutionary exercise. All thinking and organizing is necessarily communal, even when viewed through the lens of the individual. Like the struggle it documents, this book was produced by a generous and capacious collective. Following Wilson Gilmore's advice, I have tried not just to document Sostre's ideas and work but to explain the conditions and motivations that led many people whose names we do not know to throw their energy into the work of those we do.

While writing this book, I scrawled on a dry-erase board: "Write a book worthy of a life lived." Most days, for years, I felt crushed by the enormity of the gap between Sostre' life and my efforts to narrate it. Each day the chasm felt wider. While in Buffalo on a research trip, I read *We*

Make the Road by Walking, a conversation between the radical educators Paulo Freire and Myles Horton. The title itself embodies the emphasis on concrete action and creative experimentation that Sostre lived by. Freire said: "I think that one of the best ways for us to work as human beings is not only to know that we are uncompleted beings but to *assume* the uncompleteness."[43] I added "assume the uncompleteness" to the board. The two phrases have balanced one another: on one hand, a respect for the gravity of the undertaking; on the other, the humility to know this is an opening and not an end. I have done my best to write a book worthy of the life of Martin Sostre and those who struggled alongside him, while assuming the incompleteness of that task, our lives, and revolutionary struggle itself. This book sits at a fulcrum in time, with my gratitude to all the ideas, sacrifices, and struggle that came before it, and my humble anticipation of all that comes after.

1

"My Qualifications Are as Follows"

From his jail cell in Buffalo during the spring of 1968, Martin Sostre penned a revolutionary résumé. Sostre's four-page letter, addressed to the Honorable Stokely Carmichael (later Kwame Ture), outlined his skills in service of a new revolutionary Black nationalist government.[1] "In addition to offering my support and best wishes to our new Government, as a Revolutionary Black Nationalist I am offering my services to you in any capacity whatsoever," he wrote. "My qualifications are as follows." Sostre listed expertise ranging from stocking books to waging guerilla warfare, public speaking and communications to constitutional and international law, basic French and Spanish to prison smuggling and police countersurveillance. He anticipated that by the time this letter reached Carmichael, he would have been "legally lynched" and instructed him to respond directly to his defense committee instead. With greetings to other political prisoners H. Rap Brown (later Jamil al-Amin) and Huey Newton, and a pledge to liberate them should he be released from prison first, Sostre closed with the sincere "hope that some use be found for some of my experience which was acquired at a great cost."[2] As he predicted, he was sentenced to 31–41 years in prison by an all-white jury later that week, just two days shy of his forty-fifth birthday.[3]

Interspersed in Sostre's letter, as in others he sent supporters during his confinement from 1967 to 1976, are sparse yet consistent details about his life before becoming a prominent political prisoner. What lived experiences could impart such qualifications? And what had they cost, as well

as given him? He wrote that he was born in Harlem and knew "the methods of the streets"—street corner orators, picketers, riots, and gang fights. Elsewhere, he described joining the Nation of Islam as a "keeping of faith," reflecting upon the influence of the Black nationalist tradition of his youth.[4] "I got my education on the street. I listened to Vito Marcantonio, the radical Congressman from Harlem. I heard Paul Robeson and listened to Ben Davis, of the Communist Party, on street corners," he recalled.[5] He cited Lewis Michaux's African National Memorial Bookstore on 125th Street as the inspiration for his own Afro-Asian Bookshop, which was both the site of and impetus for his arrest following the Buffalo rebellion of 1967. Less frequently, he mentioned his parents' politics, noting that they frequented Club Mella, a Communist-affiliated Spanish-speaking workers' club and fraternal organization on Harlem's East Side.

To understand his political ideas and revolutionary qualifications, Sostre implied, we must first know where he came from and what he experienced in his youth. This story must be reconstructed largely through fragments in his letters from prison, which constitute most of his surviving writings. There are many reasons why Martin Sostre's life has been obscured, but none more elemental than the prison. Prisons not only destroy lives; they also mediate and erase the evidence of those lives. The same institutions that attempted to end Sostre's life have impeded its reconstruction. Sostre's personal papers contain almost nothing from the forty-five years leading up to his 1968 sentencing in Buffalo.[6] Prison also inhibited his ability and desire to look back. "A lot of things I have trouble remembering," he explained once while testifying in court. "You know, being isolated from all humanity, it is terrible."[7] Sostre's son Vinny later recalled his father as "very much forward looking. He didn't talk about the past that much."[8]

Understanding the past is essential to imagining any radical future, and Sostre's fragmented recollections were also a way of looking forward. Oral historian Zaheer Ali points out that history unfolds along two lines simultaneously: the history being remembered, and the moment of remembrance itself.[9] In reflecting on his youth, Sostre explained how he was theorizing his actions at pivotal and often traumatic transitions in his life. These shards of memory in letters written to comrades, attorneys, and loved ones from prison allow us to reconstruct the world that led Sostre to a revolutionary political perspective. His letters from prison simultaneously narrated his own history of struggle as new confrontations with

the system unfolded. They give us glimpses of a second-generation Black Puerto Rican from East Harlem who survived the Great Depression, the Second World War, and twelve years in prison before becoming—and *in order to become*—the revolutionary who wrote Ture in 1968.

Letter writing from captivity is a necessary form of survival and organizing by imprisoned people. Scholar Orisanmi Burton observes that correspondence written from confinement can constitute "community building, grassroots intelligence gathering, collective theorization, and mutual aid."[10] Facing the possibility—or even likelihood—of dying in prison, Sostre wrote assiduously to convey new ideas, organize for his release, and wage a protracted people's war against the state.[11] In his letters, he occasionally reflected upon the significance of the life he had lived, gesturing toward a kinship fractured and disrupted by the state, all while creating and trying to sustain a new chosen family. These autonomous forms of kinship are antithetical to the types of relationships sanctioned and mandated by the prison. Organizers are often required to comply with the limitations on their relationships imposed by the state. For example, Sostre's comrade Jeanette Merrill wrote to him for years pretending to be his biological sister, Leticia Sostre, to evade the authorities' restrictions on communications.[12] As the prison seeks to control, mediate, and restrict the stories people can tell and the sorts of human connections they can form, letter-writing offers a crucial antidote.

In his letter to Ture, the rather mundane fragments of Sostre's biographical sketch mingled with his hopeful anticipation that he would reverse "the sham trial given me by the power structure because of its flagrant disregard to basic constitutional principles." In fact, three paragraphs from the letter were excerpted and used as his biography in the first pamphlet produced by his defense committee, appropriately titled *Letters from Prison*.[13] For half a century, *Letters* and other pamphlets produced by his defense committee have been the primary means for the transmission of Sostre's life and ideas. Many, if not most, of Sostre's published writings were first sent as letters to outside supporters. In this way, his historical narration always had a future orientation. His eventual emancipation from prison—one of the more improbable victories of the revolutionary movements of the 1960s and '70s—was itself only possible through letter-writing. In these letters, we find glimpses of the experiences that had produced such an array of revolutionary qualifications, as well as evidence of the continual cost of their acquisition.

Martin Ramírez Sostre González was born in New York City on March 20, 1923, likely named for his paternal grandfather.[14] His parents, Saturnino and Crescencia, were married nine months earlier, not long after Saturnino's wife of five years, an Afro-Cuban woman named Victoria Herrera, died at Harlem Hospital.[15] Although both of his parents were born in Puerto Rico—Crescencia (whose maiden name was González) in a smaller eastern city, either San Germán or Mayagüez, and Saturnino in the northern capital of San Juan—they met in New York City many years later.[16] Crescencia was nearly thirteen years younger than Saturnino and twenty-three years old when Martin was born. Sostre's sister Leticia followed twenty-one months later.[17]

The only surviving document from Martin Sostre's childhood in his personal collection is this photograph from his birth year, 1923. Martin Sostre Collection, University of Michigan Library (Special Collections Research Center).

Sostre's parents arrived in the city during the first two decades of the twentieth century, prior to the much-broader migration from Puerto Rico to the US mainland during the 1920s. "They were one of the first Puerto Ricans that came here to the Barrio," he recalled.[18] Bernardo Vega, a prominent socialist *tabaquero* (cigar maker), whose memoir is one of most vivid narratives of Puerto Rican migration to New York, noticed "quite a few Black *paisanos*" (countrymen) in East Harlem when he arrived around the same time in 1916.[19] But prior to World War I, the majority of Puerto Rican migrants were middle-class and elite whites; working-class Black Puerto Ricans like Saturnino and Crescencia came in greater numbers after the war. Between 1918 and 1920, the number of island-born Puerto Ricans in the New York increased nearly fivefold, growing to an estimated 7,364. In September 1918 alone, nearly three thousand Puerto Ricans boarded ships as migrant workers for military construction in the US South.[20]

The influx was prompted by the mainland's postwar economic boom and the Jones-Shafroth Act, signed into law by President Woodrow Wilson in 1917. The act marked a new phase of US colonization of the island, which formally began with the transfer of Puerto Rico from Spanish to US control in the 1898 Treaty of Paris after the Spanish-American War. The crucial provision of the Jones-Shafroth Act was the granting of a limited form of US citizenship to all the island's residents. While it facilitated migration to the mainland, its immediate aim was to make Puerto Rican men subject to conscription, and eighteen thousand enlisted in the US Army during World War I.[21] Despite not being able to vote in a federal election or benefit from birthright citizenship, Saturnino Sostre registered at the local draft board on West 133rd Street in 1918.[22] The migration in which Sostre's parents participated, although motivated by the same forces of imperial expansion, was unusual in a decade otherwise characterized by dramatic new immigration restriction. The 1924 Johnson-Reed Act, which applied quotas to Europeans while banning entry to almost all Asians, represented the nativism of the era.[23] As historian Roger Daniels has emphasized, the issue was not simply the number of immigrants but "which kinds" would be admitted.[24]

Immigration restriction has always been an expression of both xenophobia and antiradicalism. Indeed, the two were knotted together. The Immigration Act of 1903, also known as the Anarchist Exclusion Act, facilitated the state's targeting of anyone who "disbelieves in or who is opposed

to all organized government" and was expanded with the Immigration Act of 1918. These laws provided the legal foundation for mass deportations of radicals during the Palmer Raids of 1919–1920, when anarchists such as Emma Goldman and Alexander Berkman, whose thinking and deeds both later influenced Sostre, were arrested and expelled from the country.[25] The restrictive immigration policies of the 1920s were so deeply imbricated with this right-wing reaction to the growing number of southern Italian immigrants that, as historian Andrew Cornell argues, during the early twentieth century " 'anarchist' functioned as a racializing term." The Johnson-Reed Act reduced Italian immigration by more than 90 percent almost overnight.[26] The imposition of immigration control had dramatic consequences for US radicalism as well as the integration and consolidation of whiteness among European immigrants. The quotas were deliberately designed to discriminate between western Europeans, who were seen as assimilable, and those from southern, central, and eastern Europe, who were regarded as racially alien and politically suspect. For Puerto Rico, which was a crucial military outpost in the Caribbean but whose predominantly nonwhite population did not fit US visions of a white settler ethnostate, this created an ambiguous colonial status.

The sudden change in Puerto Ricans' legal status prompted their first mass migration to the mainland.[27] Many brought with them memories of centuries-long struggles for self-determination against slavery and colonialism. No doubt shaped by the experiences of these Puerto Rican migrants, including his parents, Sostre's understandings of the interconnection between internal and external forms of colonialism later led him to proclaim himself a "Black Viet Cong" during the height of the Vietnam War and to describe the East Side of Buffalo as a "ghetto-colony." Puerto Ricans held a contradictory position in the city and on the mainland, recognized as US citizens rather than foreigners but often racialized as Black, regardless of their position in Puerto Rico's complex hierarchy of class and color. As historians Lorrin Thomas and Aldo Lauria-Santiago document, Puerto Rican migrants "struggled with obstacles particular to their peculiar political status." Although they were officially defined as citizens after 1917, "they were still often treated as *alien*, both unassimilable and dangerous."[28] The specific racism and language discrimination they met on the mainland created grounds for both unity and tensions with Black migrants from the US South and other African diasporic communities in New York City, and Harlem in particular.

During the 1920s, the number of Puerto Ricans living on the mainland increased nearly fivefold, from 11,811 to 52,774. Eighty-five percent of these new migrants lived in New York City.[29] Many settled in Harlem, where nearly half of all Puerto Ricans in the US lived by 1930.[30] At the same time, 87,000 Black people also moved to the neighborhood, while nearly 120,000 predominantly second-generation Jews and Italians left, as they were being assimilated and no longer categorically excluded as non-Protestants and racialized ethnic minorities. Among the nearly 40,000 Black people born outside the US who also made their home in New York City by 1930, most settled in Harlem.[31] Island-born Black Puerto Ricans like Saturnino and Crescencia felt more at home when other immigrants and migrants arrived as their children were growing up.

Harlem's dramatic transformation, which took place during Sostre's childhood, turned the neighborhood into a "city within a city," the single largest Black community in the United States and the "urban capital of the Black diaspora."[32] This process was marked by racial violence and turf wars, including the "gang fights" Sostre mentioned in his letter to Ture. "In those days," he remembered, "you couldn't cross the neighborhood out of that ghetto, the whites would beat you up if they catch you in that neighborhood." Sostre described Park Avenue as the dividing line, with whites to the west and Italians to the east, "so everybody stays corralled."[33] Hemmed in between Fifth and Madison Avenues was a Puerto Rican neighborhood held captive in "semi-slavery," with boundaries policed by white gangs and white police who were "vicious and racist."[34]

Other Puerto Ricans recalled these violently defended boundaries. Louise Delgado and her family immigrated from Puerto Rico the year Martin was born. As an eight-year-old in the predominantly Jewish and Italian neighborhood of East Harlem, she recalled fights between Italians, Jews, and Spanish-speaking migrants over access to community spaces such as swimming pools.[35] Author Piri Thomas, a Black Puerto Rican Cuban who grew up in Spanish Harlem, recounted similar battles over ethnic boundaries in his memoir, *Down These Mean Streets*. "Poppa moved us from 111th Street to Italian turf on 114th Street between Second and Third Avenue," he recalled.[36] One day, his mother sent him to the Italian market on 115th and First Avenue, "deep in Italian country." There he was jumped by a gang of Italian kids led by a character named Rocky, whom he ultimately had to fight to win respect in the neighborhood. The intersection where the market was located, which Thomas called "stompin' territory,"

was just one block from the Sostre family's apartment in 1940.[37] Decades later, Thomas and Sostre, born just five years apart, became friends and spoke together at a high school in New Jersey.[38] Sostre later reflected that *Down These Mean Streets* could have been a memoir of his own life.[39]

Within the boundaries of Puerto Rican settlement in East Harlem during this period delineated in sociologist Lawrence Chenault's classic 1938 study *The Puerto Rican Migrant in New York City*, the Sostres moved from a half mile north in 1925 to its heart by 1930, and a half mile east by 1940.[40] As Chenault observed, "The population in a community such as Harlem is constantly changing. The Puerto Rican group itself has constantly been expanding and extending its neighborhood of settlement since the first entrance of Puerto Ricans into East Harlem."[41] Bernardo Vega's memoirs recount a vibrant scene: "Our people lived in the streets. . . . Singing and laughter were heard everywhere in El Barrio and across Harlem. The sidewalks were filled with groups playing checkers and dominoes. Others would make their way, laughing and joking, toward the lake in Central Park. On every other corner the men who sold *piraguas*, or snowcones, did a thriving business."[42]

The possibility and promise of jobs on the mainland drove this first migration. On the whole, the 1920s were known for affluence and a booming popular culture, with low unemployment rates and little or no inflation. The US had become the world's leading industrial center, its factories accounting for half of global manufacturing output.[43] Organized labor won significant gains in industrial workplaces, such as the eight-hour shift at US Steel in Gary and the five-day week instituted by Henry Ford in 1926. Chenault wrote that "practically all reports which reach the worker in Puerto Rico emphasize the great difference in wealth, wages, and opportunity. . . . Almost everyone has some friend or relative, or has known someone, who has gone to the United States and secured employment."[44] But abundance was relative and uneven, and it was rarely enjoyed by the recent Puerto Rican migrants who had settled in East Harlem and Brooklyn. "Even in the prosperous years before the depression," Chenault documented, "employment was one of the major problems, if not the major one, of the Puerto Rican in New York."[45]

Sostre's parents found work in the occupations commonly available to Puerto Rican migrants during the interwar years. In the years leading up to the Great Crash of 1929, Saturnino worked as a merchant seaman, traveling between New York and Havana, Cuba, on the SS *Orizaba*. The ship

was requisitioned by the government for use in World War I but refitted in 1924 and operated by the New York and Cuba Mail Steamship Company, known as the Ward Line. These jobs were a direct result of US imperialism and the colonial status of Puerto Ricans. The Merchant Marine Act of 1920, colloquially known as the Jones Act (not to be confused with the Jones-Shafroth Act), required that all goods transported by ship from the US be carried on vessels owned and crewed by legal permanent residents and citizens. Under the Jones-Shafroth Act, Saturnino qualified.[46] Recognizing the interconnections between maritime commerce and warfare during World War I, politicians passed legislation that offered new economic opportunities for citizens like Saturnino while simultaneously deepening the colonial relationship of the island to the US by mandating dependence on mainland goods and labor.

The ambiguous and shifting racial and national identities assigned to Saturnino during his employment as a messman on the SS *Orizaba* capture the liminal position of Puerto Rican migrants during this period of US nativism and expansionism. The chair of the US Shipping Board, created by Congress in 1916 to regulate the shipping industry, argued that "the merchant marine should not only be wholly owned by Americans but that its personnel should be entirely American."[47] Although race was unstated, whiteness was implied. Saturnino's citizenship was an advantage in finding work as a merchant marine, but his racial classification was ambiguous. In the ship manifests that recorded his passages through New York's ports, Saturnino was variously described as a US citizen of unspecified race, a US citizen whose race was Spanish American or Puerto Rican, or a US citizen with "P. Rico" in parentheses and Spanish American as his racial identity.[48] That no manifests identified him as Black speaks to the unsettled nature of racial, ethnic, and national categories during this period. Designations such as "African or "AF. Black" were reserved for sailors of African descent from European nations such as Holland and Great Britain, and from the US, but never used for those from Spanish-speaking countries, who instead were more likely to be categorized by language or nationality.

His work on the SS *Orizaba* likely exposed Saturnino to a wide range of radical ideas.[49] Although the ship's passengers were predominantly white New York elites vacationing in Cuba during the winter, its crews were transnational, multiracial, and working class.[50] The internationalist movements of the Universal Negro Improvement Association (UNIA)

and the Industrial Workers of the World were widespread among mariners and dockworkers during the 1920s. Notably, it was while working as a merchant seaman that Ho Chi Minh first attended a UNIA meeting in New York City.[51] Havana, like New York, was a node of radicalism. Scholar Kirwin Shaffer argues that the Cuban capital was "the primary hub for migrants and exiles who founded radical organizations, published the majority of the newspapers, and coordinated much of the networking." Given US control of Panama and Cuba, ownership of Puerto Rico, and occupations of Haiti and the Dominican Republic, "anti-imperialist forces had no shortage of targets."[52] The same ships that funneled tourists and goods throughout the Caribbean islands and US mainland were vehicles for anticolonial transnational organizing.

Sostre recalled his mother, Crescencia, making "clothes with a sewing machine," as a seamstress and capmaker.[53] Although neither the 1930 or 1940 census listed her as employed, census records and labor statistics tended to underreport women's homework. In part, this was because women often produced piecework for smaller shops that contracted with larger manufacturers. One seamstress in East Harlem recalled: "You get a certain section of the dress and you do a certain amount of that section to fix the dress. And they paid you twenty-five cents a garment or sixty cents a garment. That's what they call piecework and you made as many of them as you can and they added it up and that's what they pay you."[54] Chenault remarked that "during the earlier years of the migration, such as 1925 or 1926, this type of work constituted a rather important source of earnings for many of the Puerto Rican families." In 1925, 17 percent of the city's dressmakers and seamstresses lived in East Harlem.[55] By the early 1930s, the Labor Department estimated that about 20 percent of employed Puerto Rican women in New York City were needleworkers.[56]

Although they earned no more than six to eight dollars a week, many women took homework since it could be done alongside caring for their families and raising children.[57] Especially during Saturnino's long absences at sea, this would have likely been Crescencia's only way of earning money. During a four-month period between March and July 1928, for example, Saturnino was on ships all but fourteen nights, usually with one night at home before another fourteen at sea. Perhaps because of such strains, as well as the onset of the Great Depression, Saturnino was working as a janitor in an apartment building by 1930, and later as a housepainter and carpenter.[58]

Sostre grew up in a cosmopolitan center of the Black diaspora. Harlem was home to a Black cultural, artistic, and political movement that was internationalist in both its participants and its projects.[59] By his birth in 1923, it had already produced the New Negro movement, the Harlem Renaissance, and what historian John Henrik Clarke called the "largest mass movement among Black people that this country had ever seen": the UNIA.[60] Under the leadership of Marcus Garvey and Amy Ashwood Garvey, the organization, with millions of members and more than 1,200 branches in over forty countries, made its headquarters in Harlem.[61] The Sostre family's apartment during the mid-1920s, at 27 East 132nd Street, was just a few long blocks from the epicenter of radical Harlem.[62]

The square block from the intersection of 135th and Seventh Streets extending east to Lenox Avenue was an extraordinarily rich Black cultural and political scene. At either end of the block, orators gathered on soapboxes and stepladders each spring and summer to address crowds sometimes as large as a thousand. Clarke remembered that upon arriving in New York in the early 1930s, the corner of Lenox and 135th was considered the "junior" or "undergraduate" corner, and what became known as "Speakers' Corner" at 135th and 7th Avenue was reserved for "the senior" or "elite" speakers.[63] "You had to speak first on Lenox Ave," he said, "and could do so for years before you could get to Seventh Ave."[64] Speakers had arranged hours, days, locations, and time limits, even moving to different locations in the same day. Much of the tradition of soapbox oration was brought from the anglophone Caribbean, where it reflected Afro-Caribbean storytelling traditions and was cultivated amid the architecture of public squares surrounded by legislative halls. In Harlem, it matured and, as one scholar observed, had been "thoroughly assimilated" by the 1930s.[65]

A heterogenous and politically contentious array of Caribbean men sparred on topics including political philosophy, history, economics, literature, astronomy, and drama. Richard B. Moore, for one, was born in Barbados and moved to the US in 1909 to further his education. He became a prominent figure within the African Blood Brotherhood (ABB), a socialist group founded by Cyril Briggs in 1919, and the two eventually became influential members of the Harlem division of the Communist Party USA (CPUSA).[66] Hubert Harrison, who was born in 1883 on the

island of Saint Croix in the Danish West Indies and immigrated to the US in 1900, addressed "the masses on soap-boxes from Wall Street to Washington Heights," and his book *When Africa Speaks* (1920) was sold and discussed in barbershops across Harlem.[67] A close friend of Moore, Harrison was dubbed the "father of Harlem radicalism" by labor organizer A. Philip Randolph, who also cut his teeth on the stepladders of 135th Street. Randolph was unusual among the street corner orators, having been born and raised in Florida. A prominent socialist and newspaper editor who led the nation's largest Black labor union, the Brotherhood of Sleeping Car Porters, Randolph also was an aspiring actor and helped organize the Shakespearean Society in Harlem before throwing himself more fully into labor organizing.

Other speakers were committed Garveyites. Carlos Cooks, who was born in the Dominican Republic and migrated in 1929, followed in the footsteps of his family, who were members of the UNIA. Cooks became a longtime leader within the organization before eventually forming his own African Nationalist Pioneer Movement in 1941. Garvey himself, who made his base in Harlem after migrating from Jamaica and delivering speeches in thirty-eight states, made a name for himself by speaking on 135th Street.[68] As one contemporary recalled, Garvey "could throw his voice around three corners without batting an eyelash."[69] One of the few women street corner orators was Audley Moore, who relocated from New Orleans to Harlem in the 1920s to join the growing UNIA.[70] Moore, who later became known as "Queen Mother," was drawn to the Communist Party for its defense of the Scottsboro Boys—a group of Black teenagers falsely accused of sexually assault and facing the death penalty in Alabama—and become "one of the best known women leaders" in Harlem.[71] Although Garvey, Moore, and other orators later moved into positions of formal leadership within local and national organizations, the street speaking tradition itself represented a rejection of hierarchy and the respectability politics of professional-class Black leaders.

A young Sostre witnessed this eloquent oratory. "They used to have people talking in the street," he recalled. "Crowds would gather, and they would talk politics."[72] Listening to Italian socialist Vito Marcantonio, who was an outspoken proponent of Puerto Rican independence, and actor and activist Paul Robeson, Sostre remembered that "it made sense, but it didn't really catch at the time. I was too restless."[73] Their power, however, stayed with him long into adulthood. One frequent customer of the

Afro-Asian Bookshop in Buffalo remembered stepladder speeches over a loudspeaker in front of the bookstore, some of which were likely given by Sostre.[74] During the 1967 rebellion for which he was scapegoated, Sostre recalled making "political hay in denouncing the police brutality going on outside to the large crowds in the store. Then, after a rousing speech, I would go to the shelf and pick up an appropriate book or pamphlet."[75] A decade later, during his initial years out of prison, Sostre delivered dozens of speeches and lectures at political rallies, churches, and college campuses. Always speaking extemporaneously, Sostre would move fluidly from topic to topic. His wife Liz, an English teacher, remembered anxiously sitting in the audience at a talk hosted by Michael Meeropol, the oldest son of the martyred Communists Ethel and Julius Rosenberg: "He went off the track completely, at least I thought, and I thought he was going to lose the audience completely . . . and he's still going on and on—I look at the audience and they're totally attentive and interested. Then at some point, he veers the discussion . . . and he's totally on topic and ends beautifully."[76] He "told stories with great energy and descriptive power," Meeropol reflected.[77] Although he was not known as a fiery speaker, Sostre always had a commanding presence—a skill he observed and likely absorbed from the streets of Harlem.

Street corner orators represented the outdoor face of an intellectual and political life that was woven throughout libraries, fraternal organizations, meeting halls, storefronts, and other public spaces across Harlem. Author James Weldon Johnson wrote in 1930 that never had Black Americans had "so well established a community life."[78] Harlem supported a range of "independent literary clubs, booklovers gatherings, and public forums that encouraged debate and discussion of political, economic and social issues that captured the community's attention."[79] Especially prominent sites included the Harlem YWCA and YMCA, bookstores such as the Blyden Society and Lewis Michaux's African National Memorial Bookstore, and the 135th Street Harlem branch of the New York Public Library (NYPL).

Just one block from "Speakers' Corner," the 135th Street branch of the NYPL was the "center of Harlem's public life."[80] Housed in a multistory neoclassical building at the corner of Lenox Avenue, the library blossomed during the 1920s under the leadership of Miss Ernestine Rose as an artistic hub and community gathering space.[81] Rose was born in 1880 to Euro-American parents and raised on Long Island. In 1908, she

began working at the NYPL branch on the Lower East Side in a predominantly Chinese neighborhood. To serve the people around the library, Rose acquired books in Chinese; later she exhibited works by local artists at other branches where she worked. She argued that a library must not "Americanize" different ethnic groups but, rather, understand the "history, traditions, and literature of each nationality that the library expects to serve."[82] Rose brought this approach to the Harlem branch, and in 1920 the library was singled out in the NYPL's annual report for its work with children and employment of Black staff. Recognizing that 95 percent of library patrons were Black, Rose hired five Black assistants by 1925 (half of the total), including Pura Belpré, the first Puerto Rican woman hired by the NYPL.

Rose recruited Belpré after noticing the growth of a Spanish-speaking population near the library during one of her walking tours.[83] A Black Puerto Rican around the age of Martin's mother, Belpré had recently migrated to live with her sister on nearby 139th Street.[84] She later wrote her own children's books, publishing *Pérez y Martina*, a romance between a cockroach and a mouse, in 1932. As one radio feature noted, the book became the "first Spanish language book for children published by a mainstream U.S. press." Belpré also traveled around the city to host bilingual story times, often with puppets.[85] By this time, the Sostre family had moved fifteen blocks south, where they were physically closer to the Puerto Rico Literario, established in the summer of 1929 at the 115th Street library branch in an office secured by Belpré.[86] Its aims—"cultivating Spanish letters, promoting an interest in study, and upholding the faith of Puerto Rican youth in the cause of independence"—would have likely appealed to Sostre's parents and other first-generation migrants hoping to instill a commitment to Puerto Rican self-determination in their children.

Harlem was also home to burgeoning study groups, literary societies, and debate and lecture forums dedicated to the history of the African diaspora. The "Negro History Club," for example, began meeting on Tuesday evenings at the Harlem YMCA as early as 1928. Founded by educator Willis Nathanial Huggins—a former Garveyite who worked tirelessly to promote Black history in New York public schools and helped to institute the first Black history library through the Harlem Evening School—this coeducational club began with fourteen members.[87] Huggins was a close friend of historians Arturo Schomburg and Joel Augustus Rogers,

neither of whom were university trained like Huggins, who in 1932 was the first Black student to receive a PhD from Fordham University. Like Schomburg and Rogers, the club viewed the "study of Negro History as a community enterprise."[88]

By the early 1930s, the group formally became the Blyden Society, named for the Pan-African scholar Edward Wilmot Blyden.[89] Huggins also connected the group to the Blyden Bookstore, adjacent to Speakers' Corner, where they began hosting small community sessions on research, writing, and African history.[90] It included Howard University professor William Leo Hansberry, who was born in Mississippi in 1894 and among the first US scholars to study precolonial African history and culture. He taught and mentored another member of the club, Kwame Nkrumah, a Ghanaian student and Pan-African revolutionary whom Sostre would eventually study.[91] One of the youngest members of the club was John Henrik Clarke, who was born in Alabama and moved to New York at age eighteen in 1933. He met Schomburg and Huggins during his visits to the 135th Street Library and later described the club as "a graduate level history department with some of the most important figures in Black history . . . in the middle of Harlem."[92]

Other members of the club included Rogers, the poet Claude McKay, and occasionally the Trinidadian Marxist historian C. L. R James.[93] A few years later, the "Saturday Night Seminar in Negro History" began meeting at 139 West 125th Street, perhaps under the influence of Lewis Michaux's new bookstore.[94] For those of Sostre's age, the "Junior Study Group" on Black history met at the 135th Street library.[95] During the mid- to late 1920s, Black Communists such as Grace Campbell, Cyril Briggs, and Richard Moore also cooperatively ran the Harlem Educational Forum, a debate and lecture series devoted to questions of labor and racial justice.[96]

Whether or not Sostre attended these study groups, lectures, and debates, he was surrounded by unprecedented discussions of the history and politics of the Black world. African and African American history was then absent from most formal curricula at any level. Instead, it was circulated, shared, and studied on street corners and in bookstores, libraries, and other public community forums. Perhaps most importantly, many of these scholars were not university trained. Terms like "self-trained" or "autodidact," common descriptors for them, are misnomers that reinforce the mythical divide between individual study *outside* the university and collaborative study *within it*. Instead, those who met in these spaces—while

predominantly men—were committed to the idea that group study should be accessible to the community and did not require preparation at an exclusionary academy. Clarke described his education by Huggins and Schomburg: "I was learning from these masters outside of college, certain things no college would ever [have] given me. . . . I am talking about not just the recitation of facts, but what it means in relation to the world."[97] These foundational commitments—to the political education of youth, intergenerational mentorship, and community study—would all become fundamental principles of Sostre's organizing and activism throughout his long life.

2

"Hardcore from the East Side"

The Harlem-trained African historian John Henrik Clarke once explained that "there is no easy way to study history. . . . It is necessary to understand all the components of history in order to recognize its totality. It is similar to knowing where the tributaries of a river are in order to understand the nature of what made the river so big."[1] Depression-era Harlem was a river of Black radicalism. Clarke was eight years Martin Sostre's senior, and he and Sostre would later correspond, in the 1960s, when Clarke was editor of *Freedomways* magazine in New York City and Sostre was distributing revolutionary books in Buffalo.[2] All along, the two were surrounded by overlapping, intersecting, and sometimes competing worlds of Black and Puerto Rican nationalism, Pan-Africanism, socialism, and Communism, embodying the tributaries Clarke described that merged to create the Harlem radicalism that shaped them both.

Sostre spent his life seeking out and borrowing from different political traditions. He continued to read, organize, and experiment, identifying with revolutionary Black nationalism, Marxism-Leninism, and eventually anarchism. But that trajectory was never neat or unidirectional. He wrote Puerto Rican nationalist political prisoner Lolita *Lebrón* in 1973: "I am a Socialist, but I am also an inheritor and a follower of the philosophy and revolutionary action of Betances and Pedro Albizu Campos," who advocated Puerto Rican independence.[3] In an interview later that year, he explained that he considered himself "a nationalist and a socialist."[4] These movements, with all their tensions and contradictions, played an

important role in developing what Sostre later described as "an original Black political ideology."[5]

Historian Winston James has suggested that no two figures better represent these tensions in Harlem than Arturo Schomburg and Jesús Colón. Schomburg was the most prominent Puerto Rican in the community. A bibliophile and scholar, he collected approximately ten thousand books, newspapers, and manuscripts, which were purchased by the Carnegie Corporation in 1926 to form the core of the 135th Street Library, later known as the Schomburg Center for Research in Black Culture.[6] Schomburg, who migrated from San Juan in 1891, became what James called the "most conspicuous Black Puerto Rican in New York City." Referred to as "Doctor" Schomburg out of respect for his encyclopedic knowledge, he was a fixture at the 135th Street Branch, spending three or four days a week there working at the library and participating in its vibrant social life.[7] However, fellow Puerto Ricans such as Pura Belpré recalled that the two never discussed their "shared heritage and mother tongue."[8]

To more recent migrants like Colón, who arrived in New York in 1918 as a socialist who organized with the *tabaqueros*, Schomburg's focus on Black history seemed like a political betrayal. He commented that "something happened whereby Arturo shifted his interest away from the Puerto Rican liberation movement and put all his energy into the [Black] movement."[9] Colón was apparently not alone in positing that Schomburg had turned from the Puerto Rican struggle.[10] As scholar-activist Lorgia García Peña writes, "Despite his incredible success, Schomburg always lived in between two forms of unbelonging: Black and migrant."[11] Schomburg himself did not see these two strands of himself as in conflict. For example, in 1932 he lectured on "The Negro in Spanish America" at the 135th Street Branch.[12] As he explained to a young Clarke, who was so influenced in high school by his essay "The Negro Digs Up His Past" that he sought out Schomburg at the library: "Sit down, son. What you are calling African history and Negro history is nothing but the missing pages of world history."[13]

These distinctions between Blackness and Puerto Rican identity may have perplexed the young Sostre. His family was listed on the 1930 and 1940 censuses as Black, and we do not know how they self-identified. By 1930, however, the family had moved to 35 West 117th Street, a block that was both solidly Black and Spanish speaking.[14] Sostre ultimately saw

no contradiction between the struggles of Black people in the US and Puerto Ricans, as he represented both. When asked later in life whether he gravitated toward identifying as Black or Latino, he responded: "I had the best of both worlds. I used to be in both. I used to gravitate from one to the other, and they both respected me."[15] Instead, he saw them—and later those of the peoples of Vietnam, Palestine, Cuba, Nicaragua, and throughout the global South—as parts of the same worldwide struggle against the oppressive forces of racism, capitalism, and colonialism.

Black organizers and intellectuals during the Great Depression struggled with a different tension that also animated much of Sostre's political development: how to formulate a socialist vision that centered the liberation of Black people. The onset of the Depression had added urgency to political debates in Harlem and provided ample opportunities to mobilize people around their everyday concerns with work, housing, education, and policing. The neighborhood soon became the "national center of Black labor activism."[16] According to historian Mark Naison, during the Depression "Harlem experienced an unprecedented explosion of protest activity. . . . Mass marches for Scottsboro, 'Don't Buy Where You Can't Work' campaigns, rent strikes, relief bureau sit-ins, unionization drives, rallies against discrimination in education and cutbacks in the WPA—all became *common* features of Harlem's political landscape."[17] In 1929, Cyril Briggs initiated "National Negro Week," which included the honoring of Black revolutionaries, demonstrations against Jim Crow businesses, and discussions of the so-called Negro question in Communist Party groups.[18] In 1931, the Harlem Housewives League launched a campaign demanding that chain stores in Harlem employ Black people. The Harlem Labor Union was created the following year.[19] The Tenants League, led by Communists Richard Moore and Grace Campbell, organized demonstrations demanding rent control and created committees building by building to fight for lower rents and repairs, regularly holding meetings at the 135th Street Library.[20] Many labor historians consider the 1930s the high-water mark of the organized left in the United States. Cheryl Greenberg observes that in Harlem this energy "burst the confines of traditional politics" and created "remarkably fluid" boundaries between new and old forms of activism.[21]

One of the organizations responsible for this remarkable ferment was the Harlem branch of the Communist Party. What had been a "marginal phenomenon" in Black political life for most of the 1920s,

Naison argues, became a socialist organization that "touched the life of an Afro-American community [more] profoundly" than any before or since.[22] Much of its growth was a result of the party's embrace of the Black Belt thesis and its mass mobilization in defense of the Scottsboro Boys. Drafted with the help of Black Communist Harry Haywood and adopted by the Third International at the Sixth World Congress in 1928, the Black Belt thesis argued that Black people in the United States constituted an oppressed nation within a nation with the right to self-determination.[23] This idea held particular appeal given that most Black Americans still lived in the "Black Belt" region of the South.[24] Naison argues that "the campaign to free the Scottsboro boys, more than any single event, marked the Communist Party's emergence as a force in Harlem's life."[25]

In 1931, nine Black teenagers were accused of raping two white women on a train traveling from Chattanooga and Memphis, Tennessee. After surviving a lynch mob in Scottsboro, Alabama, all but one of the "Scottsboro Boys"—13-year-old Roy Wright—were sentenced to death by an all-white jury. The biased verdict and severe penalties led the International Labor Defense (ILD), the legal arm of the Communist Party USA, to represent them on appeal. Through the activism and international speaking tour of Mrs. Ada Wright, the mother of two of the defendants, the case became what scholars have described as a "central episode in the global racial politics of the 1930s."[26] During the early 1930s, which marked the height of the CPUSA's support of Black American struggles against Jim Crow, lynching, and the criminal legal system, Harlem became the epicenter of this activism.[27] In 1932, Harlem Communists established the Scottsboro Unity Defense Committee and hosted a major dance benefit, which over a thousand people attended.[28] A Scottsboro "Tag Day" was held across New York to raise support funds that same year.[29] According to Naison, "From soapboxes, pulpits, and podiums, Black and white Communists made the details of the Scottsboro case a part of the daily consciousness of the community."[30] It was this mass mobilization, along with the Black Belt thesis, that attracted former Garveyites such as Audley Moore to the CPUSA. Moore became a prominent Harlem branch organizer from the 1930s until 1950, even helping Harlem Communist Benjamin Davis win election to the New York City Council in 1943.[31] "In a little more than two years," Naison concluded, "the Scottsboro movement had helped transform the Party from a political 'outsider' in Harlem into an important

force in the community's life."[32] Although at the time Sostre was a few years younger than the defendants, we can see why, having come of age amid a swirl of international defense activity, Sostre later declared confidently that despite a virtual life sentence he would ultimately be freed by the "universal forces of liberation."[33]

In 1933, the Central Committee of the CPUSA designated Harlem a "national concentration point." But Cyril Briggs and Richard Moore, who were largely responsible for the party's local growth, soon became victims of the national party's organizing campaign. The two were pushed out after party organizer James Ford arrived that year with the intention to "wage a struggle *within* the Harlem Party against nationalist tendencies."[34] Audley Moore, who remained and was listed as a section leader in a 1940 Harlem Communist Party organizing manual, ultimately departed in 1950.[35] She would go on to become an important founder of the modern reparations movement and continued to emphasize the importance of Black people developing our "own independent thought concerning Black struggle."[36]

The Communist Party in Harlem was an important backdrop to Sostre's youth. The East Harlem office, at 171 East 116th Street between Lexington and Third Avenue, was about a half mile from the apartment Sostre lived in as he entered high school.[37] His parents must have been aware of its activities, given his recollections that his father was "always criticizing the system and racism."[38] They were also likely aware of the Puerto Rican Nationalist Party, whose leaders in New York officially affiliated with those in Puerto Rico in 1930 and established their headquarters in Harlem. The party claimed over eight thousand members and maintained close relationships with other local leftist organizations like the CPUSA.[39] But it was another Communist space that Sostre remembered best: "My father belonged to a Marxist or Communist social club whose name I still remember as being Club Julio Mejias [*sic*]. . . . It was located on the second floor of a corner building."[40] Sostre's clear recollection of the club's name and location nearly forty years later likely reflects the prominence it had during his childhood. When the club opened at 1413 Fifth Avenue in the early 1930s, it was just one block from his family's apartment.[41]

A quarter of Harlem's Black residents were, like the Sostres, Caribbean immigrants. During the 1930s, they created a web of political centers, clubs, and fraternal organizations to meet the needs of their

communities.[42] As a musical venue, fraternal organization, and cultural center, Club Mella was all of these. The club's namesake was the revolutionary founder of the Communist Party of Cuba, Julio Antonio Mella, who was forced into exile by the Machado government and assassinated shortly before Club Mella's founding. Cuba was a center of revolutionary and anti-imperialist ferment in the 1920s and '30s, and many Puerto Rican nationalists and leftists took refuge there. "The transnational anti-imperialism of the early Caribbean Communists also existed in links between Puerto Rico and New York City," Kirwin Shaffer notes. "Puerto Rican nationalists found allies in Cuba but especially in New York."[43] In the 1930, the Puerto Rican nationalists living in New York officially affiliated with the Party in Puerto Rico and made their headquarters in Harlem.

Henry Glintenkamp, *Club Julio A. Mella (Cuban Workers' Club)*, 1937, oil on canvas. Chrysler Museum of Art. Courtesy of the estate of Henry Glintenkamp. Henry Glintenkamp, American, 1887-1946 Oil on canvas Gift of Walter P. Chrysler, Jr.#71.2248

These leftists connected through New York City institutions like Club Mella. Historian Nancy Raquel Mirabal has identified the club as one of twenty-four Spanish-speaking *logias* (lodges) that comprised the Cervantes Fraternal Society of the International Workers Order (IWO) in the United States. Thirteen of these were in Harlem. They played an important role in supporting a mutual aid network among many Spanish speakers in East Harlem. Regardless of race or occupation, members could receive health, employment, and disability insurance. By the time the club closed in 1940, for example, the IWO had paid its Spanish-speaking members $14,000 in life insurance and nearly $8,000 in disability.[44]

The *logia* also featured a women's auxiliary, Club de Damas, which met every Thursday night to discuss issues affecting "la mujer moderna."[45] Club de Damas was unusual because it offered women their own political and social space, rather than expecting them merely to support men's activities. Mirabal notes that by offering childcare and classes for women textile workers, the group simultaneously "reinforced their commitment to working-class immigrant women and challenged what continued to be a gendered and male-dominated discourse on labor." The founder of Club de Damas, Josefina Cepeda, emphasized: "Gone are the petrified looks and gestures of disgust of our male comrades as we attend a particular meeting of interest to us as mothers and wives."[46]

In his few recollections of his parents' politics, Sostre has contrasted their degree of interest but spoke dismissively of both. He described his father as a " 'talking' Marxist" who was "always criticizing the system and racism" but "never did, that I know of, engage in any political activity." "That was just his ranting in the house."[47] About his mother, Sostre was more unequivocal: "She wasn't political."[48] Sostre characterized her as "a very compliant person" and attributed this passivity to her Catholic faith. "She had all these crosses and burning incense and every time it thundered she would say, 'It's Santa Barbara.'" Sostre's perceptions of this adult inaction extended to Club Mella. He remembered his mother notifying him that the "dinner's ready" and sending him to the club to fetch his father. "I'd go there, they'd be playing cards," he remembered. "As far as I could see them when I was a kid, it was just a social club that they used to hang out."[49]

How accurate were these characterizations? Sostre was about ten years old when Club Mella opened. Would he have recognized his

mother's involvement in a formation like Club de Damas as political? What was the political role of a community center and card games for poor migrant families in East Harlem during the Great Depression? Sostre's depictions are reminiscent of those by Malcolm X in his *Autobiography*, which portrayed his father Earl as a militant Garveyite preacher and his mother Louise as self-sufficient but separate from the male-dominated political arenas of the pulpit and the Universal Negro Improvement Association. It was only after Malcolm's death, when historians located Louise's articles in the UNIA's paper, *Negro World*, that her political role as a committed Garveyite came to light.[50] Although we do not know the full extent of the Sostre family's involvement at Club Mella, thanks to recent scholarship by Mirabal and Ariel Mae Lambe, we are able to reconstruct the place they likely frequented and better understand its social, cultural, and political function in the community.[51]

Sunday nights at Club Mella were open to the public. Cubans, Puerto Ricans, and South Americans danced the rhumba and *son Cubano* on the third floor. Although dances were occasionally held to benefit groups such as the club's baseball team, political causes were near the surface on even the most social of evenings. The Spanish-section leadership of the IWO emphasized that its clubs should be "connected to radical movement."[52] For example, a "Game for Spain" doubleheader soccer match between German and Spanish immigrants, and the Local 1549 Machinists versus the Local 905 Painters, raised funds to support the Spanish Loyalists in their fight against General Francisco Franco and his fascist regime.[53] Another benefit supported strikers with the Food Workers Industrial Union who were picketing the Hotel Commodore.[54] Although women were admitted for free, they were given the option of donating their fifty-cent admission fee to the anti-fascist fight in Spain.[55] Film night at Club Cubano featured a screening about May Day and the presentation of a banner to the international brigade of soldiers fighting in Spain.[56] The Red Dancers, formed by the Jewish American left-wing choreographer Edith Segal, performed alongside a lecture by organizer James Ford.[57] In more ways than one, the club remained committed to the communist politics of its namesake, whose portrait, described by one journalist as "heartbreakingly young and handsome," hung over the bandstand. Mella's mother even spoke at the club five years after his death.[58]

El Club Mella was a hub of cultural and political activity throughout its decade-long existence. Writing under what was likely a pseudonym, journalist Mississippi Johnson described it as "a real workers' club," with a small restaurant that "helped feed the seamen during the Spring strike," newspaper clippings pasted on the walls recounting stories of Cuban soldiers fighting in Spain, and a small glassed-in bookshop featuring communist books in Spanish.[59] Johnson's journalistic portrait of "Club Cubano," along with the visual representations of Communist painter Henry Glintenkamp and cartoonist Bill James, who contributed sketches for Johnson's article, offer outsiders' views of the club in 1937, as Sostre entered his teenage years. James's cartoons depict scenes of the club's social life, with musicians performing, couples dancing, and families eating. Johnson added that "children run about the dance floor." A vivid painting by Glintenkamp captures the multiracial and mixed gender character of the venue, with food and drinks, and perhaps the bookshop and newsstand Johnson described in the far back corner. Above the door next to a closed fist is the phrase *El Machete*, the name of the Mexican Communist newspaper.

The club was particularly active as a center of transnational organizing during the Spanish Civil War, which energized many on the left as armed socialists, communists, and anarchists seized land and factories in opposition to Franco and his fascist supporters, Hitler and Mussolini. As Lambe points out, a poster featured prominently in the center of Glintenkamp's painting "marks the vibrant connection between the Cuban club and the Spanish Republic in 1937."[60] The Spanish Civil War, Andrew Cornell argues, "captured the attention of radicals the world over, as it so directly—and gruesomely—staged the intensifying ideological conflicts of the day."[61] Solidarity with Spain was widespread in Harlem. As journalist George Streator put it at the time, "Spanish freedom and Negro freedom were made to be synonymous."[62] The Abraham Lincoln Brigade was comprised of volunteers from a variety of political backgrounds who came together to fight against fascism. Italian American volunteer John Tisa remembered being directed uptown to El Club Mella, where he found "others like myself, with passports, listening to briefings and impatiently eager to leave for Spain."[63] As the war raged on, one volunteer quoted a Cuban soldier in the Lincoln Brigade: "Write to the Mella Club. The Club Mella, will you? Tell them 'Chicago' said to send more men!"[64]

Although El Club Mella was predominantly a community of first-generation Spanish-speaking migrants, it was multiracial and multilingual. Not surprisingly, it was also active in defense of the Scottsboro Boys. In 1934, the club hosted a mass meeting featuring speeches by Scottsboro defense organizers Williana Burroughs and Joseph Brodsky of the ILD team.[65] That same year, Julio Mella's mother called for solidarity with the mothers of the Scottsboro Boys from the pages of the *Daily Worker*.[66] And just as Cuban soldiers sent word back with journalists to El Club Mella, Ford reported that when visiting Spain he shook hands with a Black volunteer in the Lincoln Battalion who asked that he bring greetings to the Julio Mella Club.[67] Yet, as a search by historians for an unnamed Black Brigade volunteer who was assumed to be African American but was found to likely be a Black Cuban reveals, the internationalist struggles against capitalism and fascism were never neatly divided by race, nation, and language.[68] Club Mella was a place where such boundaries blurred and connections were made.

While the social and political lives of his parents were more closely linked to the Spanish-speaking and leftist community embodied in El Club Mella, the space that had an outsized impact on Sostre's early life was a Black nationalist bookstore owned by Lewis Michaux, known in the neighborhood simply as "Michaux's." Originally from Newport News, Virginia, Michaux settled in Harlem in the early 1930s after working as a deacon at the church of his older brother, Elder Lightfoot Solomon Michaux, an independent Holiness preacher who invited white people to his services in defiance of segregation laws. Michaux was in his mid-forties when he started the bookstore—the same age Sostre would be when he started his bookstore in Buffalo two decades later.

Both stores began modestly. Michaux arrived in Harlem with a bust of Booker T. Washington and a copy of his autobiography, *Up from Slavery*. After selling books from the back of a wagon, the National Memorial Bookstore, which took its name from his brother's thousand-acre settlement—the National Memorial to the Progress of the Colored Race in America, located on the James River in Virginia—opened in the early 1930s with only four other books: works about Harriet Tubman, Sojourner Truth, Mary McLeod Bethune, and George Washington Carver.[69] It was one of the first brick-and-mortar Black-owned bookstores in the United States since David Ruggles had opened a bookshop in New York City a century earlier.[70]

The revolution in Black-owned publishing was still decades away, and books on the African diaspora were rare.[71] As Michaux recalled, "Nobody was writing books on the so-called Negro then, other than hymn books and bible books."[72] Despite the dearth of available texts during Sostre's youth, John Henrik Clarke observed that space itself was "the main gathering place for Harlem nationalists."[73] The store's exterior, which had become iconic by the 1960s, boldly claimed that it was a "World History Book Outlet on 600,000,000 (Six Hundred Million) Colored People."[74] Like the famous Speakers' Corner ten blocks north at 135th Street, the corner in front of Michaux's became known first for its stepladder orators and later for its mass rallies organized by the Nation of Islam's Mosque No. 7 and its charismatic minister, Malcolm X. Harlem Square, as it came to be called, was a place where, as historian Joshua Clark Davis described, "a hodgepodge of Communists, labor activists, social democrats, and Black nationalists (including Michaux himself) delivered impassioned speeches in front of the store."[75]

Interior of the National Memorial Bookstore. From left to right: Lewis Michaux, his sister Margaret, Olive Batch (later Micheaux), and a shipping clerk listed as Miss Duffy, undated, c. 1945. Courtesy of Vaunda Micheaux Nelson.

A rare surviving photograph of the interior from these early years shows a variety of books stacked in a long narrow shop, surrounded by framed prints and pamphlets.[76] In the back of the store was a spacious reading room available at no charge. As the Black-owned weekly *Amsterdam News* recounted, "Anyone may come in, pick up whatever book strikes his fancy, and read for as long as he likes." In addition to selling "Negro greeting cards," commemorative stamps, books, and prints, it was also billed as "Harlem's most complete lending library." This community library appeared tenuous at first due to the loss of unreturned books. But Michaux soon instituted a deposit system whereby a book could be borrowed for three cents a day, and readers would receive their full deposit back once the book was returned.[77] Michaux's commitment to bookstores as a community space had a profound effect on Sostre, who would go on to establish similar spaces in and out of prisons throughout the remainder of his life.

Like Arturo Schomburg before him, Lewis Michaux earned the honorific "professor" for his extensive knowledge. In a 1970 interview, he called himself a "professor in my own field," pointing out the value of experiential knowledge: "I have nothing against the college knowledge, but don't overlook a man's experience that has lived with a thing. Now if you're going to jail and want to know what's going on in the jail, don't ask the jailer. See the man where he's pulling time."[78] Not only does Michaux's example demonstrate his fundamental belief that all people have valuable forms of knowledge regardless of their formal education; it also captures a relationship between knowledge and power. While the jailer and the jailed shared physical proximity, only the captive could adequately theorize confinement. Michaux's example of radical, accessible, community study as well as his belief that people's experiences were valuable forms of knowledge they themselves could analyze, became bedrocks of Sostre's political practice.

"I am a high school drop-out, having completed two years," Sostre wrote Stokley Carmichael in his 1968 letter[79] He carried this status as a badge of honor the rest of his life, understanding from Michaux's example that he was a revolutionary theoretician who could draw from his own experiences.[80] Textile High School, which he attended until tenth grade,

was located at 343 West Eighteenth Street, between the West Village and Chelsea—worlds away from the Sostre family's apartment in East Harlem. Opened in 1931 as a vocational school for textile trades, it featured a textile museum, a mill in the basement, and a yearbook called *The Loom*. The school was intended to train its students in all aspects of the industry, from design and production to manufacturing and retail. One program allowed students to run a department store for the day.[81] But Sostre found the work easy and the school's pedagogy frustrating. He remembered learning about George Washington and being taught that if the US relinquished its conial control of Puerto Rico, "we would starve to death."[82] Sostre left school, figuring he should be making money instead.[83] He came from several generations of carpenters on his father's side and wanted to work as a builder in the construction trades.[84]

When Sostre dropped out of high school at seventeen, he found work in the garment industry, but it was not in management or retail.[85] Instead, he was relegated to a low-paying job pulling heavy racks of clothes for long blocks from the factory to distributors. "You had to pull it by hand in the street," he remembered. "Cause you couldn't do it on the sidewalk. That was real back-breaking. They must've weighed about, maybe 150 pounds."[86] Unfortunately, his time learning the textile trade may have best served him in the job he was assigned as a machine operator in the Clinton Prison garment shop in upstate New York a decade later, earning just thirty cents a day.[87] Sostre cycled through a series of odd jobs in the early 1940s, ranging from a parks and cemetery groundskeeper to a spring maker.[88] He later claimed to have been a gang lieutenant during his teenage years.[89] When his son Vinny asked him what his favorite movies and sports were as a kid, Sostre remembered little entertainment besides "going to the local bars and hanging out in the street."[90]

Sostre described himself as "hardcore from the East Side," and remembered himself and his sister Leticia as "survivors" who managed to get through the Great Depression in Harlem.[91] "The lumpen is the class that I relate to, that I come from," he later explained. "[They are] the detonators of the revolution as far as I'm concerned. It's the lowest and most oppressed class."[92] No sooner had Sostre survived the Depression than he confronted the war. On December 8, 1941, the United States formally entered World War II, one day after Japanese planes attacked the US imperial outpost at Pearl Harbor on the island of O'ahu. Within a few days, Germany and Italy declared war on the United States and Congress

lowered the draft age from twenty-one to eighteen.[93] Martin Sostre—not yet nineteen years old—entered the US Army.[94]

Sostre was one of over three million civilians inducted into the military in 1942, half a million of whom were Black.[95] Tens of thousands of white police enlisted voluntarily. As historian Stuart Schrader writes, "The war, and preparation for it, turned cops into soldiers." They were allowed to enlist because "planners believed civilian police would be crucial for the military police's expansion."[96] That expansion was immediate and exponential. When the Military Police Corps became a permanent branch of the Army in 1941, there were two thousand military police (MPs), a mere fraction of the total military at 0.21%. By the war's end, that number had mushroomed to two hundred thousand, representing 2.24% of those serving in the military.[97] One of these soldiers-turned-cops was Martin Sostre.

The so-called Good War was an experience in cognitive dissonance for most Black soldiers. The white supremacy of the fascist enemy in Europe persisted in—and even drew inspiration from—the United States.[98] As the Marxist historian C. L. R. James pointed out in 1939, "When Roosevelt and other so-called lovers of democracy protested to Hitler against his treatment of the Jews, Hitler laughed scornfully and replied, 'Look at how you treat the Negroes. I learned how to persecute Jews by studying the manner in which you Americans persecute Negroes.'"[99] The democracy supposedly being safeguarded and spread abroad was denied Black Americans at home. This paradox was encapsulated in the popular "Double V" campaign initiated by the nation's largest Black newspaper, the *Pittsburgh Courier*, which called for victory against fascism abroad and over racism at home. Although many joined the mass mobilization of the March on Washington Movement—ultimately securing Executive Order 8802 banning racial discrimination in defense industries and the federal government, along with the establishment of the Fair Employment Practices Committee—still others resisted the draft entirely. One such resister was William Worthy. Just a few years older than Sostre, Worthy later became a prominent anti-imperialist journalist and one of Sostre's key supporters. Several hundred men in the Nation of Islam, a movement with which Sostre affiliated a decade later, also refused conscription, becoming the single largest group of Black war resisters.[100]

There is no record of how Sostre felt about the war or his participation in it. But when he told a packed courtroom in Buffalo at the height of the Vietnam War that "racism and militarism are two claws of the same

hawk," he may well have been describing his experiences during World War II.[101] Black soldiers were forced to run a gauntlet of racist violence, both military and civilian, extreme and quotidian. This included lynchings and beatings, as well as daily fear and confusion as many soldiers encountered the unfamiliar and intricate racial apartheid of the segregated military and the Jim Crow South. Years before President Truman signed Executive Order 9981 desegregating the armed forces, military Jim Crow caused Black troops what scholar Thomas Guglielmo described as "unspeakable suffering, humiliation, even death."[102] Even blood donations were segregated.[103] As historian Robert Jefferson stated, "Black GIs found themselves assigned to remote outposts where they faced long days, weeks, and months of intense isolation, stultifying boredom, and pernicious racism at the hands of white officers, enlisted men, and military police."[104] Ulysses Lee, a Howard University graduate who enlisted the same year Sostre was drafted, recounted the flood of questions a Black soldier faced upon arriving at a new post: "Would he be served if he tried to make a purchase at the main post exchange, or was there a special branch exchange for Negro units? Which theater, which bus stop, which barber shop could he use? Where could he place a long distance call? Which prophylactic station could he use? Was he free to enter the main Red Cross office? The gym? The bowling alley? Would the station cleaning and pressing concessionaire accept his soiled clothing? How would he be received in the nearby camp town?"[105]

According to the highest available estimates, only about 20 percent of the 1.5 million Black military personnel were ever stationed overseas.[106] Instead, most were subjected to the indignities of daily life in the segregated military, while training for years without the likelihood of deployment. The War Department received a steady flow of reports on low morale, desertions, suicides, and other mental health crises among Black soldiers.[107] "The twin traumas of war and racism exacted from many Black servicemen and women an immense and incalculable physical, emotional, and psychological price," Guglielmo concluded. One former Black officer called his experience in the Jim Crow military as a form of "mass sadism."[108]

A fire at the National Personnel Records Center in 1973 destroyed tens of millions of military personnel files, including Sostre's.[109] His military experience comes into focus only through files documenting his two court martials, the second of which ended in his dishonorable discharge.

In August 1943, the twenty-year-old corporal from East Harlem began his assignment policing a segregated unit *in Orlando, Florida. Stationed at* the South Camp of the *Army Air Forces School of Applied Tactics, Sostre described his beat* as the "downtown colored section of Orlando," likely the historic Black community of Parramore.[110] He reported to MP headquarters just a few blocks from Griffin Park, one of the first Black public housing projects in the city, whose construction had displaced hundreds of Black families just a few years before he arrived.[111]

Florida was a dangerous place for a Black Puerto Rican from Harlem in uniform. Just a few years earlier, taxi driver Lee Snell was lynched less than an hour from Orlando after accidentally hitting and killing a white child riding a bike.[112] In 1949, four Black men who became known as the Groveland Four were falsely accused of raping a white woman and beating her husband. One was lynched by white residents while trying to escape; the three others were sentenced to death or to life in prison.[113] The Ku Klux Klan was active throughout Central Florida, with membership likely in the tens of thousands. The Imperial Wizard of the Klan even retired to Miami during the 1940s.[114]

Although there are few accounts of the experiences of Black MPs, one glimpse comes from Lee, who served as an education officer during the war and wrote the bulk of his study *The Employment of Negro Troops* between 1947 and 1951, although it was not published until over a decade later.[115] In it, he documented the rising frustrations of Black soldiers and violence against them. Best known among these were the race riots in Detroit and Harlem, as well as the "zoot suit" riot in Los Angeles, when thousands of white soldiers roamed through the streets of LA beating and stripping Black and Mexican Americans of their suits.[116] But there were also daily skirmishes on public transportation as Black soldiers defied racial apartheid. "Verbal abuse, shovings, slappings, and stabbings became everyday happenings," wrote historian Harvard Sitkoff.[117] Most of these disturbances were followed by newspaper publicity and a campaign in the Black press for armed Black military police.[118]

In other words, the creation of Black military police units was a response to the growing need to control Black soldiers while mitigating the fallout caused by white violence both by police and by civilians.[119] Amid the heightened stakes of the war, where US racism was being deployed domestically and internationally as evidence of the nation's hypocrisy, violence by Black MPs was more likely to be viewed as proper

police work rather than opposed as racist brutality. There was no evidence that Black police reduced violence. Instead, like their successors—Black civilian police—these MPs were an early experiment in insulating and maintaining white supremacy through the "violence work" of a select group of Black people.[120]

By July 1942, with "little uniformity in procedure, organization, or training," the military had established twenty-two Black MP units, ranging between a few and sixty-five police in a detachment.[121] Sostre joined the military police in 1943, which Lee described as the "high point both of incidents of violence and of official concern."[122] There were over 240 reports of organized racial violence, most initiated by white police or deputized white civilians.[123] These statistics did not include other forms of police violence like the events that resulted in Sostre's first court martial.

In just his second month on the force, Martin Sostre was patrolling South Parramore Avenue with another MP. According to Sostre's account during his court martial, they "encountered an unruly soldier who disobeyed our orders for him to straighten his tie."[124] Another solider whom they suspected had been drinking approached them and began complaining about treatment from police. "You MPs been beating up a lot of fellows around here, but the first one that hit me with a club I am going to kill him," said Herbert Turner.[125] Sostre and the other cop urged Turner to move on, warning that they would arrest him if he continued to intervene. Sostre and his fellow officer claimed that Turner then reached in his pocket for a knife.[126] Sostre clubbed Turner several times, including a blow to his head, before Turner managed to get away. An hour later, Sostre was asked to identify an unconscious soldier in a Jeep on the way to the hospital. "That was the last I saw of Herbert Turner," he testified.[127] Within a few days, Turner had died of a skull fracture and brain hemorrhage. An investigating officer determined Sostre's actions were "in the performance of his duties as a Military Police" and deemed Turner's death a "justifiable homicide."[128] A court martial which was recommended for Sostre's protection found him not guilty.[129]

It is unclear how much longer Sostre remained an MP.[130] One report quoted in his FBI file indicates that he was eventually removed from duty but does not say when: "This EM (enlisted man/member) was a Military Policeman and did a pretty good job until he became very officious. He began to use his MP nightstick too freely. . . . He was cautioned never to

use the nightstick unless absolutely necessary. He replied that the nightstick was given to him to use and he would use it as he saw fit. He was then removed from the MP duty."[131] Although Sostre was acquitted by the court, others in his unit seem to have felt otherwise.

Four months after his court martial, Sostre believed that his life was in danger and requested a transfer. He explained that his role as a cop had made him "extremely unpopular."[132] "An MP is about the most disliked person there is in the army," he said.[133] Sostre attributed these threats to Turner's death in particular. "Since that time I have noticed the attitude of the people down there change toward me," he said.[134] "[I] saw people pointing at me and looking at me hard and on a few occasions a few people asked me, 'What did you kill that soldier for?'"[135] A few days after Sostre's complaints, a superior recommended his transfer: "It is my opinion that this man will be physically harmed by the colored troops of AAF Tactical Center if he is allowed to remain here."[136] But Sostre was told that he would need to wait for a shipment of Black troops to arrive before he could transfer, and the situation deteriorated.[137]

In the ensuing months, Sostre was beaten up and hospitalized after he reported on a "racket with the MP force—taking money illegally and using favoritism."[138] Shortly after his release from the hospital, Sostre was having a drink at a popular bar, Pinkston's Smoke Shop. According to the testimony of witnesses that evening, Sostre physically bumped into Edwin Banks, a Black soldier whom Sostre considered "a habitual delinquent" and whom he claimed to have arrested nearly a dozen times.[139] The two briefly exchanged words before Sostre punched Banks and then stabbed him in the side. The bar's owner, who knew both men, described Sostre taking out a blade "like lightning."[140] Banks then stumbled out of the bar to the nearby MP station.

Sostre's story diverges sharply from that of those who testified against him. According to his account, Sostre did not encounter Banks until leaving the bar around 11 p.m. to walk to the MP office to talk to some friends. They brought in Banks, who identified Sostre as the one who stabbed him.[141] Banks's friends arrived soon after and identified Sostre as well. In his court martial hearing, Sostre was given the option to remain silent, testify under oath and be cross-examined, or offer an oral or written statement not under oath. He chose to the last to "get all of the facts in." In it, he described a collusion between Banks, his friends, MPs, and the bar owner, all of whom held grudges against him from his time as an MP.

"Things look pretty bad for me; I was swindled," he argued. "These people have implicated me in the case and I wasn't even there. They just saw their chance as all of them had something against me."[142] In words that would later resonate with his arrest in Buffalo, he ended his statement: "Yes, sir, this is a hell of a frame-up."[143] Sostre's account is impossible to reconcile with the testimony of the witnesses. Perhaps for that reason, he was sentenced on April 28, 1944, to three years at Fort Jackson in South Carolina, a month after turning twenty-one. In early 1945, he was transferred to Camp Gordon Disciplinary Barracks in Georgia, a concentration camp for foreign prisoners of war that was being converted to a processing center for those discharged from the military.[144]

In the few instances that he recounted his dishonorable discharge later in life, Sostre recalled that he stabbed someone in a company brawl in Georgia.[145] The lengthiest description comes from an interview with his son Vinny just a few years before his death. There, he recalled a fight where "they rounded up everyone, and they said 'Okay, we're going to put you in a combat unit overseas, and this will erase your record.' And I refused. So, I finished up with a dishonorable discharge."[146] Perhaps Sostre was referring to another fight while he was stationed at Camp Gordon, which would explain the barter to erase his dishonorable discharge. It may have simply been that this frame-up paled in comparison to the one in Buffalo, becoming the truncated story of a brawl. Whatever his reasons or the actual circumstances of the stabbing, Sostre never mentioned killing Herbert Turner or his role as an MP to any comrades or family. Like many veterans, he hardly spoke of the war at all.

Sostre did, however, draw lessons from his experiences. In a 1968 essay from solitary confinement, he explained that Black cops were used to "blur the visibility of white exploitation." Comparing it to the tactic of using Indigenous troops to control colonized people, Sostre wrote that "any Black cop or soldier patrolling the Black community on behalf of the white oppressor is nothing but a Black traitor being used to suppress his own people."[147] In the 1980s, Sostre would go on to mentor teenagers in Paterson, New Jersey, who were not much younger than he had been when drafted into World War II. In a packet he mailed them at Christmas was a news article about US troops deployed to Honduras by President Ronald Reagan to help overthrow the Sandinista National Liberation Front in bordering Nicaragua. Next to the photo of a Black US soldier, he wrote: "This fool Uncle Tom trained by his oppressor to

kill was ordered to Honduras to kill Hispanics who never harmed him, while his own family is being subjected to genocide in the Black ghettos of the U.S.A."[148]

There are no records to indicate how Sostre felt about his two years of military service or his role as a military cop. But his later critiques of imperialism, war, white supremacy, and policing have should be understood in relation to his own experiences within these structures of violence. "The dog-fights for world markets among the imperialist powers during World Wars 1 and 2 resulted in everyone's head being bloodied except the monster's," Sostre wrote of the United States. "All the monster did was lay in cut during the fight until the combatants exhausted themselves, then moved its tentacles in, delivered the final blows and grabbed off huge chunks of real estate, industries and world markets."[149] The same analysis could extend to the Black MPs who patrolled the boundaries of white supremacy during this imperial expansion. The heads bloodied were those of Black soldiers such as Herbert Turner and Martin Sostre. Turner lost his life. Sostre had a criminal record that followed him until his own death.

Sostre's experiences during World War II exemplify the difference between harm and crime in relation to state power. Sostre's court martial file begins with a 1975 letter responding to a request from the district attorney of Clinton County, enclosing copies of both trial transcripts. By then, Sostre was a revolutionary political prisoner facing a possible life sentence for trumped-up assault charges against prison guards for resisting a rectal search—a refusal he saw as necessary to maintain the final vestiges of his dignity and personhood. As a cop acting in self defense as an agent of the state, Sostre's killing of Herbert Turner had been sanctioned as a "justifiable homicide." As a prisoner defending himself against agents of the state, his resistance was criminalized and deemed punishable through death by incarceration. These stark differences remind us of the state's monopoly on legitimate violence. Crime is not synonymous with harm. Instead, it describes the state's capacity to punish.

In the summer of 1946, Martin Sostre was dishonorably discharged and given a ticket back to New York. "I got to the streets with lotsa talk and no skills," he recalled.[150] Soon he found ways to make money: "I started

hustling, just like everybody else out there on the street. Drugs and a couple of stick-ups. Eventually, I was busted and went to jail, and I came out. And there was no other place to go, especially when you're an ex-convict, that's even worse. Because you can't give any account of yourself, your background. What they ask you about when you have a job, you know? So, I started hustling again."[151]

A young Martin Sostre, likely just home from the war, c. 1946. Thank you to costume designer J.R. Hawbaker for consulting on the approximate date of the photograph. Martin Sostre Defense Committee Papers, courtesy of Ellie Dorritie and Buffalo Workers World Party.

Heroin use had skyrocketed in the postwar years. More than half of the people in country using heroin resided in New York City, three-fourths of them African American and Puerto Rican.[152] During this time, Sostre ran an after-hours gambling club where marijuana was sold.[153] Between 1946 and 1951, he was arrested multiple times and spent time at the federal detention headquarters in New York City and the US Public Health Service Narcotics Hospital at Lexington, Kentucky, for marijuana possession.[154] In 1948, he was sentenced to eighteen months' probation on the condition that he "submit to treatment" in Lexington "and remain therein until pronounced cured of drug addiction."[155] During this period, the admissions of Black "patients" at the prison rose from 7 percent in 1947 to 32 percent just three years later.[156] Ninety percent of those admitted were, like Sostre, from urban areas.[157] On September 25, 1950, Sostre was arrested on a homicide charge.[158] He spent an entire year in jail without going to trial, only to be released on five dollars' bail.[159]

During this time at the Manhattan Detention Complex, better known as the Tombs, Sostre made an acquaintance that changed his life.[160] Julio Pinto Gandía was a revolutionary lawyer who acted as attorney for Pedro Albizu Campos, president of the Nationalist Party of Puerto Rico. He even served briefly as president of the party while Campos was in federal prison in Atlanta.[161] Shortly after finishing his own five-year sentence in federal prison, Gandía was again arrested as a war resistor during World War II for refusing to acknowledge the "military, illegal government" under which the US held Puerto Rico.[162] When asked about "evading" service, he responded: "I do not evade anything. I simply refuse to fight as a slave to an imperialist power. I will fight as much as needed, but only for the freedom and the independence of my people."[163]

In November 1950, Gandía was arrested again for his suspected connection to an attempted assassination of President Harry Truman the day after a Nationalist uprising in Puerto Rico known as the Jayuya Revolt. Gandía's comrades Oscar Collazo and Griselio Torresola carried out the plot at Blair House, Truman's temporary residence during White House renovations. Torresola was shot dead by a White House police officer, and Collazo received a death sentence that was later reduced to life in prison. One newspaper sensationally called the attempt "the biggest Secret Service gunfight in U.S. history."[164] Gandía and another comrade were both arrested later that month for their alleged involvement in the plot.[165] It was during this period that Sostre met the bespectacled revolutionary.

"There on the 7th floor was Julio Pinto Gandía," he remembered. Gandía, then in his early forties, was dressed in a black suit. It was "very shiny and worn and [he] told us it was the only suit he owned," making Sostre feel ashamed of the money he felt he and others had frivolously spent.

Sostre was rarely interviewed about his political influences, leaving us to speculate about the extent and content of his conversations with Gandía. But thanks to an oral history interview recorded nearly a half century after their meeting by sociologist Juanita D*í*az-Cotto, we have a glimpse of their exchanges. "Him and I walked back and forth, you know, in the little aisle that they had there," Sostre recalled. "We used to talk and he used to tell me about Puerto Rican independence, about Don Albizu Campos." Although he had listened to dynamic street speakers such as Paul Robeson and Vito Marcantonio in Harlem, Sostre remembered that it was with Gandía in the Tombs that it "really began to sink in."[166] Given the parallels to Sostre's trajectory, the impact of meeting a Puerto Rican socialist lawyer with a decades-long commitment to armed revolutionary struggle and national liberation on the twenty-seven-year old without any history of activism seems to have been profound. "It was he who opened my mind to the struggle," Sostre remembered.[167]

By 1954, Gandía was out of jail again and helped plan and coordinate an armed action in the US Congress by Rafael Cancel Miranda, Irvin Flores, Andrés Figueroa Cordero, and Lolita *Lebrón.*[168] At trial, he acted as his own attorney and was sentenced to six months for contempt of court. Gandía explained that it was not his intention to be contemptuous, "but I cannot answer questions which violate my moral code and code of honor."[169] Sostre would later attribute his philosophy of "action and not merely of speech" to Gandía's comrade Campos.[170] But it was Gandía himself who had made him aware of this tradition of armed national liberation struggle, propaganda of the deed, and the revolutionary potential of learning law. Their chance meeting in a Manhattan jail would be mirrored nearly two decades later when Sostre met and mentored a young Black Power activist named Lorenzo Ervin—a chapter that would take place at the federal detention headquarters near where his own journey toward radicalism began.

Despite his revelations in the Tombs, there was no obvious way of entering into revolutionary struggle when Sostre was released from jail. Instead, he continued to sell drugs—by this time, marijuana, cocaine, and heroin.[171] According to the state, he was a "contact man for the nation's

biggest distributors" and connected to the "top echelon in narcotics."[172] It is unclear how true these claims were. But it is possible that Jorge Favela, who was later listed as a friend of Sostre's in prison surveillance documents with an address in Tijuana, Mexico, was the well-known drug trafficker Jorge Favela Escobar.[173] Escobar was known as "the Godfather," and his name was, according to one historian, "rarely whispered in public." As one of the first distributors to move into cocaine after accruing considerable wealth in the opium trade, Escobar was "obsessively discreet" and always traveled under an alias. When he was arrested in 1976, he was carrying ten false IDs.[174] If connected, this could have made Sostre an alluring target for the state.

In 1951, a year before Sostre was arrested, Congress passed the Boggs Act, establishing the first federal mandatory minimum drug sentences. Where previously drug sentences were capped at five years with no minimum requirement, Boggs set a five-year minimum and ten-year maximum for repeat offenses. As historian Jessica Neptune states, these "were the most punitive laws the federal government had ever made to control and limit drug use."[175] Amid a moral panic about drugs and a wave of new, harsher drug laws, Sostre was arrested in March 1952 in a Bronx subway station with nine ounces of heroin valued at over $1,350 (over $14,000 today). He was given a low bail after promising to name accomplices. Instead, he jumped bail and fled to Mexico City. There he was arrested again but, after feigning sickness, escaped from a hospital. Finally, according to the *New York Times,* the district attorney claimed Sostre purchased a home in Mexicali, just over the US-Mexico border, and planned to convert opium to heroin with the help of a chemist. Soon after, Martin was arrested in San Diego, California, and returned to New York, where he was held on $50,000 bail. When asked by the DA if he used narcotics, Sostre replied: "I'm too smart for that. Only suckers use the stuff."[176] He would later interrogate statements such as this and implicate himself as a "parasite." "I thought I was a big man making easy money," he reflected. "But I understood I was spreading the poison of drugs in El Barrio, poisoning my own people."[177]

On December 8, 1952, Sostre was sentenced to an indeterminate term of six to twelve years for possessing and distributing nine envelopes of heroin.[178] He believed he had received a stiffer sentence because he had refused to name his connection.[179] Eventually, by maintaining a clean disciplinary record in prison, Sostre managed to secure an early appearance

before the parole board.[180] But instead of being released two years before reaching his minimum sentence, he would ultimately serve the full twelve years plus an additional thirty days for contempt of court. This was a direct consequence of his politicization and identification as Muslim, both of which made him a target of state repression. Having spent most of his twenties in the military, hustling, and in and out of jail, Sostre's long-term imprisonment and parole denial profoundly shifted his direction. "Living in the streets by your wits makes you alert," he said. "In [prison] I decided to put that sharpened awareness to another purpose."[181]

3

The Politicized Prisoner

Later in his life, Martin Sostre would tell stories about the execution of Julius and Ethel on June 19, 1953, while he was imprisoned at Clinton Prison. The couple, who were accused of conducting espionage for the Soviet Union, became the only US political prisoners to receive the death penalty during the Cold War. Their oldest son, Michael Meeropol, then ten years old, told the press: "You can quote me. The judges of the future will look back upon this case with great shame."[1] The judge who sentenced the Rosenbergs was Irving Kaufman—the same judge who, two decades later, would severely truncate, on appeal, Martin Sostre's landmark prisoners' rights victory in *Sostre v. McGinnis*. After his release in 1976, Sostre spoke at Carnegie Hall, at the invitation of Meeropol, on behalf of the Committee to Reopen the Rosenberg Case.[2] There, he called Kaufman a murderer and described the Rosenbergs' execution as a "legal lynching."[3] Sostre subsequently gave a talk in Buffalo that positioned him in this long line of political prisoners: Italian anarchists Sacco and Vanzetti in the 1920s, the Rosenbergs in the 1950s, and himself in 1967.[4]

But decades before Sostre was widely considered a political prisoner or was called upon to defend and speak about others, he became a politi*cized* prisoner—someone whose radicalism was the product, rather than the cause, of their confinement. "Jail changed my consciousness, my social and political awareness," he said.[5] Before his imprisonment, he recalled, "I was just [a] street hustler out there trying to be an illegal capitalist."[6] From 1952 to 1964, Sostre was incarcerated at Sing Sing (where the Rosenbergs

were held), Clinton, and Attica. The system had a long tradition of repressing and murdering radicals. During those twelve years, Sostre joined—and eventually deepened and extended—a counter-tradition in New York State prisons that turned repressive spaces into sites of radical organizing. He embraced Islam, studied widely, taught himself law, and began practicing yoga: "For the first time I had a chance to think, and began reading everything I could—history, philosophy, and law."[7] He developed the intellectual, moral, physical, and spiritual strength to withstand and combat the escalating repression of the state.[8]

Exactly who should be recognized as a political prisoner has been contested within radical movements, as well as by those who oppose them. The 1971 Attica uprising was a flashpoint in this debate. A year after Attica, abolitionist scholar and activist Angela Davis argued in a collection of essays profiling political prisoners—Martin Sostre among them—that "in the context of class exploitation and national oppression, it should be clear that numerous individuals are compelled to resort to criminal acts, not as a result of conscious choice . . . but because society has objectively reduced their possibilities of subsistence and survival to this level."[9] Others opposed this broad definition. Prison officials organized a panel about political prisoners at the annual conference of the American Correctional Association and demanded that incarcerated people "be circumspect in their application of the term."[10] The state's special commission on Attica charged that those adopting this definition prevented "meaningful, constructive" relationships between the imprisoned and their captors.[11] Some revolutionary theorists such as James and Grace Lee Boggs even derided what they called the "political prisoner syndrome."[12]

Martin Sostre's own views on political imprisonment were fluid. For example, in his essay "The New Prisoner," he argued that "we are all political prisoners regardless of the crimes invoked by white racist oppressors to legitimize their kidnapping us from the ghettos and torturing us in their cages."[13] Interviewed not long after, however, he called for a distinction between "a political prisoner in its classical sense, and a *politicized* prisoner, one who has become politically aware while in prison, even though the original crime that he committed was not a political crime."[14] Later, after his release in the 1970s, he would urge supporters to prioritize political prisons when advocating people get involved in defense of the Puerto Rican Nationalists: "There's a lot of injustices, but we got to have our priorities as to which is the greatest injustice."[15]

Sostre's experiences as a politicized prisoner who later became a political prisoner "in the classical sense" are certainly instructive. But this transition was not so clear-cut. Even during his first sentence, the state responded to his defiance and acts of resistance by increasing his imprisonment to the full extent of the law. As he pointed out, "Had my sentence not expired in September 1964, while in Attica solitary confinement, I probably would have spent many more years under torture."[16] His identification as a Muslim and lawsuits against the state were the primary causes of his continued confinement.[17] In other words, a decade before he was framed in Buffalo for running a revolutionary bookstore, Martin Sostre was already imprisoned for his political beliefs. What best determines whether a person is a political prisoner is not their beliefs and actions but what the state does in response.[18]

"My prison experience really politicized me," Sostre reflected.[19] "I got a taste of how brutal and vicious and lawless the system is."[20] Through his radicalization, he changed the horizon of incarcerated people's struggle and laid the foundation for the prisoners' rights movement that emerged in the 1960s and coalesced at Attica in 1971.[21] His politicization highlights the process by which oppressed people analyze their experiences and develop a radical praxis necessary to change those conditions. As organizer Mariame Kaba points out, "Just having an identity that is oppressed is not the same as having an analysis of the forces that oppress us."[22] Sostre and others in the Nation of Islam (NOI) developed an understanding of their own intersecting positions as Black incarcerated Muslim men through their experiences with state repression. In doing so, they transformed the meaning of imprisonment itself: from individualized punishment to shared oppression. As Sostre later wrote, "The struggle for liberation begins with the individual whenever and where she or he is oppressed."[23] For him and other Muslims in New York, that place was prison—and later, more specifically, solitary confinement.

Founded in Detroit during the Depression, the Nation of Islam's presence in prisons emerged during World War II, as members of the organization did not see themselves as citizens of the United States and identified with Japan as part of a global majority of color. During the war, nearly two hundred Muslim men served time in federal prison for refusing to register with the selective service, claiming instead to be "registered with Allah." Although they became the largest group of Black conscientious objectors during the war, they represented a relatively small portion

of a much-larger movement to resist the war.[24] Federal prisons became sites of protest and political cross-pollination, with objectors constituting one-fifth of all their captives. Six thousand conscientious objectors flooded these facilities during this period, the majority of whom were Jehovah's Witnesses. A smaller portion of radicals committed to racial justice and nonviolence occupied most of the attention of prison officials. In fact, compared to these radical war resistors and civil rights activists with whom they were incarcerated, most prison officials considered Muslims in the Nation to be "model prisoners.[25] But Elijah Muhammad, who was understood within the Nation as the Messenger of Allah, and other Muslims who served time during the war, learned from their incarceration that prisons were fertile grounds for politicization and recruitment.

The most notable of these politicized prisoners was a young Malcolm X, who joined the Nation in 1948 while incarcerated. The twenty-five-year-old wrote a letter from prison to the Massachusetts state commissioner reporting censorship of Black history books and an inability to correspond with Muslims outside. "Does this unwarranted persecution stem from the ignorance of the administration here; or are they receiving their orders from the state house?" he asked.[26] That same year, he and other imprisoned Muslims demanded cells facing Mecca and refused to shave, eat pork, or receive typhoid vaccinations.[27] Just two years younger than Sostre, Malcolm was also a former hustler who had also survived the Great Depression in Harlem. Most importantly, he spoke the language of the lumpen class that Sostre most identified with. "Because he was a street person like me," Sostre recalled, "I really dug what he was talking about."[28]

Malcolm was released in 1952, the same year Sostre entered prison, and quickly established a national reputation as a dynamic speaker and organizer. By the mid-1950s, he was giving weeklong lecture series that drew thousands to Muslim temples across the East Coast and Midwest.[29] Many of the issues he raised while incarcerated—censorship, religious freedoms, and bodily autonomy—would become the basis of lawsuits and resistance by Martin Sostre and other Muslims later that same decade. The dynamic of state repression and prisoners' politicization that characterized the growth of Islam in New York had already been established in Massachusetts some years earlier. Malcolm X wrote his brother: "All of the opposition was, after all, helpful toward the spread of Islam there, because the opposition made Islam heard by many who otherwise

wouldn't have paid it the second thought . . . the more the devil openly opposed it, the more it spread."[30]

Politicization is a lifelong process, not a singular event, and it is often sparked by immediate circumstances interpreted through the lens of earlier experiences. The seeds of Sostre's radical consciousness were planted by his experiences in East Harlem, World War II, and confinement in the Tombs with revolutionary Puerto Rican political prisoner Julio Pinto Gandía. Like Malcolm X, the thinker he most admired, Sostre entered prison with exposure to radical movements, even if he did not yet think of himself as political. "Like brother Malcolm X," he wrote, "I tried to educate myself in prison. I became a Muslim in prison because its Black nationalist tenets appealed to me because of similarities to the Black Nationalism I had picked up in Harlem as a kid listening to the speakers in front of the Black bookshop on 126th Street and reading about Marcus Garvey."[31]

Many of the practices by Muslims inside reflected the Black radical collectivity modeled during Sostre's youth in Harlem. Their study groups, which pooled material and intellectual resources on the African diaspora, resembled the Negro History Club, Puerto Rico Literario, and the Blyden Society. Speakers in the prison yard lectured on topics ranging from Islam to current events, and lessons were conveyed by word of mouth, drawing on oratorical traditions that extended from Africa to the Caribbean public square and the Harlem street corner. And scrapbooked newspaper clippings on African independence movements that circulated within a communal library reflected Lewis Michaux's book cart and lending library on 125th Street. Sostre later recalled that his experiences in prison "heightened [his] consciousness" and "taught [him] how to deal with the system better."[32] If growing up in the radical political context of Harlem laid the foundation for Sostre's revolutionary life, his experiences with repression and organizing in prison led him to develop many of the critical tools to put his politics into practice.

When Martin Sostre signed the receiving blotter at Sing Sing Prison on December 8, 1952, he listed his religion as Catholic.[33] He may not have given much thought to the matter; Sostre had, after all, been baptized and confirmed as a child, and was raised Catholic. Over the course of his imprisonment, however, Sostre's registration as a Catholic would

become a central point of contention in federal court. "I tried to have the registry changed from Catholic to Islam," he told a judge in 1961. This request, along with one to "have Islamic services in prison," was rejected by the warden of Clinton Prison, J. E. LaVallee, and became the bases of a foundational case establishing the religious rights of incarcerated people, *Pierce v. LaVallee*.[34]

There is little record of Sostre's first years in prison before joining the Nation of Islam in 1956. By his own description, he was a "model prisoner," educating himself and maintaining an "exemplary record" with the hopes that he would go home before his minimum sentence was met through earned good time.[35] After completing orientation and studying drafting for a short while, he was assigned to the weave shop at Clinton Prison in Dannemora, New York. There, he secured one of its most coveted jobs: machine operator. Garment production was the prison's primary industry. In 1959, for example, the state reported that "yarn and cloth, and the shirt and clothing departments, employ more than a third of the population."[36] Over seven hundred imprisoned workers finished cotton cloth that was then hemmed and cut it into material for various garments, including men's suits and topcoats.[37] The workshop was also part of the reproductive labor of the prison system, producing "parole clothing for other institutions" and "a new line of elastic waist band trousers" for the Department of Mental Hygiene.[38] Production was so high during this period that, according to the annual inspection report in 1960, space in an industrial building was being converted into a new garment shop.[39] Sostre's position was one of the highest-paying jobs for incarcerated men. He earned twenty-five to thirty cents a day, which he estimated amounted to $60 in annual income (around $550 today).[40] Meanwhile, the prison reported sales totaling $680,188 that year (over $6 million today).[41]

Sostre spent most of his money purchasing law books—a collection that would later expand when he inherited the law library of another jailhouse lawyer who was released.[42] Like many who become politicized inside, Sostre's education began by poring over these texts to get himself out of prison. "At the time I came to prison, I wasn't politically aware of the forces and the classes that control people's lives," he later said. "At that time I didn't know that the law was oppression politicized and being used by the ruling class to oppress and eliminate dissidents. I began studying it, thinking that if maybe I found a loophole in my case I would be able to get out."[43]

A weaving machine at Clinton Prison similar to those Sostre would have worked with as a machine operator, February 19, 1954. Photographs of Clinton Prison (B0095-77fl), Box 18, Folder 10, New York State Archives.

The little evidence that exists on how he taught himself law reveals a grueling process of self-instruction and imitation. The first record of his study is a request in 1954 for the transcript of his second court martial for the stabbing of Edwin Banks: "I was never offered a copy of my trial minutes nor did I know at the time that a copy was due me."[44] In 1958, via his father, Sostre reached out to the Legal Defense Fund of the National Association for the Advancement of Colored People (NAACP) for

support. This correspondence was referred to Constance Baker Motley, then working with the LDF, "to determine whether or not there is some legal assistance they may be able to give."[45] Although nothing seems to have come of his entreaty, Sostre would eventually be represented by the NAACP in his legal appeal to overturn his frame-up, and Motley, eventually appointed to a federal appeals court, would rule in his favor a decade later in a landmark prisoners' rights over his cruel and unusual punishment in solitary confinement. In 1963, Sostre wrote the wrote the dean of law at the University at Buffalo, Jacob Hyman, requesting a copy of Hyman's brief from one of the cases on religious freedom Sostre had filed.[46] After hand-copying and returning it, he thanked Hyman, explaining that "not only has your trial brief really enlightened me as to the entire issues in this controversy—with all its ramifications, but this masterful brief, to me, represents an education, an entire course of study in Constitutional law and Civil Rights. I shall take full advantage of this knowledge." Sostre did not limit his study to texts on jurisprudence but would instead copy briefs, opening arguments, evidence, and summations. From Hyman's materials, he hoped to "have the entire survey of the case, from the point of view of both parties, and . . . be able to glean and infer—from the references to the testimony contained in both briefs, enough information to allow me to perceive exactly what transpired at the trial."[47]

Sostre read widely during these years, but it was his firsthand experiences with the criminal legal system that most politicized him. "More than all the other books—that ranged from Hindu religion to José Martí," journalist Marlene Nadle wrote, it was the law that "made him realize the discrepancy between what was supposed to be and what was."[48] As a jailhouse lawyer, Sostre learned as much about the function of the law—both as an oppressive force and a subversive tool—as about its mechanics or procedures. He analyzed power and its pressure points. He knew that wardens and guards held vast control over the lives and bodies of imprisoned people, for it was they who raided his cell, censored his mail, threw him in solitary confinement, and obstructed his access to the courts. But in the eyes of the state, Sostre would learn, it was the governor who held the power that supposedly offered the necessary checks and balances on these repressive measures but in fact colluded with them. The first pivotal lesson had been his parole hearing.

On September 25, 1956, Sostre appeared before the parole board. Despite having earned enough time off his sentence to go before the

parole board more than two years before his minimum sentence was reached, the board put him off for three more years.[49] According to Sostre, rather than consider his unblemished disciplinary record, the all-white board sought admissions of guilt from him regarding other pending indictments.[50] His mother, now living in Los Angeles, pleaded to the governor to intervene: "I am a sick person and I can't work. . . . He is the only son I have."[51] In response to his denial, Sostre filed one of his first lawsuits against the state—*Sostre v. Mailler*—charging the board with racial discrimination. He signed his appeal "Martin X Sostre," signaling his recent identification with the Nation of Islam.[52]

In early July 1959, Sostre wrote a letter to the newly elected governor, Nelson Rockefeller, asking him to investigate his denial and pending appeal. Striking an uncharacteristic note of appeasement, he recounted his exemplary behavior inside. "In my seven years [of] incarceration I have never seen a comparable case of an inmate with a perfect record who has made the effort to rehabilitate and educate himself that I have made and be treated as harshly as I was," he wrote.[53] A decade later, Sostre would make Rockefeller his chief target, charging him with maintaining concentration camps in a case that would conclude in a landmark victory for prisoners' rights.[54]

The conciliatory tone of Sostre's 1959 letter reflected his effort to appeal to his audience. But it also signified the important role his parole denial played in his radicalization. A month later, he was thrown into solitary confinement and charged with being part of a "criminal Muslim organization." As punishment for his escalating actions against the state, he was then tortured in solitary confinement for nearly five years. As he explained in his letter to Rockefeller, "If it is the Parole Board's function to make a man bitter by this treatment I must admit that they have succeeded in their endeavor."[55] Sostre's parole denial punctuated his growing realization that the criminal legal system did not adhere to its own rules but instead persecuted prisoners for political reasons. It also likely strengthened his belief that bringing people to court to witness this outlaw system in action would heighten their political consciousness.

If his affiliation with the Nation of Islam is viewed as a juncture, Sostre had gone from the possibility of release after four years to serving his full twelve-year maximum sentence, nearly half of it in solitary confinement. In that process, he became a political prisoner. As another incarcerated Muslim, Thomas X Bratcher, testified in court, "The fact is

these Muslims have been placed in segregation not for violating prison rules but because they are Muslims."[56] In June 1960, Sostre was transferred with other Muslims to the solitary confinement gallery at Attica Prison, where he remained for the remainder of his sentence. During that time, he undertook the herculean task of moving cases for religious freedom and basic constitutional protections through the courts while sleeping naked on concrete floors and undergoing tear gassings, food deprivation, and other forms of torture. "Neither the application of barbaric conditions, the threat of savage brutality or death, or the coercive power of the most massive repressive apparatus of the state—the Attica medieval fortress prison," Sostre later reflected, "can defeat the human spirit when it is fully committed to resist oppression. On the contrary, such repression not only heightens the will to resist, but forges the very weapons which escalate the struggle."[57] During the years between his parole denial in 1956 and his release to Buffalo in 1964, Sostre sharpened those weapons through yoga, communal study, and participation in a burgeoning and active Muslim community in New York State prisons.

By 1957, prison officials in New York had taken note of incarcerated Muslims when four prisoners at Attica requested the Qur'an.[58] A few years later, in response to a series of lawsuits Sostre drafted against Warden LaVallee and State Commissioner Paul McGinnis, the state escalated its surveillance and repression.[59] In the summer of 1959, the Nation of Islam erupted into the national news after the airing of the Mike Wallace and Louis Lomax television series *The Hate That Hate Produced*. The program sensationalized the Nation as "Black supremacists" not unlike the Ku Klux Klan and introduced the framework of "reverse racism" that would characterize liberal understandings of Black nationalism for decades to come. As oral historian Zaheer Ali argues, the documentary television series marked "the first major example of Islamophobia in the mainstream U.S. media."[60]

A month after *The Hate That Hate Produced* aired, Muslims at Clinton Prison had their communal library raided, and Martin Sostre and others were put in solitary confinement. By 1960, Commissioner McGinnis and other state officials had met "to coordinate the information received from

the various institutions with the central file of the state police."[61] This system tracked individuals suspected of being Muslim through a card index from admission through parole and consolidated wardens' reports into monthly missives from the state prison inspector. These reports included updates on court rulings, reviews of books and articles on the Nation of Islam, and surveillance of fasting by incarcerated Muslims during Ramadan. By 1961, the inspector estimated that the state held three hundred Muslims in its prisons. In large part due to Sostre's influence, that number would double in just three years.[62]

The reasons Sostre embraced Islam are not well documented, and his explanations shifted as his relationship to the Nation of Islam changed. "There were no other radicals in prison at that time," he later explained. "They were the only group with a formed ideology. I went for the political part of the Muslims. The religious part didn't interest me."[63] In an interview conducted in 1993, long after he had left the Nation and denounced the group for becoming "model prisoners and cooperators," he would claim that he had strategically converted to Islam "in order to fight the Muslim case."[64] Subsequently, in 2012, Sostre would describe himself as a follower of Malcolm X and express no recollection of having ever reading the Qur'an.[65] In court in the early 1960s, however, he testified to having "embraced the religion of Islam" in 1956, requested his first Qur'an a few years later, and made his profession of faith—or *shahada*—in 1959.[66] In any case, his continued involvement in the life of the Nation of Islam after his release in 1964 seems to indicate that whatever drew him to the organization transcended the immediacy of his legal challenges. What seems certain is that the Nation, which referred to itself as the Muslim Brotherhood in New York prisons during this nascent period, offered Sostre a militant, disciplined vehicle with a great deal of collective autonomy and reflected the Black nationalism familiar to him from his youth.

Sostre was part of a small group of Muslims in New York prisons who created a vibrant community despite being denied basic religious rights, including the right to read the Qur'an, receive religious instruction, worship five times a day, maintain a halal diet, and observe holy periods such as Ramadan. Since few letters from Sostre's first prison term have survived, one of the best snapshots of this community at Clinton comes from his courtroom testimonies. Although he may have accentuated his earlier privileges to dramatize the terrible deprivations that took place

after filing his suit, the testimony of Sostre and other Muslim plaintiffs offers a portrait of the robust political, religious, and social world they created during the late 1950s in New York prisons. It also documented the torturous conditions that followed.

Virtually all aspects of Muslim life and property inside Clinton Prison were autonomous and communal. Books, pamphlets, and scrapbooks were stored in wooden lockers in the yard that they constructed and were controlled by a Muslim librarian. Food was purchased with shared funds and prepared using a community oven and stove. The treasurer made sure those needing toothpaste or books were provided for. These forms of communal care were especially important for those who, like Sostre, lacked strong outside support. He would later recall that he did not receive a single letter, visit, or food package during his twelve years inside.[67]

The shared "courts" at Clinton Prison are visible in the center right of this 1969 aerial photograph, forming a "U" around the football field. Clinton Prison and Dannemora, Box 1, New York Office of General Services Design and Construction Design Division, Aerial Photographs and Drawings of New York State Buildings and Sites (B1782), New York State Archives.

Sostre was a voracious reader and regularly checked out books from the two available libraries: a Catholic library and the "school library." Both required prisoners to fill out a card and have the book brought to their cell, making the development of a shared library controlled by Muslims at the prison crucial.[68] They culled information from books, newspapers, and magazines and assembled it in scrapbooks. "Anything that pertained to the religion of Islam we would put in the books, clippings and all that to make up for the literature we didn't have," Sostre said. They stored these scrapbooks, along with a dictionary, the Bible, an Islamic prayer book, and *The Messenger* magazine, which was edited by Malcolm X, in lockers in the yard.[69]

Although not much survives to suggest what Sostre was reading during the late 1950s, Sostre's testimony about confiscations offers one small window. Among the items seized were a dictionary, law books, textbooks, newspapers, government publications, and "several other pamphlets and publications too numerous to mention."[70] In the context of the recent independence of Ghana and Guinea, many of the texts centered on African anticolonial struggles. Sostre noted "about four" pamphlets he had ordered from the US Government Printing Office on Africa, as well as special issue of *Holiday* travel magazine dedicated to the continent, which featured an illustration of a Black statuette on the front cover.[71] These texts were far less radical than those Sostre would fight to access in the landmark case of *Sostre v. Otis* over a decade later—a difference that points to his political evolution as well as the seismic changes in global politics that made such texts available, especially the underground print revolution of the late 1960s. What remained constant was the concerted effort of the prison system to control not only the bodies but also the minds of its captives.

Muslim activities centered around a shared area called a "court," which they used collectively, in lieu of any official space to worship (which they were denied). "In order to ensure the continuous possession of headquarters (the court) upon which the Brotherhood centers its activities," an internal document read, "it shall be the duty of every member to have his name entered in the yard sergeant's file as co-owner of the court."[72] James X Walker explained that high on a hill above a football field, "everything that we participated on this plot of land was open to anyone who wished to see it."[73] Sostre remembered that "Muslims could congregate in, cook there, or sit down and talk or read, do whatever they wanted to. That is

where we used to hang out."[74] Joseph X Magette described their plot as seventy yards wide and fifteen yards long, paved with stones and equipped with a stove for cooking and an oven for baking. "There were certain foods they didn't serve us in the dining hall that we would more or less join together to purchase . . . so that we could cook it ourselves."[75]

Producing halal meals was a major concern given the heavy reliance on pork in the prison diet. Eating in the yard also shielded Muslims from surveillance because the state monitored whether or not each prisoner ate pork, as a way to classify them. During Ramadan, for example, officers were required to submit reports on who was consuming pork "in order to check the authenticity of the Muslims."[76] Over a decade later, when a radical commons was created by incarcerated people in D Yard at Attica, one of their demands specified that those "wishing a pork-free diet should have one, since 85% of our diet is pork meat or pork-saturated food."[77] This was a direct legacy of the organizing by Sostre and other imprisoned Muslims.

Study was also a communal endeavor. The group offered classes at the court in history, mathematics, social studies, and current events, featuring a blackboard for illustrations. Both to get around censorship and to accommodate all reading levels, many of the lessons were learned through memorization and recitation. Sostre was the group's Spanish instructor and secretary. Another Muslim taught Arabic.[78] "Each of us had an assigned task," Sostre recounted. "All of us cooperated in pooling our knowledge with the little literature we had in order to keep the religious instructions going in the court."[79]

Lessons were passed by spoken word and committed to memory.[80] Masia Mugmuk, who joined the Nation at Auburn Prison around this time, recalled learning in this way.[81] He remembered that Malcolm X gained visitor access to the prison by pretending to be a Christian minister and passed along information to Mugmuk's mentor, Ned X Hines[82]

> [Hines would] open up with an Islamic prayer, and then we'd start talking about different subjects, current events. . . . He'd give us time and give us lessons to read and study. He had to smuggle the lessons to us. We couldn't just bring the papers down. We had to hide the papers, put them in your pants or something. Then you'd bring [it] back to your cell and then you studied. Got to memorize it in seven days. After seven days, and after seven days you got to

> [re]cite the whole lesson. Then they'd question you on the lesson, what it pertains to. Like *Message to the Blackman* [*in America*] by Elijah Muhammad, that book was memorized before it ever came out. They had Mr. Muhammad's speech and some of the stuff was smuggled in, and they was able to take lessons out of the [news] paper, and they'd make lessons out of it.[83]

"When I first learned how to read after three months of studying," Mugmuk recalled, "I started reading books like [J. A. Rogers's *100 Amazing Facts about the Negro*] when they started allowing us to get books in the institution. When I first read that book, I said, 'I've already got that knowledge. [Hekima] gave it to me verbally.' "[84] Muslim prisoners also memorized the prison handbook, which outlined rules and regulations, so that they could quote from it when targeted by guards.[85]

These forms of communalism were, and remain, criminalized in prisons. While possession of religious literature was sometimes permitted, sharing it was not. Auburn Prison rules, for example, stated that "inmates are allowed to wear a shawl and a cap, but must keep them in their cells."[86] Drafting your own legal petitions was allowed, but helping someone with their legal work would result in time in solitary. Rule 21 at Attica stated that "inmates are prohibited except upon approval of the warden to assist other inmates in preparation of legal papers."[87] Even sharing newspapers was forbidden.[88] Prison authorities responded to these attempts at communal survival with individualized punishment.

The opening salvo came in April 1959 with the solitary confinement and transfer of Teddy Anderson, who had acted as a witness for Sostre's *shahada* and owned the only Qur'an in the prison. Sostre understood the state's actions as retaliation for their lawsuit. "Right after we submitted the written petition," he recalled, "Anderson, the one who had the Qur'an, was placed in solitary confinement as an agitator." Then, he "disappeared."[89] Although the state denied punishing Muslims for their religious beliefs, its own documents indicated otherwise. One report noted that when Anderson was transferred from Clinton to Auburn that May, he was "placed in segregation because he started an agitation about the Moslem Religion among the prisoners."[90] Anderson's transfer did not have the intended effect. Instead of quelling Muslim organizing, it expanded it. Sostre estimated that between April and the confiscations of literature in mid-August, the community doubled from twenty to forty. In order

accommodate, they expanded the court. "As we grew the court grew," Sostre remembered. By June, they had combined four courts to host their meetings.[91] As part of these developments, he helped to revise an older set of rules governing what was known as the Muslim Brotherhood into a new formal constitution.[92]

This six-page document was an intricate vision of a disciplined and democratic organization within one of society's most repressive spaces. "By drafting this document," writes constitutional law scholar Sarah Gordon, "the organizers of the [Muslim] Brotherhood declared they were more completely bound to each other and their aspirational vision for redemption through faith than subject to the controls of the prison warden and his guards."[93] The constitution, finalized just before Anderson was put in solitary, detailed the aims, objectives, duties, organizational structure, discipline, and communication of the group.[94] It described the group's mission as the "vigorous, intellectual vanguard of the struggle for complete unity among our brothers . . . to build and train leaders for the future struggle so that each member upon his release shall be so equipped, that he will be able to successfully organize his own group or be an asset to any organization he may join."[95] Much of the constitution's language seems to reflect Sostre's influence.

Each Muslim had an equal vote, and to protect against "reduction in our ranks" through releases, transfers, and solitary confinement, every officer's position was bolstered by two assistants who could immediately take their place. "By this method our organization is indestructible," the constitution read. It "shall always maintain its continuity; and shall frustrate the enemy's attempt to destroy it, since as soon as a member is drafted [transferred] to another prison it is his duty to organize there a Muslim Brotherhood upon the same lines as the present organization, thereby spreading the unifying and awakening force of Islam among all brother inmates in all the New York State prisons."[96] When Muslims were released, they were expected to send money, packages, books, and literature to those inside, and to make the struggles of those still imprisoned known outside.[97]

While the constitution offered a powerful vision of communalism and solidarity, it drew sharp lines around who could participate in that vision and disciplined those who violated it. Indeed, it is telling that "any person who is a known informer or a homosexual" was ineligible. While homophobia was certainly prevalent and not publicly condemned, this

equivalence of homosexuality with treason mirrored that of the state; the US government barred people perceived to be queer from the civil service as potential security risks because they were susceptible to blackmail.[98] Some of these measures may also have been designed to avoid collective punishment for individual acts. In the prison, gender and sexuality were strictly policed and surveilled. In 1959, it was common for prisons to hold queer people in solitary confinement. For example, the annual report at Clinton the following year reported forty-three "homosexuals were segregated in F-Block."[99] When asked about this clause in their constitution in court, Sostre said, "Of course we didn't want any homosexuals to be—" but was abruptly cut off by the judge, leaving us to wonder about the motivations and rationale of imprisoned Muslims.[100]

It is sometimes difficult to see practice in a statement of principles. But the document remains a powerful snapshot of the disciplined structure and communal principles of the Muslim Brotherhood at a key moment in its development into the Nation of Islam. In August 1959, not long after the constitution was drafted, it was among the materials confiscated in a raid on the Muslim locker in the Clinton Prison yard. Arousing considerable concern among prison officials, the constitution was used by the state in subsequent trials as a key piece of evidence to denounce the Nation as an illegitimate group that was not entitled to religious freedom.

The transfer of Teddy Anderson and seizure of the Nation's literature would mark the beginning of an onslaught of state repression. Soon after, Martin Sostre would be accused of being part of a criminal organization and punished with solitary confinement and the loss of sixty days of earned time.[101] A month later, he would be charged with possession of legal transcripts from another prisoner's trial.[102] Weeks after that, he would be charged with writing and distributing Muslim literature.[103] Criminalizing his acts of solidarity and mutual aid, the state would ultimately banish Sostre to solitary confinement for most of his remaining sentence. There, he would turn even this individualized punishment into a communal one while managing to sue the state and help establish the first-ever constitutional protections for incarcerated people.

4

The Political Prisoner

When he woke up on August 15, 1959, Sostre found his cell door locked. As someone passed by on the catwalk that divided the gallery of single cells, heading to breakfast, he asked them to notify an officer because "a lot of times they forget to open the doors." He soon learned that he was "keep-locked," a restrictive punishment where someone is locked in their cell.[1] Sostre was eventually taken to see the principal keeper (PK), where he was handcuffed and informed that he was being put in solitary confinement as part of a "criminal Muslim organization."[2] The reprisal was part of a larger sweep of Muslims at Clinton following the raid and confiscation of religious materials from their shared locker on the yard.[3] Such repression was a direct response to their lawsuits against the state.

At that time, it was widely understood that prisoners did not have constitutional rights.[4] Since *Ruffin v. Commonwealth* (1877) had described an imprisoned person as a "slave of the state," courts rarely recognized prisoners' right to contest their treatment or prison conditions. The so-called hands-off era, which described this reluctance to acknowledge the constitutional rights of incarcerated people, was nearly a century old by the time it was successfully challenged. Aided by Sostre's legal expertise, Muslims in New York began filing lawsuits claiming violations of their religious rights and successfully initiated the first major organized prison litigation movement. Sostre prepared templates for himself and other prisoners, even writing challenges to the state commissioner under the names of his comrades.[5] As one judge observed at trial, "These

complaints were drawn the same day, same thing. Apparently even the wording is practically identical."[6]

It was precisely the combination of Sostre's legal skills and his willingness to make them communal that threatened prison officials. Sometimes writing briefs from memory without access to legal records, Sostre and his coplaintiffs would go on to win a determination in *Pierce v. La Vallee* (1961) that federal judicial oversight of religious rights for those imprisoned, however limited, was necessary to guarantee this constitutional "preferred right." The federal judge presiding in the case also understood that this was a coordinated effort. "These are not cases where uneducated, inexperienced and helpless plaintiffs are involved," he noted. "These applications are part of a movement."[7]

What was legally innovative about these cases was their resuscitation of Section 1983 of the Civil Rights Act of 1871, which allowed someone to sue those acting under state authority for violating the US constitution. Resurrected through *Monroe v. Pape*, a Supreme Court decision just a few months before *Pierce*, Section 1983 opened the way for claims by incarcerated people upon the courts. In 1960, only 280 cases were brought under Section 1983; by 1970, the number had increased over 1,000 percent to 3,586.[8] During the summer of 1964, the basic constitutional rights of incarcerated people were solidified in *Cooper v. Pate* (1964), making an impact on the prisoners' rights movement that sociologist James Jacobs has likened to that of *Brown v. Board of Education* on the civil rights movement.[9] A month later, *Sostre v. McGinnis* won a similar determination securing the free exercise of religion in New York.[10] *Pierce* was among the precedents cited in both decisions.[11] By 1972, state prisoners had filed more than three thousand civil rights actions. That number had more than doubled to nearly seven thousand by 1976. On the eve of the Prison Litigation Reform Act in 1995, which aimed to roll back this increased access to the courts, federal courts heard almost forty thousand prisoners' rights cases per year.[12]

Solitary confinement, as prison officials were well aware, made it nearly impossible for jailhouse lawyers like Sostre to function. "We were locked in our cells twenty-four hours a day with no light bulbs, no pencils, no pen," Sostre recounted.[13] During this time, he could not purchase anything from commissary and received only one piece of letterhead each week. A guard handed out pencils, which had to be returned immediately after the letter was written.[14] "The Warden took all of our materials,

he took legal paper, he took pencils, he took pens, he took law books," Sostre recalled. "I wasn't allowed to prosecute my cases."[15] All outgoing litigation also needed to be stamped by a notary public, who only came on designated days of the week and would then forward the papers to the correspondence office to be mailed.[16]

"The hole," as solitary confinement is colloquially known, was the state's primary mechanism of discipline and torture. Before being taken to a floor of solitary cells, Sostre and others each spent twenty days in a single cell known as a "strip cell."[17] These first weeks in solitary were particularly torturous. A strip cell was "mutilated . . . everything is taken out of it."[18] SaMarion described sleeping with a blanket "on a concrete floor with only a pair of winter underwear, pair of socks, no sanitary facilities whatever." Prisoners were forced to defecate in a paint bucket, which was emptied once a day. Food rations were cut in half. Thomas X Bratcher lost almost fifty pounds while in solitary, which included time in a strip cell.[19] James X Walker, who spent over a month in similar conditions at Attica, described his time there as "a constant threat and terror campaign twenty-four hours a day."[20]

More than a decade later, Sostre would reflect that "the struggle to exercise a First Amendment 'preferred' right took from 1958 till 1971, thirteen years of torture, suffering and death at the hands of racist outlaw savages who recognize no law except that of force, violence and murder."[21] By 1964, Sostre would be listed with other Muslim prisoners in a report by the Congress of Racial Equality (CORE) as those who could "testify to gassings, strip-cells and other deprivations" at Attica. There, according to the report, officials "employ[ed] savage brutality on the inmates in order to terrorize and intimidate them and thus maintain discipline through fear."[22] Sostre would continue to deploy the law as a weapon, later using legal challenges to draw outside attention to oppressive systems and hidden forms of state violence, while carving out necessary breathing room for revolutionary organizers inside. However, the utilization of the courts in these ways would only made possible by the foundational legal victories secured by Sostre and other Muslims in the Nation of Islam during the early 1960s. When he later said, "I have been through hell and I know how to fight the devil," Sostre may well have been describing these years and their lessons.[23]

Shortly after the mass reprisals of August 1959, Kiongozi (James X Pierce) received a message from Clinton's warden, J. E. La Vallee, which he shared with Sostre. "We have no objection to your embracing the Moslem faith as a religion," La Vallee wrote. "However if you are using religion as a cover to accomplish some ulterior motive, it will not be permitted.... Let me hear no more out of you about the Qur'an."[24] The notion that the Nation of Islam was not a legitimate religion but, rather, a guise for a politically subversive movement would become the linchpin of the state's arguments against religious protections for incarcerated Muslims over the next half decade. A month later, the warden wrote Sostre personally: "I have no knowledge of any religious restriction. Suggest you and your friends take the matter up with the Protestant Chaplain."[25] They did, and the chaplain recommended he send his petition to the assistant attorney general in the nearby town of Plattsburgh. By October, Judge Stephen Brennan and the Court for the Northern District of New York had granted Sostre, SaMarion, and Pierce permission to commence their actions against Warden La Vallee in forma pauperis, which allowed an indigent person to bring suit without liability for court costs.[26] The state would soon retaliate again.

Even after Sostre and others were thrown in solitary, Muslims continued to meet on the courts in Clinton Prison yard. On December 25, 1959, despite freezing temperatures, a small group gathered as they normally would on Fridays for *Jumu'ah*. According to prison guard John Emery Duquette, who was monitoring nearby, one of the Muslims who had been placed in isolation, Samuel X Williams, proposed a takeover of the solitary gallery by Muslims. For this, he was returned there. Four days later, seven more Muslims were taken to disciplinary court and lost 360 days of earned time.[27] This loss of a full year of earned time appears to have been the harshest possible sanction of its type. According to the prison's annual records, only eight people lost that much time during 1959, and at least seven of them were Muslim. In fact, the repression of Muslims at Clinton between August and December 1959 marked a dramatic uptick in the use of solitary and lost time as punishment by the state. For example, the prison reported a total loss of 19,685 earned days between July 1, 1959 and September 1960—5,000 more days than the year before or after.[28] This figure alone attests to the seriousness with which the authorities regarded this collective Muslim presence.

Solitary and the revocation of earned time worked in tandem to

disrupt organizing while extending people's sentences. Discipline began with an initial loss of earned time, such as the 360 days Williams and others lost. Then prisoners lost three additional days of good time for each day in solitary. Good time could not be earned back until they were released into the general population.[29] Sostre lost an initial sixty days of earned time for the charge of belonging to a "criminal Muslim organization." This loss of time was one of the first of a half dozen disciplinary charges he accumulated while in solitary confinement between August 1959 and his transfer to Attica the following June.[30] It was through the combination of solitary confinement and lost time that Sostre went from the possibility of early release to a maximum sentence.

In early 1960, Sostre was given a series of psychiatric evaluations in preparation for his second parole hearing. At the time, he had two pending lawsuits against the state, including one against the parole board.[31] These meetings produced a bizarre set of documents, ranging from IQ scores, Rorschach inkblots, and Wechsler-Bellevue tests to notes on conversations with Sostre about solitary confinement and the repression of Islam in prisons. In them, evaluators described Sostre as "a man of SUPERIOR intellectual capabilities" and a "psychopathic personality with pathologic emotionality."[32] Psychologists fixated on a comment he made about doing something "dramatic [to] bring his plight to the notice of the world outside the prison" and recommended placing him in a hospital for observation. Sostre later explained that he was referring to a hunger strike.[33] The use of psychiatry to medicalize dissent would become a recurring theme in Sostre's struggle. Despite their pathologization of protest, the psychiatrists nevertheless declared their own tools useless: "This man is so involved in the legalistics of his case and is of such a personality pattern, it would be almost pointless to think in terms of psychotherapeutic alteration of basic personality structure. Close supervision in parole appears mandatory."[34] In effect, when challenged, the state could only pathologize, punish, and surveil.

By early 1960, the majority of Muslims at Clinton were in solitary confinement. State officials were frantically responding to the growth of the Nation of Islam and its mass litigation strategy.[35] Commissioner McGinnis and his colleagues set up a centralized tracking system for all suspected Muslims in New York prisons, housed within the State Police's Bureau of Criminal Investigation (BCI).[36] They internally circulated a list of the Nation of Islam's mosques, on which Buffalo's Temple No. 23,

located at 1412½ Jefferson Avenue, was underlined. Five years later, Sostre would open his Afro-Asian Bookshop in the same building.[37]

Prison officials in California, Kansas, Michigan, and Pennsylvania also coordinated their surveillance of Muslim captives. With lawsuits against the warden of Clinton now winding their way through the courts, McGinnis and Martin Dillon of the BCI reached out to other agencies to find out everything they could out about two attorneys, Jawn Sandifer and Edward Jacko, who had been tapped by the Nation of Islam's headquarters in Chicago to represent Sostre and the other Muslim plaintiffs.[38]

That same month, Sostre and Pierce were moved to an even more repressive solitary gallery called E-6. Sostre's copies of his court cases and decisions were taken from him, and he was allowed only a copy of the Christian Bible.[39] He and others in E-6 snuck in a few sheets of paper and made out what was called an interview slip to the PK asking him to meet with them to explain why they were being denied pencils, pens, and grievance slips. A guard "tore it up," Sostre said.[40] He and three others remained in E-6 until his transfer to Attica on June 28, 1960.[41]

Sostre would later describe these forms of solitary confinement in court as "two different types of discipline. . . . One was punitive, that was solitary confinement, whereas E-6 was a more coercive type of punishment."[42] Although all prison discipline is coercive, Sostre distinguished between confinement that was meant to punish behavior and that which sought to break a person's spirit and force them to submit. This separation of coercion from punishment likely stood in contrast to his later, anarchist thinking, according to which all coercion is illegitimate and must be opposed. For Sostre, living through these gradations of punishment and coercion enabled him to better understand their fundamental connections to one another.

Solitary confinement is often alluded to as a "prison within a prison." But this description fails to capture the continuum of torture deployed to punish Sostre and other Muslims in New York State. One deprivation at Clinton was called the "dark cell." There, people were made to strip completely naked and given half a cup of water and a slice of bread three times a day. Joseph Magette described a "crack under the door of the block cell about an inch high and through this crack, the cold air comes, and that was the most miserable part of the thing."[43]

Along with his study of law, Sostre began "reading and studying Indian scriptures" and practicing yoga to withstand the isolation of

solitary confinement.[44] "The floor was so hard and cold that I could sleep only ten minutes in one position," he later said. "In order to deal with this, I taught myself yoga."[45] Although Sostre became a yogi in the late 1950s, most of his writings and discussions about yoga are from decades later, so it is difficult to know how he viewed his practice during this period. Only two images he drew in prison remained in his possession at his death. In one, he meticulously drew the steel grid pattern of his cell bars from his position inside. The other, "in my cell," portrays him in a standard single cell as someone on the outside looking in would see him. As he sits in a meditative half lotus pose reading a book, another is open next to him with a dozen others—likely legal materials—stacked on the floor.

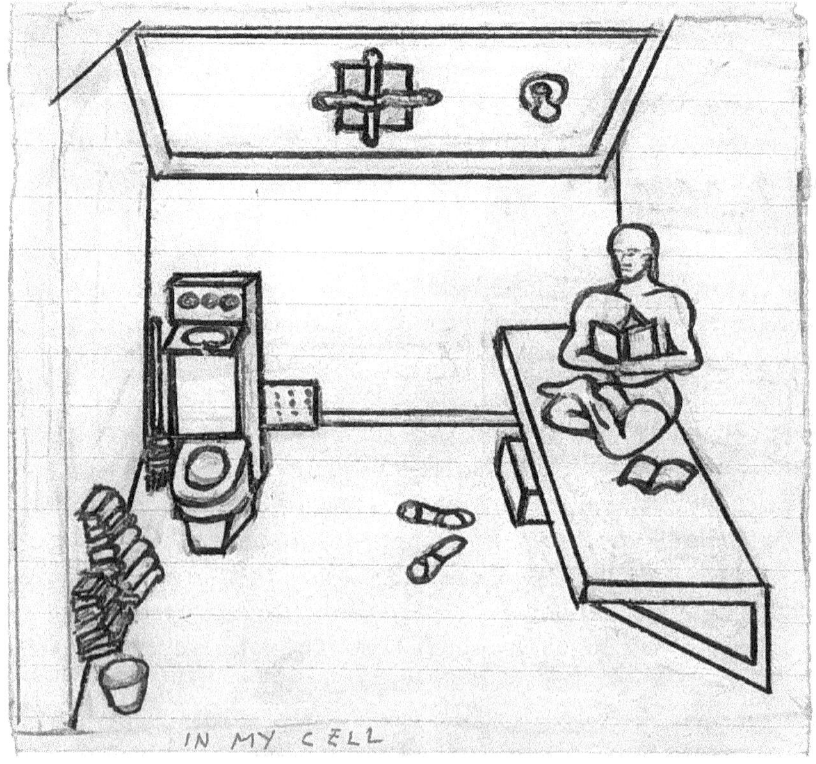

Martin Sostre, "In My Cell," undated. Martin Sostre Collection, University of Michigan Library (Special Collections Research Center).

In a 1976 interview, he described a daily routine that began with washing up, cleansing his nasal passages, and doing yoga.[46] He practiced "just enough yoga exercises to keep myself physically and mentally fit" and distinguished this approach from that of traditional South Asian yoga by rejecting notions of personal enlightenment, nirvana, or reincarnation. Sostre viewed yoga as a way to steel himself against the daily violence of prisons: "I have been able to resist and keep my spirit from being broken to a large degree because of my physical and mental discipline, and to me this is a weapon." Moreover, he saw yoga as he did study and litigation—as personal practices that served collective liberation.

Sostre is among a long line of activists, including Angela Davis and Rosa Parks, who similarly understood meditation and yoga as forms of individual survival in pursuit of collective freedom. "I started practicing yoga and meditation when I was in jail," Davis recalled, "but it was more of an individual practice. Later I had to recognize the importance of emphasizing the collective character, of that work, on the self."[47] Parks also practiced yoga for decades, beginning as early as 1965, and shared the practice with her family and community.[48] Feminist scholar Stephanie Evans, who has chronicled Parks's yoga, notes that "self-care is too often discussed as selfish" and that meditation and yoga should be viewed as part of the "sustainable struggle for human rights."[49] Although Sostre later criticized the ways yoga could produce inactivity and obedience, warning that it could become "passive" and "faddish," "trapped in the rut of outworn political clichés and unproductive acts," he continued to practice for the remainder of his life.[50]

Between 1959 and 1964, Sostre remained trapped in solitary confinement. To break subjects who refused to be coerced and disciplined, the state created a labyrinth of escalating forms of torture designed to make them comply. A decade later, having found that such measures still failed to extinguish prisoners' resistance, the state would turn to psychosurgery, shock therapy, psychotropic drugs, and other behavior-modification techniques. Martin Sostre would become one of their first targets.

Despite their extreme isolation, Sostre and other Muslim prisoners found ways to organize and keep their cases moving through the courts. Over the next several years, Sostre would testify twice in Judge Stephen Brennan's US District Court for the Northern District. Solitary confinement would become a center of debate in both.

After overcoming countless legal barriers and spending over a year in solitary confinement, Sostre, SaMarion, and Pierce finally testified in court on October 20, 1960. It is unlikely that any of those in the court that day—plaintiffs, defendants, attorneys, or judge—could have anticipated the duration or magnitude of the battle ahead. Paul McGinnis, for example, had just entered his second year as commissioner when he was called as a witness on behalf of Clinton warden J. E. La Vallee. A decade later, amid widespread prison rebellions, he would be ordered by one Judge Constance Baker Motley to pay Sostre thirty-five dollars for each of the 372 days he had spent in solitary confinement. However, all of this lay beyond the horizon when Sostre and others testified that October. The idea that a judge would have anything to say about prison punishment was anathema to the courts, a point Judge Stephen Brennan made clear at the trial. "I will not try out prison discipline," he said; "I don't want to interfere with prison regulations."[51]

With litigation looming, prison officials had worked to make the issues coming before the court as narrow as possible. Earlier that year, Commissioner McGinnis had issued a memo to all wardens, superintendents, and directors making it permissible for an incarcerated Muslim to purchase four different versions of the Qur'an, none of them the version Sostre and others requested.[52] He and his co-plaintiffs refused them, both because they did not contain the original Arabic of their preferred translation and because they rightly recognized that accepting it could make their upcoming case moot.[53] Represented by Jacko and Sandifer, whom the Black-owned New York City weekly *Amsterdam News* described as "two of Harlem's most prominent civil rights lawyers," the plaintiffs argued that their solitary confinement and loss of good time constituted punishment for their religious beliefs. The hands-off logic of the courts was deeply entrenched, however, and Judge Brennan repeatedly frustrated any attempts to bring out these larger issues of punishment. Instead, he returned to the simple issue of access to the Qur'an, which he regarded as resolved. "You are asking to purchase the Koran. Now, the Warden says you can have the Koran. Well, what is there left for me to litigate?" he asked.[54]

It was clear from the outset that the court would not rule in the plaintiffs' favor. Sostre had hardly opened his mouth before he was

reprimanded. The judge chastised him to slow down, before finally telling him, "Mr. Sostre, you are going to do what I tell you. When you don't want to do it you can leave." Sostre had waited over a year in solitary for the opportunity to testify. He responded confidently that his constitutional rights had been stripped from him. When it came to bringing forward the corresponding evidence, he asserted, "I am going to have a right to that before the Court."[55] Brennan responded, "You have no right to tell me how to try your case, and I am not going to let you, and if that is your attitude I will dismiss your case right now." Jacko pleaded with Sostre not to speak unless he or the judge asked him directly to do so.[56] Although Sostre was the target in this exchange, Brennan's racist hostility ran through the entire trial. He regularly referred to the plaintiffs and their counsel as "you people" and berated Jacko to "be a good little boy."[57] By the time Sostre and other Muslims took the stand, the judge had made it clear that he regarded the case as "so much to do about nothing. It is rather pathetic."[58]

A case that had taken years to reach federal court was dismissed in a day. Judge Brennan diminished their torture as no more than having "been inconvenience[d] for a week or two or a month or two."[59] In his estimation, the Muslim Brotherhood was not a religion, nor was their punishment in solitary confinement a result of their religious beliefs.[60] Having suffered a year in solitary only to be told by the judge that his torture constituted a "very minor" harm, it would have been understandable if Sostre had concluded that the courts were not a worthwhile tool. Instead, he would spend the next decade using them to expand the capacities of imprisoned people to survive and fight for liberation.

For Sostre and the other plaintiffs, the case offered valuable lessons and created openings for future litigation. Foremost among them was clarity regarding who to sue. "The action only involves La Vallee, nobody else," Judge Brennan had explained. "The Department of Correction is not here." Although Commissioner McGinnis had testified in court as a witness, he was not a party to the suit. "It seems to me that if you wanted something, to get a decision that would bind them," the judge had said, "No. 1, you would have to bring in the Department of Correction."[61] The second lesson had to due with the trial's scope. Their plaintiffs' repeated attempts to bring solitary confinement and lost earned time before the courts clashed with the hands-off doctrine, which had long made the judicial branch a reluctant arbiter of prison discipline. Thus, almost exactly a year later Edward Jacko filed on behalf of his clients again, this time

adding Commissioner McGinnis as a defendant.[62] In the meantime, for Sostre and his comrades, solitary confinement continued to be a central site of struggle against the state as they continued their efforts to bring constitutional claims before the courts.

When Thomas Bratcher was transferred to Attica Prison in May 1961, he found sixty Muslims in the Nation of Islam already there. At least one in ten of them, including Martin Sostre, were in solitary confinement. In a petition to Commissioner McGinnis from around this time, Bratcher contended that "Muslims at this very moment are being punished in segregation or 'protection' solely because they professed and practiced the religion of Islam." The petition was signed by thirteen prisoners before it was confiscated by guards.[63] The following month, prison officials learned of "a general sit-down strike among the Muslim inmates to create a sympathy for Sostre."[64] By November, Bratcher had joined Sostre and SaMarion in "a pact not to go down [to general population] until the religious persecution of the Muslims cease."[65]

These takeovers of solitary confinement dated back to Samuel X Williams's proposal at Clinton in late 1959, for which he and seven others had been put in "the box." Sostre pointed out to other Muslims that these reprisals had the opposite of their intended effect. "They took over the box and converted eight," he explained. "The Warden became afraid of putting any more dead brothers in the box for fear that they would be raised upon coming into contact with us. So his whole security system broke down."[66] (The phrase "dead brothers" was used by Muslims in the Nation to describe Black men without "knowledge of self," whose consciousness had not yet been raised, and who had yet to accept the teachings of the Honorable Elijah Muhammad.) "Now he is up tight because there are Muslims in all three galleries so if a dead brother comes up to the box [he] will have to be placed in a gallery with a Muslim," Sostre wrote in a letter to James X Ritchie.[67]

The strategy spread. When Ritchie was placed in solitary confinement in early 1962 for speaking about Islam on the yard, Joseph X Magette and sixteen other Muslims volunteered to join him by "keep-locking" themselves, presumably by refusing to leave their cells. "If he was put in segregation because he was speaking his religion," Magette said, "I was

committing the same act each and every day . . . so it would only be justice if I was pla ced in segregation along with him." A few months later, Magette organized another sit-in, in which another sixteen or so Muslims requested to be keep-locked in their cells.[68] These protests used the least restrictive form of solitary confinement, keep-lock, to turn the general prison population gallery into a kind of de facto solitary block.

Sostre and other Muslim prisoners decided they would collectively resist solitary confinement through solidarity, knowingly defying prison rules restricting their study and practice of Islam until they filled the solitary unit at Attica. As Sostre explained, "The box is the only weapon that the wardens have to maintain discipline in prison. When the box ceases to work, the entire disciplinary and security system breaks down."[69] This strategy resembled, and even predated, the better-known "jail, no bail" tactics of the Student Nonviolent Coordinating Committee and other civil rights groups in the South, which filled the jails until no more demonstrators could be arrested and held because there was nowhere to put them without releasing those who were awaiting trial on their personal recognizance.[70]

For years, Sostre recalled, the wardens had been putting "one or two Muslims in the box every month." When another Muslim in the general population needed to be disciplined, they would release one from solitary. "In other words, he kept manipulating the brothers like monkeys on a string." Solitary confinement was by design an individual punishment meant to disconnect people from their community. To try to survive solitary confinement alone constituted a tacit consent to the rules that governed it, thereby reinscribing its power. To collectively reject that consent by filling solitary so prison officials could no longer use it to govern was one way to empty it of power.

As Sostre's second chance in court approached, he and others attempted to make these forms of prison discipline a justiciable issue. SaMarion and Bratcher also filed a lawsuit against Warden Wilkins and Commissioner McGinnis modeled closely after Sostre's petition, which he had enclosed in a bar of soap and passed on in the shower room. Both Sostre's template and SaMarion and Bratcher's suit alleged that more than thirty Muslims had been, or were currently, in solitary because they discussed Islam or had literature outside their cells.[71] In October 1961, Sostre and other Muslims at Attica claimed to "have taken over the box and [the warden] is anxious to get us out of the box, especially with the

big trial coming soon. So don't let him clean up for we are living proof of the religious oppression complained of in our writs."[72] Just as they hoped to use solitary confinement as evidence of their oppression in the courts, the state used their purposeful takeovers of solitary to claim the Nation of Islam was not a legitimate religion and in fact constituted a threat to the security of the prison.

By the time Sostre appeared before Chief Judge Stephen Brennan's court a second time in November 1961, his reputation as a jailhouse lawyer preceded him. Assistant Attorney General William Bresinhan characterized Sostre as a "prolific drawer of legal papers."[73] The judge began the proceedings by noting his "experience with these gentlemen, especially Mr. Sostre."[74] Sostre admitted in court that he had prepared the templates in solitary confinement for his co-plaintiffs Pierce and SaMarion.[75] As in the previous trial, although this time over two full days of testimony and cross-examination, Sostre was reprimanded by Brennan for writing the judge directly rather than through his lawyers, for interjecting, and for talking too quickly. His rebuke is revealing: "Witness, you have not learned discipline yet after all your years in prison."[76]

One of the lengthiest exchanges between the judge and Sostre focused on his letter describing their takeovers of solitary confinement. Along with the Muslim Brotherhood's confiscated constitution, one of the state's key pieces of evidence at trial was a legal template and letter from Sostre and other Muslims describing their theorization of solitary confinement as the prison's central mechanism of repression. Judge Brennan asked Sostre why he felt he had the right to distribute contraband in solitary confinement in the form of a legal petition smuggled in soap. Sostre defended his actions under the "doctrine of legitimacy of purpose," trying, it seems, to draw upon English legal precedent to claim that the need for courts to intervene in religious persecution superseded any violation of prison rules because the principles of natural justice meant preventing the authorities from abusing their power. When the judge pressed Sostre on what he meant by "his whole security system broke down," Sostre explained that he meant that in order to "stop the Muslims from growing or expanding," the warden needed to put them in solitary confinement. The crux of Judge Brennan's questioning was his assertion that if Sostre and others had refused to leave solitary confinement and, instead, attempted to fill it, then they were actively participating in the same persecution from which they claimed to suffer. Frustrated by Sostre's unwillingness to cede this

argument, the judge resorted to the analogy of a child being reprimanded: "When a lad is punished, very often he will go in and say he will a good boy and the punishment is alleviated." Sostre responded: "By the same analogy the boy is being told what he is punished for."[77]

Running through Sostre's testimony was his anti-authoritarianism and commitment to bringing out the internal contradictions of prison authority and the courts as they failed to practice their own stated principles. Although he was over a decade away from identifying as an anarchist and saying that "you have to break the law to get justice," Sostre already understood law as a form of domination of the many by the few.[78] As political philosopher Ruth Kinna points out, part of the tyranny of law is that "submitting to [it] involved the suspension of individual judgement."[79] Sostre continually asserted his own right to make moral and ethical judgments that compelled him to resist the laws and interests of the state. "You see, Mr. Jacko," a frustrated judge explained to Sostre's attorney, "what seems to run through this case, if I understand this witness right, he feels he can violate prison discipline under conditions which he feels are justified."[80] While Sostre's fight for the free exercise of religion has been read most often as a form of constitutionalism or prison reform, it carried at its core what Russian anarcho-communist Peter Kropotkin identified as two of the central principles of anarchism: individual sovereignty and the moral obligation to resist authority.[81]

Despite these frustrating exchanges with an overtly racist judge, the *Amsterdam News* proclaimed the trial a "major victory."[82] In the US Court of Appeals for the Second Circuit, a two-thirds majority reversed and remanded Judge Brennan's decision, ruling that if Sostre and other Muslims were being punished because of their religion, they could seek redress in federal courts as a violation of their rights under the Fourteenth Amendment. The door was now ajar. That same year, over a hundred court actions were brought by incarcerated Muslims in what the *New York Times* called a "widespread legal attack on the state's prison system."[83] A few years earlier, the notion that a state prison commissioner would stand in court and answer to the judicial branch for the treatment of prisoners had been almost unfathomable. Now, Commissioner Paul McGinnis was the defendant in multiple lawsuits filed by Muslim prisoners across New York State. In January 1962, the Court of Appeals ruled in another case Sostre had helped to prepare that the state had violated section 610 of its Correction Law and called for a federal court hearing.[84]

In late 1962, Malcolm X testified in Buffalo for two days as an expert witness in *SaMarion v. McGinnis*, yet another case for which Sostre had provided legal templates. Sostre was again a subject of discussion. William Bresinhan, the assistant attorney general, declared at the outset that the "whole prison system of the State of New York is on trial."[85] He then pressed Malcolm X about the letter Sostre and others wrote about takeovers of solitary confinement: "We say this document, which was found in Attica Prison, written by Sostre, shows that Sostre and other Muslims are using the Muslim movement and the Muslim religion for the purpose of destroying prison discipline."[86] Malcolm strategically suggested that Sostre's comments were a result of "improper religious instructions," and Judge Henderson ultimately ruled that, regardless of its orthodoxy, the Nation of Islam was undeniably a religion and its practitioners were thereby entitled to the right to free exercise of religion, even in prisons.[87] The Nation of Islam packed the Erie County courtroom throughout the trial and publicized photographs of the plaintiffs in manacles and leg irons. Its official organ, *Muhammad Speaks*, noted that the trial was "taking on the proportions of one of the most significant court cases on religion in the history of American jurisprudence."[88]

Such legal victories came at a high cost. Most of Sostre's surviving letters from these years in solitary confinement contain desperate and frustrated pleas to court clerks asking for receipts and updates on the status of his cases. Throughout all this legal wrangling and ping-ponging between state and federal courts, he was subjected to an ongoing campaign to silence him. "The spiritual and physical aspect of the struggle," he later reflected, "involved years of torture in solitary confinement, beatings, tear gassing while locked in cages, bread and water diets, and many other barbarities inflicted by the State to break our spirit, health and resoluteness, and to coerce other prisoners from joining our ranks."[89] Six months before being released, Sostre wrote Thurgood Marshall, then a judge on the US Court of Appeals, that he "and at least eight other Muslims are now being tortured, starved, and harassed in the dungeons of solitary confinement at Attica Prison solely because [we] are Muslims." The deprivations were total: undernourishment and deliberate contamination of food, denial of medical care, confiscation of legal documents and religious texts, obstruction of legal paperwork, and denials of exercise and yard privileges. In one lawsuit, he argued that the "slow starvation coupled with forcing him to sleep on a cold and hard concrete floor while stripped of his clothes,

and depriving him of the means of maintaining basic sanitary hygiene, and denying him physical exercise, sunshine, and fresh air" constituted "remnant[s] of medieval forms of torture."[90]

Sostre routinely had to act as his own counsel and was sometimes forced to submit appeals from memory. As he explained to Marshall, "Persecuted Muslims are caged up like animals in dungeons 24 hours a day and being starved, while the *SaMarion* lawyers are outside eating steaks. They are in no rush." He accused state judges and prison officials of colluding to drag these cases on until he and the other plaintiffs abandoned their resistance: the "delay sought is merely the usual stalling tactic employed to break down the Muslims and force them to withdraw their court actions and to buy time in which to establish and implement a state sponsored 'white' Islamic religious service pursuant to the 'new' rules on religious worship."[91]

Finally, during the summer of 1964, two legal decisions, separated by little more than a month, fundamentally advanced the rights of incarcerated people in the United States. Sostre played a role in both: first, by establishing the important precedent of *Pierce v. La Vallee* cited in *Cooper v. Pate* and, second, as the plaintiff in *Sostre v. McGinnis*. These cases solidified the application of the Bill of Rights and the First Amendment to imprisoned people and opened the door for judicial intervention into prison conditions and discipline. Legal historian Margo Schlanger concludes that by 1964, "the federal disinclination to meddle in prison operations—labeled, after the fact, the 'hands-off doctrine'—was dead."[92] Soon after these decisions were handed down, Sostre's maximum sentence expired. He was transferred from Attica on September 18, 1964, to spend an additional thirty days for contempt of court at Erie County Jail.

Sostre would later write that his "singleminded struggle in the Muslims cases was a stage and mission which was concluded successfully."[93] He would soon settle in Buffalo, starting a new life and fulfilling a dream of opening a revolutionary bookstore that would do for the Black community and young people on the city's East Side what the bookstores of Harlem and communal study in prison had done for him. But in the surveillance files established as a response in part to his organizing inside, state police would waste no time in sharing possible Buffalo addresses for Sostre and described him as "a rabid Muslim."[94] Although Martin Sostre would later reflect that he was "a stranger in Buffalo," he was no stranger to state authorities.[95]

5

"A Power Base of Revolutionary Political Philosophy"

As Martin Sostre served his final thirty days at Erie County Jail on a contempt of court charge, state officials were preparing to hear *Bryant v. Wilkins* in the courthouse across the street. The lawsuit was another prisoners' rights case that he had a hand in drafting, and the imminency of the trial—combined with Sostre's presence in Buffalo—triggered a wave of panic among authorities.[1] With memories still fresh from *SaMarion v. McGinnis*, when Malcolm X had testified as an expert witness and newspapers had decried the shackling of Muslim plaintiffs, a judge now "insisted that there should be no display of manacles or shackles on the litigants in court."[2] He moved the trial forty-five miles away to Warsaw, New York, where state police hoped that "transportation and employment" would limit Muslim courtroom presence.[3] Meanwhile, the sheriff of Wyoming County met with state police, anticipating numerous arrests. They proposed using ten school buses to transport hundreds of potential detainees and transforming a local high school gymnasium into a mass holding cell.[4] Less than a year had passed since police in Birmingham, Alabama, made international headlines for turning fire hoses and dogs on children protesting racial segregation. Now, state officials in New York prepared for similar violence directed at Muslims attending a trial over the constitutional rights of prisoners.

Martin Sostre was at the center of these anxieties. State officials, in particular, feared he might attend the trial and "be considered a leader if violence should occur." An interview by state police with William

Bresinhan of the district attorney's office best captured these apprehensions. Sostre was described with a mix of fear and contempt shared by many officials: as a "self-styled attorney who has fought relentlessly for Muslim rights" and who is "full of hate."[5] In March 1965, Justice Lawless rendered a decision in *Bryant v. Wilkins* that would have been unimaginable half a decade earlier. Citing section 610 of the State Correction Law and the New York State Constitution, Lawless warned that religious rights would be trampled if "the Commissioner of Correction is permitted to restrict religious exercises to those sects which he judges worthy of recognition." The judge directed Commissioner McGinnis to "prepare and promulgate" revised regulations that would be consistent with the federal and state constitutions as well as the "spirit and intent" of state correction law.[6] This victory joined others made possible by Sostre's organizing and litigation, for which he had been made to suffer dearly.

Meanwhile, Sostre was opening a new chapter of his life at the age of forty-one. Shortly after his release in October 1964, he found a job at the Bethlehem Steel plant near Buffalo. A few months later, he married for the first time. By the time of the *Bryant* decision, he had saved enough to establish the city's first revolutionary Black bookstore—the first of three he would open over the next several years.[7] From the beginning, the Afro-Asian Bookshop was an extension of other forms of Black community space and radical study in his life, which were also targeted and disrupted by the state.[8] Through trial and error, he transformed the fledgling store at 1412 Jefferson Avenue into what he called a "power base of revolutionary political philosophy."[9] The bookshop's literature reflected the anticolonial, internationalist perspective embodied in its name. Sostre carried the speeches and writings of Fidel Castro and Pedro Albizu Campos, and journals such as *African Opinion*, *Peking Review*, and *China Reconstructs*.[10] Mao's Little Red Book and the autobiography of Ho Chi Minh were displayed in the window to attract passersby.[11] Sostre later described it as a "community center" where people could use the phone, borrow money, or get change for the parking meter. One customer remembered Sostre as "warm and kind and smart and welcoming." "It was a beautiful place," she said, "[and] became like a home away from home."[12] Like Michaux's, the bookstore Sostre emulated, the Afro-Asian Bookshop became an accessible space dedicated to radical political education. Later, he would write proudly that the bookstore was "becoming the mecca for politically motivated local youth,"

drawing visitors from hundresds of miles away, such as Rochester, Syracuse, and Toronto.[13]

Sostre's three years in Buffalo (1964–67) coincided with historic political ferment and convergences among social movements. Rejecting the incrementalism, nonviolence, and focus on demanding change from the state that characterized the civil rights struggle, a new generation organized for Black Power. The escalation of the United States' imperial war in Vietnam became a lightning rod for the student movement and the New Left. Along with better-known radical campuses in Berkeley and Ann Arbor, the State University at Buffalo (UB) was home to one of the most active campus movements of the late 1960s.[14] Students fought to remove Reserve Officers' Training Corps (ROTC) from campus, resisted the university's relocation from the city center to a suburb, opposed a contract with the US military to improve jet engines on fighter planes and bombers, and organized to free a group of draft resistors who—inspired by Sostre—burned their draft cards, becoming known as the Buffalo Nine.[15]

"There was amazing unrest," UB student Dan Bentivogli remembered. "But to me, the struggle in the Black community over the moving of the UB campus to Amherst, over the tearing up of a major boulevard through the Black community to put up a highway—these were big community issues that I got involved in."[16] Federally funded "urban renewal" projects were underway in Buffalo, serving predominantly white, middle-class suburban communities and downtown developers while deepening racial segregation, contributing to freeway pollution and noise, and cutting off small businesses that had once thrived along business strips such as Jefferson Avenue, where the bookstore was located.[17] Buffalo's economy, which had been based on shipping, steel, auto, chemicals, and aircraft, was declining. Decades of virulent anticommunism had weakened trade unions. Amid decreasing working-class radicalism, the Buffalo branch of the Socialist Workers Party broke with the SWP to form the Workers World Party (WWP) and its youth affiliate, Youth Against War and Fascism (YAWF).

Sostre and his bookstores would help to connect these interrelated struggles. Indeed, he embodied their intersections: he was a steelworker, antiwar veteran, and criminalized Black Puerto Rican business owner on the city's East Side. No other bookstores in Buffalo carried antiwar and Black Power literature, making his bookshops a central point of convergence for these movements. As historian Malcolm McLaughlin remarks, Sostre appealed to "students and to local youths alike and that enabled

him to achieve something valuable and, in itself, remarkable: he brought those disparate groups together under one roof and around a common set of causes."[18] His success in promoting the political education of Black youth and fomenting collective resistance to oppression seemed to confirm the state officials' fevered nightmares of Black insurgency.

Historian Dan Berger has described the carceral state as "anticipatory violence masquerading as responsive force."[19] This description encapsulates the state's approach to Sostre's presence in Buffalo. From the moment of his arrival, multiple state and federal law enforcement agencies watched anxiously as he embedded himself in Buffalo's radical communities, then connected and expanded them. The authorities projected their fears of Black rebellion onto Sostre and responded to his organizing with a preemptive force that they justified with fictions they created.

Within just two days of his release, Sostre landed a unionized job at Bethlehem Steel, making a solidly middle-class wage of $135–146 a week (roughly $61,000–65,000 a year in today's dollars).[20] The day he was hired, a supervisor at the company shared his application with the FBI. In it, Sostre had laid out a personal history largely based on his own life, with changes to key facts that would have likely hurt his employment chances. Sostre told the company he had received a high school diploma before earning an honorable discharge after four years in the military. Then, he claimed, he had worked for his family's painting and contracting business for ten years, took a job at "Crescent Dress Factory" in New York City in 1956, and worked at "Seaco Mills" in 1961.[21] The FBI soon discovered that Sostre had in fact been dishonorably discharged and found no evidence that the companies Sostre listed ever existed.[22] One memo warned that "he should be approached with caution inasmuch as he was convicted by court-martial for assault with a dangerous weapon, to wit: a knife."[23] The FBI's local field office and the Buffalo Police Department subversive unit established a liaison to share information about Sostre, and state police circulated his mug shot. They even made a "camouflaged telephone call" to the home of Willis Bryant's mother, where he was staying.[24] While his job was apparently not imperiled by these revelations, state surveillance of his activities deepened.

Located in the far western corner of New York State, where the shores

of Lake Erie meet the US–Canadian border, Buffalo was then the easternmost of the industrial cities on the Great Lakes. Its economic, demographic, and social history resembled other cities that are thought of as Midwestern, such as Milwaukee, Gary, Toledo, and Cleveland. The city was in a pivotal period of economic and demographic transition when Sostre arrived, epitomizing the postindustrial transformation from "smokestack town to an emerging service and high tech city," in the words of urban planning scholar Henry Louis Taylor, Jr.[25] Although relatively few African Americans settled in Buffalo during the First Great Migration, wartime production during the 1940s produced job opportunities, and the Black population doubled from 3 to 6 percent. By 1960, the city was 13 percent Black.[26] This influx of Black Southern migrants was accompanied by white suburban flight and the beginnings of deindustrialization. The overall population of the city dropped by nearly 40 percent from 1950 to 1978.[27] When Sostre settled in Buffalo in October 1964, the city was in the midst of losing fifty-one thousand residents over a six-year period. Yet almost twenty-five thousand Black people moved to the city during the 1960s.[28] This demographic transformation was bound up in the shift from an economy based on industrial employment to one dominated by the service sector.[29]

As Buffalo declined in both industry and population during the 1950s and '60s, its Black communities were repeatedly displaced and increasingly confined to the Ellicott, Masten Park (Cold Spring), and Fruit Belt districts on the East Side of the city.[30] Sostre's first apartment was located in the Fruit Belt above the High Street Delicatessen.[31] The neighborhood was racially segregated, and white police represented an occupying army. Revolutionary activist Jaan Laaman remembered that even in a white working-class neighborhood on the West Side as a kid "without any radical politics, or even too much concept of white supremacy and all that kind of stuff, you just knew that the cops were white, and they would mess with you, and if you were not white, you're going to get messed with even worse."[32] "Every thug I knew in the neighborhood became a cop," Dan Bentivogli recalled.[33] The segregation on the East Side and on the police force was so stark that one state trooper charged with spying on Sostre wrote, "This is a predominantly Negro community and proper surveillance could not be conducted."[34]

Although Buffalo's position as a port city was in decline and its once-thriving industry was being consolidated, the driving force of the

local economy remained Bethlehem Steel. Its Lackawanna plant six miles south of Buffalo's downtown, then the second-biggest steel manufacturer in the world, employed nearly thirty thousand workers.[35] One history of the steel mill describes the period from 1940 to 1967 as the "long boom," when its growth and profits reached record levels.[36] In 1966, Bethlehem produced nearly seven million tons of steel.[37] The escalation of the war in Vietnam multiplied the demand for workers, as heightened production coincided with the drafting of the young men who typically held these jobs. Laaman was still a teenager when he took a job at the steel mill in the mid-1960s. He recalled a giant billboard on the highway from downtown Buffalo to Lackawanna that said "Bethlehem Steel Hiring Now" with directions to the employment office. He was one of the young white people who visited Sostre's Afro-Asian Bookshop, and later became a political prisoner as well.[38]

The jobs given to Black men by Bethlehem Steel were the most dangerous and grueling. Vincent Copeland, a white former welder, grievance officer, and newspaper editor, was fired in 1950 for leading wildcat strikes in protest of the company's practice of hiring new white workers rather than promoting Black furnace workers. Copeland recalled waking up at 5:15 a.m. to travel from Buffalo to the plant on cold winter mornings and "curs[ing] the fate that condemned you to work there."[39]

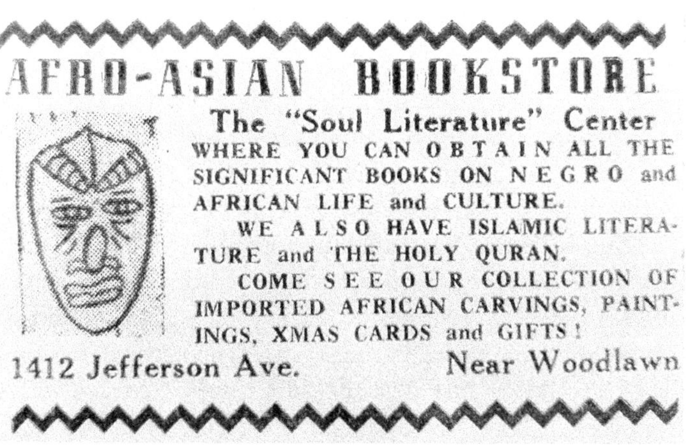

Advertisement, *Buffalo Criterion*, June 22, 1966. Buffalo Public Library, Grosvenor Room. Reproduction by permission of the Buffalo and Erie County Public Library, Buffalo, New York.

Fifteen years later, Martin Sostre was hired into those same conditions. He painted a grisly scene in a letter to NAACP executive director Roy Wilkins: "Here Black men endanger their lives and health everyday by working in 140 degree heat, burning their bodies with white-hot coals, sheets of roaring fire, and splashing melted steel, filling their lungs, pores and eyeballs with smoke, coal dust, and chemical gasses, all the while sweating out the salt from their bodies until their working clothes become stiff and white with the encrusted salt."[40]

But this was only Sostre's first shift of the day. His second shift was at his fledgling Afro-Asian Bookshop, which opened in March 1965 in the building that formerly housed the Nation of Islam's Mosque No. 23.[41] Sostre would later characterize these early days in Buffalo and at the bookstore as a lonely time. He had no relatives in western New York State. His family of origin had dwindled and dispersed from New York City during his years inside; his mother, Crescencia, had passed away during his incarceration, and his sister Leticia moved to Los Angeles.[42] "I was working alone, without any experience, political connections, money, friends," he wrote.[43]

Indeed, Buffalo may have seemed an odd location for such an endeavor. Black radical journalist William Worthy described the city as having "long been stagnant, corrupt, reactionary and culturally insipid," calling it "isolated and off the beaten path."[44] To Sostre, it was merely politically underdeveloped, and therefore an ideal site for building radical community through a political bookstore. But his feeling of isolation was also indicative of the rupture happening across the country in Muslim communities. Sostre opened the bookstore at a particularly volatile moment in the history of the Black freedom movement and the Nation of Islam—just weeks after Malcolm X was assassinated by members of the NOI in collusion with the state.

Sostre's depiction of himself as disconnected from any community was both real and constructed in hindsight. It reflected the traumatic break he experienced from his political home during this early period in Buffalo while obscuring his embeddedness in a community he later denounced and distanced himself from. When he was released, he immediately connected with the community he had made in prison. Consistent with the Muslim Brotherhood's constitution that he had helped to write, which emphasized staying in touch with those still behind walls, he continued to communicate with his comrades inside.[45] In January 1965, he married Alberta Richardson, Willis X Bryant's sister, but they soon

separated.[46] This rupture', too, may have been a result of the turmoil within the Nation of Islam.

According to FBI surveillance, Sostre remained connected to Buffalo's Muslim community for nearly a year and well after Malcolm X's assassination. Between March and November 1965, he was reportedly present at six public meetings and seven meetings of the paramilitary men's division, the Fruit of Islam (FOI). That summer, he tabled at an Afro-Asian Bazaar sponsored by Mosque No. 23 with books by James Baldwin and Richard Wright on display. The next month, he spoke at an FOI meeting about the importance of being exposed to Elijah Muhammad's writings while "in the dungeon."[47] Sostre even partnered with a friend, likely from the Mosque No. 23 community, to run the bookstore. Despite being "a politically sophisticated Black nationalist with plenty of revolutionary enthusiasm," Sostre found the man "too square and inflexible" to connect with young customers in the store.[48]

By late 1965, Sostre had permanently left the Nation of Islam. According to one FBI source, he had been expelled by Minister John Strickland for refusing to donate "substantial proceeds of the Afro-Asian Bookstore" to the mosque. Yet he continued to carry copies of *Muhammad Speaks* at the store, although one of his comrades recalled him saying he got threats from local Muslims for selling Malcolm X's writings.[49] Sostre would later write that when he got out of prison and "saw that the Muslim movement was not the Revolutionary Black Nationalism that our youth was following and that the Muslim movement was so alienated from the Black masses that in all of Buffalo they could only muster 60 registered Muslims, both men and women, I gave it up."[50]

Sostre made his assessment on the brink of a new revolutionary period. The following year, Huey Newton and Bobby Seale formed the Black Panther Party for Self-Defense in Oakland, and civil rights organizations like the Congress of Racial Equality (CORE) and the Student Nonviolent Coordinating Committee (SNCC) embraced Black Power. In 1966, the US Selective Service conscripted nearly four hundred thousand men into the military—the highest total during the Vietnam War—provoking outrage and fueling the growing antiwar movement on campuses across the country. Students affiliated with Students for a Democractic Society (SDS) and YAWF would invite Sostre to speak on campus and frequent his bookstore. The NOI seemed disconnected from this ferment. Sostre judged the Nation in Buffalo the way he had in prison: by its organizing capacity

and mass appeal rather than its ideology. Malcolm X's assassination likely reinforced his skepticism about its effectiveness. It was in that context of frustration and disillusionment that Sostre set about answering what he saw as the most pressing question: "What must a Black revolutionary do to command the allegiance of the militant Black youth?"[51]

The opening of a Black-owned revolutionary bookstore in 1965 made Buffalo an outlier among US cities. As historian Joshua Davis notes, at the time "major centers of Black population such as Atlanta; Washington, D.C.; Oakland, California; and New Orleans . . . did not have a single Black-oriented bookstore." He estimates that between 1965 and 1979, the number of Black bookstores rose from roughly a dozen to nearly one hundred.[52] This wave of Black-owned bookstores was part of the nascent Black Power movement and consistent with its emphasis on building autonomous Black cultural and political institutions. Many had a commitment to distributing what Colin Beckles called "Black counter-hegemonic information." In broader terms, we might describe this as revolutionary political education. These bookstores acted as community spaces—a Black commons of sorts. Whether they were explicitly anticapitalist, making money was rarely their primary purpose; most barely managed to stay in business.[53] "We don't define profit in terms of money," explained Charlie Cobb, a SNCC organizer and cofounder of Drum and Spear Bookstore in Washington, DC. "The profit is the patronage of the community."[54]

Sostre's bookstore exemplified these principles. From the books he carried to the clientele he attracted, the bookstore aimed to raise consciousness and spread revolutionary ideas in the community, particularly among young people. He later wrote that he hoped to make his bookshop the "main library of dissent and protest literature in Buffalo."[55] His use of the term "library" was deliberate. Like Michaux's, it featured a reading room with lounge chairs where "you could come in and sit down and take a book off the shelf, read it and go through it and put it back and walk out."[56] Patrons were welcome even if they did not buy anything. Sostre sat and talked at great length with anyone who came in. "His idea was to make the bookstore a hangout, especially for young people," said one visitor.[57] "It was more like a library," another remembered.[58] As a socialist and outspoken critic of "Black capitalism," Sostre reinvested any meager profits

it earned back into the bookstore. His was one of the earliest examples of a Black-owned, anticapitalist, community-oriented bookstore in what would become the golden era of Black radical bookshops.[59]

Located near the prominent intersection of Jefferson and Woodlawn Avenues, the bookstore was part of a historic strip of Black-owned businesses. "All of your needs could be met at some point on Jefferson," local resident Jean Adams remembered. "When we were young teens, Jefferson was where everything was happening."[60] Joseph Clore, a teenager who patronized the store, also remembered the Avenue as "the place to be." His mother's hairdresser was a few doors down, and he was intrigued by the books displayed in the window of the Afro-Asian Bookshop. Directly adjacent Sostre's bookstore was the white-owned Woodlawn Tavern, whose mostly Black clientele sometimes used his shop as a community space. One of these visitors was Arto Williams, who would use the toilet or the phone, and sometimes buy a book. He once left a freshly cleaned suit for Sostre to watch.[61] Another person who came to the bookstore by way of the tavern was a former classmate of Williams, Geraldine Robinson.[62] Both would come to play an outsize role in some of the most consequential political events of the 1960s in Buffalo, the ramifications of which would be felt for decades to come.

NOW!-- YOU CAN OBTAIN THE MOST SIGNIFICANT BOOKS ON NEGRO LIFE AND CULTURE AT THE
AFRO-ASIAN BOOKSTORE
1412 Jefferson Ave. near Woodlawn
THE CENTER OF "SOUL LITERATURE"
ALSO:
AFRICAN GREETING CARDS • NEWSPAPERS • MAGAZINES
THE HOLY QURAN By M. ALI and Y. ALI • STATIONERY
ISLAMIC LITERATURE • AFRICAN CARVINGS • GIFTS

Advertisement, *Buffalo Challenger News Weekly*, September 9, 1965. Buffalo Public Library, Grosvenor Room. Reproduction by permission of the Buffalo and Erie County Public Library, Buffalo, New York.

Robinson and her friends had been out at the Woodlawn when they "stopped in [the bookshop] and started talking to Martin." "I invited him over to my house and that's how it all began," she remembered. Born in 1943 in Columbus, Ohio, she came from what she described as a "close-knit family" with six other siblings. Her mother moved them to Buffalo when Robinson was young, using earnings from a job at Bethlehem Steel to purchase a house on East Utica Street in the Cold Spring neighborhood, less than half a mile from Jefferson Avenue. By the time Robinson met Sostre, she was in her early twenties, had children of her own, and was living in an apartment nearby.[63]

For over a year, Sostre had been working at the steel mill during the day to cover rent, light, and phone bills, opening the bookstore only at night.[64] Sales, though steady, remained very slow. The store was stocked mostly with material on the history, culture, and politics of the African diaspora. "Although some of the books were by Black nationalist writers, some by Marxists and others by traditional Negro writers, they did not sell," Sostre wrote. He soon experimented by adding novels by Richard Wright, James Baldwin, and LeRoi Jones (later Amiri Baraka), but these alone could not make the store self-supporting. Eventually, he added large African lithographs and woodcarvings. A hand-drawn advertisement in one of city's Black-owned newspapers, the *Buffalo Criterion*, showed the eclectic range of the bookstore.[65]

"I was continuously plagued by two main problems," Sostre wrote. The first was making the store financially self-sufficient. The second was "how to convert the shop into a political center for the Afro-American youth." He was at an impasse, wondering whether to work from dawn to midnight at the bookshop and quit his job at the steel mill, taking the risk even though the store was still not breaking even. While weighing this decision, Sostre was walking down Jefferson Avenue and saw a group of young people standing in front of a record store listening to the loudspeaker outside. "The idea struck me as I watched them stomping their feet with the beat and enjoying the music. This was it!" The next day he bought a used record player, a loudspeaker from a TV repair shop, and fifty dollars' worth of records (roughly $500 today).[66]

People started coming into the store, especially teenagers, to request specific records. "In conversation, I would explain to them the tenets of Black nationalism, socialism, and Afro-American history. I would illustrate my points by showing them photos and cartoons from books and

magazines on the shelves. I taught continually—giving out pamphlets free to those who had no money. I let them sit and read for hours into the store. Some would come back every day and read the same book until they finished it. . . . A month later, I quit my job at Bethlehem." Recalling the bookstores and city blocks of his own youth, Sostre created an exterior space with a loudspeaker and stepladder orators to draw crowds of young people to the shop. In addition to Sostre's own speeches, one store-goer recalled representatives of CORE speaking out front about Black empowerment and community control.[67] Pamphlets, selling for as little as a quarter (a few dollars today), served "as introductory manuals into revolutionary thought" and stimulated conversations.[68] Working sixteen-hour days, seven days a week, Sostre was finally able to meet his costs and take sixty dollars a week in salary.

This success was also due to Robinson, who earned twenty-five dollars a week running the East-West Bookshop—enough to pay for a babysitter for her five children while she worked.[69] Robinson was closer in age to most of the shop's customers than Sostre was. Listening to the Black radio station, she would write down hit songs for him to purchase as 45s. She carried rock and roll, jazz, and spirituals for the older customers in the neighborhood. The records were so successful, she recalled, that her store covered the rent for the two others Sostre owned, including the main one at 1412 Jefferson Avenue.[70] One of the final newspaper advertisements for the bookstore reflected this shift, announcing the "long awaited" release of *Malcolm X Speaks Again* on record, featuring his famous speech "The Ballot or the Bullet."

It was the writings and speeches of Malcolm X that were the most effective in connecting with young people. "Of the thousands of titles which at one time or another passed on to and off of my shelves, one name attracted the Afro youth more than all the rest—Malcolm X," Sostre later wrote.[71] In late October 1965, eight months after Martin opened the first bookstore, *The Autobiography of Malcolm X* was released. It quickly became the primary introduction to Malcolm X's thought and ideas.[72] "They would listen to Brother Malcolm because he was one of them, he talked their language," Sostre reflected: "the language of the ghetto street where the black youth are freely able to express themselves without biting their tongues. All the qualities that black youth are in time with."[73]

Carol Ann Aiken (later Karima Amin) was among the young people who were drawn to the bookstore. She was seventeen years old when the

store opened, and would later fondly recall *The Autobiography of Malcolm X* as one of the first two books she bought with her own money. The other she purchased from the Afro-Asian Bookshop was *The Mis-Education of the Negro* by Carter G. Woodson. Although Amin lived in Cold Spring on the East Side, she attended a predominantly white high school on the North Side, where she was active in sports, academics, and other extracurriculars. She described the branch library on East Utica Street as her "home away from home." On her walk there, she would pass Sostre's bookstore. Her parents warned her: "Don't go to that place. They're dealing drugs out of that place. Bad people frequent that place. Homeless people are hanging around that place." She defied them, and soon it became another second home. "Sometimes I stayed at the bookstore and never got to the library," she recalled decades later. Amin would occasionally bring a friend or browse and ask questions about authors. Some days, she rushed in and out because she had schoolwork. But on others, she would "just sit and read, or talk to Mr. Sostre for a few minutes. I never wanted to monopolize his time. There were lots of people who wanted to spend time with him and talk to him and learn from him." She described the store as "a beautiful, warm, welcoming place, a place where I wanted to be, and where I felt I needed to be."[74]

NOW IN BUFFALO

MALCOM X SPEAKS AGAIN

THE LONG AWAITED LONG PLAY ALBUM

PRESERVING HIS WISDOM & LOGIC
EXCITING! INFORMATIVE!
GET YOUR COPY NOW AT THE–

Afro-Asian Book Shops

1412 JEFF. AVE. (near Woodlawn)
289 HIGH ST. (at Orange St.)

Advertisement, *Buffalo Challenger News Weekly*, October 27, 1966. Buffalo Public Library, Grosvenor Room. Reproduction by permission of the Buffalo and Erie County Public Library, Buffalo, New York.

The first few times sixteen-year-old Joseph Clore went by the bookstore, it was closed. Sostre was still working full-day shifts at the steel plant then, opening the shop only at night. After several attempts, Clore finally caught Sostre when the shop was open. "I went in and began to talk to him, and from then on, I would stop by whenever I could," he said. Clore remembered a mix of African history and politics, Marxist literature, and books on Asia. Fifty-five years later, he even remembered the title and author of a book he purchased—William Pomeroy's *Guerilla and Counter-guerilla Warfare*—which introduced him to the resistance movement led by farmers against the Philippine government during the 1940s and '50s. Clore would sit and talk with Sostre, recalling, "It did plant a seed in me to do more reading." Clore and Amin represent just a few of the Black people in their teens and twenties who visited the store. But Clore also knew that Black youth were not the only ones taking notice. "I was telling him—even at sixteen, I knew—'The cops are watching you, man, so be careful. Be very careful.' "[75]

Just months after opening in March 1965, Sostre was visited by two men who identified themselves as FBI agents. Several months later, two more detectives appeared, this time from the Buffalo subversive unit. "Nice place you got here, Marty," one said. "You're doing all right for yourself since you got out of prison. What are you doing now behind this bookstore front?" When Sostre defended his constitutional right to sell whatever literature he wanted, the detective replied: "A law-abiding citizen doesn't get involved in hate literature and communist propaganda." When he reiterated this right, the cop replied, "O.K., Marty, have it your way."[76] These visits were made at the instruction of Police Commissioner Frank Felicetta.[77] As Clore pointed out, the fact "that a little, snotty-nosed, wet-behind-the-ears, sixteen-year-old punk like me can say, 'Hey, Martin, the cops are watching you'" meant that "everybody knew the cops were watching him."[78]

At this moment of swelling insurgency in Buffalo, Sostre's bookshops were instrumental in bringing radical social movements together. One local revolutionary organization experiencing a rebirth was the Marxist-Leninist Workers World Party. Vincent and Libby Copeland, Sam Ballan (known by his pen name Sam Marcy) and his wife Dorothy (Dottie),

and Rosemary and Milt Neidenberg were longtime local activists who had been building the Buffalo branch of the Socialist Workers Party since the 1940s. But this nationwide Trotskyist organization was preoccupied with class struggle, and they thought it failed to recognize the significance of national liberation movements in the Third World and the radical potential of unrest among Black people in the United States that was based in local communities rather that the organized labor movement. Profoundly affected by the Cuban Revolution, they left the SWP and formed a new organization, the WWP, in 1959.

The WWP was internationalist, antiracist, and supported Black self-determination. The group rejected the view that students and young people belonged to the "petty bourgeoisie," instead creating and nurturing its youth affiliate, Youth Against War and Fascism. The WWP was led by the prolific Sam Marcy, whose presentations in New York City were tape-recorded and played to Buffalo branch members gathered around a kitchen table. Year later, Bob McCubbin, a UB student who joined YAWF, would remember the lectures as "very useful in terms of deepening my political understanding."[79] Marcy, born in eastern Russia in 1911, had been subjected to the anti-Jewish pogroms of the anticommunist White Guard. His family had settled in Brooklyn and Marcy had moved through the Communist Party USA and SWP before eventually cofounding the Workers World Party. During the early years of the Cold War, he had developed and promulgated an analysis of "global class war," which argued that wars of national liberation were in fact class wars. He wrote in 1950: "In this war the geographical boundaries are social boundaries, the battle formations are class formations, and the world line of demarcation is the line rigidly drawn by the socialist interests of the world proletariat."[80] This essay and Marcy's "Destiny of American Labor" (1953) were circulated within the WWP and known together as the "global class war documents."[81]

The WWP in Buffalo, which had its foundations in interracial, left-wing unions and progressive coalitions, was centrally concerned with opposing imperialism and allying with the Third World abroad and at home. McCubbin emphasized that the Buffalo cohort differed from SWP branches, which tended to be composed of middle-class intellectuals. "They were workers," he recalled, "the most proletarian branch of the Socialist Workers Party."[82] Emblematic of this were Edward and Jeanette Merrill, white workers with backgrounds in interracial union

organizing and local civil rights campaigns against hiring discrimination, school segregation, and housing displacement.[83] Originally from rural Maine, Ed had moved to Buffalo in 1951 looking for work. There, he had met Jeanette Fusco, an Italian American who had grown up locally. Soon after the WWP's creation, when most of its founding members moved their headquarters to New York City, the two set about rebuilding Buffalo's WWP branch. Ed had worked at Bethlehem Steel and later at the Wickwire plant in nearby Tonawanda until the latter steel mill closed in 1964. Jeanette was a technician for the telephone company. Both had been surveilled and red-baited by law enforcement long before meeting Sostre. Ed was blacklisted from the factories, and Jeanette would eventually leave her job teaching Spanish because she felt the constant FBI harassment was unfair to her students.[84]

The same state police unit that watched Sostre identified the Merrills in photographs from a town hall with Governor Rockefeller.[85] Then, they watched anxiously as these revolutionary organizers converged. In response to deindustrialization and the repression and decline of radicalism in labor unions, Ed and Jeanette focused their organizing for the Buffalo WWP on the nearby campus, concluding that "the workers weren't moving but the students were."[86] They quickly developed a chapter of YAWF, recruiting young radical students such as McCubbin, Bentivogli, and Jerry Gross (later Ross).[87] This group would later form the core of the Martin Sostre Defense Committee.

In 1964, two years after the University at Buffalo was absorbed into the state university system, the House Un-American Activities Committee (HUAC) investigated suspected communists on and off campus.[88] Hundreds of students protested in the rain outside the hearings, chanting "rain, rain, go away; take HUAC with you today."[89] "For the first time in the university's history," according to historian Kenneth Heineman, "a large number of students had been mobilized around a political issue. This demonstration also signaled the birth of a new campus spirit."[90] Although she was not a student, Jeanette Merrill was among those in the streets that day.[91] The Buffalo campus rapidly became become a place where dissent and antiwar activism flourished.[92] "There was very little student interest in conventional college life," Gross recalled. "It seemed like once the war started up, everybody took sides."[93] In 1965, students launched a campus chapter of Students for a Democratic Society (SDS) with the help of sociologists Elwin "Ed"

Powell and Sidney Willhelm. That April, an eleven-hour teach-in on the Vietnam War drew 1,500 students.[94]

For students like McCubbin, who had arrived on campus in 1960, the political shift was palpable.[95] His father had died when he was eight, and McCubbin came to the university planning to get a degree and a job to escape from poverty. In his first semester, he met Neidenberg, a WWP comrade and lifelong friend of Jeanette Merrill. Hearing Malcolm X speak on campus, McCubbin recalled, also had a "profound effect" on him.[96] Gross was another white student who was radicalized in this environment. He was, by his own admission, a "very straight" guy with a "brush cut" when he came to college and enrolled in a premed program. Gross was born in Buffalo, and his father owned a fur company in Lafayette Square, where he later participated in massive antiwar demonstrations and eventually in protests supporting Sostre. His family moved to what he described as the "very suburban, lily-white conservative neighborhood" of Tonawanda. At UB, he started taking philosophy classes and founded a student group called the Atheist Philosophical Society, which, he acknowledged in retrospect, was "just a group of one, really." After running into problems getting recognized by the student council as a "faith group," it became known as simply the Philosophical Society. Under its auspices, Gross would later help publish the first pamphlet of the Martin Sostre Defense Committee, *Letters from Prison*.

Gross was soon recruited as chairperson of YAWF by the Merrills, and the Philosophical Society was used as a front to host campus events.[97] The Merrills were interested in bringing together the active antiwar and campus movement with labor organizing and civil rights struggles in Buffalo. Gross remembered that when SDS supported a strike at Bethlehem Steel, it "got the attention of the FBI[, which] didn't want an alliance forming between the steelworkers and the students on campus." By this time, he had moved to an apartment in the Italian district of Buffalo on the Lower West Side, near the Merrills. Gross attended the study groups and meetings at their home, eventually receiving a small salary from the WWP to pay rent and continue his organizing.[98]

Sostre and his bookstores became a point of connection for these different movements and his appearances on campus furthered this cross-pollination. In December 1966, he delivered a lecture sponsored by the Socialist Club in which he played selections from the record *Malcolm X Speaks Again*.[99] In early 1967, he was advertised as "Martin

X, proprietor of the Afro-Asian Bookshop," as part of a slate of speakers announced by the newly formed Socialist Club on campus.[100] It was during an SDS event at UB that McCubbin first met Sostre. "They realized that Martin was an important person, and they invited him to speak," McCubbin would later remember.[101] Sostre's presence impressed him, just as Malcolm X's had years before. Gross, meanwhile, became acquainted with Sostre at his bookshop on Jefferson Avenue, later recalling, "He had a smile that would light up a room." Gross began stopping by the store periodically, eventually meeting Robinson, who was often in the store with her children.

By 1967, Sostre began to dream beyond his small chain of revolutionary bookstores. That May, he put down a deposit for a one-hundred-dollar Gestetner mimeograph machine, with plans to begin a community newsletter called the *Afro Freedom Fighter* (*AFF*). He envisioned this "dynamic, socialist-oriented Black nationalist weekly" would grow into a tabloid-sized newspaper. Sostre planned to recruit volunteer writers, reporters, and typists, including high school students to make stencils, until the paper could pay for itself. He even poached a local journalist, who may have been Garfield Hinton of the *Buffalo Challenger*, claiming he quit one of the "establishment Black newspapers" because of editorial censorship. When people visited the store, Sostre proudly showed them the mimeo machine and announced a "genuine grass-roots community newspaper completely run and published by the militant youth of the community—by us 'little people.'" "With the launching of the *AFF* and other political activities," he hoped that "the vacuum in leadership which exists in the Black community will be filled."[102] A month after he purchased the mimeograph machine, the people of Buffalo took to the streets.

On June 26, 1967, Buffalo became one of the nearly 160 cities that erupted in response to police violence and other forms of organized abandonment during what became known as the "long, hot summer." The Kerner Commission, established by President Johnson that July to investigate these uprisings, categorized Buffalo as one of eight major disorders that summer, at a scale equivalent to the better-known revolts in Newark and Detroit.[103] The 1967 rebellions ushered in what historian Elizabeth Hinton has called a "period of sustained political violence." Between 1968 and 1972, several thousand uprisings were used to justify the distribution of hundreds of millions of federal dollars to local police

in order to discipline insurgent Black communities.[104] The rebellions were used to rationalize an unprecedented escalation of police power, forever changing the landscapes of US cities as well as the lives of those targeted by state repression.

The week of the uprising, a photograph on the front page of the *Buffalo Challenger* showed a car being flipped over outside the Woodlawn Tavern.[105] Directly next door, just outside the photograph's left frame, was the Afro-Asian Bookshop—an illustration of the bookstore's physical and political location at the heart of the Buffalo uprising. Located in the middle of the three long blocks on Jefferson Avenue between East Ferry and East Utica streets, where much of the rebellion took place, the Afro-Asian Bookshop became both a refuge and a site of politicization. Sostre kept the store open until 3:00 a.m., providing sanctuary from the tear gas and police violence in the streets as well as a space to analyze what was happening outside. "The shop stayed packed and the cops outside didn't like it, but there was nothing they could do," he wrote. "Needless to mention, I made political hay in denouncing the police brutality going on outside to the large crowds in the store. Then, after a rousing speech, I would go to the shelf and pick up an appropriate book or pamphlet."[106] Sostre later remembered a Black teenager running into the store from a cop he had called a "pig." Outnumbered by the twenty people or so inside the store, the officer simply shook his fist and yelled at him: "I hope you're proud of this."[107]

Early in the morning of July 2, 1967, the first relatively quiet night since the rebellion began, smoke began to billow out of the Woodlawn Tavern next door. Patrons from the bar poured into the streets to escape the smoke. Firefighters, whom Sostre claimed were "in collusion with police," then turned their high-pressure hoses on the bookstore, shattering its windows and soaking much of its inventory. Similar destructions took place elsewhere that summer. Days after the rebellion in Detroit later that month, Ed Vaughn's bookstore was similarly targeted. Opened in 1959, Vaughn's was one of the earliest Black-owned radical bookstores, predating even Sostre's. Although Vaughn was away at the Black Power Conference in Newark during the uprising itself, police considered his store a cause of the disorder. They broke out windows and destroyed portraits of prominent Black leaders on the wall, then came back the

following night to plug up the sink and flood the bookstore. Vaughn received an outpouring of support, with donated books arriving from all over the world. Vaughn's became more popular than ever.[108] So too did the Afro-Asian Bookshop.

In the weeks that followed, the store continued to draw people in, their memories fresh with the revolt. While the bookshop had not dramatically changed, the conditions had. In Sostre's words: "I had something concrete that was currently happening right outside for everyone to see—namely, the invasion of the Black community by droves of white armed police who were indiscriminately shooting tear gas and bullets, beating up and arresting Black men, women and children and committing other depravities. All that was missing were the cattle prods. No one could argue against these concrete facts!" Sostre estimated that sales during the six weeks surrounding the rebellion matched those of the previous six months combined. He described the two weeks after the revolt as the "best I ever had—politically."[109]

Front page of the *Buffalo Challenger*, July 6, 1967. Buffalo Public Library, Grosvenor Room. Directly to the left of the Woodlawn Tavern just outside the frame is the Afro-Asian Bookshop at 1412 Jefferson Ave. Reproduction by permission of the Buffalo and Erie County Public Library, Buffalo, New York.

The morning following the fire at the tavern, Jerry Gross found Sostre in front of his bookstore sweeping away broken glass. Gross suggested getting students at UB to donate books to restock the store. He eventually gathered several hundred new and used texts on campus, setting up the first version of what would later become the Afro-Asian Bookshop in Exile.[110] Meanwhile, confronted daily with the sheets of plywood covering the openings where the windows had once been, Sostre recognized an opportunity. Inspired by *dazibao*, or "big-character posters," which had become popular during the Chinese Cultural Revolution and had played a major role in protests at Peking University the previous summer, he began posting articles and photos on the plywood. He later explained, "What I had done was to convert the entire front of the building on the southwest corner of Woodlawn and Jefferson into a huge community bulletin board and each day I would paste new articles and photos cut from newspapers, magazines and pamphlets on the board to keep public interest alive."[111]

People in the community began to bring clippings about other uprisings and revolutionary leaders to post. "This—to me—was tangible proof of the approval of the bulletin board by the community," Sostre wrote.[112] Through his creative experiments with stepladder speeches, records and loudspeakers, wall posters, and the community bulletin board, he used cultural production outside the store to bring those on the streets into the books, pamphlets, and conversations happening inside. In doing so, Sostre successfully drew upon the lessons of booksellers before him who had understood, as he later put it, that "culture is a weapon."[113]

During these weeks, Sostre saw more patrol cars and state officials outside the store than ever before. One morning, he found the posters ripped down. A local taxi driver working the night shift told him that police had torn down the posters the night before. "Our activity had come to the attention of the high officials," Sostre noted.[114] Indeed, during this time the Buffalo police began working in cooperation with state police and the FBI to surveil the bookstore from a second-floor window across the street.[115] They also developed a relationship with Francis Beverly, a woman who occasionally helped Sostre at the bookstore.[116] By early July, she was placing multiple calls a day to Sergeant Gristmacher of the Buffalo Police Department, who described her as "very cooperative."[117] Just days before the raid, he relayed to Amico, head of narcotics, that this "informant said that she would supply us with as much information as she could but that she would not testify in court."[118] Unaware of this betrayal,

Sostre continued to repost articles and photos outside the store to replace those being torn down by police as a "sort of battle developed between the cops and me during the five days preceding the raid."[119]

Meanwhile, another public battle raged over the meanings and causes of the Buffalo uprising. UB sociologist Frank Besag and a team of interviewers who produced *The Anatomy of a Riot*—the only study of first-person narratives about the uprising "focused specifically on the perspectives of Buffalo's Black residents"—identified three major explanations for the uprising that were in circulation: the "outside agitator hypothesis," the "random hoodlumism hypothesis," and the "broken promises hypothesis." The first two explanations were constructed and disseminated primarily by mainstream media, the police, and the mayor's office, and were "widely accepted" by white Buffalonians.[120] Despite having lived in Buffalo for several years and not being mentioned by any of the 138 interviews in the study (although he himself was interviewed), Martin Sostre soon came be conveniently framed by cops and journalists as personifying both narratives. This was predominantly due to the efforts of local police. As Amico wrote in a five-page memo to Commissioner Felicetta: when released from prison, Sostre "came to the city of Buffalo solely to incite trouble, extortion, arson and engage in illegal large scale narcotic activity."[121] From jail, Sostre was scapegoated in local newspapers as "the man who incited East Side riots."[122] Meanwhile, leftists in Buffalo insisted that the disturbances were a righteous rebellion against oppression. It was the "accumulation of these grievances—and not 'hoodlumism' as the press and city officials have been quick to shout—that makes a rebellion," YAWF flyers argued.[123]

Sostre later remembered the Buffalo rebellion as the moment he first identified with anarchism. In one of his only explicit reflections on it as a political ideology, he wrote, "Although I've been an anarchist by nature all my life, the full impact of this fact and how beautifully fulfilling anarchism is didn't hit my consciousness till the long hot summer of 1967." He described a "tight-knit group" of anarchists who met at the bookstore each night to discuss what was happening in the streets. "[We would] enthusiastically discuss what we saw on TV and the news we read and heard about the revolutionary anarchist acts spreading from city to city. . . . It was only a matter of time before what was in our consciousness would burst forth into objective reality."[124]

Looking at the accomplishments of "more advanced comrades" in other cities, he remembered, "We took care of very heavy revolutionary

anarchist business."[125] Citing a similar claim in a letter to his attorney in which Sostre wrote that he "singlehandedly organized a group of brothers and took care of mucho revolutionary bis," historian Malcolm McLaughlin has speculated that Sostre may in fact have been an active participant in the uprising.[126] Similar references to "revolutionary activity" and "mucho business" appear in Sostre's other letters and writings. Certainly direct action and street rebellion were consistent with the emphasis Sostre placed on what anarchists have called the propaganda of the deed—a political action meant to catalyze revolution by serving as an example to others.[127]

In his anonymous interview for Besag's study immediately following the uprising, Sostre's reflections resemble these later ones, although he was less explicit about his role in rebellious actions.[128] In the interview, he described acts of police violence, including shots fired into the Woodlawn Tavern next door and a "gas bomb" that landed in front of his bookstore.[129] The deeper origins of the rebellion, according to Sostre, stemmed from predatory white business owners and the misleadership of the Black political elite. White shop owners were "syphoning off all the money and taking it out of the neighborhood and sucking the neighborhood dry." "I don't see too much of a future now for the white businessman, not the way things stand now," he told the interviewer. "The rest of them are going to be burned out if our grievances are not [addressed]."[130] Meanwhile, he argued, "so-called Negro leaders are the ones really responsible for the Buffalo revolt of June 1967, by playing down and refusing to articulate in plain and unequivocal language the real wants and needs of the Black community."[131]

While the political establishment ultimately labeled the rebellions of the 1960s "spontaneous" to deny their political meaning, Sostre saw these revolts' lack of top-down leadership as central to their significance. "The rebellion was a spontaneous thing, unlike what they put in the papers—that I was paying them to riot, using the basement to teach them how to make molotov cocktails and all of that," he said. "What was that if it wasn't anarchism. Anarchism is the spontaneity of the people."[132] Sostre came to understand anarchism as a natural response to oppression that was often stifled by hierarchical organizations, which relied on discipline by leaders. Reflecting on the meaning of the Buffalo rebellion, he wrote, "Only when the people's revolutionary spirit is liberated from the strictures of the party-line strait jacket and restored to its natural free state will the real revolution occur."[133]

On July 14, 1967, a Friday evening less than two weeks after the rebellion, two state troopers took their post above a dentist's office on Jefferson Avenue with a camera and telescopic lens.[134] Across the street, the windows of the Afro-Asian Bookshop were still boarded up from the fire next door at the Woodlawn Tavern. Sostre and Beverly were working when Arto Williams—the shop regular who used to drop in to Sostre's bookstore to use the phone or bathroom—and a Black undercover cop named Lewis Steverson entered the store. Williams approached the counter and told Sostre, "I want to rap with you a minute," darting his eyes toward the undercover cop. Following his cue and not wanting to interfere with his business, Sostre asked to speak with Williams in private. Steverson obliged and left the store.[135]

Williams then handed Sostre fifteen dollars, which had been marked with a florescent pencil invisible in normal light, asking that he hold onto it—just as he had once requested Sostre do for his freshly laundered suit.[136] After giving the money to Sostre in the bookstore, Williams left and reconvened with Steverson. "As I turned to walk out the door of the bookstore," Williams later testified, "I put my hand into my pocket as though I was putting [drugs] in my pocket, but the drugs were already there and had been before I went into the store." He and Steverson then met up with Gristmacher, and Williams handed Gristmacher a glassine envelope of heroin he had purchased earlier that day with money from the cops. The two initialed the envelope and dated it July 15, 1967.[137] According to a detailed arrest report prepared by New York State Police, the alleged sale took place at 10:00 p.m.—an account that would notably change at the trial the following year.[138]

What Sostre didn't know was that Williams had been released from jail that very morning on the condition that he would frame him. Weeks earlier, Williams had written a letter to the police inquiring how he might get out of jail, where he faced a felony for stealing an air conditioner. Soon, he was visited by Sergeant Gristmacher and asked for the names of people selling drugs in Buffalo. Although Williams complied, the sergeant "didn't seem interested" in the names he gave, instead pressing for information about Sostre, whom he believed was the cause of the uprising.[139] After pausing for a moment, William assured his cooperation. "What was on my mind was getting out of jail," he later testified.[140] "I

didn't come out of the jail thinking I was going to bust just anybody. I knew who I was going to bust."[141]

That Friday, Williams was released and given cash by Gristmacher, which he used to buy a bag of heroin and get high. After stopping by his parents' house, he got high again near the bookstore. He remembered eating an ice cream cone while waiting for Gristmacher and Steverson to arrive.[142] After the exchange in the bookstore with Sostre and Beverly, it was approaching midnight when Gristmacher drove to the house of Buffalo City Court Judge Joseph Sedita (the brother of then-mayor Frank Sedita) to get a search warrant. In his application, the cop swore that he had "information based upon facts received from a reliable informant" who had "given true information in the past and this information has resulted in several arrests." He additionally claimed that an informant—presumably Williams—had purchased heroin from Sostre at least ten times over a two-week period, despite only recently having been introduced to Williams, whom he had released from jail that morning.[143]

Just after midnight, Sostre was in the back of the store readying for closing when he heard a "stampede of people coming in." He heard Robinson, who had only recently arrived at the store, yell "stick-up." Thinking the store was being robbed, he ran to the front in time to see her get hit and knocked into a chair. Sostre fought with several of police officers, none of whom was in uniform. Gristmacher was among them. Sostre was beaten with a blackjack and eventually arrested along with Robinson, and two young people in the store who were charged with frequenting a place selling narcotics.[144]

It was not long after their arrest that J. Edgar Hoover instructed the FBI's Counterintelligence Program (COINTELPRO) to "expose, disrupt, misdirect, discredit, or otherwise neutralize" Black liberation movements.[145] The following year, he expressed special concern over the "increase in the establishment of black extremist bookstores" and ordered field offices to "locate and identify black extremist and/or African-type bookstores in its territory and open separate discreet investigations on each to determine if it is extremist in nature."[146] Although COINTELPRO would later come to epitomize state repression, Sostre's frame-up is best understood as part of a protracted and multifaceted war on Black radicals that predated and outlived that particular program of government terror. From the day he arrived in Buffalo, Sostre had been subject to surveillance by the FBI and state and local police. A few years later, with

rebellion in the air, he and Geraldine Robinson became the latest victims in an escalating war on Black revolutionaries. There was no denying the state's temporary victory. "They have destroyed our only Black political, intellectual and historical center—the depository of the writings of all our militant Black writers and leaders," Sostre reflected painfully.[147] "They accomplished their mission of destroying the bookshop."[148]

6

"The Court Is an Arena"

Within hours of the raid and the arrests of Martin Sostre and Geraldine Robinson, police had begun fabricating stories and feeding them to local journalists, who uncritically reprinted their claims in Buffalo newspapers. In one prominent article, Sostre was accused of conducting $15,000 in weekly drug sales and using his basement to manufacture and distribute Molotov cocktails.[1] Michael Amico, who was in charge of the Narcotics and Intelligence Bureau, claimed to have motion picture evidence of drug sales and alleged that Sostre had started the fire at the Woodlawn Tavern. Just days before Sostre's appearance before a Grand Jury, Police Commissioner Frank Felicetta testified before the Senate Internal Security Committee in the nation's capital on the causes of the Buffalo uprising, describing Sostre as a "prominent figure in the recent disorders."[2] Like Amico, who had characterized him as a violent drug trafficker distributing "bombs to hoodlums," Felicetta referred to Sostre as "Mr. X," a dog whistle meant to stoke white anxieties about militant Black Muslims.[3]

The all-white Grand Jury brought these assumptions with them. All but two of the nineteen jurors had read headlines and stories about Sostre's role in the uprising and as a "dope peddler," and many admitted during jury selection that they had followed Felicetta's testimony in Washington, DC. Nevertheless, the judge dismissed motions to disqualify them on the basis of bias produced by pretrial publicity.[4] Sostre's fight to secure bail was shaped by this media hysteria. Facing a litany of charges including illegal sale and possession of narcotics, inciting a riot,

first-degree arson, resisting arrest, and second-degree assault, Sostre's bail was set at $50,000 ($400,000 in today's dollars).[5] By the time of his trial the following year, however, the arson and riot charges were dropped, the motion picture footage could not be found, and the drug charges were reduced to a single fifteen-dollar bag of heroin supplied by a police informant. Sostre would later lay out how the criminal legal system masks its own political nature: "They can afford to make everything legal. They can pick juries, pay off witnesses, tie up courts for years. They can frame you up on criminal charges so that way you won't be able to prove that you're a political prisoner."[6]

Unable to post bail, Sostre remained in jail for nearly eight months before the state finally brought him to trial in March 1968. There, he acted as his own attorney, denouncing the trial as a farce and refusing to cooperate with what he and others considered a "legal lynching." Rather than pursue what is termed a "legal defense"—in which the defendant pursues acquittal by refuting aspects of the alleged crime—Sostre offered a political one.[7] "The court is an arena," he said. "It is a battlefield—one of the best. We will use these same torture chambers, these same kangaroo courts, to expose them."[8] Sostre's trial ushered in a new stage of his organizing. "The second phase of the struggle has now shifted to the courtroom—the ritualized extension of the establishment's coercive apparatus," he wrote University at Buffalo students who, inspired by his resistance, had burned their draft cards to protest the war in Vietnam.[9] He described this apparatus vividly:

> The robed former anti-labor, company-lawyer, racist-goon sits on an elevated platform to force all in the room to look up to him as if to a deity or monarch on a throne. Within reach of the elevated goon is the Holy Bible with all the awesome powers of heaven and hell within its covers ready to be unleashed upon the (credulous) heads of those below. Upon this book are sworn the goons and their agents—to gospelize their lies. Capping the entire circus is the bird of prey and the American flag—symbols of imperialism and slavery.[10]

"Dissent has come to the courtroom," he told the audience at his trial, "just as it has come to all levels of society, in the streets, in the universities, in the homes."[11]

Sostre saw the courts as he did other tools of oppression: as a weapon to be turned against those who wield them. "By challenging and exposing for public scrutiny every unlawful and underhanded act of oppression employed by the rulers, I am alerting everyone to these methods and raising serious questions which will have serious legal, political and moral implications," he explained. "I have found this to be the most effective method of fighting the oppressor."[12] By putting the state on the defensive and using the courtroom to unveil hidden contradictions, he hoped people would come to see courts, and the "ritualized extension" of the coercive state they represented, as illegitimate and vulnerable.

Sostre exposed the racism and fascism of the criminal legal system at every stage, using his frame-up as a case study of the law and state repression. At bail hearings, he presented the results of surveys he conducted while he was held at Erie County Jail, noting the capriciousness of bail and its reproduction of racial and class oppression. When he was committed to a psychiatric hospital to evaluate his competency to serve as his own attorney at trial, Sostre cross-examined the doctors and revealed how psychiatry acts as an arm of state repression. "I am trying to show the people of Buffalo, that this is the method used to suppress all those fighting against suppression," he told the court. "Now, they are using the psychiatrists and drugs besides the blackjack and frameup and the jail."[13] Finally, Sostre refused to cross-examine the district attorney's ten witnesses—and a police informant—and decried the trial as a sham until the judge ordered him bound and gagged. As his comrade Bob McCubbin noted, Judge Marshall was "faced with a serious problem. How could this stage play of which he was principal architect and director have any semblance of a real trial if there was to be no defense?"[14] Sostre thus forced the state to perform its play without the cooperation of the accused. "If we don't resist, none of these tactics will be uncovered," he explained.[15]

Neither a constitutionalist nor a legal reformer, Sostre viewed the courtroom as a site of struggle to unveil the contradictions of the state and raise the consciousness of those outside. He believed that the cost of acquiescence was always greater than resistance. "Law is changed every day," he reminded the audience in the courtroom. "That is the only way laws get changed, by resisting unjust laws, because if you do not oppose these laws, you let the fascists continue to take over our entire government."[16] Sostre paid a high cost for his resistance. "Rarely in the annals

of American law has a legal proceeding been so infected with unfairness and prejudice," contended one legal brief.[17] Yet, despite being sentenced to 31–41 years after being convicted by an all-white jury, Sostre concluded that "all this has been worth it. . . . Just the exposure of the methods that the state officials will go to in order to frame a man."[18]

Two weeks after Martin Sostre was arrested and accused of inciting a riot in the streets of Buffalo, he participated in—and likely organized—a takeover at Erie County Jail.[19] The "sit out" strike of late July 1967 occupied and controlled a corridor of the four-story jail. Two dozen prisoners prevented their automatic cell doors from closing by jamming library books between the door and wall. For two nights, they played cards and came and went freely in the central gallery between their cells. The strike was intended to call attention to their grievances, including demands for an outdoor recreation space, longer visitation and television time, copies of local newspapers, and an end to mail censorship. Given his own difficulty accessing coverage of his case and sending and receiving mail, Sostre may well have been responsible for crafting the last two.[20] Authorities claimed the protest was prompted by "one ringleader," assuring the public that it represented a small minority of the hundreds detained at the jail and that there was "no indication of violence and no necessity of force."[21]

Shortly after the strike ended, Sostre wrote a series of messages to his supporters on the back of legal petitions he drafted for himself and his codefendant, Geraldine Robinson.[22] In his letters, he disputed the accounts of the mainstream press, which portrayed him as the singular cause of the rebellion in Buffalo, and encouraged people outside to continue to resist.[23] Sostre called upon students for support and restated his constitutional right to sell radical literature whether it was unpopular or not. "If this is a crime," he wrote, "then I must always be a criminal."[24] He penned a lengthy retrospective on the Afro-Asian Bookshops, detailing his attempts to bring in young people despite ongoing intimidation and repression by police and the FBI. His reflections remain one of the only existing accounts of the bookstores. "Should I not be freed and should our enemies who framed me succeed in putting me away for thirty years," he declared, "I would not mind so much if I knew that this report has

contributed in any degree toward a knowledge of how to organize the Black youth of this country."[25]

These letters would inaugurate the most prolific and sustained period of Sostre's writing. Nearly the entirety of his documented political thought—mostly letters and essays—woud be composed during the nine years of captivity following his 1967 arrest. The earliest of these, written during his eight months at Erie County Jail, were not only critical in fighting for his release but offered an important counternarrative to the state's explanation of the Buffalo uprising and his role in it. The varied audiences Sostre addressed reflected the segmented communities the bookshops sought to intertwine. He now called upon these groups to come together in support of him and Geraldine, directing all contributions for legal fees and court costs to go to Robinson, who had been released on $5,000 bond, and be collected in a defense fund. That same month, the Martin Sostre Defense Committee was formed. Sostre's dispatches from jail would eventually be compiled in *Letters from Prison*. The campaign to free Martin Sostre had begun.

Geraldine Robinson, c. 1968. William Worthy papers, MS.0524, Special Collections, The Johns Hopkins University.

While Sostre worked feverishly from jail to reduce his bail and locate his witnesses, his defense committee coalesced outside. The founding members of the MSDC had sat at Ed and Jeanette Merrill's dining room table listening to tape-recorded talks by Sam Marcy of the Workers World Party. Jerry Gross, then twenty-three, was elected chair. Jeanette Merrill was its secretary.[26] According to one MSDC pamphlet, the committee was formed in "an atmosphere of reaction and repression almost unprecedented, even in the right-wing, banker-dominated city of Buffalo."[27] Gross recalled that the early committee was "basically a front group of Workers World Party and anybody from the community who would show up at a meeting." Bob McCubbin considered it only natural that he would join both. "It wasn't like I could join the defense committee without joining the party. That didn't bother me because I had so much respect for them."[28] This was not true for everyone, however. Another committed comrade, Sharon Fischer, eventually joined the committee, but was not part of the WWP or its affiliate, Youth Against War and Fascism.[29] Robinson continued to organize while awaiting her own trial and caring for her five children.[30]

It would be difficult to overstate the imbalance of power between the state, on one side, and Sostre, on the other. Gross remembered that at first, he was "flying by the seat of [his] pants."[31] Using the Philosophical Society as cover, the MSDC screened *Come Back Africa*, a documentary about South African apartheid that helped launch Mariame Makeba's illustrious career, to a crowd of roughly 250 people on campus. Admissions, along with sales of African art objects salvaged from the bookstore, raised $125. One Buffalo woman hosted a chicken-fry benefit. Contributions often came in one dollar at a time. "Very seldom was an individual donation of $5.00 received," Sostre noted. "Every dollar raised was from the natural muscle of little people."[32] During an event with Dr. Martin Luther King Jr. at the massive Kleinhans Music Hall, the group distributed thousands of pamphlets.[33] They also held bookfairs, an important predecessor of the more permanent Afro-Asian Bookshop in Exile.[34] Over the eight months leading up to his trial, a dozen or so dedicated comrades—most of them college students and blacklisted and surveilled WWP organizers, along with a single mother of five with serious charges hanging over her head—leafletted, sold books and buttons, and hosted bake sales, concerts, and film screenings to raise funds and publicize the case.

In late October, Sostre acknowledged the forces against him. "Let's look at this realistically Jerry and let's face the facts," he wrote his defense

chair. "You, Jeanette, Geraldine and others have been running yourselves ragged making untold sacrifices for 3½ months . . . and what did you raise? $900?" At this rate, he estimated, it would take his committee over three years to raise the money for his bail. Sostre pointed out that "Rap Brown would not be out if he had to depend on 50 cent and $1.00 donations to get him out."[35]

His supporters corresponded with him regularly, showed up at hearings, and picketed outside the court during his trial. They did all this while caring for their families, working low-wage jobs, and trying to make ends meet on welfare while being harassed by police. As one MSDC pamphlet recounted, "Tremendous contributions of time and money were made by many so-called 'little' people who, working all day, had little time to spare and, underpaid, little money to give either."[36] Their efforts would not prevent Sostre from being given a virtual life sentence the following year. Yet, despite their small numbers and the massive power structure they were up against, the group helped raise Sostre's struggle from a local campaign calling attention to a particular injustice to a national cause célèbre. Although it would take years to bring much of this work to fruition, its seeds were planted during this initial period of struggle.

After the trauma of his arrest and facing an uncertain future, Sostre expressed a mix of defiance and lament in his letters from jail. He bemoaned not being able to resume his former job at Bethlehem Steel to take financial pressure off his defense committee. In the aftermath of the rebellion, Sostre also longed to be in the streets organizing. "The time, circumstances, mood and responsiveness are perfect for organizing the Black masses," he wrote. "They would listen now like they never would have listened before."[37] Sostre still hoped to launch the *Afro Freedom Fighter* newspaper from the back room of the East-West Bookshop: "Everything is in readiness awaiting my return. . . . The time has never been riper for helping my people than it is now."[38]

By early October, he was forced to shift attention away from the bookstore and newspaper and toward securing his immediate release, as he and his comrades suffered several major setbacks. After his supporters painstakingly raised $550 and convinced a prominent local firm to take his case for far less than their typical $2,500 retainer, the firm dropped

Sostre as a client after only a few hours of court time.[39] Believing the lawyers caved to political pressure, Sostre tried to recoup some of the money.[40] Meanwhile, word had spread that Sostre's "key witness," Francis Beverly, had been intimidated by police and fled town.[41] "I cannot afford to make mistakes," Sostre wrote Gross. "We already made two which may be sufficient to hang me." He did not know that the person he was counting on to testify on his behalf was a police informant who had helped secure his arrest. Desperate to locate the other four witnesses in the store that night, he instructed his committee to concentrate their efforts on securing his bail.[42]

The next day, Sostre appeared in court as his own attorney and explained to Judge Frederick Marshall that he had no alternative but to represent himself.[43] "You crackers have taken my rights," Sostre said. Calling the city "Buffalo-Mississippi," he chastised the judge for repeatedly interrupting him when he was speaking, and pointedly asked him, "Why don't you get the rope?" Marshall assured Sostre that he would consider a reasonable bail amount while threatening to gag him.[44] Just a year earlier, the federal Bail Reform Act had passed with near-unanimous support. In principle, historian Melanie Newport points out, the legislation was meant to "encourage attorneys and judges to consider defendants' social context and discourage pretrial detention."[45] This reform came more than a decade after law professor Caleb Foote had sounded the alarm about the discriminatory nature of bail. In his 1954 study, he had found that bail was largely decided by "custom or intuition" and therefore was often "used for punishment purposes."[46]

The new law only pertained to federal cases, however, and thus Sostre remained bound by this racist and classist practice. "Your Honor is well aware," he told one judge, "that bail is discriminatory. The rich man is able to sign a check for $5,000 but a poor person may not be able to make $500."[47] He argued that even the same bail amount was discriminatory when applied to Black people because their earnings and assets were lower than those of white community members.[48] To make matters worse, he was targeted for his political commitments. One judge even suggested that Sostre's bail might have been set so high because of his connections to "Hong Kong and the Viet Cong."[49] Sostre replied, "The fact that I am here belies that, doesn't it, your Honor? A man with financial connections from overseas would not be in jail eating baloney sandwiches for four months."[50]

Sostre pursued multiple strategies to secure bail. First, he surveyed a dozen people held on his floor at the county jail, finding that even those held for murder were given lower bail.[51] But even after presenting this evidence and receiving two bail reductions, the initial $50,000 prescribed by the DA prejudiced negotiations such that even his $12,500 bond remained woefully out of reach.[52] Another idea he outlined was a paid bail subscription, whereby supporters would send twenty-five dollars each, be given a coupon, and returned their money after he was released.[53] Underscoring his unlikely odds, his committee began using five dollars of the fund each month to play the state lottery.[54] He eventually instructed supporters to liquidate the store, selling off a heater, records, and books.[55]

In early December 1967, Jerry Gross, who chaired Sostre's defense committee, was arrested along with hundreds of antiwar protesters in New York City. He had been ordered to report for his induction physical and decided to participate in the national "Stop the Draft Week." Gross was charged with disorderly conduct, resisting arrest, and operating sound equipment without a license.[56] Over fifty students in Buffalo mailed back their draft cards as an act of civil disobediance that week. In response, Sostre emphasized that the "anti-war struggle and the struggle of Afro-American people against oppression is precisely one and the same struggle" and proposed they communalize his fund to support Gross and other antiwar protestors in Buffalo.[57] "I want our Fund to be just like us—active," he wrote Jeanette Merrill. "Since we are activists our Fund should be a living, active fund."[58] Sostre imagined that the money could be recycled as people were bailed out and the funds were returned by the court. "We must look out for our own and let the militarist-oppressors know that our ranks is like a brick wall—one brick supports the other," he concluded.[59]

The idea of community bail first emerged in the 1920s, when the American Civil Liberties Union established a fund for radicals targeted by sedition laws.[60] The International Labor Defense provided another foundational Depression-era example by creating a centralized bail fund to support prominent victims of legal lynchings like Sacco and Vanzetti and the Scottsboro Boys. In the early 1950s, the Civil Rights Congress pooled resources to emancipate those "charged with political crimes" during the second Red Scare.[61] By the second half of the twentieth century, two types of funds predominated: those aimed at supporting a specific political cause or action, and those intended to reduce jail overcrowding.[62] According to scholar-activist Angela Davis and her coauthors of *Abolition.*

Feminism. Now, a third type of fund emerged while Davis was incarcerated at the House of Detention in Manhattan in the late 1960s when she was held for over a year on murder and other charges after guns belonging to her were used in the Marin County courtroom takeover by Jonathan Jackson and other members of the Black Panther Party. Outside supporters raised money for imprisoned people to collectively allocate to anyone in need, "one of the earliest instances of bail campaigns for people with no public profile."[63] Although Sostre conceived of his defense fund to benefit political prisoners in particular, it was in this same spirit that, from within his jail cell, he attempted to establish a community bail fund that could be activated on behalf of other incarcerated people.[64] As Sostre formulated these ideas, his case suddenly began to move after nearly five months at a standstill. In a December 10 letter to his committee, he predicted that the court would attempt to call his sanity into question for deciding to represent himself. The following day, Judge Marshall ordered that he be committed to Meyer Memorial Hospital for a psychiatric evaluation.[65]

One of the first people Dr. Howard Wilinsky examined in his new role as chief of forensic psychiatric services at the hospital was Sostre. Despite the passage of over a half century, he instantly recalled Sostre as "quick witted" and "very irascible . . . very angry at having been committed."[66] During separate examinations with Wilinsky and another psychiatrist, Michael Lynch, Sostre related aspects of his childhood and background but placed "particular emphasis on his current legal situation."[67] During the 1960s, doctors and lawyers often conflated Black protest with psychosis. As psychiatrist Jonathan Metzl argues, white anxieties about civil rights protests "catalyzed associations between schizophrenia, criminality, and violence," particularly for those associated with Black Power.[68] Sostre understood this well, writing that "psychiatrists, doctors, hospitals and insane asylums have always been employed by oppressors to intimidate, remove, and destroy those who oppose them."[69] The decision by Wilinsky and Lynch to diagnose Sostre with "paranoid personality disorder" despite deeming him fit to represent himself at trial underscores this point.[70]

Sostre spent nearly two weeks at the hospital refusing medication, reflecting that while his "lectures on Black Power, Vietnam, American racism and oppression to the other patients were not appreciated by the psychiatrists and hospital staff . . . I planted a few good seeds before I left."[71] Finally, after nearly seven months in jail, which culminated in a dark, solitary cell for prisoners held under observation, Sostre was brought to court to confirm the psychiatric report. According to his evaluation, not only had Sostre demonstrated his competency to stand trial; he had made clear his legal strategy. "He knew that his essential posture before the court was argumentative and placed demands upon that court that . . . legal counsel would not," Wilinsky and Lynch recorded.[72]

On February 19, 1968, an all-white group of eighth graders visited Judge Marshall's courtroom for a class trip intended to teach them about the justice system. As they left, they were met with an indelible image that epitomized the system's racism, as Martin Sostre was brought in wearing manacles connecting his arms and waist.[73]

Sostre began by cross-examining the two psychiatrists who had evaluated him at Meyer Hospital, and eventually called the judge himself to the witness stand. Although Marshall attempted to confine Sostre's interrogations to the issue of whether he was competent to stand trial, Sostre raised questions of power and moral conscience, showing how psychology was used as a weapon of state repression. He also hoped to create a court record that would facilitate a successful legal appeal.[74] In compiling and publishing excerpts from the trial records in July 1969 as *Martin Sostre in Court*, his defense committee, too, created a persuasive account of injustice in the criminal legal system they could use in organizing on behalf of Sostre and other political prisoners.

Sostre began by probing the psychiatrists about their understandings of race. He deftly demonstrated that while his race was noted in their evaluations, they gave little or no consideration to the effects rac*ism* might have on either their assessment of him as a "paranoid personality" or his actions. The psychiatrists neither accounted for their own possible racial biases nor assessed whether Sostre's responses to oppression could be characterized as "normal," rather than "paranoid." Sostre cited academic articles on the effects of racism on Black people's mental health, in particular drawing upon sociologist Horace Cayton's "Psychology of the Negro under Discrimination."[75] Published in an anthology on sociological approaches to mental health, Cayton's article drew a parallel between being Black in America and being a "soldier under battle conditions," opening with this basic premise: "The Negro in the United States in an oppressed minority. This oppression, based in some sections of the country on law, is further reinforced by tradition and custom. It finds its final sanction in the application of force and violence."[76] When Sostre asked one psychologist whether he had read any articles on racism and its effects on mental health, the doctor said he did not understand the phrase "racism." Sostre substituted "racial discrimination," but to no avail. Finally, he told the court incredulously: "Here is a psychiatrist who does not know what racial discrimination means."[77]

Whenever Sostre referred to Black people as an oppressed group, Judge Marshall routinely sustained the prosecution's objections. He ruled that whether psychiatrists recognized racial discrimination was "irrelevant to these proceedings," prompting Sostre to call him "Mr. Hitler." Sostre's cross-examination revealed the underpinnings of the psychologists' subjective evaluations of paranoia. Would not the mental state of a person who is opposing racism and militarism be different from one who is supportive or apathetic? Would a person who protests the "senseless slaughter of our youth in Vietnam" or the "oppressed Black man in this racist society" be considered abnormal? Judge Marshall deemed Sostre's inquiries immaterial and told Sostre they differed in their opinion of relevance. Sostre rejoined: "Of course you differ. You are the ones that are in power."[78] Finally, after Sostre demanded that the judge take the stand, the hearing was adjourned.[79]

In the most basic sense, Sostre's lengthy cross-examination of the psychiatrists who had evaluated him was a success. Since he had already been deemed fit to act as his own legal counsel, he used the hearing to expose the ways that psychology was being mobilized as a tool of state repression. One exchange clarified this particularly well. Sostre recalled a conversation with one of the doctors about the use of mace (pepper spray) in place of physical beatings. "I can almost quote you word by word," he said: "'Mace is better than the club, isn't it?' " But, Sostre warned, "just because they use mace does not mean they are going to abandon their club; it will be used as another additional terror weapon along with the dogs and guns and clubs."[80] Psychiatry, like mace, was being deployed as a softer form of violence within the criminal legal system to coerce and control those who resisted it.

Sostre's argument captured the limitations of liberal reform. He understood that new, more "humane" forms of state violence did not fundamentally alter the system. Instead, they were incorporated into an ever-growing arsenal of state domination. Years later, Sostre would resist more invasive experimental "behavior modification" programs—a euphemism for torture—that extended the use of psychological techniques.

Martin Sostre finally stood trial on March 4, 1968. The courtroom was packed to capacity, but not with supporters. As if reversing the Nation of Islam's strategy of filling the courtroom, police now jammed the room. University at Buffalo sociology professor Ed Powell recounted: "The courtroom had been packed to exclude [Sostre's] own supporters: the Sheriff's Department alone supplied 40 men, some 50 detectives, an undetermined number of FBI agents and 25 court attendants called in for special duty."[81] Jeanette Merrill observed that many Black supporters were "never allowed into the trial because of 'lack of seats' . . . a large

Martin Sostre Defense Committee members Jerry Gross, Ed and Jeanette Merrill, Geraldine Robinson, and Karl Meller picket outside Sostre's trial in Buffalo, New York, March 5, 1968. Center for Legislative Archives, National Archives and Records Administration.

percentage of the few seats available were taken up by plainclothesmen who placed themselves conspicuously throughout the court room so as to intimidate supporters present."[82]

Although outnumbered, Sostre's comrades were a vocal contingent. The MSDC distributed flyers explaining that the courtroom had become a "platform for denouncing, publicizing, and exposing racial injustice and oppression."[83] Outside the courthouse, a half dozen supporters, including McCubbin, Gross, Robinson, and the Merrills, marched in a circle carrying signs reading "Southern Justice—Northern *Style*" and "Support Black Freedom. Free Martin!"[84] Inside the courtroom, the judge angrily demanded Sostre face him when he would occasionally rise to address the audience.[85] Marshall began proceedings on the second day by denouncing all attempts at communication between the defendant and the crowd. "There will be no applause, there will be no demonstrations," he declared.[86] As Sostre was led out of the courtroom, one attorney said he had never witnessed such a display of support for a defendant.[87]

Despite the commotion, the trial was a contrast from the hearing held several weeks earlier, at which Sostre had cross-examined witnesses and called the judge to the stand; now he sat silently, except for occasional outbursts drawing connections between racism and the war in Vietnam or side remarks about the absurdity of the case. An all-white jury had been selected without any examination by Sostre or the court. "I am not participating in this mock trial and I object to all the proceedings," he told the judge.[88] When police informant Arto Williams testified, Sostre asked the judge if he had to sit through such a farce: "I would just as soon go to prison. I have good books to read."[89] Marshall rarely asked questions of the prosecution or witnesses, but he instructed the jury to disregard Sostre's periodic interjections that the trial was a sham.[90]

Over the course of three days, the prosecution brought forward nine cops, a police chemist, and a stool pidgeon to lay out the state's argument that Martin was selling heroin from his bookstore. First, Williams testified that he received fourteen dollars in marked bills from Sergeant Gristmacher (inconsistent with the fifteen dollars police claimed to have provided) and walked into the bookshop on the evening of July 14, 1967, with state trooper Lewis Steverson in plainclothes. According to Williams, Sostre refused to "do any business" when someone he did not know was present, so Steverson waited outside.[91] The two state troopers who had been surveilling the store from the second-floor window across the street then claimed that they watched the sale take place through a telephoto lens, although they had no photographs and the store's windows were boarded over. Gristmacher said that he returned to the store just after midnight with a search warrant and several police and FBI agents. The final witnesses testified to raiding the bookstore, recalling that Sostre ran into the back office and swung at one of them with a box cutter. It was then, they said, that a filing cabinet in the bookstore produced a glassine envelope with a white powder, which was brought to the chemist for positive identification as heroin. In the meantime, Robinson was arrested by an FBI agent, who said he took the bills marked with police initials in ultra-violet light pencil from her purse.

The state's testimony reproduced much of its narrative of the arrest from the previous year but changed its chronology in significant ways. The original arrest report prepared by state police claimed that Williams purchased heroin from Sostre at 10:00 p.m., after which Gristmacher secured a search warrant and returned with the FBI and state troopers shortly past midnight on July 15. Six months later, the timeline had been compressed, and police now claimed that Williams and Steverson entered the store just fifteen minutes before the raid with a search warrant secured earlier that night. Importantly, this placed Geraldine Robinson at the bookstore during the time of the alleged crime instead of Francis Beverly, whom Sostre believed to be his key witness but was in fact a police informer unwilling to testify at trial. This flipping of the timeline managed to protect the state's "source" while implicating Robinson, who could have been a formidable witness on Sostre's behalf.[92] Sostre pointed out the incongruity of time at trial, as the witnesses tried to conform with each other and maintain this new story. "They can't even get the time straight. Jesus Christ," he remarked. But the judge interrupted: "No cross examination. The defendant waives his right to cross examine."[93] Unfortunately, without an attorney, the state's obvious inconsistencies went uninterrogated. As one legal brief summarized: "The prosecution simply put on its witnesses, they told their stories . . . and walked off the stand."[94]

The following week, in order to trigger the harsher sentencing applied to repeat felony offenders, a second all-white jury was empaneled to determine whether he was the same Martin Sostre who had been convicted of the 1952 heroin charge. Although Sostre exercised his constitutional right to remain silent on the issue of identification, he turned this two-day trial into a debate on the law and conscience.[95] Judge Marshall repeatedly told the jury to stick to "facts," warning them that "issues of law are not for the jury."[96] When Sostre asked a juror whether he would obey the law regardless of conscience, the judge interjected: "That's his duty and his obligation."[97] Sostre disagreed: "It is our moral obligation and duty to resist tyranny." Marshall had already warned Sostre, "Control your tongue," and charged him with contempt of court. Sostre persisted, telling Marshall, "We are resisting, not only in the courtroom, but in the streets. . . . This is war now, and you know it."[98] The judge ordered him gagged and removed from the courtroom. When Sostre returned in handcuffs, he had a white towel tied over his mouth and was surrounded by six guards.[99]

When Sostre was finally ungagged, he returned to question the jurors about law and conscience.[100] Using the Vietnam War, urban rebellions, and the War on Poverty as examples, Sostre laid out a moral dilemma and asked them how they might respond:

> Let us say we got an order from the Pentagon to send another million men over there [to Vietnam], and then another million, and another. Are we to obey this order because it is given by the powers-that-be? The federal government says yes. But you are an individual. Let us say that because of that law your own life is placed in jeopardy and that all your resources are eaten up, that the law is causing racial strife in the cities because the revenues are being used for war instead of being fed into the cities to pay for the reparations due to the Black people for the long-inflicted injustices. Would you obey the law to the letter in this case or go along with your conscience?

All but one of the jurors stated that they would obey the law. When he responded that he would "apply my own thinking," the judge told him to leave the jury box.[101] Sostre argued that challenging unjust laws was an ethical duty. If doing so was criminalized and not met with resistance, the result was authoritarianism.

Engaged in political theater, Sostre interacted with spectators throughout the trial. He believed that uncovering the state's tactics in the courtroom was essential to politicizing those witnessing the unfolding frame-up. Sostre told Black youth watching to "sock it to them." A Black woman was removed for verbally objecting to the court's blocking his questions.[102] The trial ended with Sostre insisting on its political nature, despite the courts' pretense that it was simply a "criminal" matter.[103] When Marshall demanded that "social issues" not be interjected into the proceedings, Sostre replied: "This case is a social concern. . . . It is racism we are fighting—white racism."[104]

The racism that had been thinly veiled behind a veneer of judicial proceduralism throughout the trial became explicit in the judge's final statement to the court. Calling Sostre a "narcotics peddler" who preyed upon his community, he closed: "You are going to get justice, what you are hollering for. You know and everybody knows, from your actions in this court, that you are a vicious and violent person, and you are motivated by nothing more than hate and you have now been unmasked, defrocked and your plan to disrupt the judicial system, and pervert our laws, has miserably failed." The judge's defensiveness and virulent language of the defendant as a "vicious" dope peddler was, on the contrary, a perverse confirmation of Sostre's success in the courtroom. Over the course of eight months in jail and three trials, Sostre had managed to "unmask" and "defrock" the state's fascist repression. That the judge felt it necessary to reveal the supposed "criminal" truth in a criminal trial shows how effectively Sostre had turned the court into a political arena. As he stood and received his sentence, he already had his legal appeal in hand.[105]

7

A Single-Minded Struggle for Prisoners' Rights

The night following his sentencing, Martin Sostre was isolated on an otherwise-empty cell block at Attica.[1] "The whole block was dark," he said. "It was abandoned, so I hollered out . . . and there was no answer." Fearing that his presence at the prison would cause unrest, prison officials requested he be shipped to Green Haven Prison outside Poughkeepsie, nearly four hundred miles from his supporters and defense attorney in Buffalo.[2]

Just a few months after he arrived at Green Haven, Sostre was called into Warden Harold Follette's office, where he sat with a stack of Sostre's mail. Follette questioned him, especially disturbed by Sostre's repeated mentions of the Republic of New Africa (RNA), and claimed that his reference to being freed by the "universal forces of liberation" was evidence of an insurrectionary plot.[3] He also accused Sostre of possessing "contraband," which included pages torn from the *Harvard Law Review* and a document Sostre was translating into Spanish for another Puerto Rican prisoner.[4] According to New York law, wardens had "unfettered discretion" to continue long-term confinement until they deemed that the prisoner had been reduced to "submission and obedience." Citing his supposed violations of the "Inmate's Rule Book" and his "attitude [of] defiance," Follette committed Sostre to indefinite punitive segregation, where he would remain for 372 days.[5]

Prison officials were as anxious about Sostre's presence as state police had been when he arrived in Buffalo years earlier; they kept him under close surveillance, punished him for his political views, and isolated him from comrades on both sides of the walls. During his year in solitary, Sostre was held in a single six-by-eight-foot cell twenty-four hours a day "in virtual incommunicado."[6] He was permitted one hot shower and shave a week, and one hour a day of recreation in an enclosed yard. To receive these "privileges," he was required to submit to a "strip frisk" that included stripping naked, bending over, and undergoing a rectal examination, ostensibly to prevent contraband. He refused the rectal search, forfeiting his hour outside his cell. As Sostre pointed out, the "examination" was a pretext for dehumanization, as he was not allowed to have anything inside his solitary cell beside law books, toothpaste, and a toothbrush.[7]

Sostre responded in the ways he knew best—with collective organizing, revolutionary optimism, and unremitting efforts to use the law against the state. We are "militants at war with the vicious power structure," he reminded his defense committee secretary, Jeanette Merrill. "In war against him we must be just as vicious as he is. . . . I am going after Rockefeller and his top goons."[8] In August 1968, Sostre filed a pro se complaint seeking $1.2 million in injunctive relief and damages from the governor of New York and three other state officials for their violations of his constitutional rights: freedom of political expression, the bar on deprivation of liberty without due process of law, effective assistance of counsel, and freedom from cruel and unusual punishment, which were guaranteed in the Bill of Rights; and racial segregation in prisons, which transgressed the Thirteenth and Fourteenth Amendments' guarantees of equal rights regardless of race. Sostre's lawyer, the radical attorney Victor Rabinowitz, described the case as "an encyclopedia about what is wrong with prison systems."[9]

The impetus for Sostre's lawsuit was not only his own torture but the beating and death by suicide in August 1968 of Ray Broderick, another incarcerated person in the solitary unit. Workers World Party member Rosemary Neidenberg explained to a branch meeting in New York City that Sostre's "aim is to fight the solitary confinement problem in a manner that will establish a precedent."[10] Sostre wrote from prison, "Ray's death cannot go unpunished for anyone of us could be the next Ray."[11] Just as his litigation with the Nation of Islam during the early 1960s marked a "stage and mission concluded successfully," he recalled this period as a "single-minded and single-handed struggle for prisoners' rights."[12] Sostre saw the courts and his solitary cell as interconnected terrains from which he could expose the state and mobilize people to oppose it.

Using the court as a battlefield required a range of weapons. Sostre constantly repositioned himself vis-à-vis the state to remain on the offensive. A year earlier, he had refused a court-appointed public defender and seized the opportunity to put the state on trial. Now, his civil suit against prison officials was heard in the court of Judge Constance Baker Motley, the first Black woman ever appointed to the federal judiciary. Not only were the governor, prison commissioner, and warden all named as defendant, but the courtroom was turned into an arena in which the state was forced to explain its actions. Spectators even flipped the tradition of standing for the judge, instead rising every time Sostre entered the room.[13] Amid this spectacle, Sostre showed "very clearly that the political and judicial super-structure of this system is destroyable," said Benjamin Ortiz of the Movement for Puerto Rican Independence.[14] One radical newspaper observed that even among a flurry of high-profile political trials including those of the Berrigan Brothers, Ahmed Evans, the Chicago Seven, Huey Newton, Angela Davis, the Panther 21, and Wounded Knee, Martin Sostre's "stands out because he is on the offensive."[15]

The state's intense repression during this period allowed Sostre to broaden his base of support. This dynamic defined one of his core political strategies: "You escalate, we escalate."[16] In a letter to a supporter, he later explained how his resistance that year led to new horizons of struggle:

> When I was being tortured in solitary confinement in Green Haven, and I informed several prisoners of my intention to challenge in Federal Court the atrocities being inflict[ed] upon us and to sue for damages, several counselled me to "cool it." They told me that I was already busted in solitary and that the last thing I should do was to antagonize Follette; that I had 41 years to do and should concentrate on my case, otherwise I would never get out of prison and may even get killed by antagonizing the man who had absolute power over me and who was known for his sadism. Had I listened to that negative, cowardly counsel I never would have objectified the sweeping prison reform effected by the Motley decision. In war there must be casualties, we can't have it nice and cozy and safe in this struggle.[17]

Sostre believed that a singular act of resistance aimed at an oppressive system, even from prison, could unearth contradictions and create new terrains of struggle. Others would join the resistance, forcing the state into a more vulnerable position, which it then sought to combat through even more reactionary measures. This dialectic was ongoing, swelling the masses of those resisting, making them more aware of the other everyday forms of violence they encountered and putting the state in an increasingly defensive and precarious posture.

Although it is understandable that Sostre later characterized this period of intense isolation and severe repression as a "single-minded and single-handed struggle," it was also one of expanded support and multifaceted organizing. His comrades established the Afro-Asian Bookshop in Exile (AABE), which provided revolutionary political education alongside information and updates on his case. Black radicals Mae Mallory and William Worthy organized on his behalf and mentored his defense committee, bringing his case to national attention and expanding its links to the organized left. And in searching for an ideological and organizational home through the Workers World Party, the Republic of New Africa, and the Black Panther Party, Sostre sharpened his critiques of centralized, hierarchical leadership and deepened his interest in anarchism and autonomous organizing. Throughout this period, the state's surveillance, infiltration, and censorship intensified. What often felt like a solitary struggle was in fact a collective war on all fronts.

The establishment of the Afro-Asian Bookshop in Exile was among the highest priorities Sostre impressed on his supporters as he went to prison.[18] The AABE emerged from several projects: first a book fundraiser after the destruction of the original bookshop; then bookfairs to raise bail money and disseminate information leading up to Sostre's trial. In April 1968, it became a semipermanent fixture on the University at Buffalo campus.[19] Sostre articulated the bookstore's goals in a letter from Green Haven to his defense committee: "Besides the income it brings in for our legal expenses, it is a sower of seeds in the struggle against the power structure."[20] He emphasized that it must be "action-oriented" and "not only . . . attract and train the active segment of the community but . . . spur to action the passive and fencesitters."[21]

Jerry Gross recalled that for the first few months, they had "just a table or two tables in the student union piled with books."[22] In July 1968, the Martin Sostre Defense Committee published *Letters from Prison*, which included excerpts from nearly forty of Sostre's letters and several of his longer essays written from jail. They used the AABE as a central distribution hub. The Bookshop in Exile continued to grow, eventually overflowing its allotment of tables inthe student union, featuring prominent backdrops of Sostre's profile, political posters, and copies of the *Black Panther* with artwork by Emory Douglass. A banner at the top proclaimed: "Long Live the Memory of Ho Chi Minh—The NLF is Going to Win."[23]

For Gross and Bob McCubbin, running the AABE soon became a full-time job.[24] "People would come and look at it and talk to us," McCubbin recalled. "We'd tell them about any upcoming meetings or any developments in the case. That went on all day, every day, for a couple of years." The two even traveled to New York City to buy rare books from the basement of Lewis Michaux's bookstore, which had developed from the small shop of Sostre's youth to become what historian Joshua Davis described as the "best and biggest Black-interest bookstore in America."[25] At the end of each day, the AABE was packed away into a small storage room that Black custodial workers had secured for the committee.[26]

Mae Mallory, c. early 1960s. Courtesy of Mallory Merrill Siljegovic

Geraldine Robinson occasionally staffed the AABE while preparing for her own trial and parenting her children.[27] When Robinson had been arrested in July 1967, she was pregnant with Sostre's child; however, the pregnancy had ended in a miscarriage.[28] Now hundreds of miles away, Sostre attempted to remain connected. In April 1968, she was briefly hospitalized, and Sostre inquired about her health and studies, asking if she had been to the doctor and whether she was still getting her subscription to *Workers World* and other radical literature.[29] He also worried about her five kids, all still under the age of ten. "It is very important that they get the right children's books at an early age to counter the poison being fed them in school by the power structure," he wrote. "I'm glad their little minds are being fed right."[30] In October, the state targeted her with neglect charges and attempted to take custody of her children.[31] Social workers accused her of failing to feed and clothe them adequately and claimed she herself "always dresses in high fashion in expensive clothes."[32] Sostre gave her a check for the last twenty-four dollars in the bookstore account, which she deposited in his commissary. The welfare department, regarding this as income, deducted it from her check. He returned the money "so her kids would not be short on food that month." The incident taught him "how closely enmeshed are all sectors of this racist society."[33]

Afro-Asian Bookshop in Exile at the Norton Union, c. 1968. From left to right: Jerry Gross, Geraldine Robinson, and Bob McCubbin. William Worthy papers, MS.0524, Special Collections, The Johns Hopkins University.

Meanwhile, at Green Haven, Sostre struggled to find an attorney he trusted with his appeal. Having already been betrayed by the Buffalo firm that had abandoned his case after only a few hours of work, he believed his current lawyer was also not up to the task. "He is completely blind to the issues involved," Sostre wrote his committee. "He has no concept of the vicious nature of the power structure—his oppressors and opponents."[34] Sostre reached out to the radical civil rights activist and attorney Conrad Lynn, but his letters were returned.[35] Finally, they had a breakthrough. Late in the evening on April 18, 1968, Jeanette Merrill excitedly scrawled notes after a phone call with activist Mae Mallory: "She was at founding meeting of Republic of New Africa . . . met a woman attorney—Miss Franklin. . . . Interested in your case."[36] The story of how Mallory connected Merrill with Franklin illustrates the shared history that linked radicals on the white left and those in the Black freedom movement.

Mallory was a seasoned radical who had herself recently been a political prisoner. Born in Macon, Georgia, in 1927, she had moved to Harlem with her mother at the age of twelve. In the early 1950s, she briefly joined the Communist Party as a factory worker but was quickly disappointed. Frustrated with male chauvinism among Black nationalists and the classism and moderation of the NAACP, she organized a group of Black mothers challenging New York City's inferior, segregated schools. In 1958, she was one of one hundred parents who pulled their children from the public junior high and founded an alternative "Freedom School."[37]

The following year, she learned of the suspension of Monroe, North Carolina, NAACP leader Robert F. Williams by Roy Wilkins and the national office for Williams's outspoken commitment to armed self-defense. "I got up and went in the streets and organized some support for Robert Williams, a man that I had never met," she would later recall.[38]

Williams found broad support among Harlem's radicals, developing relationships with Conrad Lynn, Malcolm X, John Henrik Clark, Queen Mother Moore, Yuri Kochiyama, and others. He became a regular visitor at Michaux's bookstore, and he and his wife Mabel were supplied with guns and funds from their comrades in the North.[39] Mallory was embedded in this network, including the Cultural Association of Women of African Heritage, which conducted a takeover of the United Nations building to protest the US-backed assassination of Congolese independence leader Patrice Lumumba. Mallory was arrested during the action after hitting a security guard on the head with her shoe.[40]

By the early 1960s, Monroe's militant NAACP chapter had transformed into the Negroes with Guns movement and begun publishing the *Crusader*, a radical internationalist newsletter.[41] In August 1961, Freedom Riders associated with the Congress of Racial Equality traveled to Monroe as part of a broader challenge to segregation on interstate buses throughout the South. The Williamses and other Black advocates of self-defense in Monroe distinguished themselves from these nonviolent protestors from outside the community. Mallory's biographer Paula Marie Seniors notes that "by venturing to Monroe, the Freedom Riders dismissed [their] methods of survival . . . bringing a cacophony of chaos and inciting white supremacist violence." Bringing machine guns and military rifles purchased from a Harlem gangster, Mallory and writer Julian Mayfield headed to Monroe to support their comrades there.[42]

Tensions in the community were high, and during the time Mallory was staying with the Williamses, they wound up safeguarding a local white supremacist couple from potential violence after the latter haphazardly drove into their neighborhood. Despite giving them sanctuary in their home, the activists soon faced a white lynch mob who accused them of kidnapping and were forced underground to escape. Mallory and Robert Williams had a disagreement about how she had handled the situation in Monroe, and she was "unceremoniously dumped" in New York. The Williamses successfully fled to Cuba, but Mallory was arrested by the FBI in Cleveland, Ohio and charged with kidnapping.[43]

In 1961, members of the New Orleans NAACP, the Negroes with Guns Movement, and the WWP formed the Monroe Defense Committee to support Mallory. She spent much of the next two years in the Cuyahoga County Jail while her committee furiously distributed her writings from jail and launched a massive letter-writing campaign on her behalf.[44] As historian Ashley Farmer explains, Mallory's ideas at this time reflected a blend of left-wing politics and "her burgeoning interest in Black nationalist frameworks and principles."[45] These views all had a home in the WWP, and eventually Mallory won her case and returned to Harlem, where she soon lent her support to Sostre.

The movement to "Save Mae from the KKK," Farmer says, "fostered relationships between older and younger Black radicals and introduced them to national aspects of the Black freedom struggle."[46] It also provided white radicals like the Merrills with a framework and experience in defense work that they used in their efforts to free Sostre and Robinson from a legal lynching. Jeanette took dozens of photographs documenting the campaign, ranging from picket lines to casual portraits of Mallory after she was acquitted. Merrill and other more seasoned WWP organizers struck a balance between providing guidance to student activists like Gross and McCubbin and letting their younger comrades learn from their own mistakes. When asked if the MSDC chose tactics based on what had been learned from the Mallory campaign, Bob McCubbin responded, "Absolutely."[47]

Merrill was elated after Mallory told her that Joan Franklin was willing to represent Sostre.[48] Franklin was a young attorney with the national office of the NAACP and an assistant to its longtime legal counsel, Robert Carter.[49] She had received a BA in political science and a law degree from Wayne State University before serving in the Peace Corps in Nigeria in the early 1960s. In 1964, she had won an internship from the Eleanor Roosevelt Memorial Foundation to work in human rights at the NAACP legal defense fund.[50] Sostre was more interested in her affiliation with the newly formed RNA, which elected her as the minister of justice.[51]

For three days in March 1968, five hundred activists had gathered at the Black Government Convention in Franklin's hometown of Detroit, where several dozen signed a document declaring the formation of an independent Black state that remained—at least temporarily—an internal colony of the United States.[52] Franklin's role, as she later described it, was to hold the US accountable for illegal trusteeship of Black Americans and "systematic tyranny" before international tribunals and to outline a new legal system for citizens of the RNA, which included prosecuting spies within it.[53] Sostre pledged his allegiance to this new provisional government, whose president-in-exile and second vice president were Robert F. Williams and Betty Shabazz, the widow of Malcolm X.[54]

A few months after the conference, Sostre wrote Franklin about the possibility of her serving as counsel on his appeal. Describing himself rather humbly as a "layman untrained in law," he outlined possible avenues for overturning his conviction but expressed confidence that her "trained legal mind [would] uncover" enough material for a "half dozen reversals."[55] In other letters to Franklin, he indicated his interest in the development of the RNA's Black Judicial Code and emphasized their shared political commitments, sending his regards to Mallory and

Williams.[56] With such "intelligent and capable" people guiding the RNA, Sostre believed, its "rapid development and emergence as a potent world power [was] assured."[57]

For several months in the spring of 1968, Sostre regularly wrote Franklin and Mallory with updates about his legal research.[58] The three also managed to secure an attorney for Robinson and attempted to change the venue of her trial.[59] On June 24, the same week that police commissioner Frank Felicetta again traveled to Washington, DC, to deliver detailed testimony on Sostre and his WWP comrades to the House Un-American Activities Committee, Sostre mailed a series of legal documents to Franklin.[60] It was the next day that Sostre was questioned by Warden Folette and thrown in the hole for over a year—from June 1968 to August 1969—until Judge Motley ordered his release through a preliminary injunction.

Joan Franklin, undated. William Worthy papers, MS.0524, Special Collections, The Johns Hopkins University.

What can be known about this year is based almost exclusively on legal materials: Sostre's complaints, courtroom testimony, and letters to counsel. He had virtually no visitors, and most who attempted to see him were turned away.[61] He requested that Gross and Robinson be placed on his correspondence list, but the warden refused.[62] While Sostre had been writing to Jeanette Merrill under his sister Leticia's name, the prison caught on in June 1968 and removed her from the approved list, severing the last form of communication with his committee. "I am being systematically cut off from all contacts in the outside world and in the prison," he told Franklin.[63] Franklin was burdened by having to relay messages back and forth between him and his defense committee. That summer, she explained to Sostre that "it may be difficult for me to work extremely hard with the Committee as Mrs. Merrill and I do not hit it off." Careful not to undermine their case in court, Franklin asked that Merrill publish excerpts of Sostre's writings "in such a way as to appear as if I had summarized them for you and quoted certain excerpts. I want this done solely because I want to make certain that my argument as to the warden's violation of the attorney-client privilege is not jeopardized."[64]

Messages from other would-be supporters were intercepted by the state. Japanese American organizer Yuri Kochiyama, who had been among the first graduates of the Organization of Afro-American Unity's Liberation School and cradled Malcolm X's head after his assassination at the Audubon Ballroom in 1965, wrote to Sostre in March 1969.[65] She introduced herself to Sostre, whose case she had learned about from a jailhouse lawyer who was submitting a petition on his behalf. Acknowledging that she did "not know if this letter will reach" him, she assured him that she would reach out to his committee and other comrades.[66] Warden Follette diverted the letter to the local FBI office, advising that "Kochiyama is not on Sostre's approved correspondence list and this is the first letter to him from her. Needless to say, he did not receive it."[67] Among those Kochiyama vowed to contact was journalist William Worthy, who was also denied contact with Sostre but soon became a consistent champion of his case.

Worthy was a veteran activist and Black internationalist who had himself struggled with censorship, state surveillance, political trials, and imprisonment.[68] His story reveals the common experiences and perspectives that led him to support Sostre at this time. Worthy had been a conscientious objector during World War II and, in 1947, participated in the Journey of Reconciliation—a direct action campaign to test the enforcement of the recent Supreme Court ruling *Morgan v. Virginia*, which had overturned state laws mandating racial segregation on interstate travel. Worthy subsequently became a columnist for one of the country's largest Black newspapers, the *Baltimore Afro-American*, covering foreign affairs. As scholar Robeson Taj Frazier suggests, Worthy "employed journalism and foreign correspondence as transnational political practice."[69] Whether in his coverage of Black prisoners of war in North Korea and China or Robert F. Williams's exile in Cuba, Worthy's stories represented an important counternarrative to the anticommunism rampant among US journalism during the Cold War. Even his coverage of the Montgomery Bus Boycott emphasized its parallels with anticolonial movements in the global South.[70]

William Worthy, undated. William Worthy papers, MS.0524, Special Collections, The Johns Hopkins University.

Targeted by the federal government for his globetrotting anti-imperialist journalism, Worthy was denied a passport in 1957 and became what the ACLU called "a prisoner in his own country." When the State Department and the FBI discovered through their surveillance that he planned to travel to Cuba secretly to provide accurate coverage of the island's new revolutionary government, he was arrested.[71] A Committee for the Freedom of William Worthy formed, cochaired by civil rights and labor organizer A. Philip Randolph. Worthy was ultimately sentenced to three months in jail and nine months' probation. His cases resulted in two landmark decisions regarding the constitutional right to travel.[72] He saw these attacks as an extension of US imperialism and political censorship, remarking, "Travel control is thought control."[73]

Worthy followed the story of Sostre's arrest and trial for almost a year before a "chance remark" by a supporter in New York City prompted him "to delve in to the case for the first time."[74] He published nearly a dozen articles about Sostre's imprisonment and deemed his prosecution and punishment "one of the striking outrages of my journalistic experiences."[75] Worthy was among a handful of Black radicals who financially supported Sostre's defense campaign in these early years, along with Williams, Mallory, Leslie Campbell (later Jitu Weusi), and Bobby Seale.[76] Behind the scenes, Worthy wrote high-profile media contacts such as Mike Wallace, Jackie Robinson, CBS, and the *New York Times*, urging them to follow a case that would soon be a "national cause célèbre."[77] He concluded that "if ever the press was in a position to help free a man unjustly imprisoned, this is it."[78]

In September 1968, Worthy published "Sostre in Solitary" in the *Boston Sunday Globe*,[79] The four-page spread was also broadcast as a television address by Worthy and reproduced in *Workers World*. "Your case has been receiving a great deal of publicity," Franklin told Sostre shortly after it appeared, expressing the hope that a major publisher would solicit his autobiography.[80] Worthy remarked that it was possible "Sostre will be writing his own 'Soul on Ice' for a book publisher, but during rather than after his imprisonment."[81] Worthy's coverage heightened the profile of Sostre's cause and counteracted the scanty but slanderous coverage in mainstream media outlets. Jeanette Merrill wrote Worthy, "Your article and suggestions have given Martin's struggle new meaning and put the case in the national spotlight."[82]

Behind the scenes, Worthy advised Merrill and the defense

committee on how to appeal to the public.[83] For example, he sent Jeanette Merrill a pamphlet defending a young Black man falsely charged with murder—a cover-up of the accidental shooting of a one cop by another during the Watts rebellion of 1965.[84] He pointed out the effectiveness of its conventional family portrait, narrative style, layout, and explication that anyone who wanted to reproduce it could do so freely. The influence of his expert advice is visible in the MSDCs publicity for Geraldine Robinson, which included a similar portrait of her with her children.

A photo of Geraldine Robinson with her children, widely disseminated by the defense campaign. From left to right: Exzertios (7), Terrance (8), James (9), Christa (3), and Jamie (5). Box 343, Folder 19180, *Daily Worker* and Daily World Photographs Collection, Tamiment Library.

A series of photos of the Afro-Asian Bookshop in Exile, likely taken by Merrill for Worthy during the spring and summer of 1968, feature its political stance. Members of the defense committee sat behind stacks of pamphlets, books, and newsletters, along with a couple of African statuettes. An exhibit advertised the AABE as an alternative to the campus bookstore for students. Another sign proclaimed: "Defend Black Liberation with Deeds!"[85] Like its predecessor, the Bookshop in Exile soon became a target. In what Merrill described as a "modern-day book burning," two hundred-pound boxes of pamphlets and books in storage were incinerated that July by a maintenance worker who claimed he thought they were garbage.[86] The dean of students called it an unfortunate error, but Gross and others were convinced it was intentional.[87] The following year, the university resorted to more bureaucratic tactics to push it off campus. Although the AABE had handled all orders for Black history courses on campus, the university sent a letter to instructors encouraging them to buy from the official bookstore instead.[88] Citing a space shortage, the director of the student union ruled that only one table could be used per organization. In response, the Black Student Union, the Philosophical Society, and Youth Against War and Fascism combined their tables to continue the AABE.[89] A few months later, in March 1969, a group of campus activists demanded that the AABE be established as a "symbolic sanctuary" and given support for its permanent operation.[90] The student government soon passed a resolution in solidarity with Sostre and demanded permanent facilities for the Bookshop in Exile.[91]

As Sostre's committee worked to raise the profile of his case, they were surveilled, intimidated, and infiltrated by law enforcement. One of the most comprehensive archives of the Buffalo committee's activities during its first few years is in the personal collection of leftist defector J. B. Matthews.[92] Matthews had at one time been a member of the Fellowship of Reconciliation, the Socialist Party, and the American League Against War and Fascism, making nearly half a dozen trips to the Soviet Union.[93] By the late 1930s, however, he had become disillusioned and experienced what he called an "ethical revulsion against the Communist movement."[94] After popularizing the term "fellow traveler" through his 1938 memoir in which he disavowed his leftist past, Matthews launched his career as an anticommunist spy through his testimony before HUAC.[95] He eventually became its research director and worked closely with Senator Joseph McCarthy's Permanent Subcommittee on Investigations for the US Senate.

The Matthews collection gives a sense of the scope and form of anticommunist attacks on the MSDC. In a March 1969 letter, a St. John's college student identifying herself as Katherine Baker wrote the defense committee from Annapolis, Maryland, asking for literature on Sostre's case. Baker explained that she had first learned about Sostre's struggle through her subscription to *Workers World* and proposed soliciting contributions to the committee. "But we must have the facts in order to do this," she emphasized.[96] Jeanette Merrill responded gratefully with leaflets, flyers, and copies of *Letters from Prison* and "Sostre in Solitary." She was heartened to know that their campaign "is reaching all parts of the country" and reminded Baker that "the more people who become involved in exposing the frame-up, the less the racists will be able to succeed!"[97]

But there was no Katherine Baker. Elsewhere in the Matthews collection are other letters from the same alias posing as a St. John's college student. Indeed, the research director often joined radical organizations pseudonymously, with intentions of subverting them.[98] Even more mysteriously, J. B. Matthews died in 1966, a year before the formation of Sostre's defense committee. It is most likely that his widow Ruth wrote the letter. The couple had long shared their political work, hosting a salon for anticommunists at their home for over a decade.[99] After her husband's death, Ruth Matthews acted as a researcher for William F. Buckley Jr.'s right-wing newsletter, *Combat*.[100]

Other surveillance was closer to home. FBI records suggest that the small and close-knit Buffalo branch of the WWP, whose meetings often included fewer than ten people, was infiltrated. For more than a year, over a dozen meetings at the Merrills' home and Bob McCubbin's apartment were surveilled and documented. Although McCubbin recalls men whom he thought were FBI agents barging into his apartment after a demonstration and suspected a bug had been planted, at least one FBI memo suggests the informer was physically present: "I was not able to attend this meeting because of a toothache and do not know what transpired," it noted.[101]

Threats against the MSDC intensified. On July 6, 1968, three members of the MSDC received menacing notes in the mail. Jerry Gross and Ann Sterling were warned if they kept protesting, they would "get the same thing Kennedy got."[102] The Merrills received a chilling, hand-scrawled (and misspelled) note threatening the life of their three-year-old, Mallory: "This is a *warning*. Stop your suversive activtys or youre little girl will disapear [*sic*]. *Leaflets. Marches. Protests*."[103] The next night, Assistant Chief of Detectives Mike Amico and another cop came to their door at 11:00 p.m. and harassed Jeanette's elderly mother.[104] The following month, Gross was arrested and charged with assaulting a federal officer at the Elmwood Universalist Church as he and other comrades, who had burned a federal order charging them with draft evasion, occupied the church and declared it a "liberated community."[105]

Sostre's supporters understood this escalation as the state's acknowledgment of their growing success. As Jeanette Merrill wrote Worthy, "I'm sure your interest in the case, in addition to our continued struggle in Martin's behalf, has caused the police authorities and their associates to take added steps to intimidate and harass members of the Martin Sostre Defense Committee."[106] But Sostre remained physically isolated. For four months, he was held in a group of cells that housed only one other person.[107] Even when prisoners were held in the same area, they were often separated by several vacant cells and iron walls, which made it difficult to communicate without shouting.[108] Many of the sounds he did hear were of beatings and torture. They "don't beat the prisoners in the general population because it would cause a riot," Sostre explained. "So they take them up to solitary to beat their brains out."[109]

Throughout this torturous year in solitary confinement, Sostre kept a daily log of events inside and "smuggled documentary evidence out of the prison."[110] His letters to and from Franklin were his only communication with the outside world. At first, the two excitedly updated each other on relevant legal decisions and motions they were filing. Soon, as prison censorship limited their correspondence, they increasingly focused on whether each had received the other's missives.[111] One of Franklin's letters was cut in the middle and reattached with cellophane tape after all material related to the RNA and political organizing was removed.[112] Sostre saw opportunity in this repression. "This is a beautiful letter in that it will prove our allegation that this man is subjecting me to political and racial oppression," Sostre wrote her. "I have already marked this letter 'Exhibit A.' " That same day, *Sostre v. Rockefeller* was notarized.[113]

Despite his isolation, Sostre continued to shape revolutionary movements across prison walls. In October 1968, he wrote his longest essay since "Report from Jail to my Revolutionary Friends" the year prior. "Thoughts of a Black Political Prisoner in Solitary Confinement" offered a sweeping analysis of revolutionary struggle at the height of the Black Power movement. Sostre identified with both the Black Panther Party (BPP) and the Republic of New Africa, and he affirmed many of the ideas circulating widely during this period, particularly the need for community control and a Black united front. "What has just been said is not new," he acknowledged, "for it has already been said many times before, by many persons, in many places." But read in the context of his political trajectory, "Thoughts of a Black Political Prisoner" reveals the development of Sostre's ideas about Black autonomy and armed struggle.[114]

Sostre wrote his essay following the occupation of Columbia University by students protesting the Vietnam War and the violent assaults on demonstrators by police at the Democratic Party's national convention in Chicago that summer, just a few months before the election of Richard Nixon.[115] "For those of us who no longer will allow the Gestapo pigs to brutalize and slaughter our people with impunity," he explained, "there is only one correct answer to the war of extermination being waged against us by the enemy: A United Black Front." Sostre described this united front as a "natural weapon of the Black masses . . . the people's foundation of Black Liberation." "There must be total control by us of everything in our communities that affects our lives," he affirmed. He was careful, however, to distinguish between real community control and white supremacy masked by Black faces. He compared the "frantic replacement of white cops with Black" to the use of Black clerks behind the counters of white-owned business to "blur the visibility of white exploitation."[116]

Sostre devoted much of the second half of his essay to the escalating repression of Black revolutionaries and its relationship to the worldwide struggle. Frustrated by the common assertion that Black people were a minority in the United States and thus could never liberate themselves from white rule, Sostre wrote that "once the universal perspective of our war of liberation and the many fronts where it is being fought by hundreds of millions of our allies is brought to the attention of our people, they will realize that it is the oppressor, and not we, who is vastly outnumbered."[117] Anticipating the multiracial Rainbow Coalition that soon emerged in Chicago between the Black Panthers, the Puerto Rican Young Lords Organization, and poor white migrants from Appalachia known as the

Young Patriots, he argued that "although every oppressed people must, of necessity, conduct their struggle for liberation within the confines of their own locality where they are being oppressed, they must never lose sight of the universality of the war of liberation."[118] Likely informed by his own comradeship with the predominantly white revolutionaries in YAWF and the WWP, Sostre drew attention to "the two rebellions occurring simultaneously in this country, namely the war of Black Liberation, and the rebellion of the white oppressed class led by their militants against the white ruling class."[119] These interrelated movements, he believed, were allies in their struggle against their common oppressor.

Recognizing the escalating repression of Black militants, Sostre proposed securing the release of political prisoners through exchange with US state agents captured and held by other countries. "If it is true that the war of Black liberation here in the United States is one of the many fronts of the world-wide war of liberation," he wrote, "then Black political prisoners in the United States deserve the same protection accorded political prisoners in other fronts of the war."[120] It seemed logical that the revolutionary governments of Cuba, China, Egypt, North Vietnam, and North Korea would exchange captured US soldiers for Black revolutionaries held in the belly of the empire. Sostre's proposal of Black community control through a federation of tenants, workers, students, and unions anticipated aspects of his anarchist thought in the years to come.[121]

It was six months before the article was published.[122] Because Sostre was forbidden from corresponding with comrades or writing anything political to his attorney, his essay was confiscated when he tried to mail it. Yet he creatively used the law to thwart the warden's extralegal actions and smuggle it out of solitary confinement. First, he drew up a show-cause order—a formal document in a legal dispute that outlines an offense and offers the defendant an opportunity to explain themselves. "The warden has, in effect, set himself up as the political censor of constitutionally protected views of the inmates of Green Haven Prison, and goes so far as to punish inmates to solitary confinement solely because they expressed their political views in their correspondence," Sostre contended.[123] In filing the order, he brought Follette's actions to the attention of the courts while simultaneously embedding the full essay within an affidavit as evidence. The show-cause order was notarized, then sent to the Kings County Supreme Court as well as to his attorney, Joan Franklin, thereby assuring it would reach his defense committee. This is one tangible way that Sostre used the oppressive legal arm of the state as a revolutionary weapon against itself.

"Thoughts of a Black Political Prisoner in Solitary Confinement" was published by YAWF's newspaper, *Partisan*, in April 1969.[124] By the end of that year, nearly 100 Black Panthers faced the death penalty or sentences of thirty years or more, and another 155 were jailed or being sought by police. On the East Coast, they included the Panther Twenty-One, members of local BPP chapters who hadbeen indicted for a series of planned bombings that April after being coerced and framed by informants.[125] The suppression of radical movements created an unprecedented influx of people imprisoned for their political beliefs and actions.

The rising number of political prisoners was part and parcel of the broader criminalization of Black and Brown communities during the 1960s.[126] Although many scholars have dated the rise of mass incarceration to the 1970s, the previous decade was marked by both the single greatest reduction in the overall prison population and unparalleled levels of imprisonment of nonwhite people. By 1963, Black people had become the largest racial group in New York prisons. Between 1960 and 1964, Black and white people were admitted at roughly constant, albeit disproportionate, rates. After the introduction of new policing tactics such as "stop and frisk" and "no knock" raids in 1964, the numbers of incarcerated Black people rose exponentially. By 1970, almost three times as many Black people as white were sent to state and federal prisons.

On October 29, 1969, BPP cofounder Bobby Seale was bound and gagged in the trial of the Chicago Eight, as Sostre had been in his trial in Buffalo the year before. Unlike Sostre's case, Seale's earned national headlines, and drawings of him chained to a chair with a towel tied tightly over his mouth were published by newspapers across the country. Rumors soon spread through the underground press that the National Liberation Front had proposed to trade US pilots captured in Vietnam for Seale and Huey Newton, the other Panther cofounder. Eldridge Cleaver even promoted the idea from exile in Algiers.[127] In the *Black Panther* newspaper and at demonstrations, supporters rallied around the cry "Pilots for Panthers."[128] At a demonstration for the Panther Twenty-One in downtown Manhattan that November, signs demanding the exchange of "US War Criminals for Huey and Bobby" were raised alongside "Free Martin Sostre" banners.[129]

While the exact series of events tying Sostre's article to the "Pilots for Panthers" campaign is not documented, his influence was clear at the time. Sostre wrote to Franklin that the "Panthers have adopted my suggestion . . . in regards to prisoner exchange and are having me write another article on the 'U.S. Pilots for Panthers' theme."[130] Yet the Black leaders who took up this idea do not seem to have acknowledged Sostre's influence. And, while they demanded a political prisoner exchange for other, better-known Black militants, they never did so for him.[131] One can only speculate as to how Sostre might have experienced this disjuncture. All the same, it provides a potent example of how the impact of his political thinking on revolutionary movements of the 1960s and '70s has gone unacknowledged.

In the fall of 1969, as the trials of Bobby Seale in Chicago and Martin Sostre in New York City approached, the state made what Sostre considered a "defensive move" and transferred him Wallkill Prison.[132] Warden Charles McKendrick had greeted him with surprise. "What are you doing here?" he asked. "Ask your commissioner," Sostre had responded.[133] Opened in 1933 as part of a trend among reform-oriented penologists to design prisons to look like college campuses instead of industrial workhouses, Wallkill was known as the "prison without walls." It was generally reserved by prison administrators as a reward for good behavior or for so-called white-collar criminals.[134] But Sostre was not so easily deceived. He was suspicious of the motives behind the transfer, believing it was either an effort to undermine his claims in court or an attempt to set him up with a "manufactured" escape or accusations of homosexuality.[135] Although Sostre did not elaborate on why he thought he would face this accusation, his suspicions proved correct. When the warden later filed a deposition requesting Sostre's transfer to a different institution, he used graffiti that read "Sostre is a queer punk" as evidence that although there was "no evidence of overt homosexual behavior by Sostre at Wallkill . . . his selection of associates closely follows the patterns of the prison wolf or gorilla."[136] Such expressions of homophobia and anti-Black racism recast defense of personhood by assertive Black men like Sostre as sexual deviance.

Wallkill offered new organizing opportunities for Sostre, who had been held in maximum-security prisons and spent the previous year in extreme isolation. Upon arrival, he wrote his committee excitedly that he was now able to receive the newspapers of the BPP, WWP, and RNA and promised to renew his "legal and political struggle with the same intensity."[137] Within his first few months there, Sostre organized a Black Studies Program and a group called the Afro-American Cultural Society, whose internal bulletin he edited. Significantly, he also established a lending library under the auspices of the Afro-Asian Bookshop in Exile.[138] The library included nearly forty books from his personal collections, including the speeches of Malcolm X, writings by Frantz Fanon, Eldridge Cleaver, and Nat Turner, and copies of *Liberator* magazine, and was available to all prisoners.[139]

The emergence of the AABE at Wallkill marked not only an expansion of the original bookshops but also their proliferation as forms of political organizing and coalition-building. In the summer of 1969, Sostre's comrades took the AABE on the road. At the pivotal Students for a Democratic Society National Convention in Chicago that June, which led to a major split in the New Left, the AABE table gathered over 250 signatures on a petition demanding Sostre's freedom.[140] The following month, his supporters traveled to Oakland for the United Front Against Fascism conference organized by the Black Panther Party. "Hundreds of thousands of pieces of literature on Martin's case were distributed at both conferences," Merrill reported.[141] By 1970, other AABEs had emerged at universities in Boston, New York, Milwaukee, and Cleveland. The emergence of these autonomous AABEs foreshadowed the decentralization of Sostre's defense committee a few years later.

Despite restoration of Sostre's communication with the outside world, political censorship remained a central mechanism of repression. It soon become the basis of his next and final major lawsuit against the state, *Sostre v. Otis*. When Sostre arrived at Wallkill, he received 120 birthday and Christmas cards withheld during his year in solitary.[142] He demanded back copies of weekly and monthly publications that had also been withheld.[143] Although he was given copies of the *Liberator*, *Afro-American*, *Negro Digest*, and the *Buffalo Challenger*, prison administrators refused to release *Workers World*, *Muhammad Speaks*, and the *Criminal Law Bulletin*.[144] Undeterred, he renewed his subscription to *Workers World* and subscribed to *Claridad* (a Spanish-language weekly published by the Puerto Rican independence movement in San Juan), *Ramparts*, the *Guardian*, and the *Black Panther Party Newspaper*. His committee mailed him Kwame Nkrumah's *Handbook of Revolutionary Warfare*, Robert F. Williams's *Listen, Brother!*, Mao's writings, and his own pamphlet *Martin Sostre in Court*. Almost all of these were either seized or denied.[145] An entire year of *Muhammad Speaks* was thrown away because Sostre was not registered with the prison as a Muslim. A decade earlier, he had been held in solitary confinement for possessing "contraband" writings because the state did not recognize the Nation of Islam as a legitimate religion. Then, as a result of his litigation, prisons were forced to allow this material. Now he was told he could not access it because records indicated he was "not a Muslim."[146]

Sostre's defense committee responded by surveying publishers, requesting the dates of mailings and notification of any rejections. "As soon as you get confirmation from publishers that above publications are being mailed to me," he explained, "I will sue officials in Federal Court on 1st and 14th Amendment grounds—freedom of press and political beliefs and racist discriminatory banning of Black literature."[147] Sostre published an open letter addressing Governor Rockefeller directly about the censorship:

> Although prisoners are freely permitted to receive white racist, Zionist, and right-wing reactionary books, newspapers, and magazines at Wallkill Prison, and such literature is ordered and received by the prison library for prisoner use, prisoners are not allowed to receive liberal, anti-racist, and progressive literature. Your racist right-wing agents who run Wallkill concentration camp are as zealous in banning, obstructing, and destroying all political literature that opposes their ingrained white racist ideology as was the Gestapo in their book-burning of anti-Nazi writings.... In short, your outlaw agents have arbitrarily set themselves up as political and religious censors despite the protection of religious and political literature by the First and Fourteenth Amendments.[148]

In March 1970, Sostre again sued the state in Judge Motley's district, seeking an injunction and $20,000 in damages from the warden of Wallkill and Commissioner McGinnis for their interference with his receipt of literature through prison mail. A year later, the Department of Corrections established a review committee and adopted a new screening procedure. The courts ultimately found this system deficient and affirmed the constitutional right of incarcerated people to rudimentary due process, including notice of censorship and an opportunity to appeal.[149] These rights, although regularly ignored by prisons, remain one of Sostre's most important legacies to prisoners.

Meanwhile, Sostre told his legal team he had "organized another Black group in both Greenhaven [*sic*] and Wallkill," which were likely two of the first chapters of the Black Panther Party in New York prisons.[150] Sostre's affiliations were shifting during this period of rapid political change. In September 1969, RNA president Robert Williams had returned to the United States after eight years of exile. But by then Sostre had grown frustrated with the RNA's slow pace and its failure to assist his defense campaign. When Franklin assured him that the RNA "welcomed and desired" his support, he responded: "Shouldn't it be the other way around inasmuch as I am the one paying dues in prison (for my activity in behalf of the Black struggle) while they are out? Although I have constantly supported them, even while under torture in the enemy's dungeon, they have not supported me. Mae Mallory and the Panthers have been the only ones giving my committee financial support, giving my case publicity in their newspaper, and demonstrating and speaking in my behalf."[151]

The RNA itself was under attack. In March 1969, at the first national convention since its founding, a dozen armed Detroit police officers invaded New Bethel Baptist Church and exchanged fire with the New Africans (later Afrikans) gathered there. One police officer was killed and several people in the church were wounded. Police immediately arrested 142 people, including several infants.[152] Historian Edward Onaci observes that while many hoped Williams's return would "reenergize and organize" the movement, it "brought to the surface internal conflicts that had been brewing for over a year."[153] Amid intense surveillance and repression, leadership disputes, and a "constitutional crisis," the RNA was unable to support a political prisoner like Sostre. Instead, its cofounder, Imari Obadele, obliviously suggested that the movement looked "forward to the time when [Sostre] can actively participate in its efforts."[154]

As Sostre's initiation of Black Panther Party chapters in prison indicates, he had close, reciprocal ties with the BPP during this period. His committee corresponded with the party in Oakland, and the warden even accused Sostre of using the prison's hobby shop to make Black Panther symbols.[155] But his own understanding of the central role that political prisoners could, and should, play in revolutionary movements clashed with the assumptions of many groups organizing outside. Sostre had begun examining the limitations of centralized leadership, whether in the RNA, BPP, or WWP. He later denounced this model, embodied in both the nation-state and in revolutionary groups, as "authoritarian and repressive modes of social organization which require the centralization of power in the hands of a few bureaucratic functionaries."[156]

In the fall of 1969, just a few months after his transfer to Wallkill and while awaiting the trial in his federal lawsuit against New York State for its violations of his own and other prisoners' rights, he shared many of his insights about liberatory alternatives to hierarchical and fundamentally coercive structures with a young Black Power activist, Lorenzo Ervin. At Wallkill and the Federal House of Detention, Sostre was able to interact with others outside his cell for the first time in a year. Over the course of several weeks, he and Ervin engaged in long discussions about the political and philosophical perspectives that should guide Black revolutionaries. Through their conversations, Sostre helped to forge a new connection between Black revolutionaries and anarchist thought in the United States and worldwide.

Ervin, born in Chattanooga, Tennessee in 1947, was twenty-four years old—about half Sostre's age—when the two met. He had been politicized through sit-ins at segregated lunch counters and high school walkouts in his hometown during the early 1960s, having joined the local NAACP at age twelve.[157] The firehoses, tear gas, and police dogs that were deployed in response to young people, he recalled, "radicalized me for life."[158] The president of the local NAACP, who was also the school's principal, punished the student protestors, giving Ervin an early lesson in the role of Black middle-class leadership in disciplining Black insurgency.[159] Like Sostre, Ervin was drafted soon after turning eighteen. While he was in the Army during the war in Vietnam, he organized with the American Servicemen's Union, a group of active-duty soldiers who assisted others to escape conscription and find asylum in neutral countries. Ervin was apprehended, beaten, and thrown into solitary confinement in a military prison in Germany. When he and other antiwar soldiers rebelled, Ervin was court-martialed and dishonorably discharged to the US.

In 1967, Ervin began working as a SNCC field organizer and sold copies of the *Black Panther* newspaper between Atlanta and Chattanooga. He was mentored by Willie Ricks, who is often remembered for galvanizing the crowd to shout "Black Power" at the James Meredith March Against Fear in 1966. After Ervin was repeatedly harassed by local cops and heard that he might be killed, he became involved in underground activity.[160] In February 1969, he hijacked a plane to Cuba. Ervin was captured and returned to the US that September, when he met Martin Sostre.[161]

The first thing Ervin noticed about Sostre was his solitude and sternness. "He was not someone you wanted to encounter if you were not a serious-minded man," he recalled; Sostre "carried himself in a way with tremendous dignity and forcefulness."[162] After watching him carefully for a day, Ervin got up his nerve to introduce himself and discuss his case. Over a few weeks, the two engaged in intense daily discussions about politics, law, and, perhaps most importantly, how to survive prison. "Almost every day that I saw him, we would go over my case and he would give me legal advice."[163] Ervin was facing the possibility of the death penalty, and Sostre stressed the necessity of learning the law and building a defense campaign. He also gave Ervin advice that he carried with him the rest of his life: "He said, 'I don't believe in the system, but I use the system, use it against itself.' . . . It probably saved my life in many ways."[164]

Sostre introduced Ervin to the idea of anarchism. "Almost every day he regaled me about direct democracy, communitarianism, radical autonomy, general assemblies, and other stuff I knew nothing about. So I just listened for hours as he schooled me."[165] "What I'd heard of anarchists," Ervin remembered, "they were just a lazy lot of people that didn't do anything for the struggle."[166] Now, Sostre introduced him to the work of anarchist Peter Kropotkin and recommended he read *The Unknown Revolution* by Volin, a Russian anarchist who synthesized syndicalism and communism.[167] Kropotkin's ideas about forming alternative economic structures within capitalism "really excited me," Ervin said.[168] His readings helped him understand the survival programs of the Black Panther Party as a form of Black autonomous counter-structure that was undermined, in part, by the hierarchy of the BPP's central committee.[169] These conversations and ideas became the impetus for Ervin's influential book *Anarchism and the Black Revolution* (published a decade later, while he was still in prison), which has become a touchstone in the development of Black anarchist thought. "I would not be an anarchist today if I had not met Martin Sostre," he later reflected.[170]

Ervin has credited Sostre with helping him become a deeper, more independent thinker. "By the time I met him, my mind was wide open for something new," he said; Sostre "explained what that something was."[171] Ervin has been quick to note that although, unlike George Jackson, Sostre was not a prolific writer and did not receive as much national acclaim, "he was every bit as important to the development of the prison movement. . . . In the New York State system, he had done probably more than anyone to bring them to that stage of radical consciousness." After Sostre's trial, Ervin was sent back to state prison, and the two never spoke again. Ervin wrote Sostre letters from prison, but they were seized or returned. Nevertheless, the Free Lorenzo Movement built on the lessons Ervin learned from Sostre and resulted in his release in 1983. Ervin dedicated the 2021 edition of *Anarchism and the Black Revolution* to Sostre. "He changed my life," Ervin concluded, "and by extension, he changed the lives of other people."[172]

During this chance meeting between the two Black revolutionaries, Sostre was preparing for what promised to be one of the most important prisoners' rights cases in US history. His supporters dubbed the week of his trial "Free Martin Sostre week."[173] In Buffalo, Dan Bentivogli of the MSDC introduced a rally with Mae Mallory, Zayd Shakur of the BPP, and Benjamin Ortiz of the Puerto Rican Independence Movement.[174] The following day in lower Manhattan, 250 people picketed outside in the courthouse at Foley Square.[175] The energy and enthusiasm around putting the state on trial was contagious. "Martin Sostre's attempt to bring state officials to justice is a dramatic reversal of roles," wrote the *Liberation News Service*, a New Left alternative news agency.[176] Flyers framed the trial like a heavyweight title fight: "Martin Sostre vs. Rockefeller."[177]

Unlike his trial in Buffalo the previous year, when a handful of supporters had entered a courtroom packed with police, nearly one hundred comrades poured from the streets into Manhattan's federal court, exhilarated by the demonstration outside. Many were Black Panthers, Young Lords, or members of the Revolutionary Action Movement (RAM), a left-wing Black nationalist organization; also present were allies in the WWP, YAWF, and the Afro-American Teachers Association.[178] WWP cofounder Vincent Copeland, who was writing a book on Sostre, described the "festive atmosphere": "Everyone seemed to feel instinctively that this was going to be Martin's 'day in court.'"[179] As supporters settled into their seats, the clerk asked Sostre to raise his right hand and swear to tell the truth. He raised a clenched fist.[180]

Flyer, Free Martin Sostre Week, Box 17, Folder 8, MS 31, Elizabeth Olmsted Smith Papers, 1923-1975, University Archives, The State University of New York at Buffalo.

The differences from his trial in Buffalo a year earlier speak to the rapidly changing conditions—simultaneously repressive and revolutionary—of the late 1960s, which Sostre was actively shaping. The first day Sostre testified, Seale was gagged and bound in Chicago. The Panther

Twenty-One were detained nearby and awaiting trial. Even the sitting judge in Sostre's trial, Constance Baker Motley, was touched by this state repression and carceral expansion. Earlier that year, Motley had received word that the son of her first cousin, John Huggins Sr., was murdered. Her cousin John Jr. and his wife Ericka, who had met at Lincoln University in Pennsylvania, left school and moved to Los Angeles in late 1967, soon becoming active in the Los Angeles chapter of the BPP. Meanwhile, the FBI stoked a growing local feud between the Panthers and Ron Karenga's US Organization in the hopes that such measures would result in a "vendetta." In 1969, those tensions climaxed with the killing of John Huggins and Bunchy Carter by members of US on UCLA's campus. Although the extent to which the FBI orchestrated the assassination remains unclear, "evidence would emerge later showing that the state had a hand in stirring up the conflict."[181]

Judge Motley, who was nominated to the federal judiciary by President Lyndon B. Johnson in 1966, is described by biographer Tomiko Brown-Nagin as "skeptical of feminism and opposed to radical racial politics," and thus an "absolute favorite of the liberal, Democratic establishment."[182] Motley was likely familiar with Sostre's work as a jailhouse lawyer from her previous work for the NAACP's Legal Defense Fund. It was within the context of Huggins's murder and the FBI's presumed role in it that she made the "most socially progressive—and controversial—decision of her judicial career."[183] Although Brown-Nagin believes that Motley was "randomly assigned" the case, Sostre's defense committee worked with counsel Kristin Booth Glen to bring Sostre's complaint to Motley's court.[184] "In the old days when you could pick your judge," Booth Glen recalled, "I had just finished clerking and I knew her clerks, so we were able to choose her." In a 1969 letter after their first visit, she wrote Sostre, "I will begin working on the papers in your case so that we can file them, as planned, while Judge Motley is sitting."[185]

The weeklong trial testimony unfolded alongside Sostre's three main legal complaints: his punitive segregation without due process; unlawful political censorship and interference with legal mail; and the state's maintenance of concentration camps that held predominantly Black and Brown men under the rule of almost exclusively white guards and officials. Although Warden Follette had publicly contended that he had never interfered with Sostre's mail, Victor Rabinowitz and Booth Glen shared nearly twenty letters that were never sent or censored and tampered with.[186] Follette's testimony was almost incomprehensible due to its contradictions.[187] When asked in a deposition read at trial if there was a rule that a prisoner could not possess property that was not their own, he answered affirmatively but could not cite any explicit rule: "It is a thoroughly understood rule," he said. "I don't know. I haven't studied this rule book recently."[188] Follette repeatedly tried to dodge questions about sharing materials with state police and the FBI by claiming the conversations "were confidential." But Rabinowitz pointed out that these same agents "testify in this court every day in the week.[189]

Sostre's testimony on the deprivations and torture of solitary confinement were harrowing. He described the six-by-eight-foot cell with no hot water, where he remained twenty-four hours a day for over year for refusing dehumanizing rectal assaults. Sostre and others were cut off from commissary and other sources of communal aid. He and other imprisoned witnesses described state-issued socks with holes and soiled underwear. They were fed reduced rations, with meatballs made with bread and peanut butter running with corn oil.[190] With dinner served at 3:00 p.m. and breakfast at 8:00 a.m., they were essentially forced to fast each day for seventeen hours.[191] One witness said that he lost forty pounds during his confinement.[192] "The best way I can say it," Sostre explained, is that the prison "is concentrated racism in its worst form."[193]

The entire courtroom fell silent as Sostre gave an account of the death by suicide that motivated much of his case. In August 1968, Sostre and another prisoner, John Carothers, had heard someone "screaming bloody murder" in an adjacent cell. They both described the sound of a "club thunking off his flesh and bouncing off the wall."[194] After the beating, Sostre called out from his solitary cell and the man identified himself as Ray Broderick. The next day, Broderick was taken to the principal keeper and told that he had lost several months of good time. He feared he had a broken leg or ankle as well. Sostre encouraged him "not to sign anything" and dictated a legal complaint through the wall, with the help of Carothers who repeated parts to Broderick.[195] Two days after the beating, Sostre heard a guard running, followed by the sound of an oxygen resuscitator before he was told that Broderick had hung himself. "It is difficult to describe a courtroom on an occasion like this," Copeland wrote. "Everyone in the whole great room knows the prisoner is telling the exact truth: the judge, the prosecution, the defense (there is no jury) and of course the spectators. . . . It begins to seem like a play, and the State attorneys and witnesses like a team of actors playing roles they must play on pain of losing something very important to themselves if they do not."[196]

The gravity of Sostre's testimony and that of the other prisoners contrasted sharply with the absurdity of the state's arguments. To counter claims about caloric deprivation, Assistant Attorney General Mark Walsh called forward a kitchen worker from the prison who was prepared to open a jar of peanut butter to prove it was not runny.[197] When Rabinowitz inquired about the "inflammatory racist literature" Sostre was punished for having, some of which included his own writings, Assistant Deputy Warden Henry Sawner sputtered the names of Huey Newton, Bobby Seale, and Eldridge Cleaver.[198] "Do you consider the words 'Huey Newton' to be racist?" Rabinowitz asked Sawner. He replied that he did.[199] Heaving heard the tragic stories of those in solitary confinement, the courtroom audience burst into laughter when Attorney General Walsh claimed it was a "very serious thing to charge the prison officials" with the theft of $1.17 in stamps.[200] At one point, he said: "There is no proof of any damage or harm to Martin Sostre. As far as brutality—well, that is getting into the facts."[201]

The state successfully insulated Governor Rockefeller and the prison system from Sostre's third and most sweeping charge, that it operated racist concentration camps. Motley proposed that if the evidence did "show brutality, it shows it was administered *equally* to Black and white prisoners alike. Weren't two of those prisoners white who testified to brutality and conditions in the segregated confinement?"[202] Walsh argued that there was no evidence the governor "even knew that Green Haven was a prison."[203] Although these statements underscored the absurdity of the courtroom as a place of justice, it proved effective as an arena of political struggle for precisely that reason.

The *Sostre v. Rockefeller* trial illustrates the considerable shifts in prisoner organizing and revolutionary struggle from the early to late 1960s. When Sostre first sued the warden of Clinton Prison a decade earlier, he had been in a similar situation: censored, punished, and held indefinitely in solitary confinement without due process. When he attempted to raise the conditions of confinement and the loss of good time then, the judge had told him, "I am not interested in questions of solitary confinement," suggesting that if Sostre wanted a binding decision, he would need to sue the Department of Corrections.[204] Sostre and his comrades in the Nation of Islam had adjusted by filing multi-issue lawsuits against the

New York commissioner of corrections, packing the courtroom with supporters and bringing Malcolm X to testify on their behalf. Now, Sostre had gone a step further, initiating a one-million-dollar suit against Nelson Rockefeller, one of the most powerful members of the ruling class. In the process, he and other incarcerated people were able to give days of testimony to the torturous conditions they suffered in solitary confinement before a boisterous audience of revolutionary groups.

Sostre was a central figure responsible for bringing about these dramatic changes on both sides of the walls. When Judge Motley handed down her landmark decision the following spring, Sostre called it "the natural extension of prior legal victories in my struggle to safeguard the human rights of all persons in captivity." He deemed the decision "a major contribution to the Black struggle" and believed that legal actions would provide a necessary reprieve for imprisoned freedom fighters like himself.[205] Most Black revolutionaries, he wrote, are "dead, in prison, or on the lam." This "legal victory, when viewed in its revolutionary perspective, is a resounding defeat for the establishment who will now find it exceedingly difficult to torture with impunity the thousands of captive Black (and white) political prisoners illegally held in their concentration camps."[206]

Other imprisoned revolutionaries paid close attention to the trial and ruling. Sam Melville, for one, was a white insurrectionist who had grown up in Buffalo and participated in a series of bombings in 1969, including one outside the Panther Twenty-One trial just weeks after Sostre's testimony before Judge Motley. He wrote to his lawyer from Attica that summer, citing Motley's decision and quoting Lenin, to urge that they must now "move the contradiction to a higher level," further exposing the gap between the stated and actual purpose of the prison.[207] The following year, in September 1971, those contradictions would become visible on the world stage when prisoners set up a revolutionary commune at Attica prison and the state responded with vicious force.

8

The New Prisoner

By almost any measure, the state's attempts to neutralize Martin Sostre through extreme isolation and torture at Green Haven had failed. He used his 372 days in solitary to document and expose the brutality of the state's prison system in federal court, winning a foundational prisoners' rights lawsuit while raising awareness about his case and becoming one of the best-known political prisoners in the country. With its maximum-security prisons brimming with revolutionary organizing, the state had experimented with a new form of isolation, holding one of its most rebellious captives in its least restrictive prison.

During these years, prisoners emerged at the center of revolutionary struggle in the United States. Incarcerated people organized boycotts, unions, and strikes against forced labor. They successfully sued the state for reforms, and staged takeovers—in some cases running the institutions themselves. Whereas there were five reported prison uprisings in 1967, there were forty-eight in 1972.[1] And while prison takeovers were temporary, and often violently repressed, they briefly constructed prefigurative counter-structures and liberated zones from which new social orders being created by incarcerated revolutionaries were visible on a broad scale. The climax of this period—in the achievements of those inside and the savagery of the state's response—was the Attica uprising. The state's assault in retaking the prison, which killed thirty-nine rebels and hostages and was followed by the torture of many more, marked the deadliest massacre in the United States since Wounded Knee in 1890.

The years surrounding the Attica rebellion marked an intensification of revolutionary struggle and state repression across the country—particularly in New York. The kidnappings and frame-ups of Black and Brown revolutionaries in the late 1960s coincided with the state's mass criminalization of people from those same communities. New York's overcrowded jails became hotbeds of political struggle. In August 1970, incarcerated organizers at New York City's infamous Tombs took hostages and controlled multiple levels of the towering jail complex. That November, a group of prisoners at Auburn State Prison launched a work strike. In the days that followed, dozens of guards were held hostage and rebels controlled portions of the prison, releasing their comrades from confinement.[2] These interconnected revolts culminated with what Sostre called "the Battle of Attica."[3] Scholar Orisanmi Burton has termed this wave of insurgency the "Long Attica Revolt," a phrase that "names a protracted accumulation of rebellion that circulated within and beyond New York prisons for at least thirteen months prior to what ultimately *culminated* in Attica prison between September 9 and 13, 1971."[4]

During the McKay Commission's hearings on Attica, criminologist Donald Newman suggested the strategy to sequester Sostre had been successful. "You should take a look at the case of Martin Sostre," he told them. "I asked one of the officials at Wallkill as to whether he was any problem and was told 'No.' Thus, here you have a man who was so dangerous . . . that he had to spend 385 [*sic*] days in the hole, now being held at Wallkill under the lightest security in any prison in the state."[5] But this was far from the truth. Sostre used his newfound latitude to his advantage, engaging in a range of political struggles during his three years at Wallkill from August 1969 to August 1972. While there, he successfully sued the state over political censorship in *Sostre v. Otis*, organized several of the first chapters of the Black Panther Party (BPP) in New York prisons, and established radical study groups, a lending library, and several revolutionary newspapers. In 1972, Sostre attempted to form one of the country's first prisoners' unions. In response, the warden of Wallkill would file a 14-page deposition outlining his case that Sostre—whom he deemed a "serious threat to the program at Wallkill"—be transferred back to a maximum-security prison.[6]

Yet, the most revolutionary years of the Black Power and prisoners' rights movement were also some of the most difficult for Sostre. Just days before Motley's historic verdict in May 1970, Sostre broke with his longtime defense committee following their censorship of an essay he wrote for *Black News*, a community newspaper he founded and edited from prison. He considered it a significant betrayal, and it confirmed much of what he came to see as the perilous dogmatism, centralism, and hierarchy of Marxism-Leninism. Soon after, he parted ways with his attorney, Joan Franklin, and the NAACP Legal Defense Fund for their lack of commitment to prisoners' rights and political prisoners. By the end of this turbulent period, Sostre was contemplating the meaning of anarchism to his struggle and that of Black liberation more broadly.

From one vantage point, rebellions in the state's most controlling institutions—its prisons—seemed to signal that the US was on the verge of revolution. From another perspective, radical movements appeared on the brink of collapse because of violent repression by the burgeoning police state. Sostre's situation embodied these contradictions. Just months after emerging from the most isolated period of his imprisonment, he won a landmark lawsuit but lost much of his outside support. He now experienced unprecedented access within the prison but was separated from incarcerated comrades during the movement's most active period. In the summer of 1970, the publication of Vincent Copeland's book *The Crime of Martin Sostre* helped to draw national attention to Sostre's case.[7] But without a sizable defense committee to promote and distribute it, the book soon floundered, languishing in the publisher's warehouse. Amid all this turmoil, the state's key witness, Arto Williams, recanted his story and signed an affidavit admitting that he had framed Sostre, breathing new life into his appeal. By August 1972, Sostre had been transferred to Auburn prison for his attempt at organizing a prisoners' union and was again in solitary confinement. There, he drafted his longest-ever essay, "The New Prisoner."

Written a year after the Attica revolt, the essay located the roots of the uprising within the struggle of incarcerated Muslims during late 1950s and early '60s.[8] By systematically tracing the demands of the Attica Liberation Faction through decades of grievances and activism by himself and other imprisoned people in New York, Sostre offered crucial context for the prisoners' rebellion, the state's murderous response, and the counterinsurgent reforms—both cosmetic and sweeping—that followed. The opening salvo of "The New Prisoner" laid out this interdependence, warning the state that its "repression prison pacification program, *sub nom* prison reform" would "set in motion dynamic revolutionary forces that will effect the overthrow of your racist-capitalist system."[9]

The intensified struggle of the late 1960s and early '70s heightened these contradictions. Like all emergences, it was laden with the residues from previous ones. Sostre never abandoned his previous way of thinking entirely but, instead, incorporated it into a new stage—one that sought to come to terms with a different set of contradictions. He struggled through these contradictions during the years surrounding Attica, calling them a "natural progression of developing spirituality and awareness." By 1972, he had emerged in yet another new phase, embracing anarchism and reorganizing his defense campaign; he promised this stage of struggle would "make all the previous ones seem like child's play."[10] In "The New Prisoner," Sostre named a new revolutionary subjecthood not only for the movement, but for himself—one still in the process of becoming.

In early December 1969, Sostre returned from his trial in New York City to what he described as a "crush of political and legal work which piled up on me during 3 weeks I was engaged in [the] Rockefeller campaign."[11] Among these tasks was finalizing the first issue of *Black News*. Two and a half years after purchasing a mimeograph machine in Buffalo with plans to launch a radical weekly, *Afro Freedom Fighter*, Sostre now published the city's first revolutionary Black newspaper from prison. Sostre sent his first article, "Pilots for Panthers," to his committee in a series of letters, a few paragraphs at a time. "The rate at which the enemy has intensified his genocidal campaign of exterminating and kidnapping Black leaders, particularly Panthers, since the above-said article was written sixteen months ago, makes the establishment of the prisoner exchange pool more urgent than ever," he wrote.[12] Per his wishes, Jeanette Merrill mailed the very first copies off the press to the Black Panther Party's office in Oakland.[13]

The publication of *Black News* was at once a culmination and a new beginning. The paper brought to fruition Sostre's vision of creating a Black radical newspaper in Buffalo. Like his bookstore, the paper was designed to reach young people. Sostre encouraged junior high and high school students to contribute to the paper and planned to pay "newsboys" to distribute it on the East Side of Buffalo.[14] His defense committee carried the paper at the Afro-Asian Bookshop in Exile on UB's campus, and he instructed them to distribute free copies to radical student groups, in schools, and on street corners where "militant street youths hang out."[15] "It is Martin's hope that in his absence," Merrill wrote, "the Black youth (militant and revolutionary) here in Buffalo will one day make it their own."[16]

BUFFALO'S BLACK REVOLUTIONARY NEWSPAPER

BLACK NEWS

—Special Supplement—

APRIL 1970

Martin Luther King

Was A Lawbreaker-

A Tribute to his Memory
on the
Second Anniversary
of his
Murder

AN EDITORIAL BY:

MARTIN SOSTRE
POLITICAL PRISONER No. 9273
WALLKILL CONCENTRATION CAMP
WALLKILL, NEW YORK 12589

Black News special supplement, April 1970. University of Michigan Library (Special Collections Research Center).

Black News was one of the earliest Black prisoner-led newspapers in what would soon become the heyday of underground prison print culture. Due to widespread social upheaval and the innovation of the mimeograph machine, alternative newspapers multiplied during the late 1960s. Underground publications soon appeared at San Quentin, Attica, and Leavenworth.[17] As historian Emily Thuma points out, "print culture was a particularly vital organizing forum for prison activists, as it enabled their ideas to breach carceral walls and helped to form political communities that included many people who were not allowed to meet face to face."[18] By the latter half of the decade, historian Dan Berger argues, print culture was "the backbone of prison organizing."[19] *Black News* represented an opportunity to get information out of the prison, even as Sostre struggled to get it in.

For the first time since his re-incarceration, Sostre had a way to share his political views regularly in an extended form. He now published essays about international solidarity and Black student organizing, and eulogized Martin Luther King Jr. as a rebellious lawbreaker on the second anniversary of his death. "To reject the lawbreaker King image in favor of the religious non-violent image of King, is to reject King and his deeds," Sostre wrote, "not only because the real King was both religious and secular, but because he performed his greatest deeds not in the church preaching about what Jesus said 2,000 years ago, but in the streets, taking part in the contemporary struggle against the white racists' oppressive law and order."[20] Sostre's essay on King importantly critiqued the co-optation of the civil rights leader's legacy in real time, as the whitewashing of his radicalism was unfolding. It also anticipated his emphasis on revolutionary deeds that would take center stage in the years that followed.

Sostre also used the paper to exchange public messages of solidarity with the Young Lords in New York, some of whom had supported him during his federal trial in New York. Sostre called them the "detonators of the Barrio" and applauded their recent "Church Offensive," a weeks-long occupation of the First Spanish United Methodist Church, just blocks from where he had grown up in East Harlem.[21] Along with his message, he sent a check to support their free breakfast program. "We are happy to report the money is being put to good use," the central committee responded, sharing that they created a new one in his name. "We have told 'our' children about you. They have found a new hero, one who was raised on their block."[22]

The publication of *Black News* was cut short, however, after only two full issues and a couple of special supplements, totaling about fifteen pages. Although originally planned as a monthly, Sostre would soon suspend the paper on acccount of serious political differences between him and his defense committee. The fate of the newspaper, as well as his relationship with his committee, would ultimately come down to the issue of Black self-determination.

Having already published two essays about political prisoner exchanges, Sostre's interest was renewed in March 1970 when a white US air force attaché in the Dominican Republic was captured and exchanged for twenty Dominican political prisoners. In a third lengthy essay—"Black Political Prisoners Exchanged for Captured US Agent"—he again stressed the international character of Black struggle. In line with his political mentors and compatriots Julio Pinto *Gandía and* Lolita Lebrón, Sostre believed armed struggle was a necessary and central component of any serious revolution. For him, urban guerilla warfare was the natural evolution of revolutionary organizing, and he anticipated that exchanges of captured US diplomats for Black prisoners of war would catalyze those struggles. As he later wrote Lebr*ó*n regarding Puerto Rican independence: "The revolution needs organizers, writers, reporters, distributors of our newspapers and literature, paste up posters, propagandists, fund contributors, pickets, actors, speakers, etc. But, also, the armed guerilla the nucleus of our liberation army is needed . . . the military arm is too short in comparison with the political arm."[23]

In the months leading up to Sostre's article, Jeanette Merrill wrote Mae Mallory with excitement about the future of *Black News*. "Wait 'til you see this next issue? Martin refers to his editorial as 'the bombshell'—and that's putting it mildly."[24] By May, perhaps upon reading his article about the political prisoner exchange, her enthusiasm had turned to opposition. Sostre's white allies in the WWP were not prepared to carry out the program of guerrilla warfare he described, nor were his arguments about armed struggle consistent with the party's theory of revolution. More concretely, Ed and Jeanette Merrill were aware they had long been under police surveillance in Buffalo.[25] They had fought to free Mallory after her frame-up for supposedly kidnapping a white couple and received death threats targeting their three-year-old daughter.[26] Now, they told Sostre that they feared they might suffer reprisals for publishing the article. After consulting with other WWP leaders, the Merrills visited

Sostre at Wallkill and informed him of their decision not to publish the essay as it stood.[27]

For Sostre, this struck at the heart of revolutionary Black self-determination. In a four-page handwritten letter sent to the Merrills through Joan Franklin, he laid out what he believed was at stake.[28] First, he reminded them that they had never been granted control over the content of *Black News*. He had asked them to handle the mechanical and logistical arrangements but considered himself sole editor and publisher.[29] "It wasn't a freebee operation," he wrote. "I was ready, willing and able to pay my way." Sostre also considered their intimation that "we are the only ones you have, your own people do not support you" an implicit threat that their support was contingent upon their censorship of what he could say in the only outlet he had. Sostre pointed out the irony that their decision coincided with his major legal case over government censorship. To him, it felt like a startling betrayal that, evan as Judge Motley affirmed his constitutional right to freedom from censorship, he would be asked to "submit to having my Black writings to *Black* people censored by whites." Although he conceded that they were correct about his lack of Black support in Buffalo, he had developed *Black News* to address precisely this by raising Black political consciousness in western New York.[30] He explained to Franklin that he "considered their proposition that I submit to white censorship a request to sell out my struggle for Black liberation, and this I will never do."[31]

Sostre's letter ended with what he saw as the most irreconcilable point: the difference between white and Black revolutionary politics. His first article proposing a political prisoner exchange in 1968 had pointed out the entwinement of the "war of Black liberation, and the rebellion of the white oppressed class led by their militants."[32] Now, he emphasized their inherent differences. Speaking for Black people, he wrote: "Our primary concern is, and always will be, Black survival: resisting the vicious genocidal oppression systematically practiced upon 25 million Blacks right here in the United States 24 hours a day by racist whites." He denounced what he called the "pseudorevolutionary" theory of passively waiting for the "right conditions." For Black people, the time was ever present. "We have reached the fork in the revolutionary road. I can understand you turning to the right since your situation is not as desperate as ours. What I can't dig at all is your trying to coerce me to turn right with you."[33] For Sostre, the left fork meant armed struggle.

He demanded the Merrills immediately stop all work on his defense campaign, the AABE, and *Black News*.[34] Sharon Fischer, whom Jeanette described as "very dedicated to Martin and Geraldine's struggles," was tasked with taking over the committee.[35] Sostre believed *Black News* would continue its publication in New York City with its more radical base and, as if to emphasize the central role his new coconspirators, he announced he would share copies of his letter to the Merrills with the Panthers, Young Lords, RAM, and the RNA. To punctuate his point, Sostre signed his broadside to his former comrades, "In Revolutionary Struggle."[36]

A primary backdrop to the break, though it remained mostly unspoken at the time, was Sostre's growing frustration with Marxism-Leninism and the centralized bureaucracy of organizations that insisted that members espouse and express the party line as dogma, rather than treating issues as open to debate and sustained difference. The Merrills' decision not to publish the *Black News* article came after discussions with party leadership. Among them, Sostre noted, was someone the Merrills described as their "top 'tactician who in 30 years had never been wrong.' " This was likely WWP founder Sam Marcy.[37]

In September 1969, around the same time Sostre was impressing upon Lorenzo Ervin the significance of anarchist organizing, Marcy addressed the WWP at its national conference in New York City. According to FBI surveillance, Marcy forecasted this turbulence. With the trials of Martin Sostre, Geraldine Robinson, and Gross and the Buffalo Nine looming, he anticipated the difficulty of making decisions when "action is in the wind." He stressed the importance of strengthening the "center," which seemed to refer to the premise of "democratic centralism" whereby party members discuss and decide what position to adopt on a given issue and then express support for this position and work to implement it, regardless of whether they agree or not. This was called party discipline. Using the recent fracturing of SDS as a case in point, Marcy argued that "Students for a Democratic Society has no center and because of that their leadership at times loses control." He posed the question of "Russia versus China" as one example of the difficulty of developing a line that must be "disseminated to the youth so that they follow closely since it is their revolutionary spirit we are seeking if we are to succeed in the defeat of capitalism."[38]

Some months earlier, Sostre's longtime comrade Jerry Gross had been ousted from the WWP and YAWF. Gross was subjected to a "show trial" in which he was charged with criticizing the key tenets of Bolshevism, and, in particular, noncompliance with party discipline. "I was accused of insubordination by Workers World for several things," he remembered. Among them was "acting more like Martin Sostre than I should be [as] a good, loyal Workers World person; I was starting to take on some of the characteristics of Martin Sostre's anarchism."[39] Although Gross recalled picking up these characteristics from his mentor, Sostre was still years away from publicly identifying as an anarchist and continued to espouse aspects of Marxist-Leninist and Maoist thought. As late as 1972, he wrote that it was Gross who "objected to my referring to myself as a Marxist-Leninist, stating that he always considered me more of an anarchist than anything else."[40]

But the content of Sostre's mentorship of Ervin in the fall of 1969 indicates that he had already been struggling with the contradictions of hierarchical party-line formations and his belief in the revolutionary potential of spontaneous action by radicalized young people he had witnessed in the streets of Buffalo. Ironically, the allegations against Gross were similar to those made against the original members of the WWP before they broke with the Socialist Workers Party in the late 1950s. "I became a Marxist-Leninist of the party-line type and then an anarchist when I saw the continual fuck-ups," Sostre later explained. "I don't care what ideology you have, it isn't good if it doesn't afford a person, first, personal freedom on its most basic personal individual level."[41]

William Worthy wrote that Sostre's break with his WWP comrades "seems irreconcilable."[42] It might be tempting to narrate such irreconcilability through an individualized analysis that allows only two conclusions: either that Sostre was right in his refusal to compromise his values, or that he was wrong to reject those who supported his legal defense. However, consideration of the broader context surrounding the break supports another conclusion: namely, that that the rupture exemplified the white supremacist state's creation of the conditions for antagonistic differences to arise among the oppressed and their comrades. Had Sostre not been framed, he would have produced *Black News* as the *Afro Freedom Fighter* years earlier without reliance on white support. Similarly, the absence of a deeper Black radical political community in Buffalo was the result of political repression. The destruction of his bookstore, a community space dedicated to revolutionary political education of militant Black youth, prevented the young people who had participated in the uprising from developing a more comprehensive understanding of their role in anticolonial struggle. No one embodied the unevenness and tenuousness created by state repression better than the person absent from the debate itself: Geraldine Robinson.

On September 4, 1969, Robinson was sentenced for her presence at the Afro-Asian Bookshop on the night of July 14, 1967.[43] Like Sostre, she was one of the earliest political prisoners of the Black Power era, and her position as a Black woman—in particular as a Black mother—shaped the types of support she received.[44] Black motherhood acted as a double-edged sword, one she was rarely afforded to wield herself. It was often mobilized in appeals for her support, such as one advertisement calling for children's clothing, books, and toys. But it sometimes emptied her of political agency.[45] In one article, a MSDC "source" described her as "not 'political' like Mr. Sostre. . . . just a woman who is proud of being Black." The essay's author, following such cues, concluded that for "a mother of five children, political issues seem small indeed."[46] Asked decades later about her involvement in the movement when she met Sostre, she explained: "I wasn't an activist, but I knew right from wrong. . . . It got even deeper after all the things that happened. I *became* an activist."[47] After her sentencing that September, she left the court with her fist raised, telling the audience: "Don't waste any tears, and please take care of my children. Continue the struggle."[48]

Although both Sostre and Robinson had opposed the state's attempts to sever their cases from one another, the prosecution prevailed.[49] "The real reason for this severance," Sostre told the judge, "is to try to divide Geraldine and me so that he could apply pressure on one, apply pressure on the other and that way thereby splitting the defense."[50] But Robinson remained linked to Sostre's struggle, if not in the eyes of the state, then in the reality of her own material conditions and political circumstances. As Sostre had anticipated, the severing of their cases from one another successfully individualized what was indeed collective.[51] While Sostre continued to support Robinson monetarily and through legal work, at least for the moment, his decision to part ways with the WWP and fold the Bookshop in Exile was his alone, and it had implications for her and her family.

The fracture between Sostre and his defense committee raises important questions about solidarity, self-determination, and the state. What was the price of gaining support from white radicals, and what did party-line formations mean for Black self-determination? On the other hand, what were the costs for Black autonomy and which was Sostre willing to pay? He would later write unsparingly of Jeanette: "Her petty fossilized mind, hung up on outmoded Workers World Party white bourgeois ideology, failed to see that impossibility of transplanting this white bourgeois ideology to the Black community. In rejecting my Black writings directed to the Black ghetto-colony Jeanette rejected out of hand an original Black political ideology."[52]

From Sostre's perspective, armed struggle was not a revolutionary condition one waited for but an ongoing feature of the Black experience in a genocidal settler colony. Sostre's reminder to the Merrills that "the pigs don't need articles to frame militants . . . they just use guns, dope, dynamite, bombing and murder plots" embodied one of the crucial lessons of racial capitalism articulated by Black Studies scholar Otis Madison: "The purpose of racism is to control the behavior of white people, not Black people. For Blacks, guns and tanks are sufficient."[53] Ultimately, Sostre looked at the political conditions of colonized people across the world, himself among them, and saw guerilla armed struggle as the only and obvious answer. His commitment to fight according to his revolutionary principles was one he never questioned. "I am used to fighting by myself without support and money; and I am used to having those in whose behalf I am risking my life turn their back on me," he wrote. "But far from discouraging me, this makes me all the more resolute in my determination to win—and I have achieved victory under these conditions."[54]

Sostre's decision to part ways with his defense committee coincided with Judge Constance Baker Motley's ruling in *Sostre v. Rockefeller* (renamed *Sostre v. McGinnis* after charges against the governor were dismissed). In her sweeping 66-page opinion issued on May 14, 1970, Motley found Sostre's solitary confinement to be "physically harsh, destructive of morale, dehumanizing in the sense that it is needlessly degrading" and ordered that similar confinement must not exceed fifteen days and be imposed only for serious infractions. "A prisoner carries with him to prison his right to due process," she wrote, emphasizing that his punishment was primarily retribution for his legal work and political views. Through such punishment and censorship of his mail and correspondence, the prison had violated his First Amendment rights to freedom of political expression: "Basic constitutional rights cannot be sacrificed . . . in the interest of administrative efficiency."[55] This opinion altered both Sostre's own struggle and the prisoners' rights movement.

In what Tom Wicker of the *New York Times* called a "startling, perhaps historic, decision," Motley awarded Sostre $13,020 in damages and returned 124 days of earned time.[56] "If upheld," Victor Rabinowitz said, it would "result in a complete revision of every prison system in the U.S."[57] The opinion aroused immediate and overwhelming interest. Rabinowitz's firm mimeographed over one hundred copies to meet the demand, and Jeanette Merrill suggested Sostre publish the decision as a paperback book with a foreword by himself, an idea that appealed to him despite their recent rift.[58] Before even receiving his copy of the decision, Sostre wrote Joan Franklin that he imagined it could support his case that he had been denied adequate appellate review.[59]

Ironically, this victory would be followed by Sostre's break with Franklin as his legal counsel. Sostre became frustrated that NAACP had still not submitted a draft of its brief for his appeal of his original conviction, which had occurred two years before. Franklin's superiors had grown weary of his case.[60] NAACP general counsel Nathaniel Jones wrote her with concern that the costs were higher than anticipated, asking if Sostre might have other funds to support his appeal, noting his recent "substantial judgement."[61] Franklin pushed back: "It was my understanding that once the NAACP committed itself to a case it did not demand funds of individual clients both as a matter of principle and its tax exempt status."[62] Sostre never received any of his settlement, in part because Warden Follette died the month before Motley's judgment.[63] His defense committee, now comprised of a few people at best, operated on a shoestring budget and no longer had the benefit of raising funds through the Bookshop in Exile.

Franklin and Sostre disagreed on the best legal path forward. While he was confident that filing a writ of habeas corpus in federal court would result in his release, she believed this would only introduce "an intermediate step" before his appeal.[64] Behind their dispute was the imbalance of power. Sostre compared the amount of legal work he was able to accomplish with a few lawbooks in a prison library with the frustratingly slow pace of her professional legal team. He decided to move ahead with the writ on his own.[65] "I cannot take such a reckless gamble with my life at stake," he wrote Franklin.[66] "I know that they don't teach this in law school and therefore you may not dig it—it may be too heavy for you. But I also know that a great deal of precedent-setting law is made by jailhouse lawyers employing unorthodox ingenuity."[67] In retrospect, the divisions between a jailhouse lawyer fighting for his life and a NAACP attorney with a full caseload, as well as those imprisoned versus their comrades outside, appear to have been unavoidable.

In June 1970, Sostre fired Franklin and her legal team, demanding she turn over fifty dollars and all legal materials to Kristin Booth Glen of Rabinowitz, Boudin & Standard, who had represented him in the *Rockefeller* case. In several letters castigating Franklin and NAACP executive director Roy Wilkins, Sostre expressed his anger over the lack of support from Black people and organizations. "The very fact that you, who are supposed to be a Black Nationalist," he wrote Franklin, "are forcing me through your indiligence to turn to the white men to do for me simple things . . . shows that something is wrong." Sostre felt abandoned, first by white comrades and now by his Black attorney.

He explained his situation using the metaphor of being thrown overboard a ship by white people, which represented the initial frame-up. Looking up from the ocean, he saw others still on board, both white and Black. It was the white people who threw down a life raft. "Would you refuse to take the life raft because whites threw it down to you? Would you let yourself drown or be eaten by sharks because your own people on the rail refused to help you?" he asked Franklin rhetorically. "You of course will not have any reason to become a lover of whites—since it was whites that threw you overboard in the first place. But how will you feel toward those trifling Blacks that passively leaned on the rail to watch you drown—and would not even reach for one of the many life rafts on the deck?" This, he argued, was how he came to have an all-white defense committee in the first place. "Once you allow whites to take care of your business," he argued, "you will have no business—it will become white business." Claiming that Franklin could have told him plainly that she was too busy to take care of the tasks he had asked her to, he ended harshly: "My own enemies could not have sabotaged me worse. If this isn't a sell-out it would indeed be difficult to know what one is."[68]

To NAACP executive director Roy Wilkins, Sostre was less didactic. He called the organization "conspicuous by [its] absence," noting that it had not yet bailed out a single Black political prisoner. He emphasized the grassroots nature of his campaign and charged the NAACP with stealing "blood money" in the $700 retainer his defense committee had paid to represent Geraldine Robinson. His political criticism was unsparing: "You bourgeois neegrows assign a battery of lawyers and spend thousands of dollars to integrate a country club or golf course, but will not lift a finger to help a Black revolutionary brother kidnapped from the Black colony and framed by the white racist pigs."[69] Jones wrote Wilkins that he had read the latest "outburst," assuring him that the NAACP had worked diligently on Sostre's case at "considerable expense." Wilkins responded blithely that this was "typical of the thanks the NAACP has always received from those under the gun and in whose behalf we sweat in the courts. The reaction is the same as that existing long before the Sostres learned the word 'pig' which they use ad nauseum in their invective."[70]

Within a matter of months, Sostre had broken with both his defense committee and his legal team. Meanwhile, in June 1970, McGraw-Hill published *The Crime of Martin Sostre.* Following the successes of Malcolm X's *Autobiography* in 1965 and Eldridge Cleaver's *Soul on Ice* in 1968, publishers recognized the demand for prison memoirs, especially those narrated by Black men. The reception of *Soul on Ice*, for example, prompted George Jackson's attorney Faye Stender to suggest turning his prison letters into a book. The result, *Soledad Brother*, was published by Bantam Books that October and almost immediately received international acclaim, selling four hundred thousand copies in four years before going out of print.[71] The Marxist historian C. L. R. James deemed Jackson's letters "the most remarkable political documents that have appeared inside or outside the United States since the death of Lenin."[72] Since its republication in 1994, it has become one of the most coveted and censored books in US prisons.[73]

The Crime of Martin Sostre received much less publicity. Unlike *Soledad Brother*, it was not authored by its subject. Rather, the book was written by WWP cofounder Vincent Copeland, a white working-class radical and former union organizer at Bethlehem Steel who had grown up on the East Side of Buffalo before it became an almost entirely Black neighborhood. For those reasons, the book was able to capture much of the social and political context behind Sostre's frame-up. But Copeland conceded that while "Martin Sostre had a great deal to do with writing this book, it was not possible actually to collaborate with him." Most of the text was drafted during the period of his most extreme isolation, in solitary confinement at Green Haven, and Sostre only read the manuscript hastily and approved it at the *Rockefeller* trial—the first time the two men met.[74]

Although the book included snippets of Sostre's writings from prison, many of which were gleaned from defense committee pamphlets and legal documents, the authorial voice was Copeland's alone. It assumed a white readership, and Copeland addressed them in his conclusion: "You may not agree with 'our current defense program' as outlined by Martin. But Martin does not ask you to agree. Your program, white brother or sister, is easier. But it is also more difficult. . . .You must support Martin's program as you would your own."[75] Given the circumstances of Sostre's recent break with the WWP over the censorship of his political writings by his white comrades, the book's closing is awkward. Perhaps Copeland's admonition to white readers to respect Black self-determination, whether or not they agree with the strategy Black revolutionaries advocate, represents a lightly veiled critique of the position taken by Marcy and the Merrills. Otherwise, his comment reveals the distance between left-wing whites' theoretical acceptance of Black autonomy and their resistance to it in practice. As a white mediator whose voice stands in for Sostre's, which both prison officials and his white supporters outside had censored, Copeland's final words ring hollow. We cannot help but wonder if the book represented the life preserver Sostre described in his letter to Franklin, which a drowning person must grasp despite the limitations of the rescue it offers.

The Crime of Martin Sostre was banned in all New York prisons, along with his other writings. Sostre himself was forbidden from receiving it.[76] Despite its shortcomings and censorship, the book increased awareness of his case and became a touchstone for a new wave of outside supporters. Sostre continued to muse about writing his own memoir at various points in his life, but none ever surfaced.[77] For Sostre, always more interested in living a political life than narrating one, his 1972 essay "The New Prisoner" remains the closest to a written autobiographical account he left. Like many politically effective memoirs, it constructs an emergent group identity rather than focusing on the exceptionalism or individual transformation of its author. And, like Ella Baker, another organizer who lived in continuous struggle and did not leave an autobiography, Sostre focused on what the veteran civil rights organizer called "spade work"—the everyday, often unseen and unsung, work of revolutionary organizing. That fall, over a decade of spade work in New York prisons would begin to bear fruit.

By 1970, the massive dragnet of urban Black and Brown communities opaquely called "preventative detention" had packed "NYC's jail archipelago" with people who were incarcerated for months and years because—like Sostre in Buffalo—they could not afford bail.[78] With greater political repression and less churn, jails were now filled with Panthers and Young Lords who had more time to organize. Daily political education classes were held in the Tombs, where Sostre himself had first been politicized nearly two decades earlier and where the Panther Twenty-One were now held captive.[79] In May 1970, a group calling itself the Inmates Liberation Front had formed on the ninth floor, with surreptitious study groups and a handprinted newspaper called *The Inmates Forum*.[80] That August, they revolted and seized levels of the jail, some for as long as ten days.[81]

In early November, a group of prisoners at Auburn took over a microphone in the recreation yard and announced a work strike in observance of Black Solidarity Day.[82] As Sostre pointed out, many organizers of the strike had presented their demand for a minimum wage at Attica the previous summer and were transferred to Auburn as retribution.[83] These labor strikes were part of a growing effort, particularly in California and New York, to establish the first unions for incarcerated workers. The movement for prisoners' unions emerged in 1968 when incarcerated workers at San Quentin organized a "Convict Unity Day" strike that sought not only parole reform and improved living conditions but also increased wages. That February, about seven hundred people (20 percent of the prison population) refused to report to work. Over four hundred gathered outside the prison to support the strike, where they were entertained by the Grateful Dead.[84] In November 1970, at the same time the Auburn strike was unfolding, more than two thousand prisoners at Folsom withheld their labor for nineteen days despite being beaten and forced to stand naked outside. The strike produced the "Manifesto of Demands and Anti-Oppression Platform," which would become a blueprint for rebels at Attica and elsewhere. Its demands included the right to form and join unions, the establishment of workers' compensation insurance, and pay consistent with the state and federal minimum wage. Soon, the United Prisoners Union was established on the premise that incarcerated people were part of a "convicted class" who desperately needed collective bargaining rights. Over the next several years, there were unionization campaigns in more than thirty prisons across nine states.[85]

After several days of striking by workers at Auburn, the warden isolated thirteen suspected ringleaders. In protest, hundreds of Black prisoners freed the captives from isolation and captured dozens of hostages. Although they were promised their grievances would be taken seriously and no reprisals would be made, the thirteen were soon transferred to other prisons and held in solitary confinement. Another group of eighty was held in a confinement area known as "the roof." By December 1970, dozens of those in solitary confinement waged a struggle from within the most repressive confines of the prison. Others, as Sostre had done at Green Haven the year before, refused rectal searches and were beaten and tear gassed.[86] Six months after the uprising, one captive wrote: "We are engage[d] in protracted struggle at Auburn Concentration Camp."[87]

Martin Sostre followed these uprisings closely. "From Tombs to Auburn," he wrote in early 1971, "we have seen our brothers rise up as men and defy our Vicious racist oppressors." He announced a "Tet Offensive" against the prison system in the pages of a new revolutionary newspaper he called the *Vanguard*.[88] This "Black liberation newsweekly" was a four-page typed newsletter with a hand-drawn masthead featuring a Black liberation flag with a black star.[89] It outlined the key objectives for a revolutionary Black vanguard organization. The paper's Maoist influence was in keeping with the revolutionary Black nationalism that had grown out of the RNA. This armed faction aimed to engage in guerilla warfare to free liberated territories and ultimately form a Black socialist nation. "By liberation," the newsletter explained, "we mean: complete freedom from the physical, political, social, and economic control of the white racist U.S. Government, and the establishment of our own Independent Black Nation."[90] The *Vanguard*, according to Sostre, was discovered and seized by prison guards after only its third issue.[91]

During the summer of 1971, prison rebellions in California and New York had emerged that would influence the future of revolutionary struggle in prisons for decades. In July, a group calling itself the Attica Liberation Faction sent a list of twenty-eight reform demands to Commissioner Russell Oswald. Meanwhile, Sostre's comrades at Green Haven presented a list of thirteen demands, including the establishment of a prisoners' labor union. The state's refusal to engage with these demands was punctuated on August 21, 1971, when George Jackson was murdered by prison guards at San Quentin. Jackson's death was memorialized, including at Attica, where over seven hundred prisoners silently fasted.[92] Then, on September 9, 1971, a routine scuffle between an incarcerated person and a guard suddenly accelerated into a four-day takeover of Attica prison.

The story of Attica has been told more than any other prison uprising by a wide margin, but few have listened attentively to the voices of the revolutionaries who enacted it. As Orisanmi Burton points out, the dominant approach has been to draw heavily upon state sources, legitimize only the reformist demands of the rebellion, and focus attention on the retributive violence of the massacre, "craving explosive spectacles of Black suffering and death."[93] Drawing heavily upon the theorization of rebels who participated in the uprising—and Sostre, who made and interpreted it from afar—Orisanmi Burton's *Tip of the Spear* best captures the revolutionary meaning of the revolt. Through "carceral guerilla warfare," prisoners quickly captured control of D Yard and established a commune that took democratic, organized form amid the destruction of the prison's physical infrastructure and disordering of its logics.[94] Elections decided representatives from each cell block to act as "spokesmen," rather than "leaders." Frank "Big Black" Smith was voted chief of the security force to protect the hostages, rebels, and observers coming in and out to oversee negotiations with the state.[95] When issues came before the collective, they were debated in the yard and decisions were reached by volume of applause. Mariano "Dalou" Gonzalez of the Young Lords provided Spanish translation during these public forums. Taking exception to the state's claims that the rebellion assumed the form of a dictatorship that replicated the prison's forms of violence and coercion, Panther Jomo Sekou Omowale wrote that "it is difficult for people who are familiar with the dictatorship form of government to accept the fact that a group of a couple hundred people could decide things or move on things in a collective or democratic manner." As Burton argues, the "spontaneity and chaos of collective rebellion created an opportunity for forethought, plotting, cooperation, and self-organization." Several outsiders who observed D Yard described it as "true democracy."[96]

Three hundred miles away at Wallkill, Sostre and others organized a solidarity demonstration. More than half of the prisoners signed onto the rebels' demands, adding five of their own.[97] Although he was purposefully kept away from Attica, Sostre was an absent presence during the uprising. He had politicized and mentored Big Black.[98] Dalou Gonzalez wrote to their mutual comrade Sharon Fischer that "*compañero* Sostre *is* an Attica Brotha."[99] Omowale wrote to Sostre that he did "not see you or your struggle divorce[d] from my own. . . . Attica is truly all of us."[100] Despite Sostre's writings being forbidden in prisons, an inventory of materials found in D Yard after the state's massacre included his defense committee pamphlets *Letters from Prison* and *Martin Sostre in Court*, a special issue of *The Activist* magazine focused on Sostre and other political prisoners, and Judge Motley's *Sostre v. Rockefeller* decision.[101]

There were few people better positioned to analyze the meaning of Attica than Martin Sostre. In the two decades leading up to the revolt, he had spent all but three years in New York's prisons and jails. He had been politicized by revolutionary Puerto Rican nationalist Julio Pinto Gandía in the Tombs, remembered the Rosenbergs' execution at Sing Sing, had organized with Muslims in solitary confinement at Clinton and Attica to help secure the constitutional rights of imprisoned people, and had launched, in his words, a "single-minded and single-handed struggle for prisoners' rights" from his solitary cell at Green Haven. While Burton positions Attica as the culmination of at least thirteen months of insurgence, Sostre situated its roots back thirteen years.

In "The New Prisoner," written a year after the revolt, Sostre located the origins of the uprising in the struggle of incarcerated Muslims like himself during late 1950s and early '60s.[102] Part revolutionary broadside and part auto-ethnography, the essay announced a new revolutionary subjecthood, but it looked backward as much as forward. "Far from breaking our spirit in the solitary confinement dungeons of Clinton and Attica Prisons," he wrote of their struggle a decade earlier, "these dungeons became the 'foco' of rebellion which spread to every prison in the State and involved hundreds of prisoners."[103] As he explained, it was through their sacrifices in the hole during the early 1960s that "the oppressive structure was weakened and the stage for the Battle of Attica—and all its ramifications—was set."[104] By systematically tracing the demands of the Attica Liberation Faction through decades of grievances and activism by himself and other imprisoned people in New York, Sostre offered crucial context for the prisoners' rebellion, the state's murderous response, and the counterinsurgent reforms—both cosmetic and sweeping—that followed. Sostre planned to write a book chronicling the story of "how the Muslim struggled evolved into the revolutionary struggle which led to the Attica Rebellion," although unfortunately it would never be published.[105] Of the many attempts to explain the country's best-known prison uprising, few have yet to take seriously Sostre's explanation of the rebellion's deep roots in Muslim organizing that preceded it by a decade.[106]

Despite this historical erasure, the state understood these connections as they were unfolding. In 1970, surveillance reports on Muslims in prisons, which had begun while Sostre was in the Nation of Islam, were suddenly renamed "Muslim-Black Panther" reports—a shift that coincided with Sostre's and others's efforts to organize the first chapters of the Black Panthers inside. Meanwhile, FBI director J. Edgar Hoover stressed the importance of monitoring "Black Extremist Activities in Penal Institutions."[107] This escalating surveillance was accompanied by public-facing reforms as two sides of the state's counterinsurgency. The opening salvo of "The New Prisoner" laid out this interdependence, warning the state that its "repression prison pacification program, *sub nom* prison reform" would "set in motion dynamic revolutionary forces that will effect the overthrow of your racist-capitalist system."[108]

The essay was deeply informed by "foco" theory, which posited that small cadres engaging in guerilla warfare and carrying out revolutionary deeds would prompt a society-wide rebellion. Sostre positioned prisons as "training camps" and "ideological crucibles" from which revolutionary freedom fighters would emerge. Many of the article's ideas, particularly vanguardism—the idea that politically advanced cadre of the proletariat would be responsible for moving revolutionary struggle forward on behalf of the masses—and the question of the nation-state, were in tension with Sostre's growing identification with anarchism.

In the months leading up to the essay, he wrote comrades of the tension he perceived between anarchism and Black national liberation: "I am reluctant to categorize myself as an anarchist because although my philosophy of action and direct violence (along with other acts) against the State to seize and 'liberate' areas in various parts of the country and to use these 'liberated areas (fortified communes?) as bases from which to 'wage our war of liberation,' the objective of this struggle is to establish a 'black nation'—which negates anarchism."[109] Elsewhere, he expressed frustration that "most white militant and revolutionary allies get up-tight when this Vanguard ideology is expressed [and] most Black militants and revolutionaries are frightened by the reality of this Vanguard ideology which demands of them dangerous revolutionary action . . . instead of relatively safe revolutionary rhetoric."[110] In this context, the essay is significant not only for its forceful militancy and clear-eyed analysis of the state's counterinsurgency post-Attica, but as a contradictory political document of a person—and movement—in motion.

During much of Sostre's incarceration at Wallkill, the *Rockefeller* case was upcoming or under appeal. As a result, the state was reluctant to discipline him directly, lest it undermine their case in court. Instead, they punished others for associating with him. "They wanted people to shy away from me as if I were a leper," Sostre recalled.[111] Charles Daniels, who had secured what he considered a good job as head baker at Wallkill, was demoted to cleaning the cattle sheds: "I was shoveling shit for eight months because of my association with Martin Sostre." If guards found a book from "Brother Martin and it was on Black literature, you were automatically a revolutionary, and therefore you would be treated in that manner."[112] His defense committee reported Sostre was being filmed in the prison yard "as a warning for other inmates to stay away from him."[113] The state used this tactic to obstruct the study groups Sostre was leading while hoping to avoid lawsuits. By 1972, Sostre estimated that the prison had transferred about forty people for affiliating with him.[114] One of those was James Newkirk.

It had taken six years since Newkirk's first application in 1965 to be moved from Green Haven to Wallkill before he was approved. During his first year there, Sostre approached him about forming a prisoners union. Earlier in 1972, organizers at Green Haven had formed what was hailed as the country's first prisoners union.[115] There, incarcerated workers produced hospital gowns, bathrobes, slip sheets, pillowcases, baby bibs, US flags, and license plates for thirty-five cents a day.[116] The previous summer, some workers reached out to the Legal Aid Society's Prisoners' Rights Project to help them unionize. When nearly half of the 1,900 people incarcerated at Green Haven signed a request to draft a union constitution and be represented by the Society, the Department of Corrections refused to deliver nearly a thousand letters explaining legal steps to create the union. Sostre's recent victory in Motley's court provided a legal avenue for challenging this censorship as a denial of "legal mail."[117] Incarcerated union activists even used funds from the Law Enforcement Assistance Administration, a federal agency historically known for distributing billions of dollars to expand policing and incarceration at the local, state, and federal level.[118] Community activist Reverend Eugene Callender called the Green Haven union "a historic development in the labor movement."[119]

To gauge interest, Sostre began sharing copies of a *New York Times* article about the unionization efforts at Green Haven with those like Newkirk.[120] How those inside saw their labor depended on their understandings of the purpose of the prison in society. Many considered incarcerated workers "enslaved" only in the sense that they were denied fair wages and collective bargaining rights. For Black nationalists, Berger notes "that the prison constituted slavery was a question of political subjectivity, of access to social resources and civic life, *before as well as during incarceration*."[121] Race and class were often pitted against one another as the primary driver of the system rather than seen as interrelated parts of an interlocking whole.

What we know about how Sostre theorized prison labor comes largely from "The New Prisoner," which was drafted shortly after his attempt to unionize at Wallkill. In the essay, he used the phrase "slave labor" to refer to both chattel slavery and incarcerated labor.[122] Like the Attica rebellion itself, Sostre traced the development of unionizing efforts inside to the repeated intransigence of prison authorities to respect or respond to grievances. He pointed out that Attica's fourth demand, which sought the application of minimum-wage standards to imprisoned labor, "was brought to the attention of your prison officials on at least four occasions. Each time it was rebuffed and repressed—usually with force." He outlined the 1970 metal shop strike at Attica, Black Solidarity Day boycott at Auburn, and finally the July 1971 demands at Attica for higher wages just before the rebellion, pointing out that Commissioner Oswald had "ignored them and used force to repress our legitimate desire to receive some of the fruits of our labor and end the inhuman and unconstitutional treatment of prisoner in the prison-fortress of New York State."[123]

But Sostre's unionization efforts were not only met by opposition from the prison. They were also blocked by incarcerated representatives of the recently formed Inmate Liaison Committee.[124] Prisoner-led governance proliferated in the aftermath of Attica. Often called "Inmate Councils," most aimed to improve living conditions and secure basic legal rights. The councils especially appealed to prison authorities who were eager to formalize and contain prisoner organizing that otherwise threatened to be spontaneous, covert, and autonomous. As Burton points out, citing the work of sociologist Juanita Díaz-Cotto, "inmate organizations successfully encouraged incarcerated organizers to participate in an aboveground, formally regulated system of institutionalized politics that made their activities easier to surveil and control."[125] At Maine State Prison, a local committee eventually expanded into a statewide coalition, winning reforms over censorship, the right to legal counsel, and the length of solitary confinement.[126] But in other cases, councils became more obviously counterinsurgent and mirrored the state's punishment.[127] The Inmate Liaison Committee at Wallkill was an example of this. During a contentious general meeting in June 1972, they opposed the union. Within a week, Newkirk and four others were transferred. Soon after, Sostre was, too.

Although Sostre was a key organizer of the union, he was separated from those initially transferred because the department of corrections still believed he would create less trouble at Wallkill.[128] By the time he was moved to Auburn in August, attorney Lynn Walker and the Legal Aid Society had already filed suit on behalf of Newkirk and the others. Despite his not being a plaintiff, *Newkirk v. Butler* built upon the foundation of Sostre's recent victory granting prisoners the right to due process and challenged the punitive nature of the transfers.[129] His presence was palpable in the proceedings. As the judge said at one point: "We will turn to Sostre now because his name has come up a sufficient number of times in this case to make me think he may actually be a third plaintiff."[130]

Reflecting upon their thwarted unionization efforts, Sostre quoted from a judge's recent opinion in the *Goodwin* decision on Green Haven's union: "Yesterday's illegal conspiracy is today's legitimate agency and tomorrow's constitutional prerogative." He conjured the history of US labor organizing from the Industrial Workers of the World to the merger of the American Federation of Labor and Congress of Industrial Organizations. "The respectable AFL-CIO and other unions of today owe their existence to the deaths, beatings by company goons, jailings vis frameup and the sacrifice of the unionizing martyrs of the 1800s and early 1900s," he wrote. In this analogy, Sostre was a Wobbly, as the mass union led by syndicalists and anarchists was called. He considered the organizing effort his "*coup de grace* to the oppressive prison system before I leave."[131]

This renewed optimism came from a major development in his case. In October 1970, William Worthy published his final article on Sostre in *Ebony* magazine. The profile featured the juxtaposed images of a young Martin Sostre after World War II next to his mugshot in Buffalo with the caption: "Painful years have taken their toll on Martin Sostre." Noting the break with his defense committee, Worthy wrote that "visionary as ever, indefatigable, unbelievably prolific in articles, letters, and legal petitions, this extraordinary man with a touch of greatness is prepared at age 46 to go it alone—bereft of all effective support inside or outside."[132]

Serendipitously, Worthy's empathetic portrayal found resonance with one reader in California who had intimate links to the case—Arto Williams. The former police informant had enrolled in a treatment program called Tuum Est (meaning "It's Up to You") earlier that month. Williams confided in program director Hollis Candy Latson, who was formerly incarcerated for substance use, about his role in framing Sostre. "At Tuum Est I have come to understand the importance of telling the truth," William wrote in his affidavit. The director also received permission to write to Judge Constance Baker Motley on Williams's behalf.[133] Attorney Kristin Booth Glen remembers arriving in Los Angeles on the morning of February 9, 1971, during the massive the massive San Fernando earthquake, circumventing the rubble of collapsed highways to secure a signed affidavit from Williams recounting his role in the frame-up. The statement outlined Williams's agreement with Seargent Alvin Gristmacher that he would be released from jail in return for participating in the frame-up. Later that year, $100,000 worth of heroin disappeared from a police lab in Buffalo, for which Gristmacher was eventually fired.[134] With Williams's statement secured, Booth Glen rushed to the county courthouse to get an apostille, an internationally recognized seal that was necessary to make the affidavit valid across state lines for a retrial in New York.

Throughout 1972, in response to broad shifts in the movement and his immediate circumstances, Martin Sostre was undergoing a political and spiritual transformation. Declaring a successful end to his struggle for prisoners' rights, he promised to direct his "spiritual and physical energies toward the new phase which evolved from the prior one."[135] Unfortunately, only snapshots of this generative period survive. A series of typed excerpts from letters Sostre wrote to his new defense committee head, Sharon Fischer, which found their way into the archives of sociologist and activist Ed Powell, offer important glimpses of his thinking. These fragments capture Sostre grappling with the significance of the women's liberation movement and what he saw as the tensions between anarchism and Black nationalism. He was also concerned with how to strategically translate these ideas for Black and Brown youth. All of them, taken together, led him to focus on the body as a site of struggle and shift from a vision of liberation that started broad and collective and would free the individual, to one that focused on the individual and would radiate outward to the collective.

Sostre was learning about women's liberation and wrote that he "dig[s] the hell out of Shulamith [Firestone] and the feminist movement."[136] Sostre had likely read Firestone's *The Dialectic of Sex* (1970), which was among the first widely disseminated radical visions of women's liberation.[137] Firestone's emphasis on women's bodily autonomy, in particular, may have resonated with him. She argued that just as Marxism posited the proletariat's seizure of the means of production, women's liberation required control over reproduction and the restoration of women's ownership of their bodies. Her action-oriented political education through consciousness-raising groups would also have appealed to him. Following the lead of Black feminists and other radical feminists of color, Sostre wrote that only "when women are completely liberated, then the society under which this liberation takes place will really and truly represent the humanistic society which we are trying to construct." By early 1972, he had come to view "the struggle for the liberation of women as the most widespread and humanistic."[138]

Sostre also gained increased access to readings about anarchism. Prior to 1972, his readings had been limited to articles, pamphlets, and short biographical sketches. "I have never read an entire book on anarchism," he said that March. Before 1970, anarchist texts were rare and difficult to find in the United States. As historian Andrew Cornell explains, "Numerically, anarchism nearly became an anachronism during the 1940s and 1950s."[139] As late as 1968, scholar Corinne Jacker (perhaps a bit hyperbolically) wrote that "there are no books in print dealing with the history of anarchism in America."[140] By 1970, Cornell notes, "major publishing houses were rushing the works of Kropotkin, Bakunin, and Goldman back into print."[141] New works included Daniel Guerin's *Anarchism* (translated into

English in 1970), Murray Bookchin's *Post-Scarcity Anarchism* (1971), Colin Ward's *Anarchy in Action* (1973), and several books by anarchist historian Paul Avrich. Now, without naming them, Sostre reported that he "learned more about anarchism from these two books than from all the other haphazard articles put together."[142] He also credited Jacker's *Black Flag of Anarchy: Antistatism in the United States*, an academic history of anarchist thought and organization, with helping to clarify the philosophy of anarchism and its approaches to social transformation.[143]

Sostre was able to read such books because of his recent legal victories in *Sostre v. Rockefeller* and *Sostre v. Otis*. Now, he closely followed anarchist support for dancer and writer Pietro Valpreda in Italy, who had been arrested for his alleged involvement in the Piazza Fontana bombing of 1969; despite being targeted by the Italian government, he was released from prison in 1972 following massive public protests. He was cleared in 1985, and three neo-fascists were later convicted of the bombing, which they had hoped to pin on ultra-leftists. Impressed by that anarchists could muster such popular support for a revolutionary, Sostre lamented that "Anarchism is not as widespread in the U.S. as it is in Europe."[144]

But Sostre worried about how these ideas would connect with the Black and Brown youth he saw as "detonators of the revolution." "While words like anarchist, lumpenproletariat, latifundists and many other political terms from the 19th Century or earlier are correct and clearly describe a class, condition or thing, I would never use these terms in any of my agitational rap in the ghetto-colony," he wrote. "It is self-defeating to introduce foreign terms into the ghetto-colony which sisters and brothers cannot relate to. The time and effort spent in explaining these foreign terms defeats the effect of the agitational propaganda."[145] As Lorenzo Ervin's recollections in the previous chapter illustrate, it was important for Black anarchists to redefine anarchism as a universal ideology, rather than a Eurocentric one, that could be applied to their own history and conditions. For these reasons, Sostre was initially hesitant to identify as such. "Since the word 'revolutionary' is *in*, and includes anarchist (since an anarchist is a revolutionary)," he concluded, "I believe the anarchist concept can be conveyed in the ghetto-colony, with less effort, employing the term 'hard-core revolutionary' or 'Vanguard revolutionary' instead of the foreign term anarchist."[146]

By 1973, Sostre began referring to himself as a "revolutionary anarchist." His readings and conversations about anarchism and radical feminism—and more importantly, their implications for one another—helped him navigate the emerging contradictions of the revolutionary period surrounding the Attica revolt. His readings and conversations with comrades, along with recent political conflicts with white Marxist-Leninist comrades in the Workers World Party and with revolutionary Black nationalists in the Republic of New Africa, all informed Sostre's decision to expand and reorganize his defense committee into a decentralized structure and deepen his spiritual struggle against the state by once again refusing to shave or submit to rectal assaults while in solitary confinement.

After being transferred back to Auburn prison in August 1972, Sostre began drafting what became "The New Prisoner." Although he predicted that "we, the new politically aware prisoner, will soon galvanize the revolutionary struggle in America . . . and obtain revolutionary justice for all oppressed people," the prison system was using the Attica uprising to justify the construction of new mechanisms of torture to control revolutionary prisoners.[147] Only a few weeks after the massacre, prison commissioner Russell Oswald, proposed a "maximum-maximum" prison to isolate five hundred politicized prisoners while himself hiding in an underground civil-defense shelter.[148] The correlation was so plain that authorities worried these prisons might be seen as "political concentration camps." Using the language of disease, they reflected on the ways their longtime strategy of transferring prisoners was "infecting" others. Sostre himself was threatened with psychological torture through the "Rx Program," which would go on to use behavior-modification techniques on over thirty mostly Black and Brown revolutionaries.[149] Over the final three years of Sostre's incarceration, he would face a concentrated and protracted assault on his body and spirit as the state attempted to kill both, once and for all.

9

"My Spirit Unbroken"

On November 6, 1972, two years since the Black Solidarity Day actions had set the Auburn Prison rebellion in motion, Martin Sostre was interviewed there by Doloris Costello for New York City's WBAI radio. He had arrived just a few months earlier, after trying to form a prisoners union at Wallkill, yet he had already organized a strike in the Auburn license plate shop. Now, he was being held in solitary indefinitely. "The reason," he explained, "is because they're trying to make me shave a quarter of an inch beard." Sostre claimed that this arbitrary rule was not intended to verify his identity, as the state maintained, but rather "to depersonalize the prisoner." "I'm never going to shave the beard off, and this is final," he told Costello. "I'm prepared to go all the way [as] a matter of principle."[1]

In December, Sostre was transferred back to Clinton Prison for the first time in over a decade, when he and other Muslims had been held in solitary confinement after suing the warden for violating their constitutional rights to religious freedom. A move to the prison—known as "little Siberia" and "Klinton Koncentration Kamp" (KKK) for its remoteness, harsh winters, and entrenched white supremacy—was itself considered a punishment. Yet it was only the beginning. In January 1973, Sostre was forced to stand outside naked except for his shoes in six-degree weather while threatened with mace and beatings.[2] Soon, he faced transfer to the "Prescription Center," known as the Rx Program, an experimental psychological torture regime developed to neutralize and reprogram revolutionary subjects. In May, Sostre was beaten by a group of seven guards for refusing a "rectal examination" on the way to his appeal in Buffalo. A prisoner who witnessed the assault had previously overheard guards plot how "best to kill" Sostre.[3] The beating was the first of eleven that Sostre would survive. Yet he remained defiant: "They may succeed in beating me to death, but they shall never succeed in forcing me to relinquish what in the final analysis are the final citadels of my personality, human dignity and self respect."[4]

Sostre's interview with Costello just before this escalation of state violence captured the post-Attica political moment and how Sostre understood himself within it. As scholar Orisanmi Burton says, the Attica massacre was "only the most visible form of repression within a protracted campaign of prison pacification." The state was in the midst of a "reformist counterinsurgency" of ostensibly "ameliorative" changes intended to stabilize a system in crisis and deepen the carceral archipelago in New York State.[5] Burton's analysis builds upon Sostre's "The New Prisoner," in which Sostre argued that post-Attica prison reforms were "a smoke screen" for the larger "repressive pacification program."[6] Sostre acknowledged that even his Black Solidarity Day interview with Costello had been permitted only because prison officials had "very vivid memories of what happened." He was quick to point out that substantively, "nothing ha[d] changed."[7] The cosmetic reforms made by the rebranded New York Department of Correctional Services, such as beautified visitation areas, work-release programs, and the recruitment of nonwhite prison guards, were cover for a rapid militarization and expansion of the prison system. A DOCS budget of $215,554 in 1969–70 had swelled to $8 million by 1973–74.[8] "I have a list of the guns and machine guns and whatnot that were just bought with this money. It's fantastic," Sostre told Costello. "It looks like they're getting ready to fight a war."[9]

Following Attica, Governor Rockefeller requested a $12 million authorization from the state legislature, including $1.3 million for a "maximum program, maximum security" facility.[10] The state prisons were constructing an alphabet soup of control units (CUs) and special housing units (SHUs) that Sostre called "euphemisms for solitary confinement torture chambers."[11] Officials initiated brainwashing and torture regimes to isolate and discipline revolutionary prisoners while using the sterilized language of treatment. Sostre wrote in an affidavit that summer that the "State of New York has covertly set up a repressive psychiatric apparatus to impose its 'final solution' on 'selected' prisoners who challenge repressive acts of prison officials, or whose political beliefs differ from those of the administration."[12] He was one of its first targets.[13]

Sostre returning to Erie County Court for a hearing in his legal appeal, 1972. Courtesy of the Archives and Special Collection Department, E.H. Butler Library, SUNY Buffalo State.

In this context, Sostre regarded his refusal to shave and his resistance to state-sanctioned sexual assault not only as a spiritual but also an immediately physical and inherently political struggle.[14] Sostre did not see the spirit as otherworldly or divine. "I attribute it to the person," he explained, "a human quality present in everyone in varying degrees of development."[15] "Spirit is what moves people and creates political awareness."[16] Having practiced yoga for nearly two decades, he used it to steel himself against the daily violence of incarceration. Rather than seeking nirvana or personal enlightenment, Sostre described his practice as preparing him for "physical and mental combat against this repressive State in the struggle to overthrow it."[17] His resistance was meant to demonstrate the "the inability of the oppressive state to prevail over the spirituality of one man."[18]

Trapped in an escalating war between his bodily autonomy and state domination, Sostre cultivated his spiritual reserves to maintain and defend what he considered the ultimate bastions of his personhood. In a telephone conversation in May 1975, a supporter asked him: "What keeps you going? What keeps you from submitting?" He responded: "What keeps me committed . . . is the knowledge that we are winning. Not that we're going to win, that we're already winning. . . . That is what keeps up the spirit of victory—the fuel of the spirit."[19] Perhaps he misheard her question. More likely, he reframed the question. Submission was unthinkable, and victory was a foregone conclusion. Moreover, it was not a future destination but enacted each day through his refusals.

The goal of revolution, Sostre now believed, was not "to replace one State by another, it's to liberate the individual."[20] But his individual fight to maintain his personhood was inseparable from collective liberation. For him they were a single struggle on different scales. "My resistance to the state's repressive prison apparatus symbolizes on an individual level, the people's struggle against the state's subjugation," he wrote.[21] He considered individual resistance to state violence as revolutionary struggle in its most concentrated form. His assertions of bodily autonomy and identity were simultaneously necessary to his own personal freedom and symbolic of the ongoing worldwide struggle. Drawing a parallel to the national liberation movement of Vietnam, Sostre saw his struggle as a one-person version of the National Liberation Front's persistent war against colonial domination. "Mine is on a personal level, whereas the Vietnamese were fighting on a national level. They were fighting against the strongest and most developed and richest country in the whole world. That's equivalent to me fighting against the whole goon squad in the solitary confinement unit at Clinton prison. I want to show the forces and powers that I use—physical, mental, political, and legal—in order to eventually subdue the enemy and register victories, and at the same time keep from getting killed."[22]

In an interview later in life, Sostre mentioned drawing inspiration from the famous 1968 photograph *Saigon Execution*. During the war in Vietnam, among "all the injustices that were done there, like the village of My Lai . . . I remember one photograph. . . . When I was the Box I used to think about it. . . . This goon, a Vietnamese general . . . had this pistol to this Vietcong prisoner who had his hands tied behind his back, and shot him. The picture was taken just at the time when the bullet hit his head . . . and there's some smoke coming from his gun."[23] Reproduced in countless newspapers and magazines, this image of a cold-blooded execution of a prisoner of war by a general fighting alongside the US helped to turn Americans against the war.[24] For Sostre, it had deeper resonances, encapsulating how he envisioned his individual resistance as part of worldwide solidarity. Even his use of the phrase "goon" to refer to both the general in the photograph and the squads of guards who attacked him drew attention to these parallels.

Sostre recognized that his refusals would create possibilities for organizing. Even the most politically aware leftists, he had found, become so lost in "sterile ideological arguments" that they could not recognize the "concrete revolutionary deeds which are the content of liberation struggle."[25] His critique of left ideologues points to his growing identification with anarchism and its commitment to "propaganda of the deed." As the Russian revolutionary anarchist Mikhail Bakunin emphasized a century earlier, "We must spread our principles, not with word but with deeds, for this is the most popular, the most potent, and the most irresistible form of propaganda."[26] Although often identified with public direct actions, such as bombings and assassinations of the ruling class, Sostre's example of resistance to state-sanctioned sexual assault points to a more hidden form, which was simultaneously aimed at inspiring action by other incarcerated people and raising the consciousness of those outside. Just a few months after his first refusal and beating in May 1973, Sostre wrote that "revolutionary anarchism—as opposed to the strait-jacketism of cliché-oriented party-line groups—is the explicit and dynamic personal code of conscience which I follow even in prison. It is a code based on deed, and not on rhetoric."[27] He believed his resistance to assault and the escalation of violence by prison guards meant that "only those with the lowest level of political consciousness will not be able to relate to the concrete struggle I am waging against the repressive state."[28]

In mid-1972, Sostre expanded beyond a single defense committee in Buffalo into what would eventually become a diffuse network of collectives across the country. His ongoing legal challenges to individualized forms of state domination created new opportunities for people to learn about his struggle. It was out of this ferment that supporters formed new autonomous committees. In letters to members of these nascent groups, Sostre distilled ideas about revolutionary struggle through his tangible example. He explained succinctly:

> The message is clear: If the State has been unable to break my spirit and force my submission to its dehumanizing, degrading and depersonalizing laws despite its subjecting me to years of torture in solitary confinement, brutality, additional years in prison on manufactured assault charges, the comrades outside can with minimum unity overthrow the repressive state and replace it with a stateless and egalitarian society that is self-managed by the people. The struggle to smash the repressive prison system is an inseparable part of the struggle for liberation because prisons are used by the state to coerce the people into obeying its oppressive authority. Prisons and executions are used to crush the spirit of resistance of the people.[29]

When people witnessed the state's violent response to these straightforward acts, they were moved to action and encountered new forms and degrees of repression. Through this dialectical process, they changed their own individual political understandings and ways of organizing collectively.

Unable to suppress revolutionary movements through corporeal controls like solitary confinement, punitive transfer, and state-sanctioned sexual assault, the state incorporated what Burton calls a "war on Black revolutionary minds."[30] Sostre saw resistance against these attempts to incapacitate his brain and sexually violate his body as necessary, in his words, to "maintain my spirit unbroken."[31] These assertions of bodily autonomy were always outward looking. Sostre understood that the other side of coercion is consent. Only by resisting and rejecting both could people hope to be free. Through its barbaric siege of Attica, the state had hoped to demonstrate its awesome technological power over its subjects. For Sostre, the opposite was true: "All the gates and all the security and maximum-security prison, all that was taken in a matter of minutes because technology never defeats men. I mean, Vietnam proved that when people are oppressed and they are determined to move, their own technology will be swept the away as if it was made of straw."[32]

Sostre was in his third month of solitary confinement at Clinton in early 1973 when he received a received a letter of solidarity from another Puerto Rican revolutionary prisoner of war, Lolita Lebrón. A compatriot of Sostre's first mentor, Julio Pinto Gandía, Lebrón had been held captive for nearly twenty years in federal prison since participating in 1954 with three other nationalists in a revolutionary action at the US Capitol meant to draw attention to Puerto Rico's independence struggle. When she came across Sostre's address in a Black Panther Party publication, she immediately wrote to him: "Ever since I learned about your case, you have been in my thoughts and in my heart." Lebrón was particularly concerned to "read that they are torturing you in the mental program," a reference to the recently launched Rx Program at the Adirondack Correctional Treatment and Evaluation Center (ACTEC).[33]

The Rx Program was part of a swell of medicalized violence in the 1960s and '70s, which one coalition dubbed the "prison/psychiatric state."[34] But these techniques were decades in the making. Philosopher Lisa Guenther traces the origins of the behavior modification movement to anticommunist brainwashing experiments of the CIA and the Department of Defense during the Cold War: "Many of the same psychologists and psychiatrists who began their careers in the 1950s with research on thought reform went on to apply their research in the 1960s and '70s to behavioral reform in prisons."[35] The Patuxent Institution in Jessup, Maryland, established in 1955 under the Defective Delinquent Statute, marked one of the first experiments. The prison was granted full autonomy by the Department of Corrections, enabling it to involuntarily commit and permanently detain people in a rank-based system aimed at obtaining total authority through a maze of punishments and rewards.[36] Investigative journalist Jessica Mitford found that a decade after opening, nearly half of those paroled from Patuxent had served more than their maximum sentence.[37] By 1972, a hundred or more imprisoned radicals had been transferred to a federal prison in Marion, Illinois, where they were met with a series of experiments so grotesque that Marion activist Eddie Griffin described it as a "legal form of assassination."[38] The Marion Control Unit eventually become a model for the so-called supermax prison—the highest form of surveillance and authoritarian control in which people are subjected to decades of isolation—after being on lockdown for an incredible twenty-three years beginning in 1983, following the killing of two guards.[39] Although these early 1970s programs were meant to isolate, control, and pacify revolutionary captives such as Sostre, they emerged in response to prison organizing like his own a decade earlier. What the state euphemistically called "behavior modification" was first designed not to control Sostre the anarchist in the early 1970s, but Sostre the Muslim jailhouse lawyer in the early 1960s. Indeed, we can best understand the decades-long rise of the control unit and psychological torture when viewed alongside Sostre's decades-long organizing.

"The Power to Change Behavior" symposium in 1961 has been identified by scholars and activists as a pivotal moment in developing what historian Alan Eladio Gómez calls "institutionalized brainwashing, behavior modification, and torture within the prison regime."[40] In Washington, DC, high-ranking psychiatrists and other social scientists gathered with prison officials to discuss the "use and effectiveness of brainwashing and other means of persuasion" on prisoners.[41] Coinciding with Sostre's torture in solitary confinement at Attica and pending lawsuits over the constitutional rights of incarcerated Muslims, much of the conversation in the nation's capital centered around the question: "How shall we manage the Muslims?"[42] The answer was behavior modification and vast discretion over their treatment. The chair of the seminar closed the meeting by encouraging the group of prominent scholars to experiment and share their findings: "What I am hoping is that the audience here will believe that we here in Washington are anxious to have you undertake some of these things; do things perhaps on your own—undertake a little experiment of what you can do with the Muslims."[43] As former Panther and Black Liberation Army cofounder Dhoruba bin-Wahad commented in

2021, "Guantanamo Bay is the sum total of what they've been doing to Muslims in US prison for decades."[44]

Sostre was a longtime target of this repression and had warned about the growth of the prison/psychiatric state years before he was a candidate for the Rx Program. His extensive cross-examination of the psychiatrists who diagnosed him as a "paranoid personality" in his 1968 trial sought to expose the use of psychiatry as a tool of state repression.[45] Not long after, his lawsuits documented attempts to "bug" him. As he explained in his complaint against Governor Rockefeller later that year, "the term 'bug you' . . . is prison colloquialism meaning to be committed to the Dannemora State Hospital for the criminally insane, the state's worst insane asylum notorious for the frequent killing of patients by its vicious sadistic guards."[46] Sostre had first learned of the state's plan to target him while held in solitary confinement at Auburn for refusing to shave his beard.[47] He considered his transfer to Clinton's notorious Unit 14—a torture site reachable only by taking an elevator to rows of underground cells that opened like gladiator cages, from either the front or back—as "a deliberately planned retaliatory punitive transfer by prison officials. Its ultimate objective was to railroad me to the state's new Rx Program."[48] Sostre warned that this "treatment center is the prototype receiving and experimental center of the state's covert pacification program."[49]

ACTEC opened in the former site of the Dannemora State Mental Hospital, adjacent to Clinton Prison. It was "the nerve center" of the prison system's new diversification strategy, where prisoners were sent to be "studied, classified, diagnosed, experimented upon, and sorted by an international coterie of doctors, behavioral scientists, social workers, and penal experts."[50] As Orisanmi Burton explains, "as a 'diversification' institution, ACTEC operated myriad programs dispersed across several buildings, each of which contained multiple wards, floors, and wings, ensuring that captives in the same institution could have wildly different experiences."[51] The Rx Program was one of many nestled within the center and intended for revolutionaries like Sostre.

A few years after the Attica revolt, a New York State document called the Multi-Year Master Plan laid out five years of prison expenditures. Among its findings was that a minority of the state's prisoners needed "intensive prescription and control programming."[52] In an attempt to subdue revolutionary captives once and for all, prison officials introduced psychotropic drugs, insulin, and electroconvulsive shock "therapy," sensory and sleep deprivation, psychosurgery, sexual experimentation, and other forms of torture. "Having already incarcerated insurgent Black bodies, only to learn that physical capture did not equal control," Burton writes, "counterinsurgency experts tried and failed to exterminate insurgent Black knowledge, thoughts, feelings, behaviors, and even impulses."[53] Through in-depth oral history interviews and declassified documents, Burton uncovered evidence of what he calls "scientific forms of sexual grooming and rape" as well as ties to better-known CIA "brain warfare" operations such as MK-Ultra.[54] As Alan Eladio Gómez argues, such practices "muddled commonplace distinctions between what constituted punishment, rehabilitation, and torture."[55]

Political poster, Third World Students Coalition, c. 1973. Martin Sostre Collection, University of Michigan Library (Special Collections Research Center).

Although Sostre was one of the Rx Program's first targets, he successfully resisted by waging a public campaign that sounded the alarm about these new dystopian forms of mind control. Notably, this campaign coincided with both the expansion of his defense committee beyond Buffalo and the internationalization of his struggle. Dan Georgakas, a Greek American anarchist living in New Jersey, was busy writing his classic in labor history, *Detroit: I Do Mind Dying*, when his friend Ernest Nassar reached out about Sostre's case. Nassar, a Detroit-based leftist attorney, was interested in the rise of behavior modification, and the two visited Sostre in prison. When they inquired what they could do to help, Sostre replied: "Why don't you do a New York / New Jersey committee?"[56]

Advertisement for a conference on mind control, 1973. Martin Sostre Collection, University of Michigan Library (Special Collections Research Center).

Rather grandiosely labeled the regional committees for the East Coast and Midwest, these were in fact two committees founded by just two people and centered in New Jersey and Michigan, respectively. The committees operated parallel to, and often in tension with, Sharon Fischer in Buffalo.[57] But through their connections, Sostre's support quickly expanded to include leftist attorneys such as Conrad Lynn, James Lafferty, Lynn Walker, and Abdeen Jabara, and writers Tana de Gámez and Paul Sweezy. Yuri Kochiyama, whose efforts to correspond with Sostre years earlier while he was held in solitary confinement at Green Haven were thwarted by prison censors, again reached out.[58] Nassar wrote that Angela Davis and the recently formed National Alliance Against Racist

Sostre on the cover of *Palante*, a bilingual newspaper published by the Young Lords Party, January 15, 1971.

and Political Repression were committed to highlighting Sostre as one of half a dozen political prisoners during her speaking tour, and he would be traveling throughout Europe to establish defense committees in Italy, Sweden, and Denmark. The attorney assured Sostre optimistically, "Your isolation is coming to an end."[59]

Much of this support was directed toward publicizing the horrors of the Rx Program and garnering international support. "It is essential to expose this program at once through a massive educational campaign," read one call for an international letter-writing drive. Because two of the program's first potential subjects, Sostre and Eduardo "Pancho" Cruz, were both Puerto Rican, a coalition of Puerto Rican communities had "ear-marked the struggle around Pancho Cruz and Martin Sostre as having top priority."[60] The Young Lords' newspaper, *Palante*, encouraged readers to protest their planned transfers.[61] In June 1973, Sostre's supporters collaborated with Cruz's committee to host a conference on behavioral modification at the Cathedral of St. John the Divine in New York City. There, Marxist psychologist Eli Messinger warned that this program "brings us closer to an era of mind slavery and psychiatric fascism."[62] Just four days after the conference, a state memo announced that the Rx Program would be "phased out."[63]

Sostre knew this was only a temporary victory. He warned that "while our legal, political and physical struggle against the Rx program has forced the enemy to suspend operations at the ACTEC the plan now is to increase the capacities of special housing units in maximum security facilities throughout the state." He predicted that the state would "retreat from ACTEC back to the safety of the 'Box.'" There, in the maze-like solitary confinement cells of Clinton's Unit 14, he recounted the tortured screams of a prisoner who had recently returned from the Rx Program.[64] Sostre recognized that, as he had explained to the psychiatrist he cross-examined in court years earlier, "just because they use mace does not mean they are going to abandon their club."[65] A group of militant prisoners being held in the Rx Program confirmed Sostre's admonishment: "While we are dealing with the latest threats, treatments, and techniques in so-called modern penology, we can't afford to forget the old-line methods. For a pick-ax handle can be just as much a brain destroying device as psycho-surgery ever could be."[66] As Sostre headed back to federal court for his appeal hearing, he was again met with these "old-line methods."

On May 19, 1973, Sostre prepared to be transferred from Clinton to Buffalo. There, Arto Williams was set to recant his testimony in federal court and admit to his central role in framing Sostre. To leave his solitary cell, however, Sostre was required to undergo a "rectal examination." Sostre had refused and publicly repudiated this practice for over four years, a fact well known to prison officials from his lawsuits. That day, Jimmy Sullivan was working as a porter on Unit 14 when he overheard a sergeant and three guards plotting to beat up the prisoner in Cell 37. An hour or so later, according to an affidavit by Sullivan, Sostre was removed from the back door of his cell and ordered to strip.[67] The accounts of what happened next given by the guards are irreconcilable with Sostre's own because they did not recognize his right to refuse. But even the prison's incident reports as documented by guards captured his defiance: "You will have to do this again when I come back from court. You will never break my spirit and I am willing to die before I frisk voluntarily."[68]

These squads were brought in especially for beatings. "They're all football players. They don't have any small pigs on that goon squad," Sostre said. "They're all overgrown, half my age and six footers that weigh anywhere from two to three hundred pounds. Here I am in solitary confinement, buck naked and I weigh only a hundred and sixty-five pounds." According to Sullivan, Sostre respectfully declined the search. He was then knocked to the ground and punched "viciously and calculatedly" in the kidney until he was limp.[69] Sullivan was approaching his parole date after over a decade inside and knew the risks of testifying to what he had seen. But, he decided, "today is too much," and shared what he had witnessed.[70]

The strip search originated in the slave market. Historian Walter Johnson documents the continuous "stripping and examining [of] slaves' bodies" and the attention given to the word "stripped," used by buyers and traders "as if they had done it themselves."[71] Auction houses even provided separate rooms or screens for this practice, not to protect the modesty of those being sold, but suggesting that there was something shameful about it.[72] These practices continued well after the legal abolition of slavery. At Parchman Farm, a plantation-turned-prison in the Mississippi Delta described by historian David Oshinsky as "the closest thing to slavery that survived the civil war," activist James Farmer remembered feeling "consumed with embarrassment" after he and other Freedom Riders "stood for ages—uncomfortable, dehumanized" and naked following their arrests in 1961.[73]

These assaults were—and remain—common in prisons throughout the country, not just in the Deep South. While they particularly targeted protestors, they were also deployed against women and men of color and persons regarded as sexually deviant. In his history of the Women's House of Detention in Manhattan, Hugh Ryan documents public protests against physical examinations of arrested women picketers in the left-wing League of Women Shoppers in 1936, just a few years after its opening.[74] Angela Davis recounted similar searches at the so-called "House of D" in her autobiography.[75] The most publicized case, however, came in 1965 after eighteen-year-old antiwar protestor Andrea Dworkin was arrested and experienced physical and psychological torture over the course of several days at the jail. A male doctor and a trainee inquired about her sex life and drug use, and conducted physical searches with a speculum that left her bleeding for days. Dworkin's account, in the form of an open letter to the warden, was published in the *Village Voice*. She wrote that "no internal examination is conducted with such gross disrespect for the human body and for human dignity with such obvious pleasure in the embarrassment and pain of the patient/victim."[76] The account made national news and led to a slew of government investigations, the firing of the doctor, and the resignations of other prominent state officials. Leading that publicity drive was activist author Grace Paley, who met Dworkin at the protest.[77] A decade later, Paley became involved in the Committee to Free Martin Sostre in New York City.

The public outcry following Dworkin's assault was the exception rather than the rule. Despite Judge Motley's ruling that Sostre's solitary confinement at Green Haven Prison, which included strip searches and rectal assaults, was "dehumanizing in the sense that it is needlessly degrading," these rapes continued unabated in New York.[78] Jalil Abdul Alim, one of the many captives targeted after the Auburn rebellion, reported a year later that he had been beaten after refusing a rectal search and "was deaf in my left ear for more than two weeks."[79] In a statement reprinted in the *New York Times*, Auburn prisoner James Dunn reported nine guards armed with ax handles arriving outside his cell and ordering him to strip. "They forced me to undergo several consecutive frisks (examinations) in an effort to provoke me. The said officials ordered me to march (butt naked) without my clothes. I refused."[80]

The best-known instance of mass state-sanctioned sexual assault came during the Attica massacre, when the National Guard and prison guards marched naked captives across the yard, then raped and tortured them as reprisals for the uprising.[81] Among them was Sostre's mentee, Frank "Big Black" Smith, who was forced to strip and lay prone on a picnic table while his body was burned with cigarettes and spat upon.[82] Johnson argues that the routinized process of "looking, stripping, touching, bantering, and evaluating" by white slave traders and buyers provided a ritualistic communion through which "white men confirmed their commonality with the other men with whom they inspected the slaves."[83] Burton persuasively situates the retaking of Attica within this tradition of racialized sexual violence, which, like lynching and gang rape, was meant to terrorize while asserting the shared identity of participants and onlookers and reinscribing their power. The image of lines of prisoners standing naked in the yard at Attica reproduced ad nauseum in the official McKay Report, the *New York Times*, and other publications, Burton points out, "reifies the captives' status as chattel, presenting their vulnerability to sexual violence as a banal social fact."[84] "At its core," he concludes, "the massacre was a collective act of *sexual revenge* that aimed to punish the rebels and defend the racial breach within normative masculinity."[85]

Sostre's refusals are best understood within this context of sexual violence and racialized gender war.[86] After being subjected to his eighth assault, he documented the various forms of physical, psychological, and spiritual torture he had endured over the last few years under a unifying behavior modification regime carried out by those who engineered the violence at Attica:

> Physical beatings, strangulation till one loses consciousness, being forced outdoors while entirely naked and exposed to six degree sub-freezing weather, caging dissidents in cells 24 hours a day for years without receiving sun and cut off from all human contact till the victim loses his health, is driven insane, to suicide, or is spiritually broken into submission to the repressive authority of his torturers, planting contraband in the cell, formulating false assault charges against the victim of the assault, etc.—these comprise the behavior modification program currently being implemented by the same sadistic law-and-order individuals responsible for the Attica Massacre.[87]

Although Sostre did not use the word "rape" to characterize these assaults, he nevertheless highlighted their sexualized violence: "When you bend over and spread them, they'll be leering and saying, 'Yeah, look at that asshole he's got.' Three or four of them saying, 'I'd like to ram this club up in there' and stuff like that."[88] He also emphasized their dehumanizing and degrading aims. Sostre contended that these acts of violent domination were intended to coerce submission and understood his refusals as an assertion of his individual freedom, dignity, and personhood.

It is noteworthy that Sostre regularly used the gender-neutral language of "personhood" instead of "manhood," especially given the intense concern about Black masculinity generated in response to the 1965 Moynihan Report, which condemned matriarchal Black family structures as responsible for a "tangle of pathology."[89] And, while Sostre described the searches as symbolic sodomy, he did not explicitly mobilize homophobic arguments to condemn them.[90] Although Attica rebel L. D. Barkley's cry "We are men! We are not beasts" during the rebellion has often been interpreted as an assertion of Black masculinity, Sostre's emphasis on a gender-defiant personhood is consistent with some of the Attica rebels' revolutionary rhetoric. As Burton states, the revolt was "an effort to chart a new course for what a revolutionary manhood or 'humanhood,' as one survivor termed it, could become."[91]

The assaults were part of a vicious circle in which Sostre became entrapped. While the courts offered one of the few spaces to raise awareness about these brutal tactics and petition for relief, accessing them triggered more violence. To get to court from solitary confinement, Sostre had two options: to be raped or to be beaten. Often, he experienced both. Although he attempted to file a legal complaint on the day of his initial assault, it was held up for several months in the prison mail. In the meantime, the state filed its own lawsuit charging Sostre with three counts of second-degree assault for the May beating. Under New York's "persistent felony laws" (a precursor to the better-known Three Strikes laws of the 1990s), Sostre faced a second life sentence if convicted of his third felony. As Sostre pointed out, "This is a favorite device of making the victim the criminal and making themselves the victim."[92]

The contradictions were glaring. In his effort to appear in Erie County Court and overturn his original virtual life sentence, Sostre was framed again and faced a second life term. He was even denied visits with lawyers unless he submitted to the assaults. As his attorney Dennis Cunningham argued, "The prison authorities have imposed a 'Catch 22,' designed to ensure their triumph over Sostre in this case by cutting him off from legal assistance in violation of his constitutional rights."[93] Nevertheless, having just been assaulted by a goon squad of seven guards, Sostre returned to Buffalo in May 1973 for another attempt at securing his release through the courts. There to testify on his behalf was the very man who had served as the state's key witness and accomplice in framing him: Arto Williams.

It had been over two years since Arto Williams decided to recant his testimony that had helped send Sostre to prison. Williams was once again incarcerated, this time in California, and now flew back to face the man he had betrayed as well as the likelihood of federal charges for perjury. His statements undermined the state's case by showing how he had exchanged false testimony in exchange for the promise of reduced jail time. The trial also offered Sostre the opportunity to testify in court for the first time in his own defense, explaining how his bookstore had served the community on the East Side of Buffalo, including Williams. Finally, the trial aroused renewed interest in the case and offered an occasion for its key figures to come together in one place. Most of them would be interviewed during this brief period for the short documentary by Pacific Street Films—*Frame-Up! The Imprisonment of Martin Sostre* (1974). The filmmakers, Joel Sucher and Steven Fischler, helped to locate Williams and their film would soon play a pivotal role in the growth of Sostre's defense campaign.

The first time Sostre and Williams had appeared in court together, Sostre had refused to participate. The original trial had been an inexorable march of state witnesses without rebuttal or cross-examination. Now, Williams outlined the full day of the frame-up in greater detail. In particular, his exchange with Sostre in the bookstore on the night of July 14, 1967, took on a different character, as he and Sostre both explained in their testimony how the store functioned as a community space. Holding onto Williams's suit or safekeeping fifteen dollars for him were just a few examples of the ways his bookstore served Buffalo's East Side. "People used to leave packages there sometimes to give to another person or a lot of times they would leave umbrellas," Sostre said. "In fact, a couple of times some women left their kids, small kids, two or three year old kids for me to mind."[94] These details may have seemed small, or even irrelevant, to the court. But the fact that Sostre repeated them almost verbatim in an interview years later—the packages, two-year-old, and William's suit—suggests the meaning he attached to small acts of community care.[95]

Williams's testimony also revealed the ongoing manipulation of the state and its use of vulnerable criminalized informants for political repression. Just weeks after successfully framing Sostre and Robinson, Williams claimed he had purchased drugs from a Muslim in the Nation of Islam, Clarence X Torrey.[96] "Each time I was arrested I would call [Gristmacher] and he would come down and get me out," Williams testified. Gristmacher had even secured Williams a job at Bethlehem Steel and tried to convince him to speak at schools about drug use.[97] In his testimony, Williams revealed a broader web of manipulation whereby police used his substance-use disorder as a weapon against both him and their radical targets in Buffalo.

Sostre attacked the state's flimsy evidence that it claimed had been collected during police surveillance from across the street. Although the two state troopers stationed there had been unable to produce any photographic evidence at the original trial (they later admitted that the camera was not loaded), they nevertheless testified that they had witnessed an exchange of money for "something."[98] The day before the appeal was heard, Pacific Street Films recreated the state's surveillance from the second-floor office window across the street from the bookstore, revealing the impossibility of spotting a 1 7/8′ x 7/8′ glassine envelope from that distance, even with a high-quality zoom lens.[99] This reenactment was described at trial the next day by one of the film's directors, Joel Sucher. Observing the bookstore's doorway through a telephoto lens in broad daylight, Sucher testified that the angle of the window and the glare on the glass made anyone entering the store disappear after walking in a few feet. Moreover, on the night of July 14, 1967, the bookstore's windows were boarded up after the fire at the Woodlawn Tavern next door.[100] By the trial's end, the same district attorney who had used Williams's testimony to convict Sostre in 1968 suggested the informant be prosecuted for perjury, bringing the state's betrayal full circle.[101]

Despite this compelling evidence, Sostre's attempt to overturn his 31–41-year sentence in court was ultimately unsuccessful from a legal perspective. In March 1974, Judge John Curtin wrote a 23-page decision arguing that Williams' recantation was "unworthy of belief" and that "there is no reason not to believe the testimony of the police officers."[102]

The trial nevertheless advanced his cause in other significant ways. Most importantly, it provided the opportunity for the filmmakers with Pacific Street Film Collective to produce the first and only documentary about him. The effectiveness of the film lay in its juxtaposition of duplicitous state officials with its erudite and principled protagonist. Through simple questioning and probing by the filmmakers, who often feigned naivete, the film lays bare a capricious and unjust system as it crumbles under the weight of its contradictions. In this way, the directors' approach to filmmaking mirrored Sostre's courtroom strategy.[103] Years earlier, a review of WWP cofounder Vincent Copeland's book *The Crime of Martin Sostre* had predicted that "it should go a long way towards creating the kind of public indignation over this frame up that could ultimately free Sostre."[104] It was *Frame-Up!* that would ultimately play this role. The thirty-minute film proved an effective tool for creating new defense committees and introducing thousands of new supporters to both the injustice of his frame-up and his continued assertions of bodily autonomy.

Sucher and Fischler were only twenty-three years old when they set out to film *Frame-Up!* But they were already experienced directors in a mode of filmmaking they described as "a politically malleable *cinema-verité* form."[105] The two had met as children living on the same block in the predominantly Jewish and Italian neighborhood of Sheepshead Bay, Brooklyn.[106] Both began identifying with anarchism while attending Brooklyn Technical High School, an all-boys school with an authoritarian structure where 10 percent of the six thousand or so students acted as "a kind of student police force that would line up in the hallways when you changed class." Sucher was rebellious and often got into fights with antisemitic Italian or Irish kids in the neighborhood. Although he was expelled from Brooklyn Tech, he eventually graduated and attended New York University with Fischler.[107]

Their first experimental film documented a student takeover at NYU and parodied the dean of students, who was sent to break up the occupation. Its warm reception propelled them into film school, where they were mentored by Martin Scorsese.[108] The director entered their first film, *Inciting to Riot*, in a national student film festival, where it won a major prize.[109] By the time they began *Frame-Up!* they had already pioneered a style of confrontational countersurveillance filmmaking through their 1972 documentary on the NYPD's Bureau of Special Services and Investigation. "We used to see [undercover cops] at demonstrations with cameras, and that spurred our interest," Fischler said. "We turned the cameras on them and filmed a bit of their investigation of us, and we made a film called *Red Squad*." In the process of making the film, the directors were harassed, arrested, and eventually became part of the longest class action lawsuit in New York State history, *Handschu v. Special Services*.[110]

They brought this approach to Buffalo, interviewing a full cast of law enforcement, informants, journalists, defense committee members, and Sostre himself. In addition to short interviews with Williams and state trooper Steverson, the directors spoke extensively with one of the chief architects of the frame-up, Mike Amico of the Narcotics and Intelligence Bureau. "Considering us to be nothing more than straight media-type journalists, he lowered his defenses," the crew remembered. They recalled going through two rolls of film and were running low, and yet it was still "a task to get him to stop rambling."[111] They even located Manuel Bernstein, the journalist who had uncritically reprinted the police propaganda linking Sostre to drug sales and urban rebellion in the days immediately following the arrest.[112] Almost satirically, his office was a "seedy press room, spider webs and all, in the Buffalo P.D. headquarters."[113]

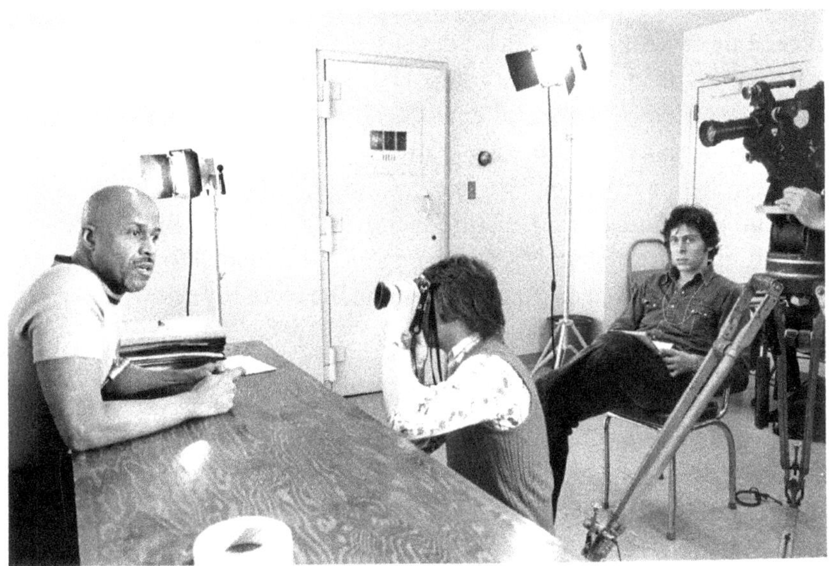

Sostre interviewed by Steven Fischler in the Erie County Jail, May 1973. Courtesy of Steven Fischler, Joe Sucher, and the Pacific Street Film Collective.

The bumbling frame-up outfit was set in stark contrast to the film's charismatic lead. Interviewed at Erie County Jail, Martin Sostre covered a range of topics, including his trial, his refusals to shave or submit to rectal examinations, and his definition of political versus politicized prisoners. He occasionally cut through the deadly seriousness of the subjects with sardonic humor or by flashing a warm smile. When rebuking the rebranding of "prisons" as "correctional facilities," for example, he quipped that "they might as well call it the Waldorf."[114] The film's most memorable scene was recorded not by Sucher and Fischler, but by a local television station.[115] In it, Sostre and the superintendent of Erie County Jail sit at small school desks separated by only a few inches. As the conversation intensifies, Sostre catches the warden in a series of lies about lighting in the cells. "Sostre's ready wit and intelligence overwhelm the prison official who cannot admit to having made mistake after mistake over the simplest details," defense committee member Dan Georgakas wrote in a review of the film. "The inflexibility of the system, its inability to admit fault, its inability to admit that prisoners know what they are talking about, is dramatically underlined."[116]

Frame-Up! took thirteen months to produce. During that time Martin Sostre continued to be beaten for his refusals.[117] He detailed the brutality of one assault in a letter to his longtime adversary, Judge Irving Kaufman: "After a short struggle in which I defended myself as best I could against their unprovoked attack, they knocked me to the concrete floor and forcibly performed the rectal examination. I was then handcuffed and harnessed with a thick 3-inch belt around my waist, to which handcuffs were attached, and driven to Clinton County Court."[118] There, he faced a second life sentence for resisting the May 1973 assault. But Sostre saw opportunity in Plattsburgh. "They've provided us with a forum to air all the barbarity and savagery that's covertly taking place in the box," he wrote his committee.[119]

Despite Sostre's revolutionary optimism, the cost of his refusals is difficult to overstate. He was denied visits from loved ones, attorneys, and supporters. He sacrificed exercise, fresh air, and the sight of trees. He was prohibited from accessing medical care for the assaults he sustained. He was literally beaten speechless. His Amherst committee outlined the direct and collateral repercussions: "He will be placed in solitary confinement, probably after a beating, etc. At this point his communication to the outside will be cut off. . . . He will have no access to a telephone and only a few letters will reach his hands. Because of this severe confinement he will be denied the opportunity to report to those who are concerned for his safety after any occasion of retaliatory or sadistic beatings, humiliations or tortures."[120] Usually stoic in court, Sostre showed a rare moment of vulnerability as he testified on behalf of another prisoner in late 1973. "I'm sorry. I have been locked in a year," he said. "I haven't even heard a radio for a year. . . . You know, being isolated from all humanity, it is terrible."[121]

Sostre outlined the difficult odds he was facing in trying to organize strikes against sexual violence through his individual acts of resistance. "Many times I was the only one resisting the rectal examination in the box," he said. "At Clinton prison which has a population of about 1,800 or 2,000, there was never at one time, more than four resisting the rectal examination." When they joined him, they were often transferred to other prisons.[122] One who refused to submit was denied his right to meet with the parole board.[123] In Sostre's exchange with Lolita Lebrón, he took the opportunity to share his frustration with a comrade who had also paid a high price for her revolutionary deeds. "We surrender to the oppressor without defying him; we cooperate with him and we receive the unjust beatings, passively. The minority that fights the oppression, doesn't receive any support by the passive majority." *Drawing a connection between US imperialism across borders and walls, he wrote that "t*he reality is that even though the enemy starts war against us in Puerto Rico, in the slums of the United States and here in jail, the majority of us remain paralyzed, without spirit to struggle, and frightened." Sostre was inspired by the revolutionary tradition established by Lebrón and other Puerto Rican nationalists. He attributed his "philosophy of action and not merely of speech" to Lebrón's mentor, Pedro Albizu Campos, and regularly "pointed out to [fellow prisoners] that if you, with 20 years of incarceration, are able besides keeping the Nationalist ideals alive which Don Pedro Albizu Campos left to us, fight for the rights of the prisoners, we in the Clinton Jail should at least, resist with vigor the oppression of these sadist guards."[124]

Some incarcerated people were moved by Sostre's challenge, however. One was nineteen-year-old Arthur Tavares. Wrongfully convicted of murder at age fifteen, Tavares had been illegally tried as an adult, and halfway through a ten-year sentence he found himself in a solitary confinement cell near Sostre. Although the two could not see each other, they communicated verbally. After Sostre returned from one beating, Tavares told him, "[If] you with your 50 years are willing to confront them, I will also resist them."[125] Sostre recalled Tavares coming back from his own beating and saying, "I'm hurting all over, but you know something, I feel good. I broke that circle of fear."[126] Sostre would later help to secure Tavares's release from prison by writing a successful legal appeal challenging his conviction as a minor.[127]Another person Sostre influenced was John "KO" Smith, a former boxer who was already resisting the searches when the two briefly crossed paths in prison. Smith watched from his cell as Sostre interacted with other organizers on the prison yard. Eventually, Sostre came to his cell window and told him about his thirteen months in solitary at Green Haven and the Motley ruling. "After I met him during my brief stay at the Green Haven prison, it did influence my thinking!" Smith would later recall, "knowing that this elder brother did the same thing!"[128]

Sostre's resistance was directed at those within and beyond the prison. He hoped his refusals would recruit others inside to join him, as Tavares had, and that the state's sadistic response would illuminate the everyday violence of the prison system to those outside and compel them to act. He later claimed, "I wasn't doing these things for anybody else. I'm not Jesus Christ. I tried to do it for myself." Yet he also said that any victories were still collective ones: "If I won a decision it would affect all prisoners. I wanted more freedom and if I won it for me, everyone would have it."[129] Sostre's deeds strengthened the resolve of those on both sides of the walls. Ernest Nassar wrote him, "Your principled struggle and personal integrity and bravery set a high standard for us. Really, it makes it easier for us to live in this Hell of Lies and carry on."[130] In the final analysis, Sostre was defending his own humanity and dignity, as well as those of others, both of which he deemed more important than the possibility of death. Within this cycle of violence, Sostre continued to find opportunity in the face of repression: "We must seize it and steadfastly use it against their own interests," he wrote.[131] His 1975 trial for assault in Plattsburgh would soon become that opportunity.

10

A Structure for the Future

Antonio Rodríguez and Marjorie Browne (now Miller) knew little about Martin Sostre when they attended his arraignment at the Clinton County Court on July 6, 1973. They had come at the urging of a young academic couple, Allyn Kahn and Kay Branagan, rare leftists in the otherwise-conservative Plattsburgh.[1] Sostre arrived in court that day having just been gang-raped and beaten by seven guards at nearby Clinton Prison. Watching him shuffle into the courtroom with tight shackles around his ankles left a lifelong imprint on the two young college students. Rodríguez remembered it as being "like watching slavery right before my eyes."[2] Sostre noticed the two young potential comrades across the wooden railing that separated them. "His large eyes and kind face looked bright and hopeful with surprise when he turned toward Antonio and me," Browne said. "It was the most penetrating gaze I ever got from anybody." Sostre quickly explained his situation and the need for local support. "He was warm yet grave in his urgent delivery," she recalled. "We walked out of that courtroom totally changed."[3] They decided to start a local defense committee.

After being supported by a single, centralized committee in Buffalo since his arrest in 1967, Sostre reconfigured his defense campaign during the final years of his imprisonment to a "federation" of autonomous groups that could work to secure his release from prison while acting as revolutionary bases for future-oriented struggle. When the Plattsburgh defense committee was formed that summer, there were only a few others scattered across the country. By late 1975, there were nearly a dozen.[4] The groups participated in street protests, vigils, and sit-ins; produced and distributed pamphlets and newsletters; raised funds through yard sales, concerts, and poetry benefits; circulated petitions and made phone calls; conducted letter-writing campaigns; and provided support in the courtroom. They also engaged in political education, which in some instances led to new political formations and campaigns. This structural reformulation epitomized Sostre's growing identification with revolutionary anarchism, which he conceptualized as a movement for collective liberation from all forms of oppression beginning with the individual. He explained to committee member Dan Georgakas: "Only when the people's revolutionary spirit is liberated from the strictures of the party line straight jacket and given free rein will the real revolutionary liberation struggle take place."[5]

The anarchist concept of prefigurative politics became central to Sostre's new political philosophy. The term is frequently attributed to social scientist Carl Boggs, who used it in 1977 to describe the "embodiment, within the ongoing political practice of a movement, of those forms of social relations, decision-making, culture, and human experience that are the ultimate goal."[6] Sostre was putting it into practice years earlier, describing it simply to one comrade: "If we do it right, it will end up right."[7] Prefiguration represented an explicit rejection of the rigidity of Marxism and the hierarchal state centralism of Leninism and Trotskyism. Although it implicitly rejected the vanguardist claim that revolution would come "from the outside" through the leadership of an advanced cadre, which Sostre had recently endorsed in "The New Prisoner," he was primarily concerned that revolutionary struggle not reproduce the fundamental flaws of the present order.[8] As he wrote one supporter, "I believe that it is indispensable that we have such a network now not only in readiness to supplant this dying repressive State but to speed its demise. Otherwise, the repressive capitalist State will be replaced by an authoritarian State and we will have to go through the same shit all over again."[9]

During the summer of 1975, in Sostre's introductory letter to a new comrade, Karen St. Hilaire of Potsdam, New York, he commended her on leaving law school and praised her understanding that "law is oppression codified." He then succinctly laid out an analysis of his past and future struggles, emphasizing that they must "organize structures or bases that are prototypes of the society we want to build. Without living, objective examples to expand the consciousness of the people and to which they can relate, no new society will replace the present exploitative one." "It is with this in mind," he wrote, "that the network of Martin Sostre Defense Committees are being organized."[10]

Historian Andrew Cornell identifies three types of prefigurative practice: personal, institutional, and organizational. The first is enacted in individual choices that stand outside social norms in order to inspire change. "The hope has always been that the nonconformist acts of a few will inspire a critical mass of imitators," writes Cornell. We can see this approach in Sostre's emphasis on propaganda of the deed and refusals to shave or submit to rectal assaults. The second is the formation of counter-institutions, such as free schools and cooperatives, that provide concrete, functional alternatives to capitalism and private property. Sostre imagined the defense committees would set up these exemplary structures, and he later expanded upon this idea by recommending the seizure of abandoned property to develop cooperative apartments, groceries, dry cleaners, and bars.[11] Forming a chain of radical bookstores continued to play a central role in his vision. "We'll never be able to compete with the oppressive state if we don't have a counter structure—a visible one, however small it may be," he urged.[12] The third is a mass organizational strategy whereby groups model the principles they hope to instill in a new revolutionary society in the belief that these organizations will "actually grow into the governing institutions of postrevolutionary social order."[13] The new federation of defense committees operated on, and experimented with, principles of horizontal, collective egalitarianism. The experiences of the Canton-Potsdam defense committee documented in this chapter give an intimate, if partial, view of these commitments and how they unfolded.

Sostre envisioned all these prefigurative elements as interconnected. "I saw my defense committees as a structure for the future," he explained, a "microcosm of the society that we're trying to build. Something concrete to show the people instead of just rhetoric."[14] Revolution would emerge first within the dominant order of an exploitative society, rather than as a singular historical event or spontaneous uprising absent the hard work of organizing. "I don't believe in no magic," he said, "that all of the sudden it's going to come out of the sky or from the ground. I believe it's going to take hard work. We're going to have to lay the foundation. We're going to have to construct it. We're going to have to act *as if* . . . In other words, we're going to have to show something tangible in order to get people to come to our side."[15] Ideally, these three forms of action would flow into one another. The principles the committees put into practice internally and the counter-institutions they created would provide the basis for revolutionary transformation of the entire society: politically, economically, and socially. At what Cornell calls the point of transition between "mid-twentieth-century anarchism and contemporary anarchism," Martin Sostre outlined his defense committees through a layered and multidimensional version of prefigurative politics, a mode of organizing that the historian argues has "become a defining characteristic of contemporary anarchism."[16]

Through demonstrations, pickets, letter-writing, sit-ins, petitions, and other forms of public advocacy—and drawing upon the Catholic left, renewed interest in US-based anarchism, and both veteran and neophyte organizers—Martin Sostre formulated one of the most successful anarchist defense campaigns in US history, which won his own emancipation against seemingly insurmountable odds while laying the groundwork for broader struggles to come.

In late December 1973, Martin Sostre appeared in New York City federal court to testify on behalf of Silas Davis, a prisoner seeking $125,000 in damages for beatings he survived while in solitary confinement at Green Haven Prison. As had now become customary, Sostre was assaulted on his way to court for refusing the rectal "examination."[17] Many of the details in Davis's case mirrored those Sostre had brought before Judge Motley. The ironies of the situation are almost too sordid to list. Sostre was beaten en route to testify about abuses similar to those he had suffered while held in the same solitary confinement cells for 372 consecutive days; the suit was heard in the same courthouse where he had won the landmark case that deemed this practice "dehumanizing in the sense that it is needlessly degrading."[18] Meanwhile, he endured his fifth assault in nearly fourteen months in solitary confinement, surpassing his earlier isolation at Green Haven in its duration and brutality. "They want complete submission," he explained in court when asked why he was in solitary for refusing to shave his beard. "They have taken everything that I have. . . . The only thing that you have left is your personality, and they even try to take that." Sostre told the judge that "there is no end in sight. I have 30 years to go, so that could very well mean 30 years in solitary confinement."[19]

For more than a decade, Sostre had used the courts to air grievances and unveil the otherwise-hidden violence of the prison. He believed that public exposure and legal rulings could at minimum provide cover and room for revolutionary prisoners like himself to maneuver against repression. But the state's counter-organizing had narrowed this window. After one beating, Sostre asked an unsympathetic judge not to summon him to court unless absolutely necessary: "The prison officials are using my court appearances to brutalize me in retaliation for my legal success against them."[20] Whereas legal precedent and the commonsense logic of the hands-off doctrine had once been enough to prevent prisoners from accessing the courts, they now used clubs and rape to intimidate would-be litigants.

It was becoming clear to Sostre that he would never secure his release through the courts. After a legal appeal in late 1973 knocked a decade off his sentence, Sostre wrote mockingly: "Break out the champagne and start celebrating for now my sentence ends in 1997 instead of the year 2008."[21] In March 1974, after Judge Curtin denied Sostre's habeas corpus application, more than one hundred people demonstrated against Governor Rockefeller outside the Statler Hilton demanding Sostre's release.[22] A coalition under the auspices of the New York City Martin Sostre Defense Committee vowed to intensify its activities.[23]

Although Sostre never abandoned the courts as an arena of struggle, the expansion of his defense committees signaled his realization that only immense public pressure could secure his release. It also reflected his disillusionment with the democratic centralism of Marxism-Leninism and his shift toward anarchism. His experiences with organizations such as the Nation of Islam and the Workers World Party had demonstrated the pitfalls of decision-making concentrated in the hands of one person or small group. He believed that hierarchical organizations co-opted people's natural revolutionary tendencies and produced uncritical subjects bound to inaction by ideology. Sostre had witnessed people whose consciousness was raised by deeds, only to have their energy captured by organizations and "quickly de-anarchized, straight-jacketed with the party-line and perverted into mindless robots programmed to obey unquestioning every directive issued by the super-ideologue party leader."[24]

Another reason for the shift was security. Although he could not have known about the surveillance of anticommunist crusader Ruth Matthews or the FBI informant documenting WWP meetings, Sostre had witnessed the impact of state infiltration on Black Power organizations and had been surveilled and framed himself. In 1975, he warned the other defense committees that a friend of Sharon Fischer in Buffalo was an FBI informant and advised them not to "divulge any confidential information to the members of the Buffalo D.C."[25] He understood that "all the pigs have to do is infiltrate the headquarters and they have the files of everyone, all the activity of the whole network." Reorganizing his defense committee structure addressed what he now saw as the limitations of centralized organizing and litigation, and expressed his conviction that a decentralized network of autonomous groups could fight for his emancipation while simultaneously building bases for broader, multidimensional struggle. In retrospect, Sostre considered the reorganization of his defense committees his first experiment in intentional anarchist organizing. "I have been trying to live an anarchist life on a personal level," he reflected, "but it was never tested in a concrete form until this defense committee was organized."[26]

The month after Sostre was denied a new trial by Judge Curtin, a New York City–based committee held a meeting at St. Mark's Church outlining a plan to establish a bookstore to act as the physical center of its activities and to make the recently completed *Frame-Up!* "available for defense use."[27] A few months later, community organizations gathered on the Lower East Side with food and music to watch one of the first public screenings of the film and to celebrate the grand opening of a final bookstore dedicated to Martin Sostre and called simply, "In Exile."[28] The all-day block party's invited guests included Angela Davis, Jitu Weisu, Gilberto *Gerena-Valentín,* Gil Noble, and Felipe Luciano.[29]

The latest (and final) bookstore-in-exile marked a renewed effort to create a physical base for political education and defense activities, which had been absent since Sostre's break with the WWP in 1970. The space was also part of a growing connection between Sostre and the Puerto Rican activist community. Established by Sostre's former comrade at Wallkill, Víctor Sanchez, and his partner María, the bookstore was located at 240 East Fourth Street in the heart of "Loisaida," a Nuyorican pronunciation of "Lower East Side" coined by poet "Bimbo" Rivas the same year the bookstore formed. Just months after opening, the Sanchezes posted a letter in *Claridad*, a Spanish-language socialist newspaper and official publication of the independence movement based in San Juan.[30] That May 1974, Sostre dissolved the defense committees led by Dan Georgakas and Ernest Nassar and ordered all funds and letters be forwarded to the recently formed New York City committee at the "In Exile" bookstore.[31] "Nothing has changed. I am in the box in the same cell," Sostre wrote that summer. "However, I am many times better off politically and legally than I was before."[32]

When reformulating his defense committees, as in all his political work, Sostre was not dogmatic about party lines or political affiliations. The early NYC committee was comprised of a constellation of organizations including the Puerto Rican Socialist Party, the *Internationalist* newsletter, the Interboro New American Movement, and the Pacific Street Film Collective. Some members were drawn to his anarchism, while others remained completely unaware of it. But as a prominent political prisoner and almost solitary Black anarchist, Sostre increasingly attracted interest from a growing, if dispersed, anarchist movement while also helping to develop and expand it. As Andrew Cornell notes, "Interest in anarchism grew in tandem with the constellation of radical social movements that fundamentally altered American society during the 'long 1960s.' " But unlike earlier periods where mass organizations and publications promoted anarchist ideas for decades, they now "came diffusely, through many channels . . . [as] activists rediscovered parts of the anarchist tradition and experimented with them."[33]

The Catholic Worker Movement's interest in supporting Sostre exemplifies this trend. Founded in New York City during the Great Depression by Dorothy Day and Peter Maurin, the movement was an unlikely synthesis of the teachings of the Christian gospels and secular anarchism. "Participants combined direct service to the hungry and homeless with nonviolent protest activity," Cornell writes. "They saw themselves working simultaneously in traditions established by Jesus Christ and the Industrial Workers of the World."[34] Around the time of his first assault in May 1973, perhaps after hearing of his struggle through an anarchist conference in Toronto days earlier, Dorothy Day wrote a letter to Sostre.[35] Soon, the *Catholic Worker* newspaper began publishing updates on his situation.[36] Lutheran pastor Dennis Jacobsen, who had recently moved to Plattsburgh to form a campus ministry, read about Sostre in its pages and joined the emerging local defense committee.

A Catholic peace group and a secular advocate of armed struggle may seem like strange bedfellows, but there were ample reasons for the Catholic Worker Movement to rally around Sostre's case. For one, the movement was founded on a commitment to moral acts of conscience, such as tax and war resistance, which often led to political imprisonment.[37] Moreover, its autonomous network of "houses of hospitality," which began by providing shelter, food, and clothing during the Depression, mirrored some of the aspirational ideas of creating autonomous bases embedded in Sostre's committees. One founder of a Catholic Worker house was Jesuit priest Daniel Berrigan, who wrote Jacobsen in November 1973 that he was "now in touch with Martin. He writes glowingly of your committee and work."[38]

By then, Berrigan was a well-known peace activist and former political prisoner, and he became a crucial supporter during Sostre's final years in prison. Berrigan and his younger brother Philip were contemporaries of Sostre, born in 1921 and 1923 respectively, in a small iron mining town in Minnesota. The two came to national prominence in 1968 when they led a group of Catholic activists (later known as the Catonsville Nine) into a draft board office in Maryland, seized over three hundred files, and set them on fire using homemade napalm.[39] Despite their differing views on nonviolence, the Berrigans and Sostre had much in common and were particularly well situated to understand Sostre's resistance due to their own political imprisonment. In 1974, Phil Berrigan wrote to Sostre that he was reading Ammon Hennacy's "book of essays on Thoreau, Paine, Berkman, Mother Jones," whom it described as anarchists. He continued, "Too bad he didn't live to add one or two chapters. One would be yours."[40]

During Dan Berrigan's eighteen months in Danbury Federal Prison, he wrote in his diary: "There is no guarantee of political or personal success. There is rather a sense of 'rightness,' of standing within history in way that confers health and creates spiritual continuity."[41] Although Berrigan did not resist the strip search with the same intransigence as Sostre, one anecdote from his comrade Jim Forest recalls the spirit with which he approached time in prison. "As Dan and I were standing next to each other and performing the syncopated, comical dance of opening our mouths and sticking out our tongues, running our fingers through our hair, lifting our balls, turning around, bending over and spreading our cheeks," remembered Forest, "Dan says to me, 'Keep smiling. When they've gotten your smile, they've gotten too much [of your spirit].'"[42] The story at once demonstrates a shared emphasis with Sostre on maintaining one's personhood as a critical form of resistance in prison and the disproportionate violence meted out against Black revolutionaries as compared to their white counterparts.[43]

The Berrigans were experienced in nonviolent civil disobedience and political theater. The Catonsville Nine used their trial as Sostre did his courtroom appearances: as a "morality play, a celebration, [and] a massive teach-in." With guidance from their radical attorney, William Kunstler, they offered a political defense by refusing to participate in jury selection and formed a local defense committee to raise funds and organize support.[44] Even the symbolic, theatrical action of burning draft records with homemade napalm had embodied propaganda of the deed. As Phil Berrigan noted, "Dan is a superior propagandist."[45] Shortly after making contact with Sostre, Dan Berrigan wrote Jacobsen with a list of ideas for his campaign, including holding vigils outside the warden's home, sending a delegation to Buffalo to confront Judge Curtin, and putting pressure on Amnesty International.[46]

Dan Berrigan proved to be a formidable fundraiser for Sostre's campaign, using his connections to raise thousands of dollars for local defense committees in Buffalo and Plattsburgh.[47] In the process of soliciting these donations, he found that some leftists did not recognize the connection between Sostre's acts of resistance in prison and revolutionary struggle. In November 1974, he sent a request to philanthropists Carol and W. H. "Ping" Ferry. The couple were known for supporting political prisoners and radical organizations, and especially valued giving direct grassroots support. Ping Ferry replied that they had no objections to funding Sostre's campaign, but he also included a critique of "self-inflicting martyrs" like Sostre that he borrowed from Detroit organizers James "Jimmy" Boggs and Grace Lee Boggs (without naming them). In fact, Ferry's indication that these were the arguments of a "Black friend," referring to Jimmy, masked Grace's role in this critique, as well as her position as a Chinese American woman. Ferry then alerted Jimmy and Grace, should they "want to take on Dan Berrigan directly."[48]

The Boggses, who had supported Sostre since his original frame-up, took the opportunity to critique Sostre's actions, writing that they believed he was "behaving like a martyr" and "building a Sostre movement." In their response, which they apparently conveyed to Sostre in a message "along the lines" of their letter to Berrigan, they questioned the premise that someone could build a revolutionary movement from inside prison and saw his actions as part of a broader "victim complex" hampering Black communities.[49] The Boggses' response was rooted in their misunderstanding of Attica as fundamentally a call for prison reform.

As their biographer Stephen Ward points out, "Their central critique was that activists who considered themselves revolutionary were mistakenly hailing Attica as 'the highest stage of revolutionary struggle' the movement had reached to date. Such a view, the Boggses argued, was misplaced because it confused '*militant struggles to reform*' prisons with the '*revolutionary struggle*' to transform the entire society."[50]

Dan Berrigan was sensitive to critiques that certain activists sought martyrdom, as it was a charge that had been leveled at him. He also acknowledged they were not the first to raise such questions about Sostre. But unlike the Boggses, he had met with Sostre for hours the previous summer to discuss his actions.[51] Berrigan believed "resistance in prison is valuable to those who resist outside" and emphasized to the Boggses the importance of imprisoned people deciding for themselves what actions were necessary to preserve their dignity. He assured them that Sostre was "struggling simultaneously at personal survival and a prisoners' movement." Elsewhere, he confided that he considered their view of Sostre "pretty disgraceful."[52]

Daniel Berrigan with his student Bill Wylie-Kellerman (to his left) at a demonstration in February 1974. Photo by Pat Barile. Box 19d, Shoot 740015, *Daily Worker* Negative Collection, Tamiment Library.

The debate between Daniel Berrigan and the Boggses underscores the ongoing question over the meaning of the Attica revolt in the revolutionary movements of this period. If understood primarily through what Sostre called the "Attica reform demands," as the Boggses did, the uprising was little more than a call for more "humane" forms of imprisonment.[53] But, as Orisanmi Burton has labored to show, the Attica rebellion was an expression of "abolitionist worldmaking" and the state's retaking was rooted in the racialized sexual violence Sostre was resisting.[54] For Sostre, these meanings were clear. Prisons were "revolutionary training camps for cadres of the Black liberation struggle," and Attica had set in motion the "dynamic revolutionary forces that will effect the overthrow of [the]racist-capitalist system."[55]

The backdrop to this debate between Berrigan and the Boggses was Sostre's own life-and-death struggle. The month Berrigan made his request, Sostre was beaten three times, twice on the same day. He described being taken to a clothing room in the cellar of the administration building on November 4, 1974, by eight guards. They held him in a chokehold until he was unable to breathe. Finally, he became unconscious. "My lungs and throat were bursting with excruciating pain—I was deliberately being suffocated." When he woke on a stretcher, he tried to ask the nurse for pain medication but was "startled at the sound of my voice . . . because it came out in a whisper." He was then handcuffed, manacled with chains on his waist, leg-ironed, and taken to court. Spectators in court saw bruises on his head, and he was unable to speak throughout the hearing.[56] Back at Clinton, Sostre was met by nine guards, where he refused another exam and had his bare foot stomped on and likely fractured. "Thus today I absorbed my 6th and 7th assaults," he wrote. "Two new elements were introduced making today's brutalizations more vicious and sadistic than all the others: strangulation into unconsciousness and kicking me while on the floor."[57]

The Ferrys ultimately found merit in both Berrigan's and the Boggses' arguments and wrote a substantial check for $2,000 (the equivalent of $11,000 today) to the Martin Sostre Defense Committee, which Berrigan promptly gave to the Plattsburgh group to support the upcoming trial.[58] But the misgivings the Boggses raised about Sostre's actions revealed fault lines within the revolutionary left and the difficulty Sostre faced in making clear the connection between his personal resistance and worldwide revolutionary struggle. His belief that individual resistance could move people toward revolutionary action, however, was soon put to the test. In the Plattsburgh trial, Sostre faced a judge and jury drawn from the conservative small town.

In early February 1975, Sostre was again transported fewer than a dozen miles from Clinton Prison to the county jail in Plattsburgh. There, he soon stood trial for his self-defense in the May 1973 assault and faced a potential second life sentence. Just across Lake Champlain from Vermont and thirty miles south of the Canadian border, Plattsburgh was an overwhelmingly white town with a population under twenty thousand. Antonio Rodríguez recalled being called the N-word for the first time in his life by a child shortly after he arrived there. When he moved to Plattsburgh in the early 1970s with long hair and wearing dashikis, his older brother warned him not to reveal he was a Democrat.[59] Plattsburgh's major industries had their origins in US imperialism, labor extraction, and human captivity: a local military base established during the War of 1812 and a prison built during the 1840s that supplied cheap labor to local mines. Over a century later, many of the prison's staff made the short commute from Plattsburgh to nearby Dannemora to work.[60] One sympathizer commented regarding jury selection, "Mr. Sostre has no peers in Clinton County."[61]

Nonetheless, this vibrant defense committee managed to build local support. Since first exchanging words with Sostre in court during the summer of 1973, Rodríguez and Browne had been joined by Antonio's sister, Sylvia, who moved into the couple's spare bedroom. Although the three had little formal organizing experience, all brought valuable skills and backgrounds to the emerging committee. The Rodríguezes had grown up in a political household in the Bronx, with parents who were Puerto Rican migrants close in age to Sostre. Their mother Juana (who used the anglicized "Jenny") was a community activist, and their father Frank was a master carpenter. Both were active in local Democratic clubs; Antonio even canvassed door to door as a kid. Anti-racism and anti-capitalism were frequent topics of discussion at the dinner table.[62] Although Marjorie had a less politicized upbringing, she and her six siblings were among the few Black youth growing up in Plattsburgh, so her childhood was itself a political education.[63] Her mother worked at the air force base, and her father opened a bar called Lloyd's Tavern around the time the committee was formed. Both were respected members of the Plattsburgh community, and the tavern became a popular meeting spot and occasionally served as a place the committee could safely gather and store flyers. Soon, Marjorie's brother Neal began dating Sylvia, and the two couples, along with Professor Kay Branagan and Reverend Jacobsen (known to most as "Jake") formed the core of the defense committee, along with students and community members such as Marilyn Taub, Louis Cafone, Betsy Boehner (now Lapenne), and Janine Migden.

Over the course of nineteen months—between the arraignment in the summer of 1973 and trial in February 1975—the group of fewer than a dozen young people worked energetically and effectively, despite a scarcity of resources. "We never had enough envelopes or enough money for stamps," Sylvia said. "But we got it done. People sometimes would send us a return letter with stamps in it, or five dollars, and that went into making more fliers."[64] Although this committee was close to Clinton Prison, they were not allowed to visit Sostre, because he refused the assaults. They also had trouble writing to him because of prison censorship.[65] At one point, Antonio traveled to New York City with Reverend Jacobsen wearing a collar, pretending to be a Catholic priest from Puerto Rico, so he could visit Sostre while he was briefly held at the federal detention center.[66]

Many of the members were newly politicized or brought into the struggle through their partners. Sylvia would thumb through the phone book, calling local colleges and universities to connect with student groups. For Branagan, the group's eldest member in her mid-twenties, the aim was clear: "Our goal was to organize a revolution." "Some support committees are like groupies," she said, but "we weren't. We were a political organization who felt that this was an important issue, but also saw it as a way to organize the comm\unity."[67] This ambition was reflected in the range of topics covered in the committee's newsletter, *New World Notes*, which began in September 1975. The "people's newspaper" used Sostre's case to raise awareness about a range of struggles, including women's liberation, Indigenous sovereignty, prisoners' rights, Puerto Rican independence, and farmworkers' union organizing.[68]

Through leafletting, panel discussions, local radio appearances, and articles in local and student papers, the Plattsburgh defense committee made the upcoming trial a local and regional flashpoint. Posters of Sostre were plastered across the town explaining his resistance in his own words: “I cannot submit to injustices even minor ones. Once one starts submitting to minor injustices and rationalizes them away, their accumulation creates a major oppression. This is how entire peoples fell into slavery.”[69] The defense committee redirected the stakes of the trial away from Sostre's guilt and toward the community's own complicity in injustice. “Reality is at our doorstep,” Neal Browne wrote in the student paper. “Blocks from our campus, not far from the bars downtown, in an old brown building, the trial will take place, the outcome fairly certain: Martin Sostre will be found guilty . . . [but] the ones who will really be on trial will be Martin Sostre's persecutors, and maybe, ourselves. The choice is ours.”[70] Others in the community wrote letters to the editor about the “special responsibility” Clinton County residents had.[71] As the trial neared in early 1975, Antonio anticipated attendees from Buffalo, Burlington, Montreal, Amherst, and Chicago. He wrote confidently, “The whole world will be watching.”[72]

When jury selection began on February 5, 1975, the committee shifted to providing local support for an influx of national attorneys and activists.[73] Sostre's lawyers were the radical attorneys Dennis Cunningham and Liz Fink, well known at the time for representing the Attica Brothers. They and their legal aides stayed in the apartments of the group's members. Marjorie Browne remembered being shaken awake one day by William Kunstler, then perhaps the country's most recognizable defense attorney.[74] Daniel Berrigan visited the first week of the trial and “galvanized a lot of people.”[75] He met with Sostre in jail, then spoke to a crowd of three hundred at Plattsburgh State, about a quarter of whom marched together from the college to the jail.[76]

With the outcome of the trial likely to be decided by the composition of the jury, members of Sostre's defense committee were tasked with finding out as much as they could about potential jurors.[77] A nearby apartment equipped with a phone and Rolodex served as headquarters. When a juror was called for questioning, committee members scrambled from the courtroom to the apartment to find information on the juror.[78] “There weren't going to be any Black people on the jury at all,” Marjorie recognized. Many potential jurors had ties to the prison; as many as nine were excluded for their relationship to prison staff.[79] Sostre's attempts to question jurors' attitudes toward strip searches and law and order were met with fury. According to one account, the judge "went into a rage, slammed his gavel down in front of Sostre, and threatened to gag him if he spoke again."[80] As in Buffalo, Sostre raised the question of law versus individual conscience. When one young juror said that she would follow her conscience, the district attorney emphasized that she must agree to follow the law rather than her own moral code and she was dismissed. Sostre wrote her a letter that evening thanking her for her courage.[81] In total, 160 potential jurors were called over nearly two weeks. Also as in Buffalo, an all-white group of twelve and four alternates was seated.[82]

Although Sostre faced a life sentence and a system stacked against him, he appeared comfortable and defiant during the proceedings. Marlene Nadle, covering the trial for the *Village Voice*, wrote that he looked "20 years younger than his 51, and radiated the low-key calm of yogi turned revolutionary anarchist." He smiled and chatted with comrades in the audience. For Sostre, the courtroom remained what Nadle called "the revolutionary's forum." The trial made Sostre's everyday resistance visible on a grander scale. Just as his refusal to submit to rectal assaults challenged other imprisoned people to either join in resistance or consent to coercion, the trial forced the people of North Country to face the injustice in their own backyard and decide whether they would turn away. According to Nadle, "The town, or at least a significant minority in it, was meeting Sostre's spiritual challenge. They were demonstrating for the first time in their lives, parading in front of the judge's windows in five-degree-below weather, holding candlelight litanies in the churches, and turning up in court to bear witness in the spectator seats." At the defendant's table, Sostre sat with Cunningham, Fink, and members of the Plattsburgh committee, constantly urging them to broaden the trial beyond himself to the underlying issues of racism and imprisonment. "His head almost always engaged in future actions rather than his own ego," Nadle wrote; "he turned Feinberg's courtroom into organization headquarters."[83]

The state responded with intimidating displays. The atmosphere was tense, and state police, undercover agents, and sheriffs conspicuously packed the courtroom and "lingered obtrusively in the hallways."[84] Judge Feinberg, who "looked like a plump Kissinger and talked like Mr. Magoo," banged his gavel in frequent outbursts of rage.[85] He reserved a special contempt for Sostre. At one point, he said he'd "rather deal with the devil's advocate than the devil," referring to Cunningham and his client.[86] The entire first week of testimony was dedicated to the recollections of the guards who had assaulted Sostre on May 19, 1973, and the prison doctor who had examined them. By the end of the trial, it was clear to everyone there that a guilty verdict was "a foregone conclusion."[87]

A group of supporters gathered the night before the verdict to discuss what could be done. They decided they would stand in silent protest after the verdict came in and Antonio would read a brief statement on the group's behalf. It was already 6:00 p.m. by the time closing arguments ended and the jury convened. After a dinner break and nearly two and a half hours of deliberation, foreperson Thelma Wood emerged with a white piece of paper: "Guilty, on all three counts."[88] It was Antonio's turn. "I hesitated for a long moment before I stood and Martin looked up at me with a questioning look," he remembered.[89] Finally, Antonio stood and began to speak: "We condemn this trial as a frame-up and an example of systematic oppression and express our solidarity and support of Martin Sostre and the struggle for freedom everywhere. We stand because we feel that we are all on trial." Others were torn about whether they should join or not. "I really had a lot of fear," Louis Cafone shared. Then he saw Sostre stand and raise his fist in the air in solidarity. "It gave me the strength to stand."[90] Dozens more joined and raised their fists. Chants of "Free Martin Sostre" began to fill the room. Tom Wielopolski, who been imprisoned with Sostre, cut through the chants when he shouted at the judge, "Fuck you pig."[91] "That is enough, Mr. Wie—" the judge interjected. "Wielopolski, pig," he responded.[92]

Judge Feinberg shouted for arrests, and police flooded the courtroom from all sides. Sylvia Rodríguez, who was five months pregnant, was trying to leave when a court official shouted, "Get that Black girl!"[93] A dozen supporters, most of them local committee members, were handcuffed and taken to jail. Some were transported to the county jail where Sostre was held. Cafone, for example, remembers talking to Sostre through the air vents.[94] Others were transported hours away to Albany due to overcrowding at the local lockup. As Liz Fink later pointed out, the protestors were completely deprived of due process and "taken, not under arrest, but under *sentence*."[95] Following the arrests, the judge turned to the all-white jury and praised them: "Each of you, Ladies and Gentlemen, has performed just like a charm."[96]

Meanwhile, the group that became known as the Plattsburgh Twelve now faced the issue at the heart of the trial: the strip search. Sylvia refused. "Not that I was so radical," she explained, "but I was thinking, what would Martin do?" Eventually, she agreed to have a woman officer search her in separate area but refused to take off her clothing. The cop, whom Sylvia suspected worked at the desk, was visibly nervous and quickly patted her down before leaving.[97] Betsy Boehner, however, was strip-searched. "I was brought into a cell and a female guard was supposed to be strip searching me. And a male guard walked in," she recalled. "All I could think about was, 'Oh my god, I might get raped.' "[98] The men faced a similar decision in Albany. "We knew that it probably would happen, and . . . had a couple minutes to talk about it," Antonio recalled. Fearing that if they resisted, they would be assaulted and charged as Sostre had, the group decided to consent to be searched. "I have to say, we failed that moral test," Rodríguez remembered. "We were ashamed about it."[99]

Attorneys Dennis Cunningham and Liz Fink with protestors outside Clinton Prison, 1975. Courtesy of Ewa and Hania Dubinsky.

We urge you to discontinue the vindictive torture and dehumanization of the rejected law-and-order Rockefeller/Wilson/Preiser regime against Martin Sostre - "Prisoner of Conscience" U.S.A.

We demand an end to his 30-month repression in solitary confinement for wearing a quarter inch long beard; and a halt to beating upon him while forcibly performing rectal searches denounced by federal courts as "dehumanizing" and "needlessly degrading."

We request his immediate transfer from Clinton Prison to one near New York City or Buffalo, near his family, friends and attorneys.

We further request a pardon or commutation of sentence for Martin Sostre the innocent victim of injustice.

From:

To:
Gov. Hugh Carey,
The Capitol,
Albany, N.Y. 12224

MARTIN SOSTRE DEFENSE COMMITTEE, P.O. Box 432, Plattsburgh, N.Y. 12901

Postcards demanding an end to Sostre's torture and a commutation of his sentence, c. 1975. Courtesy of Ewa and Hania Dubinsky.

Sostre was often frustrated by people's willingness to champion his resistance while not taking the same risks. The defense committee members who were arrested spent eight days in the county jail, made bail when a wealthy local woman donated the funds, and all but three had their sentences reduced to time served. Before these arrests for protesting the verdict, Sostre described other prisoners "like spectators sitting at ringside cheering their fighter, but afraid of becoming boxers themselves because they can't take the punishment."[100] While legitimate, this did not always capture the full picture. Many took tremendous risks to their personal safety, particularly those who testified against the state. After Jimmy Sullivan, who had been incarcerated with Sostre and witnessed the May 1973 assault, signed several affidavits recounting what he had seen, his house was firebombed and his parole was revoked. He wound up re-institutionalized, and doctors suggested he was paranoid.[101] A letter to Plattsburgh defense committee member Dennis Jacobsen a few months before the 1975 trial reveals the pressure he was under. Sullivan claimed the parole board had offered to release him if he signed a conflicting affidavit saying he was locked in his cell the day of the assault. "In other words Jake, I'd have to commit perjury to be set free. They want Martin pretty badly I guess," he wrote. "I suppose if I did I could never look at myself in the mirror again or face my peers or you. A man should not be put under such pressure in these bastilles."[102] Jimmy Sullivan and Arto Williams both testified against the state on Sostre's behalf in successive years, and both faced repression, criminal charges, and further incarceration for doing so.

Judged narrowly, it would be easy to deem Plattsburgh a defeat. Sostre was convicted on all counts, and key members of his defense committee were jailed. Many of his own committee members even felt they had failed the test presented to them. But nestled within those apparent losses were seeds of new formations and possibilities. First, the public pressure mounted before and during the trial likely prevented Sostre from receiving the life sentence that New York's persistent felon laws allowed. Furthermore, that a group of a dozen young people went to jail protesting the racist frame-up they had witnessed in court and then considered the refusal of the strip search to be a moral litmus test—whether they had resisted it or not—demonstrates the effectiveness of Sostre's efforts to bring the repression of those in prison to the consciousness and experience of those outside. These comrades did not simply bear witness to these injustices; they now willingly faced imprisonment and struggled with the implications of their actions and inaction. The trial's authoritarian conclusion accentuated what they had witnessed throughout. People saw friends and students in handcuffs for the first time.[103]

With the punishment to a Black political prisoner radiating outward to those in solidarity with him, others in the predominantly white North Country were prompted to question the reach and design of the criminal legal system. Almost a year after the trial, the committee wrote in its newsletter that "the case of Martin Sostre was not just the case of Martin Sostre. It dealt with many issues, touched many lives. Particularly in Clinton County it had tremendous social and legal implications. It exposed the inhuman conditions at Clinton Prison, made the citizens see the ugly reality of institutionalized violence and racism. . . . For many, the mask was off."[104] As in his 1968 trial in Buffalo, the events in Plattsburgh laid bare the fascism of the legal system and radicalized those who attended.

One of those in attendance was Joel Ray, a professor at nearby Clarkson University who, having recently been denied tenure, opened a coffee shop, bookstore, and music venue called Giant Steps in Potsdam, New York. For Ray, the issue at stake was power. "Sostre has been framed, imprisoned, harassed and beaten because he understands power and wants others to understand it," he wrote. "Ask yourself whether Martin Sostre's struggle is not your own."[105] Following Sostre's sentencing that March, Ray and others encouraged people interested in starting a committee in St. Lawrence County to meet at the bookstore. A constellation of defense committees across North Country soon emerged, drawing energy and outrage from what they had experienced in Plattsburgh.

Potsdam, slightly smaller than Plattsburgh and nearly two hours to the east, was home to four universities (the State University of New York at Potsdam, Clarkson, St. Lawrence University, and nearby SUNY Canton), as well as a few burgeoning communes. Interest in a Martin Sostre Defense Committee began early in 1975 after Antonio and others visited Potsdam State to screen *Frame-Up!* and talk about the upcoming trial in Plattsburgh. Many from the area attended, and two hundred people watched the documentary. After an hour and half of discussion, they announced an organizing meeting for the Canton-Potsdam committee at Ray's bookstore. Members of the newly formed group went on their local radio station to spread awareness about Sostre's case. All credited the Plattsburgh trial as a radicalizing moment. "The political structure is not what I thought it was," said Joan Lomba, a farmer from a local commune. "More things open to me every day."[106] Karen St. Hilaire, then studying criminal justice, recalled that it "was quite shocking to really be faced with the fact that our ideals weren't a reality."[107] "It was a demoralizing, disillusioning experience for all of us," Clarkson math professor Ed Dubinsky explained.[108]

Over the final ten months before Sostre's commutation, the Canton-Potsdam defense committee became one of the most active in a nationwide network.[109] The group played a crucial role in expanding and intensifying a campaign that now stretched from Buffalo in the west through Rochester and Syracuse in the Finger Lakes and central regions, north to Watertown, Canton-Potsdam, and Plattsburgh, and south to Albany and New York City. That spring, Sostre decided to make Potsdam the central mailing hub.[110] He even began scouring the classified ads and spoke with a builder about his plans to cooperatively purchase land in North Country to establish an "egalitarian non-profit commune-oriented society that will replace the present exploitative capitalist one."[111]

Like Plattsburgh, the Canton-Potsdam committee was a mix of veteran organizers and the newly politicized. St. Hilaire, for example, was shocked when she read *The Crime of Martin Sostre*. "Wow, does this really go on?" she wondered.[112] Others, such as Dubinsky and his partner Andrzeja, were more experienced. Dubinsky already had a decade of organizing under his belt. As an undergrad at Temple University during the 1950s, he had supported Democratic candidate Adlai Stevenson, later working on the presidential campaign of John F. Kennedy while a PhD student in mathematics at the University of Michigan. "In college I was at best liberal but then I went to teach in West Africa for two years," he wrote to Sostre. There, Dubinsky became politicized when he met author Julian Mayfield and other African American expatriates while in Ghana and heard Malcolm X speak in 1964.[113] Returning to the US, Dubinsky worked with the Congress of Racial Equality to establish a Freedom School as part of Mississippi Freedom Summer. "My radicalization continued," he explained, as he took a teaching position at Tulane University in New Orleans while traveling back to Laurel, Mississippi, three days a week to register people to vote.[114]

For his attempts to register Black voters, Dubinsky was beaten up by white supremacists, then arrested and convicted of assault. He explained to Sostre that because of this, it was "very hard" for him "to deal with people who doubt your total innocence."[115] At Tulane, Dubinsky became the faculty adviser to the university chapter of Students for a Democratic Society, explaining that "the job of a revolutionary is to attempt to win over as many people as he can to his way of thinking."[116] After five years at the university, and despite having tenure, Dubinsky was fired for his role in organizing against the Army's Reserve Officer Training Corps on campus.[117] While teaching in Poland, he met a chemist named Andrzeja Axt, who would have been fired from her research position at Warsaw University as part of a purge of Jewish intellectuals had she not been pregnant.[118]

Born in Belgium in 1937, following her leftist parents' flight from political repression during the 1920s, Axt was active in the Union of Polish Youth (ZMP), a communist organization for those aged fourteen to thirty-five. "I was fanatically involved in what I thought was a fight for a new world of equality," she wrote.[119] However, she was deeply disillusioned by the atrocities of Stalin and left the organization. During these years, her family was targeted in Poland, where she was beaten up and her mother was fired for being Jewish. "I suffered personally both physically and emotionally very badly from the antisemitic movement," Axt recalled. After earning a master's degree in chemistry, she was almost fired from her job at the University of Warsaw due to antisemitism, before eventually leaving Poland in 1972 to live with Dubinsky in the United States. There, she joined a women's group that grew organic food at a nearby commune and started volunteering with an experimental school on campus.[120] Both were searching for political community and purpose in rural New York when they became involved in supporting Sostre. As Ed Dubinsky explained in an introductory letter, "I have been here 3 years and I am still trying to make my contribution to the struggle."[121]

A series of surviving letters between Sostre and Dubinsky during the crucial three months between his conviction and sentencing offers an on-the-ground view of how this network of autonomous bases developed. Within them, debates unfolded over committee autonomy and collectivity, consensus versus majority rule, and the relationship between organizing for Sostre's individual emancipation and opposition to all forms of state domination. A palpable energy and optimism pervaded their correspondence. Dubinsky and others had found a renewed sense of purpose and a vehicle for their organizing. "You have already done much more for us than we have done for you," he wrote Sostre.[122] The following month, Sostre wrote with excitement: "Imagine where we'll be at one year from now!!"[123]

Each defense committee was autonomous, connected loosely by Sostre at the center. They controlled their own finances but would sometimes donate to others as needed. They all shared a basic formula outlined by Sostre: all money raised was divided in a two-to-one ratio between a savings and checking account. The former, which would earn interest, was a bail fund for the eventuality of a reversed conviction, when he would need to post bail. The latter would cover operating expenses such as stamps, printing, and long-distance calls.[124] Sostre had become frustrated from years of uneven, and sometimes unwilling, communication between older committees.[125] "Although each D.C. is autonomous," he explained to Dubinsky, "the interchange of information, literature and ideas between them is essential not only for communication and coordination of their major activities, but for building and reinforcing the revolutionary solidarity and élan without which an army of liberation cannot hope to defeat the oppressive State."[126] The interconnected and concentrated growth of the New York committees fueled camaraderie and collaboration. This would prove crucial as they coordinated a demonstration called "Break the Chains" at the state capitol that April 1975.[127]

The rally marked a year to the day since a coalition had gathered in New York City with plans to intensify and expand the network of committees. Now, the protest signaled a new direction: the fight for clemency.[128] A few years earlier, Franz Leichter was making his routine visit to Clinton Prison's Unit 14 when someone yelled from their cell, "Who are you?" When Leichter explained that he was a state assembly member, the person identified themselves as Martin Sostre and handed him a stack of legal papers.[129] A few years later, Leichter testified in Plattsburgh as a character witness. Now, he played a behind-the-scenes role pushing for a commutation by Governor Hugh Carey.[130]

Coordinated between half a dozen committees, including a chartered bus from Plattsburgh, around fifty people marched around the statehouse on April 21, 1975. Finally, state officials emerged from the building and met with representatives of the group, which included contingents from Plattsburgh, Potsdam, and Syracuse. Dubinsky wrote Sostre that the "the face of Martin Sostre was paraded around the Capitol building and plastered across the *Albany Times-Union*." Perhaps as importantly, members from these different North Country committees gathered over dinner afterward. Tom Wielopolski even came to Potsdam to stay with the Dubinskys for a few days. "It is a deep experience for me and profoundly important to find someone like Tom that I can relate to so strongly both personally and politically," Ed related to Sostre.[131] A few weeks later, he reported that they were "really developing some solidarity between Syracuse and Potsdam."[132]

But others, including Andrzeja, found Wielopolski's style domineering and raised questions about decision making among the committees. In a letter she likely never mailed, she wrote Sostre that "Tom whenever he comes tries to impose force, discipline, votings . . . 'collective decisions' as he calls it." She believed such decision-making forced people who disagree or were at different stages of political development to submit to the will of the majority. This more closely mirrored the democratic centralism of the Marxist-Leninist groups Sostre had left behind than the network of anarchist collectives he was trying to now develop. "He does not understand that by doing that he will just replace one form of oppression by another." According to her letter, a similar tension existed within the Plattsburgh group. "They could not understand that Potsdam does not vote, or hardly ever votes—that we talk and discuss and feel each other [out] till a collective decision can be made without the force of voting."[133] The Potsdam group also began to discuss hierarchies developing within the group. "There was considerable discussion at our meeting this week (and before) about the form of our group," Dubinsky wrote Sostre. "Several people (including me) felt that I had been lately taking too strong a role at meetings, preparing the agenda and running the meetings." The group decided that the agenda would be collectively decided and meetings would have a rotating chair. "In my opinion, this is a concrete step towards practicing anarchism and making ourselves into a model to begin to develop the forms that will be used after the revolution," he shared.[134] Through such discussions about horizontal organizing and, at least implicitly, male chauvinism and leadership, the Canton-Potsdam committee experimented with prefiguration, autonomy, and collectivism.

The letters between Ed and Martin captured the seeds of organizing that they hoped would blossom with Sostre's release. Early in the group's formation, a spontaneous discussion emerged about what had drawn them to the group. For most, it was the galvanizing force of Sostre's indomitable spirit. "We read some of your statements and talked about your life a little," Dubinsky wrote him. "In general there was the feeling that it was your crusade and your example that was bringing us together. Some people saw it as following your leadership, for others it was your challenge of the system in its most insidious form—the prisons, and still others talked about this being one of the most important examples of many forms of oppression."[135] The two discussed the pace of people's radicalization and the need to broaden their understanding of the forces at play. "Sooner or later we must widen the struggle to include all forms of state oppression," Dubinsky wrote. "But I don't want to push the committee too far but rather work with the group as we pass through our radicalization at the fastest possible pace."[136] Sostre agreed, but he also reminded Dubinsky that "revolutionary struggle is a multi-dimensional struggle; we must eventually broaden our struggle horizontally as well as deepen it vertically."[137] From Jefferson County Jail, while awaiting sentencing, he continued to do just that—drafting motions for a local case concerning the discriminatory jury selection process, connecting with the Watertown chapter of the National Organization for Women, and proposing grant funding for a recreation area on the third floor of the jail under the state's new so-called "humanization program."[138]

Children of the Potsdam-Canton Martin Sostre Defense Committee. Courtesy of Ewa and Hania Dubinsky.

After months of waiting, members of the New York committees gathered again in Plattsburgh on June 3, 1975, for Sostre's sentencing. There, Judge Feinberg called Sostre "schizoid and psychopathic" and sentenced him to 0–4 years, an indeterminate sentence that was added to his existing sentence from the Buffalo frame-up. Sostre pointed out that the people of Clinton County had been "bought off" by the economic benefits of the prison, but he did not consider the sentence a defeat: "Many talk of freedom, but no one has gained freedom without paying the price. So I'm happy about the whole thing." He explained to Feinberg and the entire courtroom, "I was not thinking of myself, I was thinking of all prisoners being brutalized by crimes in that concentration camp in Clinton. . . . I'm part of a world-wide struggle, I don't see myself isolated. All we want is an egalitarian society based on true justice [for which] I, and many others, am ready to give up our lives."[139] After the sentencing, the committees drove to Clinton Prison to protest outside. "We all stood there," Andrzeja Dubinsky wrote, "Plattsburgh, Potsdam, Buffalo, Syracuse in a great demonstration united by that monstrous wall."[140]

Just weeks after sentencing, Sostre wrote that "the cumulative effect of years of struggle seem now on the verge of bearing fruit. Conditions have never been as favorable for my release."[141] He was recently transferred to federal custody in New York City and, according to Berrigan, the move "was absolutely crucial. His presence electrified everything."[142] Meanwhile, his supporters were following Governor Carey across the state to apply pressure surrounding his clemency campaign. On June 15, 1975, two dozen demonstrators from Plattsburgh and Potsdam picketed outside the Clinton County Democratic Organization and presented Carey with a petition.[143] A few days later, Daniel Berrigan and twenty supporters calling themselves the "Interfaith Committee of Concern" occupied Governor Carey's office in Albany for seven hours demanding amnesty for Sostre.[144] "The only way these guys will pay attention to this case if after considerable public pressure is applied," Berrigan said.[145]

Berrigan and others formalized a Committee to Free Martin Sostre in New York City that fall, which he cochaired with Assemblywoman Marie Runyon and activist and actor Ossie Davis and coordinated with Reverend Paul Mayer. Betsy Boehner of the Plattsburgh Twelve, who had recently moved to the city, joined as part-time staff.[146] They hoped to "make this committee the focal point of a mass campaign for executive clemency," Runyon explained.[147] With considerably more resources and connections than any defense committee to date, the group gained support from political figures and celebrities.[148] The list of those championing Sostre's cause now included Ralph Abernathy, Noam Chomsky, Angela Davis, Michel Foucault, Jean Genet, Allen Ginsberg, Jean-Paul Sartre, Benjamin Spock, prominent radical attorneys and journalists, and other antiwar, labor, and human rights organizations.[149] One letter calling for his release was cosigned by Attorney General Ramsey Clark, comedian Dick Gregory, and musician Joan Baez.[150]

This widening support capitalized on Sostre being named the only "prisoner of conscience" in the United States by Amnesty International in late 1973. Jerry Ross initially contacted the organization, which was founded in England a decade earlier, while traveling through California after he fled Buffalo. In 1972, he met with their London office while visiting his sister, but he was not confident he was making inroads. He wrote home to Sharon Fischer, "It looks as if Amnesty International is really out of it as far as helping Martin as they are concentrating on Chile now and 'more pressing situations' failing to realize that New York State is practically under police state rule."[151] But persistence paid off when, a year later, the international organization announced that it had become "convinced that Martin Sostre has been the victim of an international miscarriage of justice because of his political beliefs."[152] By 1974, the organization was sending observers to Sostre's trials and featured him during its "Prisoner of Conscience Week" that October.[153]

In September 1975, Sostre's supporters launched a major mailing campaign to the governor's office. Carey had already received 738 letters, up from just four the previous year.[154] Now, the committee announced an ambitious goal of 20,000 letters: "Letters to Carey are the most important tools in our struggle to set Martin free at this time."[155] By November, Berrigan reported that the committee had received more funding and "decided in an all out effort beginning (after letters etc.) with a sit in at Gov. Carey's office in Albany, then visits by politicos and religious types. They're beginning to move, we're stressing executive clemency."[156]

With the trial over and the balance of support pressing for Sostre's release now in New York City, groups that had formed upstate in Potsdam and Plattsburgh began to expand their focus. "As you said, there are always consequences," Dubinsky wrote Sostre. "One of the consequences wrought by the Plattsburgh Kangaroos is the strengthening of the committees."[157] For the Canton-Potsdam committee, an initial step was to develop an awareness of the broader functions of the criminal legal system and its role in St. Lawrence County. Half a dozen members of the committee responded to the invitation of a local newspaper editor and began research for an investigative series on a range of issues related to imprisonment.[158] They also became active in supporting residents of nearby Watertown in cases of police harassment and brutality. A few women connected to the group began researching the conditions of imprisoned women at the St. Lawrence County Jail.[159] Dubinsky wrote excitedly that this "localizes the struggle geographically at the same time [it] expands the scope."[160]

That summer, workers were on strike at a local nursing home in North Country where a committee member was employed. When the management brought in scabs, the committee organized a group to "flood one shift change" just before the bargaining session.[161] Dubinsky reported that this willingness "on the part of the committee to branch out in these directions is now confirmed . . . [and] represents a crucial development."[162] That fall, Dubinsky wrote that he believed the time had come to divide their work between supporting Sostre and "specific useful projects here in St. Lawrence County . . . which would be our work and vehicles for building a strong base in Potsdam."[163]

The committees made connections to prisoner support efforts in other regions fighting against state-sanctioned sexual violence. For example, the Plattsburgh committee received a letter and petition from the recently formed Action for Forgotten Women (AFFW) in North Carolina. The grassroots organization was formed just a few months earlier to support incarcerated women in North Carolina, particularly Joan (pronounced Jo-Ann) Little, a twenty-year-old Black woman who had been charged with murder after she defended herself against a white guard who forced her have oral sex with him while holding an icepick to her head.[164] As historian Emily Thuma documents, the incarcerated women at the North Carolina Correctional Center for Women (NCCCW) raised a host of issues, among them the "institutional violence of routine vaginal and rectal searches."[165]

The Canton-Potsdam group planned to write individual and group letters of support and sign their petition, and the Plattsburgh committee used its first issue of *New World Notes* to call for letters and legal aid contributions to AFFW.[166] Although their connections to supporters of Joan Little and other women at NCCCW may have been limited to such acts of solidarity, they demonstrate the steps the defense committees were taking to grow beyond Sostre's struggle. They also suggest the shared networks and impact his committees may have had on similar defense campaigns. As Thuma points out, the Joan Little Defense Fund, although headquartered in Durham, was supported by other committees that were encouraged to "follow their own initiative" in what she described as a "decidedly decentralized" mobilization.[167] While most of the Canton-Potsdam committee's organizing still revolved around prison and jail conditions, they laid the foundation for understanding the Martin Sostre Defense Committee not as a vehicle for fighting for one person's emancipation from a single unjust system but, rather, as struggling on behalf of all people against various forms of state oppression. Dubinsky wrote ambitiously in October 1975 after another demonstration in Albany: "These and other activities will be our work and vehicles for building a strong base in Potsdam, that will join with the bases in all the other cities that will form the beginning of the movement that will create our new society."[168]

Around the time of the October demonstration in Albany, Sostre was visited by two psychiatrists and a parole officer in connection with his clemency petition.[169] His committees continued to escalate pressure, declaring (as his Buffalo committee had once done) the first week of December "Martin Sostre Week."[170] The week of forums, bake sales, film screenings, and festivals was punctuated by a message of support from Soviet physicist and human rights advocate Andrei Sakharov.[171] Having just received a Nobel Peace prize for his stance against nuclear proliferation, Sakharov called upon Governor Carey "in the name of all men and women throughout the world who are imprisoned for their convictions to grant executive clemency to Martin Sostre."[172] With international support mounting and a parole board hearing scheduled for December 17, the New York City committee organized a Christmas vigil outside Carey's office.[173] The following day, Martin Sostre was granted parole on his original frame-up charges. This left only his 0–4 year indeterminate sentence from Plattsburgh for Carey to commute.[174]

"A good night and ho ho ho to you." It was December 24, 1975, and the crackling of a yuletide message on WBAI radio in New York City opened a five-minute segment announcing the executive clemency of eight prisoners by Governor Hugh Carey. Among them was Martin Sostre, who would soon hear the news through the prison grapevine.

The international movement to free Martin Sostre had succeeded in the face of improbably odds. Many who had fought for Sostre's release celebrated that night what they considered his freedom. But, in a *New York Times* article on his clemency the following day, Sostre negated the separation between prison walls and the society beyond them. "For me this is a continuous struggle whether I am on the outside or the inside," he said. "If the battlefield changes, my struggle never changes."[175] Collapsing the distinction between prisoners' rights and human rights, Sostre traced this fight long before his frame-up to over two decades of repression and resistance. Although he was arguably the most successful jailhouse lawyer in US history, having won landmark cases over the rights to free speech, religious practice, due process, and basic constitutional protections for imprisoned people, he dismissed the idea that he would take the bar exam when released. Instead, he cited his political and press connections and the eight remaining defense committees across the country: "I intend to use all of this against this oppressive system."[176] Soon, a month shy of his fifty-third birthday, Sostre would reenter the world he considered "minimum security."

11

Minimum Security

On February 9, 1976, Martin Sostre left prison for the last time, having spent most of his adult life inside. In what seemed like poetic justice, he was released from Green Haven, where he had drafted one of the most significant legal complaints of the prisoners' rights movement.[1] The next day, he spoke at a press conference in New York City surrounded by many of his supporters. Wearing what would become his trademark blue jeans, denim jacket, and a navy beanie, Sostre recognized his historic release against "overwhelming odds," acknowledging the "miracle that I'm here."[2] Alongside defense campaigns for Angela Davis and Huey Newton, the movement to free Martin Sostre represented one of the most improbable, if since forgotten, victories of the Black Power era. Many of his revolutionary contemporaries were killed or in exile. Others, such as Ruchell Magee, would remain imprisoned for another half century; Magee would be released at the age of eighty-four, just months before his death.[3] Despite the euphoria of his release, Sostre was candid about what his incarceration had cost: "I know it's fashionable to say I'm not bitter. Of course I am. I lost nine years of my life."[4]

Although he was looking toward his life outside, reporters focused their questions on prisons. "Eventually, I don't believe there will be any need for [them]," Sostre responded. One journalist asked a hypothetical question about a bank robbery gone bad, prompting an audible groan from Dan Berrigan in the back of the room.[5] At this pivotal transition in Sostre's life, such questions revealed the limitations of liberal understandings of his organizing then and since. His success as a jailhouse lawyer was viewed narrowly as "prison reform," and his sweeping ideas about revolutionary struggle were distilled to this single issue. One *New York Times* article announcing his clemency dubbed him "The Prison Attorney."[6] These framings exposed a fundamental misunderstanding about the role of the prison in society, as well as about Sostre's identification as a revolutionary within a worldwide struggle against all forms of oppression.

Sostre emphasized that he was simply entering "minimum security"—moving from the maximum security of the prison to the society that created and maintained it. "The same oppressive and repressive forces exist outside as well as in," he argued. "Only inside, it's in a more concentrated form."[7] Since the prison represented a distillation of state repression, it could only be understood in relation to, not apart from, the world outside it. To abolish the prison would require a revolutionary reorganization of society itself.[8]

Sostre's experiences with surveillance and state repression on both sides of the walls underscored this continuum. He used his parole, which extended until September 7, 2001, as an example. In addition to mandatory employment and limitations on where he could live, his parole agreement forbade him from being a "menace" to society. Any speech against the government—which he nonetheless continued—could be construed as a parole violation. He even carried a copy of his parole agreement in his jacket, calling it a "contract with a gun to your head."[9] As Sostre transitioned from maximum to minimum security, his tactics and targets shifted, even as the goal remained destroying the state and creating an egalitarian society free from all forms of domination. "The battlefield has changed from the dungeons to the streets," he said.[10] "My getting out is merely phase one. Phase two is to set up shop here and continue the same struggle for human rights."[11]

But Sostre returned to revolutionary movements that were besieged and fragmented. The window for global revolt, which had seemed wide open in the late 1960s and early '70s, appeared to have closed. Carlito Rovira—who had joined the Young Lords Party at fourteen, idolized Sostre, and even became a bodyguard for him at speaking engagements—described this period as one of decline and state revanchism. "By 1975, with the end of the war in Vietnam, things went into a rapid ebb, especially with the demise of the Black Panther Party and the Young Lords. The movement had been crushed."[12] When asked about his impressions of what had changed, Sostre acknowledged that "the spirit among the masses is not at the height of the Sixties." He blamed the combination of state repression and the "shortsightedness" of the movement, which tended to focus on single issues, as well as revolutionaries who had "sold out their original commitment." Sectarian divides, political assassinations, frame-ups—all of which Sostre had himself endured and survived—had taken their toll. He was nevertheless hopeful about the development of armed resistance through groups such as the Black Liberation Army and the Weather Underground, and saw them as signs that the "underground is proliferating, building its network, preparing for the upcoming struggle."[13] Undeterred, Sostre approached this political moment and set of historical challenges as he had others: by starting where he was.

Sostre's initial years back in minimum security embodied the tension between his identification as a revolutionary organizer fighting on all fronts and the tendency for grassroots struggles to become isolated from others. Those who were paid staff members of nonprofits suffered from this tension. In 1977, Sostre worked briefly as a legal assistant for Prisoners' Legal Services (PLS) and then as an organizer for the Tenant Takeover Team and Columbia Tenants' Union. Meanwhile, during his first two years home, he delivered dozens of lectures and speeches at churches, colleges and universities, and political rallies. He also lent his support to a wide range of campaigns, from opposing city budget cuts and the death penalty to supporting the release of political prisoners and demanding the US government release the entirety of the Rosenberg files. "We are oppressed economically, legally, psychologically, culturally, psychically and by all other means deemed necessary by the criminal ruling class, to maintain themselves in power," Sostre wrote. "Since oppression is multi-dimensional, doesn't common-sense dictate that resistance to it be multi-dimensional?"[14]

Sostre's vision of fighting on all fronts was reinforced by what he encountered when he returned to New York City in 1975. The municipality was on the brink of bankruptcy. Many American cities were affected by the fiscal crisis, but the situation in New York was especially dire. Manufacturing and profitable, expanding industries had followed the white middle class to the suburbs, and the city's property taxes could not cover its essential services. By 1975, it was the epicenter and emblem of the urban financial crisis.[15] Just months before Sostre was released, the *New York Daily News* had printed the famous headline that opens historian

Kim Phillips-Fein's account of the crisis: "Ford to City: Drop Dead." For President Ford, his advisors, and many Americans in other places across the nation, the city embodied the failures of urban liberalism and the false promise that government could play a central role in addressing poverty and racial inequality.[16] Beginning with an international oil embargo and the withdrawal of US troops from Vietnam in 1973, the US had entered an economic recession. The Watergate scandal and resignation of President Richard Nixon revealed the corruption of the ruling class and marked a further erosion of the country's fabricated moral authority, a process which had begun in the minds of many Americans during the Vietnam War.

Just weeks out of prison, Sostre arrived at the offices of the New York State's Housing and Development Administration as part of his new job with State Assembly Member Marie Runyon, best known for her housing activism. Carrying a brown accordion folder with "Martin Sostre, Mail Wallkill" written on the side, he went to support a tenants union facing eviction by an absentee landlord. During the proceedings, Sostre would occasionally turn to journalist Joe Shapiro to express his frustrations: "Say we win on this building. But there are a million buildings with the same problems. We'll be here a lifetime patching things up. We're only putting on band-aids."[17] Shapiro, a journalism student at Columbia University, was writing his thesis on Sostre and conducted several lengthy interviews with the former political prisoner during this period. His notes capture both the abruptness of Sostre's transition home and the different directions in which he was pulled as he tried to find solid ground within the political struggles of the late 1970s in New York.

"It looks like there's been a war here," Sostre said to Shapiro, gazing out the window of his office on the ninth floor of the new multimillion-dollar State Office Building on 125th Street at the abandoned housing and vacant lots surrounding him. "When you've been gone a long time the change is more noticeable." Sostre's remarks read like a time capsule of New York's fiscal crisis.[18] As if time-traveling, he observed the closing libraries, rising transit fares, suburban flight, rising gas prices, and capital investments in corporate office and upscale residential buildings that characterized this new regime. Surveying the neighborhood where he grew up, he lamented the real estate trusts and landlords who "suck the tenants dry." With ominous accuracy, he predicted the destruction of shoebox houses and tenements, the dislocation of their residents, and their replacement by luxury high-rises that "only the rich will be able to afford."[19]

Although Sostre didn't mention it in the preceding exchange, he was in all likelihood aware that his office was on the former site of Lewis Michaux's bookstore, which had been the inspiration for his Afro-Asian Bookshop in Buffalo. In 1966, Governor Rockefeller had announced the building of the state offices on 125th Street between Seventh and Lenox Avenues as part of "the first surge of new development" which would turn Harlem into a "truly viable community." Along with the twenty-three-story office building, the governor had vaguely suggested the possibility of a cultural and community center.[20] Among such promises was one to Michaux—that the African National Memorial Bookstore would be allowed to relocate to the state building when completed.[21] In the meantime, the eighty-year-old bookstore owner had been forced to move his 225,000 volumes a block away during construction.[22] By 1974, Rockefeller had left office and Michaux again faced eviction by the state.[23] The following fall, the bookstore closed forever after serving the Harlem community for forty-three years. Michaux soon passed away at age ninety-one.[24]

Sostre had last been in Harlem in 1967, the year workers broke ground on the building in which he now worked, and just before the uprising and frame-up that had changed his life.[25] In a 1968 interview in *Esquire* magazine, writer James Baldwin suggested, "at the risk of sounding paranoiac," that the state building site was chosen specifically to displace Michaux's. "The Black Nationalist Bookstore is a very dangerous focal ground," he explained. "You know, it's what in Africa would be a palaver tree. It's where Negroes get together and talk. It's where all the discontent doesn't begin, exactly, but where it always focuses."[26] The forcible removal of Michaux's bookstore was emblematic of the broader forces of displacement, disinvestment, and capital extraction underway in Harlem and other urban areas across the country during the mid-1970s.[27]

In an unfurnished office with a handwritten sign with Marie Runyon's name on the door, Sostre bit his nails and looked over a list of apartments that Shapiro had brought him.[28] As he would explain to an audience a few weeks later: "Here I am, a high school drop out with a criminal record that have been away from society for nine years. That have only $40 in my pocket, which with this inflative society, you can't even buy a decent bag of groceries."[29]

Housing was one of many urgent issues New Yorkers faced under the neoliberal austerity policy that deepened under the fiscal crisis. On May 5, 1976, over a thousand City College of New York students went on strike and marched down 125th Street to the state office where Sostre's office was located. Just six years earlier, students had shut down CUNY's campuses and seized buildings, demanding the university serve the communities it occupied. They had even created a community-based institution they called the "University of Harlem."[30] One of their successful demands was the implementation of open admissions, which dramatically diversi-

Martin Sostre and Angela Davis speaking at the National Alliance Against Racist and Political Repression's "North Carolina Freedom Rally," August 12, 1976. Box 21C, Daily Worker and Daily World Negatives Collection, Tamiment Library.

fied the student body; first-year students were 78 percent white in 1969 and just 30 percent white by 1975.[31] Now, the Board of Higher Education announced its intention to impose universal tuition for the first time in the university's 129-year history.[32] As scholar-organizer Conor Tomás Reed points out, "CUNY became a national experiment in the neoliberal privatization of public goods like free college education."[33] In a speech to students, Sostre encouraged them to use the same tactics as the student strikes and takeovers of 1969, which had initiated open admissions and desegregated the university.[34] "This is war," Sostre emphasized. "Don't go for that stuff that this is too militant, because that's the only thing they understand; that's pressure."[35]

He also continued to advocate on behalf of political prisoners, hoping to build a national network to emancipate others. During his first summer home, Sostre wrote and spoke in defense of Mustafa Dzhemilev, a Crimean Tatar who spent fifteen years in a Soviet prison camp. Twenty-three years after being incarcerated at Sing Sing with Ethel and Julius Rosenberg, Sostre spoke at a tribute at Carnegie Hall sponsored by the Committee to Reopen the Rosenberg Case.[36] Sostre and their son, Michael Meeropol, spoke about "political prisoners of the 1950s, 1960s, and 1970s" at Western New England College, where Meeropol taught.[37] Sostre continued to call for the release of the remaining Puerto Rican nationalists jailed for their involvement in the 1954 action in Congress, including speeches at an event to "Free the Five" and alongside Zoraida Collazo, the daughter of of one of the Five, Oscar Collazo, at Columbia University the following year.[38] "All struggles of liberation are linked and interconnected," he reminded one audience. "Whatever serves the cause of liberation in one area of this planet affects us."[39]

Four years after being highlighted by Angela Davis during her national speaking tour for the National Alliance Against Racist and Political Repression, Sostre now shared the stage with her. Sponsored by the NAARPR, the "North Carolina Freedom Rally" called for the release of the Wilmington Ten—a group of young Black activists, many of them high school students, who were imprisoned nearly a decade on trumped up charges of arson and conspiracy—as well as an end to capital punishment and support for textile workers in Roanoke Rapids, North Carolina, who were fighting for a union contract.[40] After Davis spoke on the repression of civil rights in North Carolina, she "then yield[ed] the spotlight" to Sostre.[41] His billing alongside Davis reveals the prominence Sostre held within revolutionary movements upon his return home. The rally also captured their shared efforts to harness the energy of the individual struggles to free them from political imprisonment and transform them into dynamic mass movements following their release. Davis did so through the 1973 establishment of the NAARPR, a national organization led by Davis, Charlene Mitchell, Anne Braden, and another former political prisoner, Frank Chapman, with support from the Communist Party USA. Much of Sostre's energy, on the other hand, had been devoted to building a federation of defense committees that could act as revolutionary bases for multidimensional organizing. When he came home, the effort to consolidate these energies and pivot them toward future-oriented struggles was at the forefront of his agenda. "The show isn't over just because I got out," he reminded supporters.[42] To help accelerate this process, he gave a half dozen speech in cities where he had established key defense committees, including Amherst, Potsdam, and Buffalo. This tour was less a victory lap than an organizing expedition. With his next steps undetermined, Sostre was finally able to assess what he had helped build from behind the walls as he attempted to "weld a human force together."[43]

In his speeches, Sostre shared what he had learned, outlined his theories of revolutionary struggle, and distilled nearly a decade of organizing inside. To him, the key lesson of his defense campaign was the power of people to organize collectively and autonomously. "My getting out is living proof—not abstract, but a concrete example—of what a resolute struggle will do," he said.[44] Although careful to emphasize that there was no blueprint everyone should follow, he argued that through "struggle emerged certain principles, certain tactics, that can be utilized over and over again. . . . And that's what we're looking for: it's not no theory, it's not no rhetoric, it's not a supposition. But it's a fact, evidenced by my being here." Sostre continually reminded listeners that his victory was "not done through the courts"; it was achieved through organizing and escalating protests. "Using these same principles, the same tactics, we can not only free other political prisoners, but these same tactics against the system will also succeed in furthering the cause of liberation. Liberation from oppression, in all its manifestations."[45] He regularly thanked the thousands of supporters who printed leaflets, bought stamps, stuffed envelopes, wrote letters, signed petitions, made posters, attended meetings, screened films, and participated in demonstrations and sit-ins. "It was the sum total of all this activity," he argued, "that finally forced the repressive state to disgorge me from the dungeons."[46]

In early March 1976, Sostre traveled to Amherst for his first in-person visit with a defense committee outside New York City. Although he had had shut down that committee the previous year due to possible financial mismanagement by its chair, Zoë Best, she was present at his press conference the day after his release and likely hosted him with her four daughters in Amherst.[47] In addition to delivering a speech as part of the Distinguished Lecture series in the University of Massachusetts Amherst central auditorium, Sostre visited the Che-Lumumba School at the New Africa House on campus. Founded by students in 1972, the school's mission was to teach "Third World children" from a radical internationalist perspective.[48] Best's daughters were among the students at the school, and several parents had been active on the local defense committee. Students even wrote him letters of support while he was inside and spontaneously put on a play about his trial during his visit. Afterward, they took photographs of him with the help of one of the instructors.[49]

Broadcast on local public radio, Sostre's lecture in Amherst remains one of the few surviving recordings of his speeches. In it, he used the metaphor of minimum and maximum security to explain to the crowd of five hundred that the "same oppressive and repressive forces exist outside as well as in." He reminded them that the same state troopers who stop people for speeding on the highways tortured prisoners at Attica after retaking the prison. Sostre also emphasized how censorship works to isolate and break the spirit of those inside. "Some of you may have written me," he said, sharing that he had been given a box of thousands of letters when he was released, dozens of them postmarked years earlier.[50] Among those withheld were innocuous holiday cards, well wishes, and the letters from the children at Che-Lumumba School.[51]

Sostre's message to the audience was that it would take a range of tactics—sit-ins, leafleting, petitions, demonstrations, and more—to achieve victories such as his. Referencing the occasion of the bicentennial, he implied that this would include revolutionary violence: "Whether it's a local issue, or whether it's a long-term objective of creating an egalitarian society which is free of repression, of racism, of sexism, and all forms of exploitation, it's not gonna come on a silver platter, and it's not gonna come through moral suasion. Because if that was possible, we would not be celebrating the bicentennial this year, 'cause certainly the revolutionaries of two hundred years ago, they exhausted all means."[52]

Less than a month later, Sostre spent four days in Potsdam, New York, visiting with his former defense committee. The group, which had recently renamed itself the North County Defense Committee, most fully represented his vision for the transition from an individual defense campaign to broad-based multi-issue local struggles. Approached by Upstate People for Safe Energy Technology (UPSET) shortly after Sostre's release, the NCDC had joined the struggle against a proposed 765 kilovolt (kV) power line that would run through the region.[53] "After Martin was released, we just looked at each other and said, 'Well, what are we going to do now?'" Defense committee member Joel Ray said. "So, we started working on nuclear power."[54] First developed in Quebec a decade earlier, high-voltage transmission lines could carry nearly five times the power of a typical 345 kV line, promising more energy over greater distances at lower costs.[55] But the technology was still new, and many feared the long-term health effects and environmental degradation it might cause. The 140-foot wide, 200-foot tall steel towers required a 250-foot wide clearing along the 155-mile route.[56] The 765 kV line "became the biggest issue of the '70s for the North County," Ray recalled.[57]

Sostre's visit to North Country coincided with this transition from prisoner defense to ecodefense. In talks at Clarkson College and Potsdam State, Sostre again delivered lectures entitled "Maximum to Minimum Security," emphasizing the state's control of the lives of people on both sides of prison walls. He assured a crowd of 250 that he planned to return to North Country frequently, particularly to support the NCDC's opposition to nuclear power. "Isn't that subject far removed from prison reform?" a local paper asked. "Not for Sostre, who argues that all reforms are basically related, in trying to make a just society."[58] Although Sostre would not have referred to these struggles as fights for "reforms," his speeches nevertheless made clear to audiences the interconnection between these different forms of oppression. During his visit, he met with students and faculty for informal discussions in the student union, where the local Martin Sostre Defense Commitee had held its meetings.[59] Other photos show Sostre relaxing at the Dubinskys' home with their daughters and poring over a newspaper article with Ed about workers in Andrzeja's native country of Poland.

North Country Defense Committee logo, c. 1976, 765 kV Line Protest Collection, Special Collections, St. Lawrence University.

It had been nearly a year since Sostre wrote Ed that "revolutionary struggle is a multi-dimensional struggle," and the committee was now moving in that direction. Just a few years after its origin as a small group attending his trial in Plattsburgh, the NCDC described itself as a "multi-issue citizen action group" that cut across age, class, religious, and political affiliation. "Coalition is at the heart of NCDC activity," one pamphlet emphasized.[60] In addition to opposing the power line, the group supported Indigenous land rights, opposed highway construction, raised awareness about the dangers of nuclear power, and organized with local farmers. By late 1976, the power-line protests were reaching an apex. Over five hundred people marched against the line at Fort Covington near the Canadian border in October 1976. A few months later, twelve were arrested in a tree defense on a farm. Protesters blocked construction sites and lay in front of bulldozers. By 1978, more than fifty people had been arrested.[61] Among them was Andrzeja Dubinsky.

Not everyone saw a clear correlation between the committee's defense of Martin Sostre and the opposition to nuclear plants and high voltage power that followed. "I don't think the two issues, as issues, really touched that much," said Ray, who became among the most committed of the original defense committee members in the power line fight. Sostre "really did not have much to do with what came afterwards."[62] But for others such as Andrzeja, these campaigns could not be understood apart from one another. Just days after Sostre was sentenced in Plattsburgh during the summer of 1975, she had written him about the paradox of waiting for her citizenship so that she could be arrested rather than deported.[63] Years later, she was arrested for standing in front of a dump truck to prevent construction of the power line. After her own sentencing, she wrote that there was "a person who helped me get involved again—made it absolutely impossible for me to remain silent. Martin Sostre."[64] She identified his sentencing in 1975 as the moment she realized "there is no end to 'involvement'—be it in fighting the terrible prison system or nuclear plants or the 765 kV line." Echoing Sostre, she wrote that "one cannot separate big issues from small—rotten prison systems from tramping over peoples' rights to be free and decide in every issue, violating the laws of Nature by interfering with them, and on, and on, and on. This is all part of one big system. So that's where I am at. . . . Involved again. Probably this time for good."[65]

Soon after Sostre returned from his trip to Potsdam, he excitedly reported that the "committee is stronger than before . . . [and] emerged as a political force up in North Country."[66] Although there is no record of Sostre staying in touch after his visit, Andrzeje and Ed Dubinsky spent much of the next decade not only involved in the power-line fight but also supporting Indigenous self-determination, particularly at Ganienkeh, a sovereign Mohawk community that reclaimed land about twenty miles northwest of Plattsburgh in 1974.[67] As their daughter Ewa would later remember, "They used a letter writing campaign for Ganienkeh, just as they had for Sostre's defense."[68]

Finally, in May 1976, Martin Sostre made a long-awaited return to the city where he was framed. At a press conference at the Buffalo airport, he announced his plans to reestablish a revolutionary bookstore there. "The former one was light stuff compared to what this one will be," he vowed. He also promised to oust right-wing politicians like Mike Amico, who had since been elected Sherriff of Erie County, from office.[69] Sostre's visit coincided with International Workers' Day (popularly known as May Day), and he shared the stage with antiwar journalist and activist Don Luce at the University at Buffalo, not far from the former home of the Afro-Asian Bookstore in Exile.[70] Sociology professor Ed Powell, a faculty sponsor of SDS in the early 1960s and longtime supporter of

Sostre, wrote him an open letter that positioned Sostre alongside the martyred anarchists in Haymarket Square, Emma Goldman, Alexander Berkman, and Big Bill Hayward. "That spirit returns to Buffalo today with Martin Sostre," he wrote.[71] In speeches at Buffalo State, the Niagara Branch Library, and Lincoln Memorial Church, Sostre emphasized the far-reaching and everyday forms of repression and encouraged them to resist their complicity in it. "The only solution is to refuse to participate in these injustices against ourselves," he said.[72]

As his speeches indicate, Martin Sostre was anything but directionless when he returned from prison. But he was unsettled. He wanted to open a bookstore, but it was unclear whether this would be in New York City, Buffalo, or both. He talked of purchasing land to establish an cooperative political community, but it was uncertain if he would move to the North Country. Although he hoped to write a book, he was often working, supporting political causes, and traveling for talks. Amid all of this, he wanted children, something that had not been an option for most of his adult life. Sometime during these hectic first few months home, he married for a second time.

"She's getting married to Martin Sostre, a man who was framed for having a political bookstore," twelve-year-old Melanie Best wrote about her mother in her diary. It was just days before Sostre's speech in Amherst, and soon afterward her mother, poet and former defense committee chair Zoë Best, moved with Melanie and her other three daughters from Amherst to New York City. The six lived in a six-room apartment at 142nd and Broadway, near Riverside Park, for less than two months before Best left with her children and resettled in Portland, Oregon. Little information survives that would help to explain their brief time together or its precipitous ending.[73] What remains are fragments from the diary of Best's eldest daughter noting plays on Broadway, a trip to an art gallery, a talk Sostre gave: "one of the best ones he did." Then, a sudden departure: "We left Thursday, secretly, from New York City. But as we were going out of the building and down the elevator, Martin was going up. We only just made it out in time."[74]

Melanie recalled long calls from the road on their journey to Oregon. Some of them she documented. "Today Mom called Martin. She talked (long distance) for an hour and a half. She is very sad because Martin said 'I did not think I was that bad. And I love you.'" It remains unclear what Sostre meant by this phrase or how accurate this quotation is, filtered first through Zoë, then by her daughter on to her diary pages. But Melanie recalled other impulsive or inexplicable decisions her mother had made. Years earlier, her mother had delivered divorce papers to her father the same day they closed on their house in Amherst.[75] It is impossible to know what this relationship and its abrupt end meant to Sostre.

That same summer of 1976, Sostre decided to meet Lizabeth Roberts in person, having first communicated with her during his incarceration. For their first date, Roberts suggested the Brooklyn Botanical Gardens. Her first thought was that the five-foot-nine Sostre was shorter than she imagined. As they strolled, Roberts found him enthusiastic, perhaps even relieved, to talk about things unrelated to political organizing. Much had changed in New York since Sostre had last lived in the city during the early 1950s. "He was more than willing to play tourist," she said.[76]

During the mid-1970s, Roberts had joined the Prairie Fire Organizing Committee, a political formation that counted among its tasks supporting the activities of the Weather Underground and other clandestine groups. She was already active on the defense committee for Curtis Brown of the Tombs rebellion and soon joined the group's prison committee, which corresponded with and sent revolutionary material to people inside. She remembered sitting in her living room with those who knew Sostre well, including attorney Liz Fink and Attica Brother "Big Black" Smith. Each person on the committee was paired with comrades inside. When Sostre's name was called, Roberts volunteered. "The next thing I know, I'm calling him," she said.[77]

Born Elizabeth Roberta Slimowitz to a Jewish family in Crown Heights, Brooklyn, on March 23, 1944, she eventually adopted variants of her first and middle names. Her father was a firefighter, and her mother worked at home raising Liz and her brother George. In her early teens, she left their all-white apartment building and headed to Greenwich Village to listen to Beat poetry and read her own. She would later remember these escapes as an "unseen pact" with her mother: "I was living the life she wanted to live. She was living her life through me." By the late 1960s, she was attending classes at Alternate U., a free school and political organizing center on West Fourteenth Street. Following the Stonewall rebellion in June 1969, Alternate U. became a gathering place for the newly founded Gay Liberation Front and stayed open twenty-four hours a day to provide refuge for queer people targeted by police. Roberts remembered a poster of a political prisoner at the top of the stairs at the school. Although she concedes it was probably of George Jackson, there are days she still remembers it as Martin Sostre.[78]

In one of their earliest phone conversations while he was inside, Sostre did something that Roberts would come to consider one of his unique gifts. She expressed criticism of Prairie Fire's male-dominated leadership, anticipating that he would agree that more women should be represented. Instead, he asked her what sorts of work women did. "They take the envelopes, and they fold the literature, and they put it in the envelopes, and they lick the envelope, and they seal it so it's ready to go," she responded. "That's important work!" he exclaimed. As she explained later, it was not that he discounted sexism in the group or felt the question of gender equality in leadership was not important, but that he understood mailing materials was crucial to organizing. Indeed, Sostre owed his release from prison to such labor, much of it performed by women. But the lesson Roberts took from this early conversation was that she could never anticipate the direction he might take in answering a question. Decades later, she reflected: "Are we raising the wrong questions?"[79] By July 1976, they had decided to move in together in Manhattan Valley. Liz reluctantly gave up her Brooklyn apartment to live with him at 118 West 109th Street, where they would remain for the next forty years.

During these first years home, Sostre struggled to find a job that matched his skills and principles. In 1977, he briefly worked with Prisoners' Legal Services of New York. In the aftermath of the Attica rebellion and the McKay Commission Report, prisoners' rights clinics proliferated across the state. Among them was Prisoners' Legal Services in Albany. By 1975, the New York State Bar Association proposed a statewide legal services organization for imprisoned people. The following year, PLS became a recognized nonprofit and received a substantial grant from the Federal Law Enforcement Assistance Administration, allowing the organization to operate statewide and hire staff. Sostre was likely employed as one of nearly a dozen legal assistants who worked with thirty-five attorneys most of whom were Ivy trained.[80] The organization was divided into three sections: one covering civil cases such as divorces, another litigating civil prison conditions, and one for criminal appeals. Although Sostre was an experienced and accomplished litigant and writ writer, his day-to-day work bore little resemblance to what he had done inside. Unable to write complaints, file briefs, argue cases, or even interview people in prisons to collect the facts of the case, Sostre was relegated to the role of an office administrator. Claudia Angelos, then a recent Harvard Law graduate, later reflected critically upon the limitations of PLS for someone of Sostre's talents and background: "He couldn't do what he was doing in that cell at Clinton in that office."[81]

By 1978, the organization had become state funded, with $1 million allocated in the budget. Lynn Barclay, who started work at PLS the same year as Sostre, recalled the improbability of their work: "We really were kind of astonished every day going to work; because we were suing the state of New York, and then the state of New York was giving us money so that we could sue the state of New York some more."[82] Everyone who remembered working with Sostre at PLS agreed that although he was agreeable, funny, and pleasant to be around, the work did not inspire him. "There was no place for him," Angelos said. "He was just way ahead of his time [in] understanding . . . that the role of law and lawyers is very subsidiary and should be very in service of other forms of social change." Instead, "off he went to Manhattan Valley to become a full-time organizer."[83]

"I remember having some sort of conversation with Martin about continuing to do prison work, and he looked at me as if I was crazy," Liz recalled. "We've got to do tenant organizing. Look where we are," Sostre had told her. "Landlords are going to take all of this away from these people. They're going to make it nice, and then they're going to take it away."[84] For Sostre, tenant ownership resonated with his standing commitment to community control as well his budding interest in building prefigurative counter-structures and cooperatives. The year before, for example, Sostre had written Ed Dubinsky from prison outlining his idea of establishing a political commune. Dubinsky had replied that although the farmland was poor, there was a gutted, abandoned schoolhouse nearby that could be fixed up into a "center of political activity" with transitional housing, health clinics, and a community center for teenagers, adding, "It is a grand dream that would require much in the way of money, energy and commitment."[85] Although ultimately Sostre did not pursue this vision in the North Country, it would continue to shape his organizing for decades to come.

By 1970, more than two hundred thousand housing units in New York City had been abandoned by owners.[86] New state laws enacted in the early part of the decade, historian Roberta Gold argues, "represented tenants' worst legislative defeat since Congress ended federal rent control in 1947."[87] Organizers were nevertheless able to build upon the militant rent strikes and building seizures of the 1960s and accomplish legal tenant takeovers in buildings with absentee landlords.[88] In the summer of 1976, for instance, Sostre communicated with striking residents at Co-op City in the Bronx, which, after the longest and largest rent strike in US history, reached an agreement with the state to cede control to the 60,000-person cooperative.[89] But, as Gold notes, the "1970s chapter in affordable co-op history contains paradoxes."[90] The institutionalization of subversive tenant takeovers produced legal ownership opportunities for some residents but also "chipped away at the constituency for the rights of tenants *per se*."[91]

The Tenant Takeover Team represented one example of this transition. Following Marie Runyon's electoral defeat during the fall of 1976, her successor Ed Sullivan established the nonprofit with funds from the state.[92] Sostre was among the earliest employees of the group, which helped tenants secure legal ownership of their buildings from absentee landlords who had neglected these properties. "The city was a mess at that point," recalled organizer Gregory Watson decades later. As he explained, the city now owned two-thirds of the properties in Harlem. Rent strikes—which had long been one of the most successful tools available to tenants in fights against private landlords—were less effective against the city, which did not rely on rent. Watson had been hired on to the Tenant Takeover Team while he was a graduate student at Columbia University's School of Social Work. Despite being the same age as Watson's parents, Sostre was soon hired to work under him. Over forty years on, neither Sullivan nor Watson could remember much from this period, but Watson noted that Sostre was a "very good organizer . . . [who] had the tenants at heart."[93] Sullivan pointed out that Sostre was humble and lived among those he organized in Manhattan Valley on West 109th Street.[94]

The same summer that Martin met Liz, a young activist named Sandy Shevack was handed a flyer for a speech by Sostre while attending an anti-bicentennial celebration in Philadelphia. He had first heard Sostre's name when he was eighteen, as a second-year college student visiting with the Prisoners Council at Rahway State Prison, about thirty miles from where he grew up in Passaic, New Jersey.[95] Two years earlier, over five hundred captives at Rahway had held the warden and several guards hostage for twenty-four hours, making demands for better health care, food, and educational programs, and an end to predatory commissary sales and mail censorship. The rebellion had taken place in the long shadow of the Attica uprising. One of the reforms initiated by the Rahway revolt was the formation of a prisoners' council. At Rahway, the young Shevack listened intently to the articulate and forceful voice of the council's head, Samuel "Sammy" Williams, who had been among the Muslim prisoners who organized the takeovers of solitary confinement with Sostre at Clinton Prison two decades earlier. Shevack recalled that although Sammy shared that he had not finished high school, "he was speaking like one of the sociology professors I had." When Shevack asked how he had acquired so much knowledge, Williams replied: "When I was locked up in New York, I was politicized by Martin Sostre."[96]

Although many of the goals Sostre articulated when he came home went unrealized, his life and work developed in new and unanticipated directions as a result of meeting Roberts and Shevack. He spent much of the next forty years organizing in minimum security. The flashbulbs and publicity of his 1976 press conference had diminished and faded. But he continued activities that were threaded throughout his previous twenty years of organizing on both sides of prison walls: engaging in political education, mentoring young people, and making revolutionary struggle visible.

12

Organizing the Community

Following their first meeting in 1976, Sandy Shevack stayed in touch with Martin Sostre. In 1979, he invited Sostre to speak with teenagers after a screening of *Frame-Up!* On their drive through Passaic, Sostre began inquiring about vacant buildings and then abruptly asked him to pull over. Confused, Shevack parked the car, and Sostre led him to the entrance of 40 Market Street, a two-story commercial brick building that still bore on its facade the name of the original clothing company for which it was built in 1914. As the two peered through the windows together, Sostre asked: "What do you know about this building?" Shevack remembers it like a scene out of a Laurel and Hardy film: "I said, 'Well, it's vacant.' 'I know it's vacant,' Sostre replied. 'Go to city hall, go to the tax assessor's office, find out who owns this.'"[1] Shevack was in his mid-twenties and working to divert young teenagers in his hometown from criminalization, violence, and substance use. He was not sure why Sostre was interested in century-old brick buildings in disrepair. For Sostre, however, the connection between control over property and the power of the community was already clear.

When the two finally walked into 40 Market Street in December 1982, they could see the sky through the roof. Snow lined the floor inside. "This is an ice-skating rink," Shevack said.[2] "I've seen enough."[3] "Yeah, so have I. This is it," Sostre replied. Thinking they agreed about the extent of disrepair, Sandy began to walk out. "No, this is *it*. . . . This is the building," Sostre told him. "You don't see what I see."[4] The next year, they received enough grant funding to purchase the building at auction. Working with local teenagers, they would ultimately convert the 75-year-old structure into a community center and the base of the Juvenile Education and Awareness Project (JEAP), a nonprofit formed by Sostre and Shevack that rehabilitated vacant sites while providing local teenagers with jobs, trade skills, and political education. Over two decades, JEAP would renovate nearly half a dozen dilapidated structures in Passaic and Paterson, New Jersey, turning them into affordable housing, a community center, and a day care. Inspired by the example of the Black Panther Party's Survival Programs and Fannie Lou Hamer's Freedom Farm Cooperative, Sostre and Shevack worked with over one hundred young people to transform a landscape abandoned by private capital and the state into housing and community spaces that served the common good.

Some considered this work a departure for Sostre. As Shevack recounted, some of Sostre's comrades in Buffalo "thought when he got out he would be doing something much more political."[5] Most of his comrades from the defense committees simply lost touch with him. By the 1980s, Lorenzo Kom'boa Ervin was in the process of building his own international defense campaign from prison, modeled after Sostre's. "Some people thought he should've been marching around the community," he remembered. "But he wasn't a fool. He did what he could do."[6] Indeed, Sostre remained under the close scrutiny and surveillance of the state. Even a decade out of prison, he was described by one attorney as "literally the most hated person in the New York state prison system."[7] Although Ervin himself might not have made the same choices, he understood why Sostre did.[8]

But there was more continuity between Sostre's past and present work than many perceived. JEAP pulled together key organizing tenets and unfulfilled dreams from the three decades of Sostre's life since he had first become politicized in prison during the 1950s. Through his Afro-Asian Bookshops in Buffalo, his efforts to recruit young people to write for and distribute *Black News*, and his mentorship of young radicals like Ervin and the Young Lords, Sostre had emphasized youth political education. He had stressed the necessity of owning land and building tangible counter-institutions that served the community rather than extracting wealth from the people. As Malcolm X had said: "Land is the basis of all independence. Land is the basis of freedom, justice, and equality."[9] In Buffalo, Sostre had hoped to save enough money to buy the building at 1412 Jefferson Avenue. In prison, he had dreamed of acquiring farmland to establish a political community in New York's North Country. And when he returned to New York City in the late 1970s, he became involved in efforts to take over abandoned lots and form housing cooperatives. "We have to seize that first," he said. "You've got to have that as a base. . . . You have to control your own neighborhood."[10]

The principles of community organizing, political education, youth mentorship, and prefigurative counter-structures that were woven throughout Sostre's activism and political transformations were now the bedrock of JEAP. The project brought together many of Sostre's lifelong interests and skills: his childhood dream of working in carpentry and construction; his commitment to young people and radical political education; and his belief that revolutionary struggle required the arduous work of tangibly changing people's material conditions. And he worked with an energetic younger comrade whose talents complemented his own. Shevack likened their relationship to a puzzle whose pieces fit together. Sostre had bold ideas, self-taught construction skills, and a reputation for producing results. Shevack had earned trust from his community through his work with criminalized young people and developed knowledge as a grant writer. Thirty-two years apart in age, the two formed a formidable partnership that lasted longer than any other in Sostre's life besides that with his wife Liz. Sostre's son Vinny recalled long phone calls between the two when he was young. "That was the one person that I would consider [my dad's] friend later in life," he said.[11]

The story Shevack tells about the organization's humble beginnings at 40 Market Street encapsulates Sostre's radical optimism and political vision. He saw what could be, rather than what was. Reflecting on their work together, Shevack explained that, far from his own preconceived images of dramatic mass marches and glorified struggle, the work was demanding and unglamorous. Cutting through the false dichotomy between the utopian and the pragmatic, their work together embodied the necessary interrelationship of the two. Dreaming was an essential world-building practice. So too was actualizing it. As Shevack explained, it was about empowering communities with a combination of "hope and results."[12]

Shevack and Sostre would purchase their fifth and final building in 1987, an 86-year-old brick community center that had been deserted for years. Shevack came across the building as it burned, during his night shift as a paramedic. Sostre described it as "a pit of abomination. . . . The front door was wide open, there were crack vials all over the place. The stench was unbelievable."[13] Standing outside the abandoned, two-story building with flames licking through its glassless windows in one of Paterson's most neglected neighborhoods, Shevack now saw what Sostre once had at 40 Market Street. "When you look around in depressed neighborhoods," Shevack told a local paper, "people just see what's there and not what could be there."[14] As JEAP began construction, Sostre said: "The first thing we're going to do is organize this community."[15]

Sandy Shevack was twenty-four years old when he was interviewed for the Academy Award–winning documentary *Scared Straight!* "I was trying to explain that there needs to be not only follow-up services [for formerly incarcerated people], but there needs to be essential social change to deal with the root conditions of inequality," he later recalled.[16] In a film best known for intense scenes of imprisoned people screaming profanity at teenagers to "scare them straight," it came as little surprise when he appeared only as a name in the credits. But Shevack's connections to Rahway State Prison and the Lifers Group featured in the film, as discussed below, provided a foundation for what he and Martin Sostre would eventually build a few years later.

Sandy Shevack, born in 1954 in Paterson, had been raised in a working-class, mostly white neighborhood in nearby Passaic. He became politicized as a teenager after the assassination of Dr. Martin Luther King and joined Students for a Democratic Society and the antiwar movement while studying at William Paterson University. Shevack's brothers were both successful amateur boxers on a team called the Magnificent Seven. When a beloved trainer was arrested and wrote Shevack and his brothers from prison, it prompted Sandy to visit him at Rahway. There, he met Sammy Williams and Richard Harris, a member of the Panther Twenty-One, both of whom told him about Sostre. Later, Shevack's brother became a social worker at the prison and Sandy eventually began working with the Youth Services Bureau in Passaic, bringing teenagers to meet with what was known as the Lifers Group Juvenile Awareness Program.[17] Since they first connected in 1976, Shevack still occasionally reached out to Sostre to introduce young people to him. In the summer of 1978, for example, Shevack brought a group of teenagers from Passaic to help Sostre clean out debris from a building in Harlem. A few surviving photographs of the day show the two men surrounded by five teenagers, smiling. Shevack was unsure of Sostre's relationship to the building, but he noticed how much the young people loved being around him.[18]

During the early 1980s, Liz and Martin had three children. After losing their first, Martin Paul, to meningitis at six weeks, Liz gave birth to Mark in July 1980 and Vinny in April 1982. During this busy life at home, Shevack invited Sostre to Passaic to work with young people in a GED preparation program, where he read books, talked about his experiences, and played pool with the teenagers. Later that year, funding for the program was

Sandy Shevack and Martin Sostre with a group of teenagers outside a building in Harlem, c. 1978. Courtesy of Sandy Shevack.

eliminated. The austerity and budget cuts to social programs that Sostre had encountered upon his release in the mid-1970s were now the federal mandate of the Reagan administration. But he remained convinced, Shevack recalled, that "you need an idea first before you can do anything."[19]

Liz, Martin, and Mark Sostre. Courtesy of Sostre family.

The two turned to their friends Ben Chavis and Reverend Lucius Walker. Chavis, a former political prisoner and member of the Wilmington Ten, was then director of the Commission for Racial Justice of the United Church of Christ.[20] Walker was a committed leftist who had recently been fired from his position at the National Council of Churches for giving too much money to community organizers. He was known for his support of political prisoners, reparations for slavery, and later his active opposition to US imperialism in Nicaragua (where he had been wounded in an attack by the US-backed Contras), which found expression in his founding of Pastors for Peace to help provide aid to Latin American countries.[21] Shevack researched grants, and Sostre edited them. They workshoped their proposals to buy an abandoned city property and met with Larry Kressley from the Public Welfare Foundation at Sostre's Manhattan apartment during the summer of 1982.[22] They soon received word that they were approved for a $15,000 grant (almost $50,000 today), but there was a catch: they were required to match the funds within a few months. The two scrambled to patch together several private grants and eventually secured enough money to set about identifying abandoned buildings owned by the city.

They chose 40 Market Street, originally constructed by Joseph Bros as a clothing store. Its second story consisted of a partial loft with a balcony, leaving open a double-height portion of the ground floor from which visitors could see directly up to the roof (or the sky, as was the case when they bought it). The front facade featured a glass vestibule with an inset doorway reminiscent of the Afro-Asian Bookshop at 1412 Jefferson Avenue. The building had also once housed a candy store before becoming a vacant property acquired by the city. In January 1983, Sostre and Shevack—along with fifteen teenagers funded by a county organization called the Private Industry Council—began the nine-month demolition and rebuild.

Sostre came from several generations of carpenters, including the grandfather for whom he likely was named.[23] But here, as in his legal work, he was self-taught. "He knew nothing about construction," Liz would recall lovingly in 2012. "All I remember is he learned by doing it. And getting books."[24] When their son Vinny asked Martin, then in his late eighties, how he had learned construction, he pulled out a *Reader's Digest* do-it-yourself manual from near his chair. "That's the latest edition, and I have all older editions here also."[25]

Sostre made the long bus ride from upper Manhattan to Passaic, New Jersey, usually arriving dressed in denim, white sneakers or combat boots, and a baseball cap or winter hat. According to Shevack, "his dress was very proletariat."[26] Sostre brought a satchel full of newspapers, handouts, and other educational materials. "It was like his own personal life that he was carrying with him," JEAP participant Sharrieff Bugg would later recall.[27] Sostre used the commute as teaching preparation, sharing his interpretations of what he read in the newspaper with the teenagers when he arrived. "Riding a bus is a waste of time unless you're reading," Shevack would remember him saying.[28] Many of the young people in JEAP recalled him pulling out photos of political prisoners, including a man with dreadlocks who was likely Mumia Abu-Jamal, the activist, journalist, and jailhouse lawyer then on death row.

The teenagers would gather in front of the metal storefront shutter at 40 Market Street early in the morning on weekends. Although Shevack and Sostre were lenient about returning from lunch, they emphasized punctuality to begin the workday. A typical day often started with a lesson about a political prisoner, global event, or happenings in the local community. Teens were then assigned to an area and introduced to the tools they would use. In the first few months, the building was both the organization's headquarters and an active demolition site. "I have fond memories of the smell of mildew, dampness, it being dark and cold," said Quahim Muhammad, who entered JEAP around age fifteen, after seeing some of his older peers walking around Passaic in jeans, boots, and construction hats and asked them how to join. At lunch, they would circle up and talk. It was during these conversations that Muhammad learned that Sostre had been incarcerated. At this time, he was visiting his grandfather at Rahway every weekend. These visits eventually included Reverend *Marcus Riggins,* who was incarcerated and later married Muhammad's mother at the prison. Muhammad and his brother Lance were among the earliest participants and stayed the longest. "We actually grew up in the program," said Muhammad. Around this time, Muhammad embraced Islam, changing his name from Dion to Quahim. He credits much of the literature he encountered at JEAP with influencing his decision. *The Autobiography of Malcolm X* was the first book he read cover to cover.[29]

The book was one of many at 40 Market Street. Others included Black history classics that Sostre had once stocked in his Buffalo bookstores: Lerone Bennett's *Before the Mayflower*, Carter G. Woodson's *Mis-Education of the Negro*, Robert F. Williams's *Negroes with Guns*, and the writings of J. A. Rogers.[30] He even arranged books along the glass entrance and put posters on the windows, reminiscent of his community bulletin board in Buffalo. Youth International Party found and Chicago Seven member Abbie Hoffman, to whom the building was informally dedicated, donated books to the library.[31] It was common for young people and other members of the community to flip through a book or sit and read. "It wasn't an arcade, it wasn't a place to come and play, it wasn't a place where we played cards or clowned around," Muhammad said. "It was a place to come in and obtain some knowledge. You stayed as long as you remained actively engaged in some sort of learning." Unlike the environment of a formal school, JEAP eschewed requirements, testing, and discipline, instead regarding knowledge as an offering. "We were surrounded by literature, books. We were surrounded by handouts," Muhammad recalled. "It probably became really, for many of us, the first influence of political life on any level."[32]

The teenagers in JEAP heard firsthand from activists, organizers, and writers. An impressive list of speakers included Chavis, Hoffman, Charlene Mitchell of the National Alliance Against Racist and Political Repression, memoirist Piri Thomas, Paul Bermanzohn of the Communist Workers Party and a survivor of the Greensboro Massacre, political prisoner George Merritt, and Attica Brother Frank "Big Black" Smith. Sitting in a circle with Big Black, one of the teens asked how he became an activist. "This guy right over here," he replied, pointing to Sostre and sharing a laugh together. At another event, the teenagers traveled to Newark to see Angela Davis speak. Merritt came to the back table where they were sitting and ushered Sostre to the front, where he embraced and reminisced with Davis, much to the shock of awestruck JEAP participants.[33] Muhammad remembered that simply having this access "allowed us to fill in the blanks [and] ask questions." For many participants, the program was an invitation to learn and engage with the forces in the world that structured their lives. Later becoming an educator himself, Muhammad would reflect on how "intentional it was for them to surround us with the right tools at the right moment to make us—me—a lifelong learner."[34]

Other former JEAP members focused on the impact of having caring mentors in Shevack and Sostre, who were emotionally available. "When them two came together, it's like you had two great parents that really cared about you," recalled Tim Sturdivant years later.[35] Sturdivant first met

Sandy Shevack in court during the late 1970s when he was thirteen. Like Lance and Quahim, he was one of six children raised by a single mother. Shevack knew his mother and appeared in court that day to tell the judge he would be responsible for him. "It was like an angel had stepped into my life," Sturdivant said. "Sandy introduced me to a lot of different things," which included running, canoeing, and Martin Sostre. Sturdivant was among a group of teenagers Shevack brought to New York City to hear Sostre speak. Afterward, they all sat around a table eating pizza and drinking soda as Sostre explained South African apartheid. It was completely new to Sturdivant. Later, he was watching TV when a movie about Nelson Mandela came on. "Oh wait! I know what apartheid is!" he exclaimed.[36]

Reflecting as adults, the young people in JEAP remembered Sostre in a variety of ways. Some described him as funny, others as stern. But all agreed that he was candid and would "tell you like it is." Pedro Pagan recalled his first day at JEAP when he was fourteen. Sostre pulled him and others to the side and said: "You guys, you've got to understand: some of the people, they don't care about you. You've got to make your own way. They'll come over there and they'll fuck you." Taking Sostre literally, he turned to another teen and said he did not want to come back. But he later came to understand and appreciate Sostre's bluntness.[37] Shevack had a reputation for being loving, caring, and the more likely of the two to give participants the benefit of the doubt. Despite Sostre's reputation for seriousness, Muhammad described a "glow that came over the place" when he was around. "Once you got to know him, that sternness of him—it's like somebody took a chisel and hit him with a hammer and it just all fell down. Just humbled him into real Martin."[38]

In early 1984, Sostre and Shevack were beginning their second project together, a three-story apartment building at 180 Third Street in Passaic. Meanwhile, Sostre had become a court-appointed manager for a Manhattan apartment building just south of the George Washington Bridge.[39] For years, rent strikes had been the primary mechanism available for tenants to fight absentee landlords, but there was no guarantee that necessary repairs would be made during the strike. In 1977, the Department of Housing Preservation and Development made a little-used city housing code—Article 7A—more readily available, enabling tenants to sue landlords and a housing court judge to appoint an administrator to collect rent for repairs and upkeep. Four years later, an estimated three hundred buildings were run by administrators like Sostre.[40] The building he managed was divided into two factions. One had sued their landlord and now paid rent through Sostre. Another had organized a rent strike against the other tenants in response. On February 18, 1984, there was a dispute involving a friend of Angel Fuentes of the rent-strike faction. According to Sostre, the person broke into a third-floor apartment after an eviction proceeding. When a struggle ensued, Sostre tried to wrestle away a gun which went off and superficially wounded Fuentes in the neck. Terrified at the prospect of returning to prison, Sostre went underground for over two years.

Vinny Sostre's earliest memories are from these years. He was not yet two years old, so his recollections are mostly fond ones: clandestine meetings in Florida, including a trip to Disney World; his dad's dark sunglasses; and carrying luggage in trash bags to make it look like they were taking out the garbage when they left town. "I thought all of it was cool, as a kid," he said, recalling the search for tapped telephone wires. "Turned out, I think, they were just phone lines buried in the wall. As a kid, everything was like a treasure hunt."[41]

Shevack recalled the difficulties he faced when Sostre was gone. He was the director of a newly formed nonprofit with financial commitments and community obligations. There were cost overruns, and he borrowed money as he and the teenagers finished the apartments at 180 Third Street while paying the mortgage on 40 Market Street.[42] After working his graveyard paramedic shift for the Paterson Fire Department, Shevack would head to a building and work until evening, when he would sleep briefly before starting another shift at midnight.[43] He occasionally saw Sostre during these years, once rescheduling his night shift to drive over a hundred miles and meet for an hour in a hotel room in Atlantic City.[44]

These years were especially hard on Liz, who was left to raise their two young children. "I was working full time. I was a mommy full time. I was political full time," she said. "It was too much." When asked if she worried that Sostre might go back to prison, Liz responded: "I was so busy with so many things, I had little time to think."[45] Sostre worked odd jobs as a handyman in Miami, Florida, and sent money home. There is little documentation of this period outside of the recollections of an overwhelmed mother and comrade in Liz and Sandy, and a young child in Vinny. One of the only surviving physical documents from Sostre during this period is a masthead for a proposed Black revolutionary newspaper called *The Bomb*, which was likely never published. The fuse—attached to a bomb reminiscent of the figures he had drawn to advertise the Afro-Asian Bookshop two decades earlier—lists major atrocities in American history: "kidnapping, slavery, rape, 400 years stolen slave labor, injustice, atrocities, brutality, repression, murder, de facto segregation and racism, terrorism, unemployment, genocide."[46]

During these years, JEAP developed a relationship with a vocational program that trained and certified young people in refrigeration repair. Its founder, Anderson Lee, was born to a Black sharecropping family in a North Carolina hamlet in 1930. He remembered improvising toys out of broken wheels and tires he and his siblings found in the woods and going barefoot during the summer to preserve their one pair of shoes. After traveling during his enlistment in the Korean War, Lee decided he could no longer stomach working on a plantation in the Jim Crow South and moved near relatives in New Jersey. Lee worked as a truck driver for the sanitation department and eventually saved enough money to purchase a pickup truck of his own, which he used to deliver appliances. After watching someone repair a refrigerator, he was motivated to enroll in a nineteen-month night course, working his garbage route from 5:00 a.m. until evening, then driving to Newark for classes until 10:00 p.m. By 1964, he had begun training young people and eventually founded the Anderson Lee Vocational and Technical School. "I organized this little school, and Sandy gave me a place to hold my classes," he said.[47] Lee

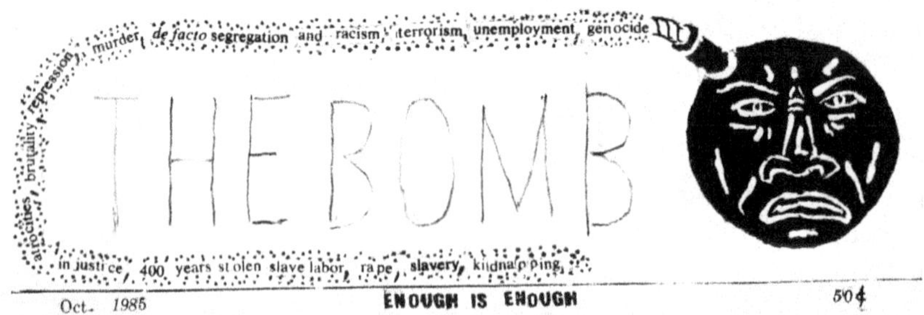

Hand drawn masthead for *The Bomb* by Martin Sostre, October 1985. Martin Sostre Collection, University of Michigan Library (Special Collections Research Center).

offered free tuition and graduated about twenty-five students a year from the ten-month course he hosted at 40 Market Street. He credited Shevack with offering the first space to hold classes and being a "vital part of enabling this program to achieve the things that it has."[48]

Finally, after two years underground, Sostre was arrested in May 1986 while doing legal research at the New York University Law School. A criminal attorney recognized him and called the police. "I was walking through the library when I saw him and stopped dead in my tracks," the lawyer, Sam Polur recounted. "I was going to put him under citizen's arrest, but I was afraid he might be armed and there were people around."[49] Despite sensationalist framings by Polur and the *New York Post*, which ran a photograph of Sostre in sunglasses next to the headline "BOOKED! Famed Fugitive Seized in Law School Library," others pointed out that Sostre's phone number and address were readily available. "We didn't know where he was," said one detective. "But we checked last night, and found that his address had been in the phonebook."[50] Sostre retained the high-profile leftist attorney Michael Kennedy and, following a nine-day trial, was acquitted of all charges a year later.[51]

Despite his two-year absence, JEAP had managed to rehabilitate two buildings in Passaic. Shevack and the teenagers had turned 180 Third Street into six one-bedroom apartments and another small building at 192 Sixth Street into two two-bedroom apartments. More than nine families had moved into the low-cost housing, much of which was covered by Section 8 of the Housing Act of 1937, which subsidized rent through the federal Housing and Urban Development department. Other apartments were rented out to those who had participated in the program, including to Jerry Patterson, whose first apartment was in the rehabilitated building at 280 Oak Street.[52] Shevack also lived in the one-bedroom apartment above 40 Market Street for fourteen years.[53]

JEAP was earning recognition for its impact on the community. "A small group is quietly but busily making a noticeable change in the city," wrote a local journalist.[54] In 1984, the organization was honored by the Passaic Chamber of Commerce. The following year, it was given a community service award. Sheila Williamson, director of the Community Foundation of New Jersey, presented the group with a $1,000 grant: "Two major necessities of the people of Passaic are safe, affordable housing and meaningful employment of teen-agers. Both these problems are creatively addressed by the Juvenile Education and Awareness Project."[55]

This recognition from the community was the result of the tireless work of the group's cofounders. Shevack would later recall constant overages and debts to the banks. Initial grants rarely covered a full project, so they were caught in a cycle of needing to show results to receive grants but needing grants to produce results. "If we couldn't get grants, we got loans. We were in debt," Shevack said. For example, 40 Market Street was used as collateral to purchase 180 Third Street.[56] They also felt pressure to finish projects, even when the necessary funds were lacking. Shevack remembered, "We needed to exhibit success to the community, which often expected failures and disappointments."[57]

Sandy Shevack and Martin Sostre inside 280 Oak Street, c. 1986-1987. Photograph by Mike Taylor. Courtesy of Sandy Shevack.

Both Shevack and Sostre regularly worked other jobs—Shevack for the fire department and Sostre as a tenant organizer in New York. Sostre was often spotted leaving for the trip back to Manhattan near midnight, earning the nickname "Night Train" from locals in the neighborhood.[58] Osvaldo Moczo, a teenager who met Sostre when he was in his late sixties, would later describe him as a "workhorse" and had trouble recalling whether Shevack or Sostre was older.[59] Shevack remembered leaving in the evening to work his night shift and coming back the next morning amazed at how much Sostre had accomplished alone. But no amount of hard work could cover the debts to banks, overages, and unexpected costs. Sharrieff Bugg remembered Sostre teaching them how to straighten out nails taken from old framing to be reused. Only reflecting as an adult did he realize this was an indication of how tight money was. By the mid-1980s, JEAP had begun using rent from the apartments to help cover costs. But the question became, as Shevack put it, "are we activists or are we real estate managers?"[60]

Shevack was working his night shift in May 1986 when they were called to a fire in Paterson. The burning building at 103 North Main Street, constructed by the First Ward Republican Club in 1901, had remained its headquarters for over half a century.[61] By the 1960s, a group called Northside Forces had taken ownership.[62] Begun in 1964 as a church club for mothers in the neighborhood, Northside Forces later ran a dental clinic, thrift shop, and low-income housing corporation. Although the program had hoped to turn the building into a recreation center, it remained vacant for nearly seven years. When JEAP sought to acquire it, a sign still hung on the burned-out facade: "Teen Activity Center. Mayor's Council on Youth. Division of Northside Forces."[63] The relationship between JEAP and Northside Forces was contentious, and it took over a year to settle the transfer of ownership.[64] But in late 1987, JEAP finally purchased 103 North Main Street.[65] Shevack and Sostre had a proven track record of four successful projects in Passaic and were looking forward to establishing a presence in Paterson. Shevack estimated that the project could be completed within six months.[66]

In early 1988, before beginning renovations, Shevack traveled to Nicaragua. He had been closely following the Sandinista National

Liberation Front when a young engineer named Ben Linder was murdered by Contras, a US-backed group funded and trained by the CIA to overthrow the Sandinista government.[67] Linder's death prompted national outrage and convinced Shevack to travel outside the country for the first time. He worked there for two weeks on a coffee farm and returned later that summer. In between his trips to Nicaragua, Shevack arranged with Anderson Lee to have refurbished refrigerators sent from New Jersey to Sandinista communities through PeaceWorks, a local group dedicated to providing support to grassroots community organizations in Nicaragua. Then, he later recounted, "I said, 'I'm going to call the newspapers up. I'm going to get a real good story, good Sandinista story.'" What happened next was "ridiculous," Shevack said, recalling his naivete.[68]

Soon, a reporter began digging into the program. "The concept was to teach city Youth Corps youngsters how to use hammers and saws to fix

Sostre holds the flag of the FSLN out a window at 103 N. Main Street. The flag was presented to Shevack during his trip to Nicaragua in 1988. Courtesy of Sandy Shevack.

up houses," Mike Fabey wrote in the first of several articles on JEAP for the Passaic *Herald-News.* "But they also learned how the United States uses its soldiers and money to tear down countries and kill innocent people."[69] Fabey managed to locate a few former participants, one of them ex-military, who claimed they were uncomfortable with the political messages coming from Shevack and Sostre. He even quoted from a newspaper article Sostre had sent to the teenagers. In it, Sostre wrote next to the photo of a Black US soldier in Honduras: "This fool Uncle Tom trained by his oppressor to kill was ordered to Honduras to kill Hispanics who never harmed him, while his own family is being subjected to genocide in the Black ghettos of the U.S.A."[70] Fabey did not mention that Sostre was an Army veteran.

Journalist Patricia Alex, of nearby Hackensack newspaper *The Record*, soon joined the fray, responding to each article published by Fabey with one of her own. In each, she pointed out that JEAP's founders had never tried to conceal their political views. Sostre argued that no one had "any right to keep these kids who live in the ghetto ignorant of the oppressive forces here. . . . If the kids understand the political forces, then they can fight to make changes."[71] During one break while working at North Main Street, the teenagers had watched a documentary about Linder's murder by the Contras. Shevack had then asked the group to consider how a $500 million war fought by the United States in Nicaragua affected them. Moczo, then seventeen years old, explained in an interview with Alex that he had previously accepted "these dumps we've got here. . . . Now my eyes are opened."[72]

The manufactured controversy over JEAP's political teachings passed, but serious practical problems emerged during the renovation of 103 North Main Street. What had been conceived as a six-month project would ultimately take nearly four years. Not only was there unanticipated damage to the building, but meeting the regulations and securing the permits required for a preschool proved much more onerous than they had expected from their experience with residential buildings. Shevack and Sostre had originally planned to rent the building to an existing preschool. When that did not materialize, Sostre decided they should run it themselves. The New World Day Care Center opened on November 18, 1991, and served eighteen children ranging in age from two and a half to five. Meanwhile, Sostre was busily making cots for another thirty-seven children.[73] He and Shevack would run the day care together for a decade, which at its height employed a half dozen staff—a director, cook, and teachers—and provided care to nearly sixty-five children. Most families were able to send their children to the day care for free by using state vouchers.[74]

In many ways, the day care center was a culmination of their decades-long partnership. It was their most ambitious project, through which they mentored several cohorts of local teenagers while converting the abandoned building into a much-needed space for early childhood education. When it opened, Sostre emphasized that New World was a tangible structure that met the material needs of oppressed communities: "One picture is worth 1,000 words. One deed is worth 1,000 pictures. And you can't get any more concrete than this."[75] "A building that was contributing to the decay of the community, is now contributing to the uplifting of the community," Shevack added.[76]

But New World also marked a notable departure from previous projects, which grew increasingly more evident over time. For almost nine years, JEAP had been transforming buildings in disrepair to serve communities of color in Passaic and Paterson while providing local teenagers with construction skills, political education, and a wage for their labor. Now, Shevack and Sostre's focus shifted away from radicalizing teens and transforming spaces to managing a day care center. However, this did not mean they left political work entirely. As Shevack argued, "Quality preschool education *is* political." New World served working parents, helping young children living in poverty to get early learning opportunities so they were on pace with children from more affluent families when they started public school; eventually it became a community institution. But running the preschool themselves meant that Shevack and Sostre were increasingly mired in bureaucratic and administrative duties while supporting the staff, students, and families, as well as maintaining the building. "Our whole emphasis was the preschool," Shevack recalled. "We were so immersed in just keeping that center going."[77]

Both together and separately, the two continued their political activities outside the day care center throughout the 1990s. They sent preschool furniture to Nicaragua and helped with defense work for political prisoners such as Geronimo Pratt, Mondo We Langa, and Ed Poindexter.[78] Sandy also served as the regional coordinator for the Free Lori Berenson Committee and stayed involved in solidarity work with El Salvador, Nicaragua, and Cuba.[79] Sostre supported those he regarded as prisoners of war with his longtime comrade Yuri Kochiyama, who had first written him while he was in solitary confinement at Green Haven in 1969.

Former Black Panther Francisco "Cisco" Torres had written to Sostre while both were incarcerated in the early 1970s, perhaps using Kochiyama as an intermediary. Sostre and Torres had been released within a few years of each other—in 1976 and 1978 respectively—and in the decades that followed, they formed a small collective to continue supporting those still inside. As Torres pointed out, while cases such as Angela Davis, the Panther Twenty-One, and even Sostre received high-profile attention, many others, including his own, remained "under the radar."[80] The collective comprised of an impressive list of revolutionary political prisoners, most of whom were also former Black Panthers, including Safiya Bukhari, Ashanti Alston, Chango Monges, Blood McCreary, Oscar Washington, Sasha Brown, Tarik Haskins, and Nat Shanks, in addition to Cisco Torres and his brother Gabriel.[81]

For Ashanti Alston, organizing with Sostre was a chance to work with an elder and thinker whom he had long respected and learned from. The former member of the Black Panther Party and Black Liberation Army had been searching for alternatives to Marxism-Leninism, Maoism, and Black nationalism while in prison, and credited Kuwasi Balagoon and Sostre with providing a valuable perspective. Balagoon was one of the Panther 21 who—like Ervin, Sostre, and Alston—moved through the revolutionary Black nationalism of the Panthers and Republic of New Africa before eventually critiquing their reliance on hierarchy, centralization, and the nation-state. Like Sostre, Balagoon was particularly drawn to Italian anarchist Errico Malatesta's emphasis on revolutionary deeds instead of rhetoric.[82] "I did not need the traditional canon on anarchism. I needed to hear it from some Black folks who I had a lot of respect for," Alston recalled.

When Alston was released, he went to the Tamiment Library at New York University in search of anything Sostre had written, from pamphlets to mainstream newspapers to the radical press. Joining the collective, he would later reflect, "was my opportunity to actually get to know the person who we all knew about but that we'd never met because we was all in different places, but who had such an impact on us, and now we were working on a project together."[83] Although Sostre was an elder in the group, his humble demeanor made a deep impression. Most collective members' names were associated with their court cases. But, according to Torres, "if you didn't recognize him by name, you didn't even know it was him." "There are other people who would let you know, 'Hey, I'm So-and-So.' He wasn't that type of person."[84] Alston remembered Sostre's excitement about doing political organizing with comrades. "I think he felt isolated, so I know that when we had actually found out where he lived and started working together, he was really happy to be working with some people around something."[85] As Alston's memories indicate, Sostre remained involved in political work outside the day care, which did not fulfill his commitment to freeing other political prisoners.

The FBI watched these gatherings of former political prisoners closely. In a 1992 memo, they described the collective as "actively involved in reforming the BLA on both the East and West Coasts and promoting and planning resurgence of BLA activity."[86] Just as state police had done thirty years earlier in Buffalo, the Bureau circulated a photo of Sostre, now in his early seventies.[87] Due to heavy redactions, little information that can be gleaned from hundreds of pages of unclassified surveillance documents. But the investigations, which were made in coordination with the Joint Terrorist Task Force formed in 1980, revealed both the ongoing surveillance that Sostre endured during his long life and a more recent part of the state's repressive apparatus: "counterterrorism."[88] "Anyone that stands up is a terrorist," Sostre explained in 2012. "You have to be very careful because now they'll kill you."

When Sostre was in his late seventies, his relationship with Shevack became strained. "The falling out between Martin and I was somewhat incremental," Shevack would later recall. Their disagreements over money and the day care came to a head in the late 1990s over the question of whether the center should seek inclusion in the state's new Abbott Program. The program was an outcome of the fifth decision in *Abbott v. Burke* (*Abbott V*) in 1998, a New Jersey Supreme Court case considered to be one of the most important in public education since *Brown v. Board*. The ruling made full-day "high-quality" preschool mandatory for all three- and four-year-olds in thirty-one high-poverty school districts and offered subsidies for participating schools.[89] New World Day Care was in an eligible district. Shevack believed that the benefits, which included lower teacher–student ratios, teaching assistants in every class, and opportunities for staff professional development and higher wages, outweighed any drawbacks. Sostre's reasons for resisting the program are not documented. It may have been his general distrust of government intervention, or he may have seen the standards set by the state, which included stricter building codes and higher formal education requirements for teachers, as impediments to community control and school autonomy.

The *Abbott* ruling, according to education researcher Colleen Malleo, "transformed the preschool teaching profession in New Jersey."[90] Prior to the ruling, 35 percent of preschool teachers in Abbott districts had bachelor's degrees; by 2003, 92 percent did.[91] But within these numbers was a double-edged incentive. The program financially supported teachers in earning their bachelor's degree in early childhood education. But teachers without a degree could lose their jobs and would be suddenly considered unqualified for a position at an Abbott-designated school.[92] The history of feminist women's health centers, childcare cooperatives, rape crisis centers, battered women's shelters, and other counter-institutions during this period offers cautionary tales regarding the institutionalization of community-based programs through state and federal grants. Compliance with government-mandated requirements led to the imposition of a professional and administrative hierarchy in the organization and replaced participatory and democratic decision-making processes that included patients, parents, and other clients with a top-down model in which directors' primary responsible was to funders.[93] But what little evidence remains from Sostre's writings and interviews indicates that he approached New World Day Care as a business, not as a community organization with shared power.[94] Ultimately, Shevack viewed Sostre's decision not to enroll in the Abbott program as the "nail in the coffin." In his words, "The whole mood in the place changed" after that. Both staff and families left for Abbott schools, and enrollment dropped to fewer than a dozen students.[95] What appeared on its face to be a souring of a twenty-year political mentorship and friendship cannot be separated from the neoliberal political economy and changing state and federal education policy.

The other factor in this rupture was the two men's differing life stages. When Shevack and Sostre met, they were twenty-one and fifty-three respectively, and neither had children. Sostre was now approaching eighty and had two college-aged children, whereas Sandy still had none. Sostre had spent most of his prime earning years in the military or prison. They also had differing relationships to the communities in which they worked. Each time Sostre made a controversial decision, the burden of mending relationships and finding new staff fell to Shevack, who lived locally. Eventually, the relationship reached an impasse, and Shevack, having already begun working as a site manager in an after-school and summer program through the Passaic Board of Education, ceded decisions over the preschool to Sostre.[96] In 2002, Sostre attempted to sell the building at 103 North Main Street without consulting Shevack or the organization's advisory board. Shevack reluctantly sued to enjoin Sostre from selling the building and requested he be removed from the board. The following year, a judge ruled in Shevack's favor. The two never reconciled.[97] Shevack reflected: "I never thought it would end the way it did, but that should not be, in my opinion, the focus" of any story about JEAP and its legacy. Instead, he emphasized that Sostre's "contribution—his energy, his intellect, his dedication—created opportunities for people who've benefited from it to this day."[98]

Today, the buildings transformed by JEAP continue that legacy. 40 Market Street is home to Angela Kidz University preschool, founded by Angela Burgos-Oliver, as well as the Bella Chanel Mentoring Program, a girls' empowerment program established by Kim Cottrell, whose brother Tim Sturdivant worked on the building as JEAP participant. The building at 103 North Main Street was purchased in 2016 by Carol Sobh, founder of the Startlet Academy preschool and aftercare program. "I look at [40 Market Street] every time I go in," Shevack said. "I was the one who said, "'This can't happen. This building is ridiculous.' . . . But there's a lot of people who are benefiting today from the work and the insight that Martin put forth. Some of them know Martin and some of them don't. But his work is living on today."[99]

By the early 2000s, Martin Sostre was in his eighties. Without a stake in JEAP or the day care center, he no longer made his regular trips to New Jersey. Instead, his family remembered him working out and practicing yoga, studying at the Columbia Law Library, and going to lower Manhattan to read at Borders (which he used like a library) and shop for deals on Chambers Street. He also closely watched the stock market, specifically

Chinese stocks, which he believed would accelerate the demise of the US and become more valuable as China rose as a world superpower.[100] His wife Liz took on an increasing role as caregiver, especially when Martin had seizures, some of which were grand mal and resulted in his blacking out entirely. His skepticism of doctors and hospitals was frustrating to Liz. Whether or not he had remembered, or chosen, to take his anticonvulsant pills was a recurring issue in the family. Liz believed the seizures were the result of a head injury he sustained while painting a ceiling. But a letter from the American Red Cross during World War II suggests he may have had seizures as a child. "When [Sostre] was one year old, at the time of teething he suffered from convulsions," it documented. "This persisted until he was seven years old, and reoccurred at rather frequent intervals, but particularly when he had even a slight fever accompanying a cold."[101]

In 2006, Martin and Liz experienced the devastating loss of their eldest child, Mark, who died from an accidental overdose at age twenty-six. Around this time, Vinny moved closer to home to better support his parents. Among the things that he did was during this period was interview his father. Crowded together in their home office with Liz offering prompts and clarifications offscreen, Vinny told his dad that part of his motivation was personal curiosity about his family's background. The other was to update his Wikipedia page. "That's the way that people are going to find out about you," he explained.[102] Indeed, it was during this period that a younger generation of organizers was beginning to learn about Sostre's legacy and connecting it to their own struggles.

Leslie James Pickering already had a decade of experience with organizing and state repression when he first encountered the story of Sostre's frame-up and the Afro-Asian Bookshops. Born in Buffalo in 1978, Pickering had moved to San Francisco to live with his aunt when he was sixteen, where he encountered zines on animal liberation and environmental justice at hip-hop and punk shows. Within a year, he was participating in civil disobedience actions.[103] By the late 1990s, Pickering had been detained a few dozen times, culminating with his scaling the Washington Monument to protest primate research.[104] After being interrogated for hours and narrowly escaping charges, he felt the need to shift tactics. Pickering became a national spokesperson for the Earth Liberation Front (ELF), an autonomous underground group that used sabotage and other guerilla tactics in efforts to prevent ecological destruction. The FBI targeted the network as "eco-terrorists" and inundated the cells with surveillance and informers. By the early 2000s, the ELF had fallen apart, and Pickering returned to Buffalo eager for a change of scene and a lower profile.[105]

Through his role as a spokesperson for ELF, he had realized the importance for communication skills, so he decided to return to school for book arts and publishing. While enrolled at Goddard College in Vermont, well known among radical activists for its "distance learning" program, Pickering was encouraged by an advisor to conduct a community-needs assessment in his hometown. With an iPod and an aftermarket microphone, he spent the summer asking hundreds of residents two things: What's wrong with Buffalo? And what can be done about it? "Everybody knew what was wrong with Buffalo," he recalled, but "they had no ability to answer the second question." That same summer, he was scouring libraries and bookstores for information about local radical history for his free community-based course on revolutionary struggle in western New York. Pickering remembers being able to find pamphlets and books still stamped with "East-West Bookshop" or "Afro-Asian Bookshop in Exile" in used bookstores around town. Eventually, he contacted Pacific Street Films and ordered a VHS copy of *Frame-Up! The Imprisonment of Martin Sostre*.[106]

In response to the survey conducted the previous summer, Pickering and others had begun hosting informal monthly events at community centers around the city aimed at educating residents about past struggles and catalyzing conversations about what could be done to fix the problems they now faced. The events often featured a film screening or a lecture before a conversation that Pickering described as "barely even facilitated." Among the topics—which included the Attica rebellion, the Young Lords, Assata Shakur, Malcolm X, COINTELPRO, the American Indian Movement takeover of Alcatraz, the MOVE bombing, and the murder of Fred Hampton—was Martin Sostre.[107]

A flyer for the screening of *Frame-Up!* at a community center on Buffalo's West Side featured the familiar mugshot of Sostre taken after his 1967 arrest. "Sostre became one of America's more prominent political prisoners and his influence remains strong on the streets of Buffalo where liberation has yet to be won," the poster read, in part.[108] Pickering recalled using more text than he would normally include, having often seen people in the community lingering to read poster. He reasoned that "even if they aren't coming, they're getting something out of it." But people were coming. And while the success of the growing community conversation series meant increased visibility, Pickering was careful, due to his past experiences with state surveillance, to turn down opportunities from local journalists and the press. Despite these precautions, Pickering later found out that FBI informers had been present at several of the events.[109]

On March 28, 2005, a week following Sostre's eighty-second birthday, the former political prisoner called into a community center in the city in which he was framed to answer audience questions. Pickering remembers a good-sized crowd, some of whom had been connected to Sostre's defense committee or visited his bookstores. A second screening was held on the East Side, just blocks from the former site of the Afro-Asian Bookshop.[110] It had been nearly four decades since the frame-up that destroyed Buffalo's first radical bookstores, and Sostre had never fulfilled his vision of returning and reinvigorating them. But his aim of raising the revolutionary consciousness of people and creating a "library of dissent" remained in the minds of those in Buffalo. Even the use of posters to spread political awareness was reminiscent of Sostre's community bulletin on the boarded-up windows of his bookstore in the aftermath of the rebellion. Unfortunately, these similarities also extended to the response of the state.

That August, the community center where Pickering had been hosting conversations on the West Side was destroyed by arson.[111] The fire left the Massachusetts Avenue Project (MAP)—the community garden and food justice organization that had allowed him to use their space—without a home. Meanwhile, Erie County was experiencing a budget crisis and targeted over a dozen libraries for closure.[112] MAP reached an agreement with a city council member to lease the recently shuttered Northwest Branch Library on Grant Street for one dollar a year. That summer, children in the neighborhood continued to show up at the library. Rather than turning them away, the organization asked Pickering if he would be interested in trying to keep it open. Using the mailing list built through the community discussions, he began soliciting donations for radical books. He planned to name it the "Martin Sostre Commemorative Collection." Then he received a call from a local journalist who wanted to write a story about the "terrorist reopening a library."[113]

A week after the reading room opened, Pickering learned from the pages of the *Buffalo News* that they were getting kicked out of the building. MAP's new executive director had told the journalist before she notified

Pickering: "The Massachusetts Avenue Project in no way endorses or supports violence of any kind."[114] When he later successfully sued for his FBI file, Pickering found the entire article in text-only form, making him suspect that the bureau had a "hand in writing the article." Pickering and others were convinced: "If we were going to continue to do this kind of organizing, we had to do it in our own space."[115] In 2012, he and his partner Theresa Baker-Pickering opened Burning Books, a radical bookstore on Buffalo's West Side, which was surveilled and targeted by the FBI for several years. Bruce Beyer, a former member of the Martin Sostre Defense Committee and himself a political prisoner who was inspired by Sostre's resistance, noted the parallels in the local newspaper. "Police agencies seem to have great difficulty discerning the difference between protecting the First Amendment rights of bookstore owners and violating them," he wrote. "If not for lawyers, I believe I would be visiting these young activists in prison rather than attending activities at Burning Books."[116]

Another young activist who took an interest in Sostre was Kazembe Balagun. As a student at Hunter College in New York City, Balagun was active in the Student Liberation Action Movement (SLAM!), a multiracial radical student group formed in the late 1990s to combat yet another wave of tuition hikes and budget cuts at CUNY campuses. His mentor, Ashanti Alston, introduced him to Sostre along with other Black anarchists such as Kuwasi Balagoon, whose last name Kazembe honors. When Balagun watched *Frame-Up!* at Hunter's Center for Puerto Rican Studies, he was struck by the significance of a film highlighting a Black anarchist of Puerto Rican descent. Later, he decided to screen it as part of the 2008 Visual Liberation film festival at the Brecht Forum, a radical countercultural space in lower Manhattan.[117] Balagun called the number listed in the white pages for Martin Sostre. "I said, 'My name is Kazembe, I'm the outreach coordinator for the Brecht Forum. I would love to show this film." Sostre replied, "Sure, I'll do it. What day?"[118]

Over one hundred people, including young anarchists of color, members of the Puerto Rican anti-authoritarian punk band Ricanstruction, and movement elders like Alston, filled the small space near the West Side Highway. Sostre's humility and sprightliness left a lasting impression on Balagun. Although offered a ride, Sostre took the subway. Balagun watched as an 85-year-old wearing an army cap, T-shirt, and shorts ran up the stairs at the forum. The thirty-minute documentary ended with a somber, black-and-white slide: "Martin Sostre is still in jail." Balagun came on stage and announced: "I'm happy to tell you that Martin Sostre is free. And he's with us tonight." After a standing ovation, Sostre took questions for about half an hour.[119]

The film showing and discussion at the Brecht on August 6, 2008, was likely the first public event Sostre had done in decades, and also his last. In 2014, he suffered a stroke. During his father's final days in the hospital, Vinny recalled the difficulty of witnessing the ironclad will that had been such a staple of his father's life as he resisted the increasingly invasive medical treatments required to keep him alive. He also recalled the respectful care his father received from some of the hospital staff when they learned of his role in the Black freedom struggle. On August 12, 2015, Martin Sostre passed away at the age of ninety-two.

Although he never published a memoir, Sostre was a meticulous historian of his own struggle. His resistance to state violence was recorded through his legal work and courtroom testimony. The foundation of his landmark victory in *Sostre v. Rockefeller*, for instance, was a daily log he kept during his 372 days in solitary confinement. He had an impeccable memory for detail, honed by preparing writs from recollection rather than reference books. Alongside these granular details, he would pull back during key transitions and theorize what he had learned through the previous stage of struggle. Many of these ideas have been preserved through his essays published in radical newspapers and his letters to comrades. Complementing Sostre's own accounts are the vivid recollections of those with whom he organized; they were gracious enough to share their stories in this book. As revolutionary political prisoner Albert "Nuh" Washington said, "a revolutionary never dies because his ideas live with his comrades."[120]

Sostre understood his life as a "continuous struggle," with an ever-changing battlefield, in a universal war of liberation against all forms of oppression. He recognized that the process of social transformation was necessarily dynamic and ongoing. "All of these acts," he once wrote, "will not just disappear. Nothing disappears in this world. Either it lies dormant awaiting the propitious moment to manifest itself, or it manifests itself in different forms and manners. Once an act or thought is set in motion, nothing can stop it."[121] It is telling that he connected acts and thoughts as forms of energy. Sostre's revolutionary life is inextricable from his revolutionary thinking. Each informed the other. In that sense, neither is ever extinguished.

Acknowledgments

Acknowledgment is much too small a word for the generosity extended to me throughout the writing of this book. I had hardly begun research while away on academic leave, when I was politically targeted and fired from my job as a professor at the University of Mississippi. A year later, I decided to leave academia. To inventory the forms of support and care that came from mentors, friends, family, comrades, and so many people I did not know during this transitional period, would not only be a futile task; it would miss the point. Our struggles are interconnected, and acts of solidarity are expressions of love, for each other and for ourselves. These acknowledgments are dedicated to the many people whose labor, care, and comradeship—both in the past and whose struggles are its subject matter, and those in the present—helped make this book possible.

The list of library workers, clerks, and archivists who supported my research is too long to catalog. A partial one includes Heather Ackerman, Kristen Diehl, Daniel DiLandro, Paul Doty, Malia Guyer-Stevens, Kailey Holtslander, Miriam Intrator, Thai Jones, Morgen MacIntosh Hodgetts, Haley Maynard, Gregory Mobley, Kate Mollan, Shannon O'Neill, Rebecca Shevy, Cynthia Van Ness, Kristen Wilson, and Marcia Zubrow.-Many went above and beyond the scope of their job, with an appreciation for the politics of this book. I am especially grateful to those who bent, subverted, and labored in the margins. Special thanks to Julie Herrada, who created a home for Sostre's personal papers in the Labadie Collection at the University of Michigan; Hope Dunbar, for making long-unavailable materials at the University at Buffalo accessible; and Addie Owens for fulfilling as many interlibrary loan requests as possible for this project.

When I was not able to travel to archives, I relied upon the support of friends and researchers. Thank you to Zoë Hopkins and Elizabeth Ross for their research early in this project. Alex Elkins generously shared materials on the Buffalo uprising, Teddie Kelly provided digital copies of *Workers World*, and Lily Sawyer-Kaplan put together helpful case summaries and supported with legal research. Thank you to Gary Kroll and Redia Spada for securing trial documents from the Clinton County Clerk's Office, and Dennis Conrow and Brendan Hornbostel for accessing files at various National Archives sites. Gabrielle Corona and Pamela Cappas-Toro translated primary source materials from Spanish for me. And Lloyd Barba and Katie Lennard went above and beyond to drive long distances, find people on Facebook, or consult with their networks.

The true archives of revolutionary struggles are maintained by those who waged them. The stories entrusted to me by Martin Sostre's comrades, family, and acquaintances are the heart of this book. A full list of those interviewed includes Ashanti Alston, Karima Amin, Claudia Angelos, Kree Arvanitas, Nellie Hester Bailey, Kazembe Balagun, Lynn Barclay, Dan Bentivogli, Melanie Best, Kristin Booth Glen, Kay Branagan, Neal Browne, Sharrieff Bugg, Louis Cafone, Paul Chevigny, Joseph Clore, Mark Demeritt, Michael Deutsch, Jethro Eisenberg, Lorenzo Kom'boa Ervin, Sylvia Federici, Richard Feldman, Steven Fischler, Dan Georgakas, Danny Gotham, Deirdre Griswald, William Harris, Dennis Jacobsen, Peter Kirchheimer, Edward Koren, Jaan Laaman, Elizabeth (Boehner) LaPenne, Anderson Lee, Franz Leichter, Bob McCubbin, Michael Meeropol, Janine Migden-Ostranger, Marjorie Miller, Osvaldo Moczo, Masia Mugmuk, Quahim Muhammad, Jalil Muntaqim, Pat Murray, Vaunda Nelson, Peggy Nemoff, Maire Osborne, Stephen Ostrander, Pedro Pagan, Jerry Patterson, Leslie Pickering, Geraldine (Robinson) Pointer, Joel Ray, Antonio Rodríguez, Sylvia Rodríguez, Mimi Rosenberg, Alan Rosenthal, Jerry Ross, Carlito Rovira, Herman Schwartz, Sandy Shevack, John "KO" Smith, Lizabeth Sostre, Vinny Sostre, David Spaner, John Steinbock, Gordon Stewart, Tim Sturdivant, Joel Sucher, Ed Sullivan, Francisco Torres, Ed Vaughn, Gregory Watson, Howard Wilinsky, and Bill Wylie-Kellerman. While some people's recollections figure prominently in the book and others show up in fragments or sometimes not at all, each informed my telling of Sostre's life in important ways. I am humbled that they shared their memories with me and sincerely hope that I have done them justice. Thank you to Penny Miller for transcribing many of these interviews.

Dozens of people also offered personal effects such letters, photographs, defense committee materials, newsletters, diaries, and FBI files. Others generously shared from their family archives. I am particularly thankful to Mallory Merrill Siljegovic, who sent beautiful color slides of photographs her mother Jeanette took; and Ewa and Hania Dubinsky, and their mother Andrzeja, who relentlessly searched for letters, photographs, and audio recordings that were instrumental in piecing together the life of the Potsdam-Canton defense committee. Listening to loving stories of people's parents and learning what Sostre's struggle meant to them and their families was one of the unexpected joys of this project. Joe Shapiro has also been a constant source of support, sharing notes and recordings from interviews as well as the photograph for the cover of this book. Finally, my deepest thanks to Ellie Dorritie and the WWP comrades who located and mailed boxes of primary sources produced by the original Martin Sostre Defense Committee in Buffalo.

There was no family more giving than Sostre's own. Vinny and Liz were open and patient with my questions and generously shared materials and family stories. When necessary, they even helped me access materials such as Sostre's medical and psychiatric files from Clinton Prison, which the state denied, citing the protection of mental health records (of course, these were records produced through the state's own efforts to pathologize and torture the person whose privacy they later claimed to protect). This labyrinthian journey through state bureaucracy was successful through the help of Brad Thomson and Wally Hike, and is indicative of the support I received from Martin's family. I appreciated Liz's honesty and candor, and Vinny gentleness and understanding, as partners on this journey. I am also grateful to Geraldine and the entire Pointer family, particularly Terrance and Mariah, for their warmth and willingness to collaborate on the ongoing struggle to exonerate Geraldine and Martin.

Jerry Ross and Sandy Shevack have been stalwart supporters and co-conspirators on this project. Jerry has remained an unflinching advocate of Martin and Geraldine since their frame-up in 1967 and has persistently sought to make their story better known for over half a century. It is easy to see why Sandy was one of Martin's closest and enduring comrades. He is a natural organizer, always staying connected and putting people in touch with one another. Without Sandy's longstanding relationships to the many young people that he and Martin mentored during the 1980s and 1990s, the final chapter of this book—and of Sostre's political organizing—may have remained a postscript.

I talked through ideas and shared versions of the manuscript at various stages with comrades who were incarcerated and their feedback and knowledge profoundly informed the analysis and arguments in this book. Many were experiencing the same forms of state repression—solitary confinement, strip frisks, censorship, legal obstruction, falsified write-ups, punitive transfers, and parole denials—that Sostre had a half-century before. This includes Bryant Arroyo, Corey Devon Arthur, Christopher Blackwell, Perry Ford, Robert Hampton, April Harris, Alvamore Alexis Irizarry Jr., Anita Krecic, Lawrence Jenkins, Antoine Lipscomb, Safear Ness, Loretta Pierre, Felix Sitthivong, John "KO" Smith, Kenneth Vogt, Antoine "Indy" Walker, Paris Whitfield, and Stevie Wilson. I am grateful for their helpful comments, kindness, and comradeship.

The writing of this book was also deeply informed, and in many ways only made possible, by my own organizing. I am especially indebted to my Study and Struggle family, who helped me create what became my political home during these years. Thank you to Geraldine Alford, Corey Devon Arthur, Jarvis Benson, Stef Bernal-Martinez, Robbie Boyd, Cam Calisch, Pamela Cappas-Toro, Andy Eisen, Rosa Flores, Robert Hampton, bex kolins, Kayla Lee, Alison Mollman, Safear Ness, Mariana Peñaloza Morales, Loretta Pierre, Charlotte Rosen, Linda Ross, Ian Scott, Maya Singhal, Jessica Sylvia, Kenneth Vogt, Paris Whitfield, Tanika Williams, and so many more for creating such a beautiful political community. More recently, this has included efforts to Free the Mississippi Five with Sarah Ball, Patrick Bannon, Tamarra Bowie, Jamie Dear, Ai Miller, Pauline Rogers, Jessica Sylvia, Stacey Williams, Tiffany Worley and the Five themselves: Lisa Crevitt, Evelyn Smith, Anita Krecic, Loretta Pierre, and Linda Ross. Lastly, thank you to the entire Haymarket Books crew—Anthony Arnove, Dan Blanchard, Julie Fain, Nicole Kim, Sean Larson, and John McDonald—that make so much of our work at Study and Struggle possible.

There were several people who worked with me to make Sostre's life and ideas more accessible and widely known during the period I was researching and writing this book. Foremost among them is William C.

Anderson, who collaborated on a variety of projects dedicated to Martin's legacy and has remained a constant friend and comrade through them all. Thank you to Lorenzo Kom'boa Ervin for his vision in proposing the Martin Sostre Institute, as well as the other forms of support and knowledge he generously lent. When I was looking for support to host a centennial celebration of Martin's life, Sarah Ball swooped in and became a lifelong friend in the process. Denzel Burke, Destine Phillips, Tommy Hagan and the rest of the young people with REAL Youth Initiative were amazing collaborators on a zine we put together about Sostre's life. I remain humbled and grateful to Mariame Kaba, Robin D. G. Kelley, and Ruth Wilson Gilmore for various forms of support they offered over the years. Thank you to Robin for his stunning foreword and to Mariame, Ruthie, Mumia Abu-Jamal, Orisanmi Burton, and Angela Davis for their generous words of praise for the book. Finally, thank you to James Coughlin and Leslie Pickering, who have put into motion efforts in Buffalo that I have only dreamed about.

Other people have been sounding boards and offered emotional support and words of affirmation. This includes Minali Aggarwal, Dan Berger, Orisanmi Burton, Walter Johnson, Austin McCoy, Derecka Purnell, Sherie Randolph, Barbara Ransby, Chandan Reddy, Dean Spade, Em Thuma, Stephen Ward, Keeanga-Yamahtta Taylor, and Jessie Wilkerson. Ursula Wolfe-Rocca labored alongside me many days at the coffee shop, always kindly letting me interrupt with some esoteric bit of history I had just learned. She also read the manuscript and offered generous feedback. Lisa Lowe deserves her own page of gratitude for the incredible support she offered during my transition away from the University of Mississippi and academia. She also made possible one of the collaborations that has been a highlight of this project for me—working with Minh Vu. Minh has been such a joyful, brilliant, and sweet research companion. I am lucky to have shared this journey with them.

I have had the opportunity to work with several wonderful editors while writing this book. I am indebted to Brandon Proia, who championed the project and signed it to the University of North Carolina Press. Dawn Durante was understanding when I approached her with my desire publish elsewhere after leaving academia; I am forever thankful for her care throughout that process. Zach, Angelica, and the entire crew at AK made me feel welcomed and excited about the possibilities of collaborating on this book together and we haven't looked back since! And from its conception and through rewrite after rewrite, Grey Osterud offered brilliant developmental editing while helping me navigate the many ethical considerations that accompany a project of this nature. Anyone who has worked with Grey knows how tremendously fortunate we are, and how impossible it is to express the appropriate level of gratitude deserved. Thank you to Sam Smith for the smart and attentive copy edits.

My parents, Steven and Lynette, have had my back more times than I can count and remain a phone call away, a seemingly small thing that is in fact so very profound. I am also thankful to Christine, Randy, Kiefer, and Nick for their enduring affection and love. Zach Norman has collaborated with me on virtually every project since we were nineteen, including the cover of this book. Zach, thank you for always being up for looking at a few hundred more possibilities with me. Cam Calisch was playing all positions during the writing of this book—comrade, co-worker, caregiver, confidant, and friend. They give widely and deeply, always with tenderness, and I have been lucky to receive so much from them. To my little moonchildren, you make me smile, kvell, and laugh every day we are together. After nearly five years of my writing, Jules exclaimed at the end with shock: "you're writing a book!?" It was a wonderful reminder that we spend our time in other worlds, sacred and splendid, for ourselves and everything our minds can imagine together. Anaïs, I look forward to creating those with you. Margaux, it would take more than another five years and a book to express my love and gratitude. Holding this, though, I hope you are reminded of all your labor and care that made it possible and my utter joy and delight in sharing my days with you.

Notes

Foreword

1. Martin Sostre, "What is to be Done?," March 9, 1976, Black Mass Communications Project Collection, Robert S. Cox Special Collections and University Archives Research Center, University of Massachusetts Amherst.
2. The *New York Times* finally ran an obituary of Sostre four years later as part of its "Overlooked" series. Alexandria Symonds, "Overlooked No More: Martin Sostre, Who Reformed America's Prisons from His Cell," *New York Times*, April 24, 2019.
3. "John Brown's Provisional Constitution" (1858), available at https://famous-trials.com/johnbrown/614-browconstitution.
4. Orisanmi Burton, *Tip of the Spear: Black Radicalism, Prison Repression, and the Long Attica Revolt* (Oakland: University of California Press, 2023), 410. See also Toussaint Losier, *War for the City: Black Liberation and the Consolidation of the Carceral State* (Chapel Hill: University of North Carolina Press, forthcoming).
5. Martin Sostre, "Armed Struggle Natural Response to Fascist Rule," Folder 2, Subject Vertical Files, Civil Liberties—Blacks—Black Nationalism—Sostre, Martin, Labadie Collection, University of Michigan, Special Collections.

Introduction: "An Original Black Political Ideology"

1. Martin Sostre to Karen St. Hilaire, June 28, 1975, in author's possession, courtesy of Anne Heidenreich.
2. Martin Sostre to unknown (likely Sharon Fischer), January 19, 1972, Box 13, Folder 13, Elwin H. Powell Papers, University Archives, State University of New York at Buffalo.
3. Martin Sostre, "Thoughts of a Black Political Prisoner in Solitary Confinement," *Partisan* 5, no. 2 (April 1969): 15.
4. Martin Sostre, "Pilots for Panthers: Assault on the Monster's Head," *Black News* 1, no. 1 (January 1970): 1.
5. Martin Sostre to Ed Dubinsky, n.d. (missing first page), in author's possession, courtesy of Hania Dubinsky.

6. Martin Sostre, "Statement on the S.L.A.," April 1974, Folder 2, Subject Vertical Files, Civil Liberties—Blacks—Black Nationalism—Sostre, Martin, Labadie Collection, University of Michigan, Special Collections.
7. Martin Sostre to Lolita *Lebrón, April 20, 1973, Mixed Materials 1, Folder 5,* Martin Sostre Collection (MSC), University of Michigan Library (Special Collections Research Center).
8. Akinyele K. Umoja, "Maroon: Kuwasi Balagoon and the Evolution of Revolutionary New Afrikan Anarchism," *Science and Society* 79, no. 2 (April 2015): 210.
9. Carlos Pisacane originally wrote this in his 1857 "political testament." Quoted in Robert Graham, *We Do Not Fear Anarchy, We Invoke It: The First International and the Origins of the Anarchist Movement* (Oakland, CA: AK Press, 2015), 191.
10. "The Open Road Interview with Martin Sostre," by David Spaner, *Open Road*, Summer 1976, 29.
11. Martin Sostre, "Some Comments on Anarchism," July 1973, Folder 2, Subject Vertical Files.
12. Martin Sostre to Ed Dubinsky, May 15, 1975, in author's possession, courtesy of Hania Dubinsky.
13. Martin Sostre, reel-to-reel tape recording with Ed Dubinsky and Jackie Sharpe (now Sauter), in author's possession, courtesy of Andrzeja Axt.
14. Devin Leonard, "Day-Care Center Is Symbol of Progress," *The Record*, December 11, 1991.
15. The most detailed are "Some Comments on Anarchism" and his interview with *Open Road* in 1976.
16. "Open Road Interview," 28.
17. In 2012, a few years before his death, abolitionist organizer Mariame Kaba published several entries on Sostre on her blog, *Prison Culture*. "To my knowledge, there has been no biography written about his life which is a real shame," she wrote. "His is a name that should be more well-known." Mariame Kaba, "Martin Sostre: Legal Advocate, Prisoner, Revolutionary . . . ," *Prison Culture*, June 12, 2012, https://www.usprisonculture.com/2012/06/12/martin-sostre-revolutionary-legal-advocate-prisoner/; Mariame Kaba, "Quote of the Day: Martin Sostre," *Prison Culture*, June 11, 2012, https://www.usprisonculture.com/2012/06/11/quote-of-the-day-martin-sostre/.
18. Martin Sostre, "Armed Struggle Natural Response to Fascist Rule," Folder 2, Subject Vertical Files.
19. Martin Sostre to Joan Franklin, June 11, 1970, in *People v. Sostre*, General Case Material, January-June 1970, Folder 100243-030-0492, Supplement to Part 23: Legal Department Case Files, Series B: The Northeast, Section II: New York, Papers of the NAACP, ProQuest History Vault.
20. Alexandria Symonds, "Overlooked No More: Martin Sostre, Who Reformed America's Prisons From His Cell," *New York Times*, April 24, 2019.
21. Martin Sostre to author, July 2013, in author's possession.
22. Linda B. Bakonyi, " 'These Babies Are Truly Our Future,' " *The Record*, October 6, 1993.

23. Martin Sostre to Lolita Lebrón, April 20, 1973.
24. Andy Cornell, *Unruly Equality: U.S. Anarchism in the Twentieth Century* (Oakland, CA: University of California Press, 2016), 287.
25. Eric Laursen, *The Operating System: An Anarchist Theory of the Modern State* (Oakland, CA: AK Press, 2021), 20.
26. "Open Road Interview," 29.
27. Cornell, *Unruly Equality*, 240.
28. Martin Sostre to unknown (likely Sharon Fischer), March 13, 1972, Box 13, Folder 13, Powell Papers.
29. William C. Anderson, *A Nation on No Map: Black Anarchism and Abolition* (Chico, CA: AK Press, 2021), 82.
30. Lorenzo Kom'boa Ervin, "We're Not Distinct from the People as Revolutionaries," interview, *Millennials are Killing Capitalism*, December 16, 2021. https://millennialsarekillingcapitalism.libsyn.com/were-not-distinct-from-the-people-as-revolutionaries-lorenzo-komboa-ervin-on-anarchism-and-the-black-revolution.
31. Ashanti Alston, interview with author, August 11, 2020.
32. Ashanti Alston, "Beyond Nationalism but Not Without It," *Anarchist Panther* 1, no. 1 (October 1999), https://theanarchistlibrary.org/library/ashanti-alston-beyond-nationalism-but-not-without-it.
33. Alston, interview.
34. Alston, interview.
35. Sostre, "Some Comments on Anarchism."
36. Damali Bashira, "Martin Sostre: What is Justice?," *Encore American and Worldwide News*, October 6, 1975, 13.
37. Quoted in Anderson, *Nation on No Map*, xiii.
38. For an introduction to anarchist critiques of the state, see Peter Kropotkin, *Anarchism, Anarchist Communism, and the State: Three Essays*, ed. Iain McKay (Chicago: PM Press, 2019); Errico Malatesta, *Anarchy* (1891; repr., London: Freedom Press, 1995); Mikhail Bakunin, *Statism and Anarchy* (1900; repr., Cambridge, UK: Cambridge University Press, 1990); and Laursen, *The Operating System.*
39. Martin Sostre, "The New Prisoner," *North Carolina Central Law Journal* 4, no. 2 (Spring 1973): 247.
40. Wilson Gilmore cautions that "as with any theoretical premise, Lorde's caveat is useful only if the elements—whose paring away enables its elegance and urgency—are added back, so that the general truth of the abstraction has concrete meaning for day-to-day life. The issue is not whether the master uses, or endorses the use of, some tool or another. Rather, who controls the conditions and the ends to which any tools are wielded?" Ruth Wilson Gilmore, "Public Enemies and Private Intellectuals: Apartheid USA," *Race and Class* 35, no. 1 (July 1993): 70.
41. Liz and Vinny Sostre, recorded conversation, May 2021, in author's possession, courtesy of Liz and Vinny Sostre.

42. Charlie Allison, *No Harmless Power: The Life and Times of the Ukrainian Anarchist Nestor Makhno* (Oakland, CA: PM Press, 2023), 5.
43. Paulo Freire and Myles Horton, *We Make the Road by Walking: Conversations on Education and Social Change* (Philadelphia: Temple University Press, 1990), 11.

1. "My Qualifications Are as Follows"

1. Carmichael had been named the honorary prime minister of the Black Panther Party the previous year.
2. Martin Sostre to Stokely Carmichael, March 16, 1968, Folder 252253-054-0001, Subgroup C, Washington Office, Series I, Administrative Files, Student Nonviolent Coordinating Committee (SNCC) Correspondence, SNCC Papers, ProQuest History Vault.
3. "Gets 31-41 Years for Dope," *Evening Times* (Sayre, Pennsylvania), March 19, 1968.
4. Warren Schaich and Diane Hope, "The Prison Letters of Martin Sostre: Documents of Resistance," *Journal of Black Studies* 7, no. 3 (March 1977): 284.
5. Arthur Dobrin, "An American Prisoner of Conscience," *The Progressive* 44, no. 5 (May 1980): 36.
6. The only documents from before this period were his father's baptism certificate and a photograph of himself as a baby. See Martin Sostre Collection (MSC), University of Michigan Library (Special Collections Research Center).
7. Martin Sostre, testimony in *Davis v. McGinnis,* 306, National Archives and Records Administration—Kansas City, Missouri (NARA—KC).
8. Liz and Vinny Sostre, recorded conversation, May 2021, in author's possession, courtesy of Liz and Vinny Sostre.
9. Zaheer Ali, commencement address, University of North Florida, April 14, 2021, in author's possession.
10. Orisanmi Burton, "Captivity, Kinship, and Black Masculine Care Work under Domestic Warfare," *American Anthropologist* 123, no. 3 (September 2021): 625.
11. I borrow this phrase from Burton, who contrasts the "carceral warfare project" of the state with what he calls "people's war" or "counter-war" of the "Long Attica Revolt." See Orisanmi Burton, *Tip of the Spear: Black Radicalism, Prison Repression, and the Long Attica Revolt* (Berkeley: University of California Press, 2023), 4.
12. Merrill explained this cryptically by letter to journalist William Worthy: "The one point that I refrained from discussing over the phone with you today is how we are able to communicate with Martin. Miss Leticia Sostre (Letty), to my knowledge, is his only living relative. She is the only person who is able to correspond with him. I would rather not discuss our relationship with her over the phone." Jeanette Merrill to William Worthy, July 4, 1968, "William Worthy" folder, Martin Sostre Defense Committee Papers (MSDCP), in author's possession, courtesy of Ellie Dorritie and the Buffalo Workers World Party. Sostre also explained this at trial. See Sostre, testimony in *Sostre*

v. Rockefeller, October 29, 1969, 68. I am grateful to Tomiko Brown-Nagin for sharing her copies of the full transcript from the *Sostre v. Rockefeller* trial, which archivists were now unable to locate at the National Archives in Kansas City, Missouri.

13. Martin Sostre, *Letters from Prison* (Buffalo, NY: Philosophical Society / Martin Sostre Defense Committee, July 1968), 4.
14. As early as the 1940s, he was sometimes referred to as Martin González Sostre, which likely reflects the traditional practice in Puerto Rico and many Spanish-speaking countries where the child takes the surname of both parents, although his name would have more likely been Martin Sostre González, with his father's surname first.
15. Death certificate, Victoria Sostre, August 10, 1921, in New York, New York City Municipal Deaths, 1795–1949, FamilySearch database, Victoria Sastre [*sic*], 1921, https://www.FamilySearch.org/ark:/61903/1:1:2W1T-8N6.
16. For Saturnino, see Birth Registration, Saturnino Sostre y de Jesus, February 22, 1886, in Puerto Rico, Registro Civil, 1805-2001, FamilySearch database, Saturnino Sostre y de Jesus, citing Puerto Rico, Estados Unidos de América, Puerto Rico Departamento de Salud and Iglesia Catolica (Puerto Rico Department of Health and Catholic churches), Toa Alt, https://www.FamilySearch.org/ark:/61903/1:1:QV1Y-JJ7M. For Crescencia, see New York, New York Passenger and Crew Lists, 1909, 1925–1957, FamilySearch database, Crescencia Sostre, 1925, citing Immigration, New York, New York, United States, NARA microfilm publication T715 (Washington, DC: National Archives and Records Administration, n.d.), https://FamilySearch.org/ark:/61903/1:1:KX9S-F6F. Although a 1925 passenger log lists Crescencia's place of birth as San Germán, Sostre later remember her birthplace as Mayagüez. Martin Sostre, interview with Juanita D*í*az-Cotto, May 25, 1993, in author's possession. I am grateful to Professor D*í*az-Cotto for sharing this interview, which was originally recorded for her book *Gender, Ethnicity, and the State: Latina and Latino Prison Politics* (Albany: State University of New York Press, 1996).
17. Leticia Sostre was born January 8, 1925.
18. Sostre, interview with D*í*az-Cotto.
19. Bernardo Vega, *Memoirs of Bernardo Vega: A Contribution to the History of the Puerto Rican Community in New York*, ed. César Andreu Iglesias (New York: Monthly Review Press, 1984), 12.
20. Cathy Cabrera-Figueroa, "Pioneras Boricua," *The Gotham Center for New York City History* (blog), July 29, 2021, https://www.gothamcenter.org/blog/pioneras-boricuas-1; *Mónica Jiménez, "'American' State of Exception: Reimagining the Puerto Rican Colony and the Nationalist Enemy Under United States Rule, 1900–1940" (PhD diss., University of Texas at Austin, 2015), 126.*
21. Harry Franqui-Rivera, *Soldiers of the Nation: Military Service and Modern Puerto Rico, 1868-1952* (Lincoln: University of Nebraska, 2018), 94–95. Also see Sam Erman, *Almost Citizens: Puerto Rico, the U.S. Constitution, and Empire* (Cambridge,

UK: Cambridge University Press, 2018); Jorge Duany, "A Transnational Colonial Migration: Puerto Rico's Farm Labor Program, *New West Indian Guide* 84, nos. 3–4 (2010), 225–51.

22. Registration Card, Saturnino Sostre, September 12, 1918, in United States World War I Draft Registration Cards, 1917–1918, FamilySearch database, Saturnino Sostre, 1917–1918, https://www.FamilySearch.org/ark:/61903/1:1:K-6JQ-LBG.
23. Mae Ngai persuasively argues that the Johnson-Reed Act "marked both the end of one era, that of open immigration from Europe, and the beginning of a new one, the era of immigrant restriction." Mae Ngai, *Impossible Subjects: Illegal Aliens and the Making of Modern America* (Princeton, NJ: Princeton University Press, 2014), 17.
24. Roger Daniels, *Guarding the Golden Door: American Immigration Policy and Immigrants Since 1882* (New York: Hill & Wang, 2004), 50, quoted in Andrew Cornell, *Unruly Equality: U.S. Anarchism in the Twentieth Century* (Oakland: University of California Press, 2016), 78.
25. Julia Rose Kraut, "Global Anti-Anarchism: The Origins of Ideological Deportation and the Suppression of Expression," *Indiana Journal of Global Legal Studies* 19, no. 1 (Winter 2012): 169–93; William C. Anderson, "Indicting Anarchism, Inventing 'Terror': From 1898 to Cop City," *Prism*, October 3, 2023.
26. Cornell, *Unruly Equality*, 46, 78.
27. This legal status also allowed for movement back and forth. For example, in July 1925, when Martin was a toddler and Leticia an infant, Crescencia traveled with both children from Puerto Rico to New York City on a five-day voyage on the SS *Porto Rico*. The fare would have been a substantial expense for the family. Tickets were about forty dollars, roughly equivalent to one month's rent at the time. New York, New York Passenger and Crew Lists, 1909, 1925–1957, FamilySearch database, Crescencia Sostre, 1925, citing Immigration, New York, New York, United States, NARA microfilm publication T715 (Washington, DC: National Archives and Records Administration, n.d.), https://FamilySearch.org/ark:/61903/1:1:KX9S-F6F.
28. Lorrin Thomas and Aldo A. Lauria Santiago, *Rethinking the Struggle for Puerto Rican Rights* (New York: Routledge, 2019), 2.
29. Lawrence Chenault, *The Puerto Rican Migrant in New York City* (New York: Columbia University Press, 1938), 53, 59.
30. Chenault, *Puerto Rican Migrant*, 4.
31. Gilbert Osofsky, *Harlem: The Making of a Ghetto: Negro New York, 1890–1930* (New York: Harper & Row, 1966), 130, 131.
32. Quotations from James Weldon Johnson, "Harlem: The Cultural Capital," 301, in Alain Locke, ed., *The New Negro* (1925; repr., New York: Touchstone, 1997), and Manning Marable, *Malcolm X: A Life of Reinvention* (New York: Viking, 2011), 53. See also Osofsky, *Harlem*, 128–29. Documenting the number of Black-identified Puerto Ricans is difficult because many resisted the label "Negro." In the 1930 census, over three-quarters of Puerto Ricans were

classified as white. See Cheryl Greenberg, *Or Does It Explode? Black Harlem in the Great Depression* (New York: Oxford University Press, 1991), 226.

33. Sostre, interview with Díaz-Cotto.
34. Martin Sostre, interviews with Vinny Sostre, 2002 and 2012, exact dates unknown. In author's possession, courtesy of Liz and Vinny Sostre.
35. Daniel Katz, *All Together Different: Yiddish Socialists, Garment Workers, and the Labor Roots of Multiculturalism* (New York: New York University Press, 2011), 132.
36. Piri Thomas, *Down These Mean Streets* (New York: Knopf, 1967), 24.
37. Thomas, *Down These Mean Streets*, 30.
38. Sandy Shevack, interview with author, August 7, 2020.
39. Sandy Shevack, email to author, May 13, 2021.
40. Chenault outlines the boundary between Eighth and Third Avenues and 98th and 126th Streets. See Chenault, *Puerto Rican Migrant*, 165. Vega, discussing the late 1920s, gives slightly different boundaries: 96th and 107th Streets, from Third to First Avenues. See Vega, *Memoirs of Bernardo Vega*, 151.
41. Chenault, *Puerto Rican Migrant*, 165.
42. Vega, *Memoirs of Bernardo Vega*, 141.
43. Workers' wages, which had remained virtually static from 1890 to 1918, accelerated 22 percent in the seven years that followed, and per capita income climbed from $520 to $681 between 1919 and 1929. William Leuchtenburg, *The Perils of Prosperity, 1914–1932* (Chicago: University of Chicago Press, 1993), 178.
44. Chenault, *Puerto Rican Migrant*, 51.
45. Chenault, *Puerto Rican Migrant*, 72.
46. As Stephanie Mercedes points out, the Jones Act "had two purposes: it declared that Puerto Ricans were American citizens; and at the same time, it limited Puerto Rico's commerce by only allowing it to sell its products to the United States." Stephanie Mercedes, "Origins of the Jones Act of Puerto Rico" (MA thesis, CUNY Graduate Center, 2019), v.
47. Peter Cole, *Wobblies on the Waterfront: Interracial Unionism in Progressive-Era Philadelphia* (Urbana: University of Illinois Press, 2013), 102.
48. List or Manifest of Aliens Employed on the Vessel as Members of Crew, SS *Orizaba*, March 13, March 25, April 3, April 15, May 1, May 15, May 29, June 10, June 12, June 26, and July 10, 1928, in author's possession, originally located through FamilySearch database.
49. "Ward Line Increases Cuba and Mexico Services," *New York Herald Tribune*, October 15, 1928; "Havana Is Ready for Early Opening of Winter Season," *New York Herald Tribune*, October 28, 1928.
50. A partial list of nationalities taken from ship manifests on the *SS Orizaba* includes crew from Spain, Norway, Cuba, Germany, Greece, Mexico, Holland, Italy, Ireland, France, Hungary, Great Britain, Costa Rica, Scotland, Russia, Venezuela, Chile, the Dominican Republic, Nicaragua, Denmark, and the United States.

51. In documenting the influence of the UNIA on Australian Aboriginal self-determination during that decade, John Maynard argues that "the role of merchant seaman in the spreading of Garvey's ideas cannot be underestimated." John Maynard, "Garvey in Oz: The International Black Influence on Australian Aboriginal Activism," in *Anywhere but Here: Black Intellectuals in the Atlantic World and Beyond*, eds. Kendahl Radcliffe, Jennifer Scott, and Anja Werner (Oxford: University Press of Mississippi, 2014), 100.
52. Kirwin Shaffer, *Anarchists of the Caribbean: Countercultural Politics and Transnational Networks in the Age of U.S. Expansion* (Cambridge, UK: Cambridge University Press, 2020), 18–19, 21.
53. Martin Sostre, interview with Vinny Sostre, 2002. In his petition for executive clemency in 1975, which was prepared by attorney Lynn Walker (presumably through conversations with Sostre), his mother was identified as a "seamstress and milliner." See Petition for Executive Clemency to the Honorable Hugh Carey, Governor of the State of New York, 3, in Executive Clemency Files, New York State Archives.
54. Olga Quinones, quoted in Christopher Bell, ed., *East Harlem Remembered: Oral Histories of Community and Diversity* (Jefferson, NC: McFarland & Co., 2013), 37.
55. Bell, *East Harlem Remembered*, 38.
56. Chenault, *Puerto Rican Migrant*, 75.
57. For more on Puerto Rican garment workers in New York City during this period, see Altagracia Ortiz, *Puerto Rican Women and Work: Bridges in Transnational Labor* (Philadelphia: Temple University Press, 1996), 56–59.
58. See 1930 and 1940 censuses, in author's possession, originally located through FamilySearch database.. See also Joe Shapiro, "In and Out of Prison: Revolutionary Politics in the '70s," *Introspect: The Carleton Journal of American Culture* 2, no. 1 (1976): 5. In his 2002 interview with Vinny, Sostre remembered his father as a painter and carpenter.
59. As Brent Hayes Edwards reminds us, that movement was a "North American component of something larger and grander." Brent Hayes Edwards, *The Practice of Diaspora: Literature, Translation, and the Rise of Black Internationalism* (Cambridge, MA: Harvard University Press, 2009), 3.
60. John Henrik Clark, "Marcus Garvey: The Harlem Years," *Transition* 46 (1974), 19.
61. Tony Martin, "Garvey, Marcus Mosiah," in *Encyclopedia of the African Diaspora: A Historical Encyclopedia*, ed. Carole E. Boyce-Davies (Santa Barbara: ABC-CLIO, 2008), 459). There is a vast literature on the UNIA and its leaders, including Colin Grant, *Negro with a Hat: The Rise and Fall of Marcus Garvey* (New York: Oxford University Press, 2008); Tony Martin, *Race First: The Ideological and Organizational Struggles of Marcus Garvey and the Universal Negro Improvement Association* (Westport: Greenwood Press, 1976); David Cronon, *Black Moses: The Story of Marcus Garvey and the Universal Negro Improvement Association* (Madison: University of Wisconsin Press, 1969); Mary Rolinson, *Grassroots Garveyism: The Universal Negro Improvement Association in the Rural South* (Chapel Hill: University

of North Carolina Press, 2007); Claudrena Harold, *The Rise and Fall of the Garvey Movement in the Urban South, 1918–1942* (New York: Routledge, 2007); Robert Hill, ed., *The Marcus Garvey and Universal Negro Improvement Association Papers* (Durham: Duke University Press: ongoing); Ula Taylor, *The Veiled Garvey: The Life and Times of Amy Jacques Garvey* (Chapel Hill: University of North Carolina Press, 2002).

62. Sociologist Ira Reid, who worked for New York branch of the National Urban League from 1924 to 1928, described Harlem during this period as "throbbing, pulsating, vibrating." See Ira Reid, "Why I Like Harlem," *The Messenger*, January 1927, 2, quoted in Kevin Mattson, "The Struggle for an Urban Democratic Public: Harlem in the 1920s," *New York History* 76, no. 3 (July 1995): 295.
63. Ralph Crowder, "Willis Nathaniel Huggins," *Afro-Americans in New York Life and History* 30, no. 2 (July 2006): 136.
64. John Henrik Clarke, "Portrait of a Liberation Scholar," 33, in *Against the Odds: Scholars Who Challenged Racism in the Twentieth Century*, eds. Benjamin Bowser and Louis Kushnick with Paul Grant (Amherst: University of Massachusetts Press, 2002).
65. Keith S. Henry, "The Black Political Tradition in New York: A Conjunction of Political Cultures," *Journal of Black Studies* 7, no. 4 (June 1977): 455–84, 461.
66. According to Mark Naison, Briggs became the "the most influential of the early Harlem Communists." See Mark Naison, *Communists in Harlem During the Depression* (Urbana: University of Illinois Press, 2005), 5.
67. L. B. Bryan, "Hubert Harrison," in "WPA Negroes of New York," quoted in Henry, "The Black Political Tradition in New York," 481; David Levering Lewis, *When Harlem Was in Vogue* (New York: Knopf, 1981), 104.
68. Grant, *Negro with a Hat*, 88–89.
69. Martin, *Race First*, 9. *For more on street speaking in Harlem during the 1930s, see Roma* Barnes, "Harlem Street Speakers in the 1930s," in *New York: City as Text*, eds. Christopher Mulvey and John Simons (New York: MacMillan, 1990), 106–30.
70. Keisha Blain, "Audley Moore, Black Women's Activism, and Nationalist Politics," *Black Perspectives* (blog), February 25, 2019, https://www.aaihs.org/audley-moore-black-womens-activism-and-nationalist-politics/. For more on Queen Mother Moore, see the special issue on her life and legacy edited by Ashley Farmer and Erik McDuffie in *Palimpsest: A Journal on Women, Gender, and the Black International* 7, no. 2 (2018). See also the forthcoming biography by Ashley Farmer, *"Queen Mother" Audley Moore: Mother of Black Nationalism* (New York: Pantheon, forthcoming).
71. Naison, *Communists in Harlem*, 136.
72. Sostre, interview with Díaz-Cotto.
73. "Radical Completes Another Building in Passaic," *The Record*, January 22, 1987. For more on Marcantonio's support for Puerto Rican independence, see Margaret Power, *Solidarity Across the Americas: The Puerto Rican Nationalist Party and Anti-Imperialism* (Chapel Hill: University of North Carolina Press, 2023), 139–41.

74. Joseph Clore, interview with author, August 6, 2021.
75. Sostre, "Report from Jail to My Revolutionary Friends," in *Letters from Prison*, 21.
76. Vinny Sostre and Liz Sostre, interview with author, June 25, 2021.
77. Michael Meeropol, email to author, June 25, 2021.
78. James Weldon Johnson, *Black Manhattan* (New York: Knopf, 1930), 159, quoted in Mattson, "Struggle for an Urban Democratic Public," 294.
79. Crowder, "Willis Nathaniel Huggins," 135.
80. Mattson, "Struggle for an Urban Democratic Public," 295.
81. Sarah A. Anderson, " 'The Place to Go': The 135th Street Branch Library and the Harlem Renaissance," *Library Quarterly* 73, no. 4 (October 2003): 386.
82. Quoted in Ann Sandford, "Rescuing Ernestine Rose (1880–1961): Harlem Librarian and Social Activist," *Long Island History Journal* 22, no. 2 (Summer 2011): 4.
83. Elinor Des Verney Sinnette, *Arthur Alfonso Schomburg: Black Bibliophile and Collector* (Detroit: New York Public Library / Wayne State University Press, 1989), 91, 134.
84. New York Passenger Arrival Lists (Ellis Island), 1892–1924, FamilySearch database, Pura Belpré, 1920, https://FamilySearch.org/ark:/61903/1:1:J669-X49.
85. "How NYC's First Puerto Rican Librarian Brought Spanish to the Shelves," *All Things Considered*, presented by Neda Ulaby, aired September 8, 2016, on National Public Radio, https://www.npr.org/2016/09/08/492957864/how-nycs-first-puerto-rican-librarian-brought-spanish-to-the-shelves. For more on Belpré, see Lisa Sánchez González, *The Stories I Read to Children: The Life and Writing of Pura Belpré, the Legendary Storyteller, Children's Author and NY Public Librarian* (New York: Centro, 2013).
86. Vega, *Memoirs of Bernardo Vega*, 156–57.
87. "Negro History Club Organized in Harlem," *New York Age*, November 3, 1928; Elizabeth Ann Botch, "History and Heroes: A Means of Social Uplift in 1930s Harlem" (MA thesis, University of Montana, 1976), 85.
88. "Y.M.C.A To Open Night School to Teach 3-Rs," *New York Age*, October 27, 1928.
89. Edward Blyden was born on St. Thomas in 1832. In 1840, he was refused admission to US theological schools and migrated to Liberia. There, he worked as a newspaper editor and college teacher. He called his vision of Pan-Africanism "Ethiopianism." Blyden later moved to Sierra Leone, where he affiliated with the Muslim community. Significantly, he came to regard Islam as a more "African" religion than Christianity and advocated that African Americans affiliate with Islam as well; see Edward Blyden, *Christianity, Islam and the Negro Race* (London: W. B. Whittingham, 1887). For more on Blyden, see Hollis R. Lynch, *Edward Wilmot Blyden, Pan-Negro Patriot, 1832–1912* (London: Oxford University Press, 1967); Richard Brent Turner, *Islam in the African-American Experience* (Bloomington: Indiana University Press, 1997); and Edward Curtis, *Islam in Black America: Identity, Liberation, and Difference in African-American Islamic Thought* (Albany, NY: State University of New York Press, 2002).

90. Crowder, "Willis Nathaniel Huggins," 136.
91. Sostre would later win a major prisoners' rights case regarding access to political publications. One of the writings to which he was denied access was Kwame Nkrumah's *Revolutionary Warfare*. See Alan Kohn, "Inmate Wins U.S. Ruling on Censoring of Literature," *New York Law Journal*, July 30, 1971.
92. John Henrik Clarke, quoted in Crowder, "Willis Nathaniel Huggins," 141.
93. Crowder, "Willis Nathaniel Huggins," 141.
94. The program included Howard University professors Emmet Dorsey and Abram Harris, Dr. Scott Nearing, and Dr. Willis Huggins, as well as Richard B. Moore. "Negro History Club Announces Program," *Amsterdam News*, March 7, 1936.
95. Botch, "History and Heroes," 81.
96. Naison, *Communists in Harlem*, 14. Campbell is omitted from Naison's list but was identified as the "chairman" in 1926 when Richard B. Moore was the secretary. See "Harlem Educational Forum Sunday Program," *New York Age*, June 5, 1926.
97. Quoted in Crowder, "Willis Nathaniel Huggins,"142.

2. "Hardcore from the East Side"

1. John Henrik Clarke, "A Search for Identity," *Social Casework* 51, no. 5 (May 1970): 263. Clarke described himself as a "young Depression radical—always studying, always reading."
2. Memo, Buffalo to New York, September 9, 1965, Martin Sostre FBI File (100-NY-154100). I am grateful to Brendan Hornbostel for helping retrieve this file from the National Archives and Records Administration—College Park, Maryland (NARA—CP).
3. Martin Sostre to Lolita *Lebrón,* April 20, 1973, *Mixed Materials 1, Folder 5,* Martin Sostre Collection (MSC), University of Michigan Library (Special Collections Research Center).
4. Maritza Arrastía, "From Prison, Sostre Urges More Struggle," *Claridad*, January 27, 1974.
5. Martin Sostre to unknown (likely Sharon Fischer), January 19, 1972, Box 13, Folder 13, Elwin H. Powell Papers, University Archives, State University of New York at Buffalo.
6. Winston James, *Holding Aloft the Banner of Ethiopia: Caribbean Radicalism in Early Twentieth-Century America* (New York: Verso, 1998), 199.
7. Elinor Des Verney Sinnette, *Arthur Alfonso Schomburg, Black Bibliophile and Collector: A Biography* (New York: New York Public Library, 1989), 148.
8. Quoted in James, *Holding Aloft the Banner*, 203.
9. Sinnette, *Arthur Alfonso Schomburg*, 23.
10. Bernardo Vega refuted this notion in his memoirs: Schomburg "later moved up to the neighborhood where North American Blacks lived, and there he stayed. This led quite a few Puerto Ricans who knew him to think that he was trying

to deny his distant homeland, but nothing could be further from the truth." Bernardo Vega, *Memoirs of Bernardo Vega: A Contribution to the History of the Puerto Rican Community in New York*, ed. César Andreu Iglesias (New York: Monthly Review Press, 1984), 195.

11. Lorgia García Peña, *Community as Rebellion: A Syllabus for Surviving Academia as a Woman of Color* (Chicago: Haymarket, 2022), 91.
12. "New York City: Social-Personal," *New Journal and Guide*, July 11, 1932.
13. Clarke, "A Search For Identity," 263.
14. See figure 2, "Settlement of Spanish-Speaking Racial Groups in Lower Harlem Area, New York City," in Lawrence Chenault, *The Puerto Rican Migrant in New York City* (New York: Columbia University Press, 1938), 95.
15. Martin Sostre, interview with Juanita Díaz-Cotto, May 25, 1993, in author's possession, courtesy of Juanita Díaz-Cotto.
16. Manning Marable, *Malcolm X: A Life of Reinvention* (New York: Viking, 2011), 54.
17. Mark Naison, *Communists in Harlem during the Depression* (Urbana: University of Illinois Press, 2005), xvii–xviii.
18. Naison, *Communists in Harlem*, 19.
19. Marable, *Malcolm X*, 54.
20. Naison, *Communists in Harlem*, 20.
21. Cheryl Greenberg, *Or Does it Explode? Black Harlem in the Great Depression* (New York: Oxford University Press, 1991), 138.
22. Naison, *Communists in Harlem*, xvii, 3.
23. Naison, *Communists in Harlem*, 17. See also The Black Belt Thesis Study Group, *The Black Belt Thesis: A Reader* (New York: 1804 Books, 2023).
24. See Willcox, "The Negro Population," 11, in *Negroes in the United States*, eds. William Hunt, Walter Willcox, and W. E. B. Du Bois (Washington, DC: Government Printing Office, 1904), which showed that in the 1900 census, nearly 90 percent of Black Americans lived in the US South and over 30 percent in Mississippi, Alabama, and Georgia alone. Although the "Black Belt" originally referred to the fertile, black soil across this region, it came to signify the Black Americans who lived and labored there.
25. Naison, *Communists in Harlem*, 57.
26. James Miller, Susan Pennybacker, and Eve Rosenhaft, "Mother Ada Wright and the International Campaign to Free the Scottsboro Boys, 1931–1934," *American Historical Review* 106, no. 2 (April 2001): 389.
27. For example, a Finnish American Communist, August Yokinen, was put on public trial and expelled after taunting Black men with racial slurs. This was seen as a watershed for the CPUSA's racial politics during the 1930. For more on the organizing of Black Communists during this decade, see Robin D. G. Kelley, *Hammer and Hoe: Alabama Communists during the Great Depression* (Chapel Hill: University of North Carolina Press, 1990); Dayo Gore, *Radicalism at the Crossroads: African American Women Activists in the Cold War* (New York: New York University Press, 2011); Erik McDuffie, *Sojourning for Freedom: Black Women,*

American Communism, and the Making of Black Left Feminism (Durham: Duke University Press, 2011); Minkah Makalani, *"In the Cause of Freedom": Radical Black Internationalism from Harlem to London, 1917–1939* (Chapel Hill: University of North Carolina Press, 2011); Lashawn Harris, "Running with the Reds: African American Women and the Communist Party during the Great Depression," *Journal of African American History* 94, no. 1 (2009): 21–43.

28. Naison, *Communists in Harlem*, 71.
29. "Scottsboro Tag Days, Sat., Sun.," *Daily Worker,* December 17, 1932. Tag days were a fundraising technique during the 1930s where canvassers would give donors a tag to wear advertising their support for the cause. I am grateful to Paul *Hébert for this information.*
30. Naison, *Communists in Harlem*, 57.
31. Ashley Farmer, "Mothers of Pan-Africanism: Audley Moore and Dara Abubakari," *Women, Gender, and Families of Color* 4, no. 2 (Fall 2016): 278.
32. Naison, *Communists in Harlem*, 88.
33. Martin Sostre to Leticia Sostre, May 28, 1968, Martin Sostre Defense Committee Papers (MSDCP), in author's possession, courtesy of Ellie Dorritie and the Buffalo Workers World Party.
34. Naison, *Communists in Harlem*, 95, 98.
35. In a 1940 political organizer manual, Moore is listed as section leader for upper Harlem and member for six years, before which "Audley was an organizer of a branch of the Workers Alliance on the Sewing Project and worked among 3,500 women, Negro and white." *A Political Manual for Harlem,* issued by the Harlem Division of the Communist Party USA, 15–16, in author's possession, courtesy of Robin D. G. Kelley. As Kelley explained, he received the manual from Don Wheeldin, who "was a longtime Black member of the CPUSA . . . [and] was a CP organizer in Harlem during the Depression and friends with Paul Robeson." Kelley met Wheeldin while the latter was living in Pasadena. Wheeldin befriended and mentored him during the 1980s. Robin D. G. Kelley, email to author, October 14, 2022.
36. Erik McDuffie, " 'I Wanted a Communist Philosophy, but I Wanted Us to Have a Chance to Organize Our People': The Diasporic Radicalism of Queen Mother Audley Moore and the Origins of Black Power," *African and Black Diaspora* 3, no. 2 (2010): 182.
37. See addresses of Harlem section offices, *A Political Manual for Harlem*, 12.
38. Martin Sostre, interview with Vinny Sostre, 2012, in author's possession, courtesy of Liz and Vinny Sostre.
39. Margaret Power, *Solidarity Across the Americas: The Puerto Rican Nationalist Party and Anti-Imperialism* (Chapel Hill: University of North Carolina Press, 2023), 137–38.
40. Martin Sostre to unknown (likely Sharon Fischer), April 26, 1972, Box 13, Folder 13, Elwin H. Powell Papers. Elsewhere, he remembered it as the home to the "Cuban Communist Party on 116th Street and Fifth Avenue." Sostre, interview with Díaz-Cotto.

41. According to Nancy Mirabal, the club was founded in 1932. See Mirabal, "Archival Dilemmas and Possibilities," *Cultural Dynamics* 30, no. 4 (2018): 347.
42. Marable, *Malcolm X*, 54.
43. Kirwin Shaffer, *A Transnational History of the Modern Caribbean: Popular Resistance across Borders* (Cham, Switzerland: Palgrave Macmillan, 2022), 98, 123.
44. Nancy Mirabal, *Suspect Freedoms: The Racial and Sexual Politics of Cubanidad in New York, 1832–1957* (New York: New York University Press, 2017), 181.
45. Mirabal, *Suspect Freedoms*, 181.
46. Mirabal, *Suspect Freedoms*, 182.
47. Martin Sostre to unknown (likely Sharon Fischer); Martin Sostre, interview with Vinny Sostre, 2012.
48. Sostre, interview with Díaz-Cotto; Sostre to unknown (likely Sharon Fischer).
49. Sostre, interview with Díaz-Cotto.
50. For example, see Ted Vincent, "The Garveyite Parents of Malcolm X," *Black Scholar* 20, no. 2 (1989): 10–13; Erik McDuffie, "The Diasporic Journeys of Louise Little: Grassroots Garveyism, the Midwest, and Community Feminism," *Women, Gender, and Families of Color* 4, no. 2 (2016): 146–70; Anna Malaika Tubbs, *The Three Mothers: How the Mothers of Martin Luther King., Jr., Malcolm X, and James Baldwin Shaped a Nation* (New York: Flatiron Books, 2021); Jolie Solomon, "Overlooked No Moore: Louise Little, Activist and Mother of Malcolm X," *New York Times*, March 19, 2022.
51. Ariel Mae Lambe, *No Barrier Can Contain It: Cuban Antifascism and the Spanish Civil War* (Chapel Hill: University of North Carolina Press, 2019); Mirabal, *Suspect Freedoms*.
52. Mirabal, *Suspect Freedoms*, 181.
53. "A Soccer Game for Spain," *Daily Worker*, December 1, 1936.
54. "Arrest 3 Pickets at Commodore," *Daily Worker*, June 13, 1933.
55. Mississippi Johnson, "Rumba and Politics at Club Cubano," *Daily Worker*, August 16, 1937.
56. "Show May Day Film Tonight in Harlem at Club Julio Mella," *Daily Worker*, May 17, 1937.
57. "Browder to Speak at Harlem Welcome to 'James W. Ford,' " *Daily Worker*, August 18, 1933.
58. Johnson, "Rumba and Politics"; Mississippi Johnson, "Mother of Julio Mella Speaks at Cuban Club," *Daily Worker*, June 4, 1934.
59. Edward Brunner speculates that Mississippi Johnson may have been a pseudonym for fashion writer, designer, and leftist Elizabeth Hawes. See Brunner, "Red Funnies: The New York *Daily Worker's* 'Popular Front' Comics, 1936–1945," *American Periodicals* 17, no. 2 (2007): 207. I am grateful to Robin D. G. Kelley for pointing this out.
60. Lambe, *No Barrier Can Contain It*, 93.
61. Andrew Cornell, *Unruly Equality: U.S. Anarchism in the Twentieth Century* (Oakland: University of California Press, 2016), 137.
62. Naison, *Communists in Harlem*, 197.

63. Lambe, *No Barrier Can Contain It*, 93.
64. Marion, "Lincoln Boys are Holding Toughest Spot at Front," *Daily Worker*, April 22, 1937.
65. "Anti-War Mass Meeting Friday," *Daily Worker*, June 21, 1934.
66. "Scotts Plea by Mother of Julio Mella," *Daily Worker*, November 16, 1934.
67. "Ford Returns from Spain Confident of Loyalist Victory," *Daily Worker*, May 26, 1937.
68. Ariel Mae Lambe, "Who Is the Mysterious 'Cuba Hermosa'? New Evidence Comes to Light," *The Volunteer*, November 22, 2016, https://albavolunteer.org/2016/11/who-is-the-mysterious-cuba-hermosa-new-evidence-comes-to-light.
69. It is not clear exactly when Michaux's bookstore opened. The earliest year cited is 1932. See Laura Harris Hurd, "Rockefeller's Promise Fails; Famous Bookstore Threatened," *Amsterdam News*, January 12, 1974; and Joshua Clark Davis, *From Head Shops to Whole Foods: The Rise and Fall of Activist Entrepreneurs* (New York: Columbia University Press, 2017), 40. Michaux's grand-niece Vaunda Micheaux Nelson points out that the name came from his brother's settlement, which was purchased in 1936, so it was likely begun after that year. The FBI dates its beginnings as 1939; see Summary Report, New York Office, June 28, 1968, Lewis Michaux FBI File (100–146759). In a 1968 interview, also in his FBI file, Michaux says that he had conducted business for thirty-five years, which would date the bookstore to around 1933. He may have begun selling books from the back of a wagon in the early 1930s and established a brick-and-mortar location under the name National Memorial Bookstore after 1936.
70. As Davis notes, "The famed New York abolitionist David Ruggles is widely credited as the first African American to own and operate a bookstore. . . . A tiny handful of short-lived Black-owned bookstores opened around the country in the late nineteenth and early twentieth centuries. These stores, however, struggled to stay in business, and few, if any, operated for more than several years." See Davis, *From Head Shops*, 40.
71. Davis writes that "from 1960 to 1964, Black presses published only 51 books, but ten years later, from 1970–1974, they published 240 books, more than four times as many." See Davis, *From Head* Shops, 54.
72. Louis [*sic*] Michaux, interview with Robert Wright, July 31, 1970, 2, Ralph J. Bunch Collection (formerly known as the Civil Rights Documentation Project, Moorland-Spingarn Research Center, Howard University, in author's possession, courtesy of Joshua Davis.
73. "Even booksellers such as Michaux, himself an ardent believer in Black nationalism, sold few works on nationalist or radical ideology in the 1940s," writes Joshua Clark Davis. See Davis, *From Head Shops*, 41, 43, 49.
74. It would later read "2,000,000,000 (Two Billion) Africans and Non-White Peoples."
75. Davis, *From Head Shops*, 41.

76. One of the visible publications in the photograph is a 1944 photo essay on African Americans, *The Negro in American Life*, sponsored by the Council Against Intolerance in America with a preface by Lillian Smith, author of the recently released *Strange Fruit*. Also visible is *Girls on City Streets*, a 1935 study of rape and sexual violence.
77. "National Memorial Book Store," *Amsterdam News*, May 4, 1946.
78. Michaux, interview with Robert Wright.
79. Martin Sostre to Stokely Carmichael, March 16, 1968, Folder 252253-054-0001, Subgroup C, Washington Office, Series I, Administrative Files, Student Nonviolent Coordinating Committee (SNCC) Correspondence, SNCC Papers, ProQuest History Vault.
80. "He was very proud he didn't finish high school," his son Vinny remembered. Vinny Sostre and Liz Sostre, interview with author, June 25, 2021.
81. "Straubenmuller Textile High School, 1919–1954," WritLargeNYC, January 17, 2023, https://writlarge.ctl.columbia.edu/view/143/.
82. Arrastía, "From Prison, Sostre Urges More Struggle."
83. Vinny Sostre and Liz Sostre, interview with author.
84. The baptism certificate for Saturnino Sostre lists his father as a carpenter. Certificado de Bautismo de Saturnino Sostre de *Jesús*, Mixed Materials 1, Folder 8, MSC. Generously translated by Pamela Cappas-Toro. See also Martin Sostre, interview with Vinny Sostre, 2002, in author's possession, courtesy of Liz and Vinny Sostre.
85. Martin Sostre, interview with Vinny Sostre, 2002.
86. In 2002, he recalled that it was two dollars an hour and in 2012 that it was not more than 50 cents an hour. Martin Sostre, interviews with Vinny Sostre, 2002 and 2012. Quote is from 2012 interview.
87. Sostre, testimony in *Pierce v. LaVallee*, heard on November 14, 1961, 55, NARA—KC.
88. Airtel, St. Louis to Buffalo, November 24, 1965, 4, Martin Sostre FBI File (100-NY-154100); Lorrin Rosenbaum and Judith Kossy, "A Question of Justice: The Case of Martin Sostre," *Index on Censorship* 5, no. 3 (1976): 3; United States World War II Army Enlistment Records, 1938–1946, FamilySearch database, Martin G Sostre, enlisted 2 Feb 1942, Cp Upton, Yaphank, New York, United States, citing Electronic Army Serial Number Merged File, ca. 1938–1946, National Archives and Records Administration (2002); NARA NAID 1263923, National Archives and Records Administration—College Park, Maryland.
89. Psychological evaluation by Dr. Howard C. Wilinsky and Michael J. Lynch, 1, in *People v. Sostre*, General Case Material, February 19, 1968, Folder 100243-029-0498, Supplement to Part 23: Legal Department Case Files, Series B: The Northeast, Section II: New York, Papers of the NAACP, ProQuest History Vault.
90. Martin Sostre, interview with Vinny Sostre, 2002.
91. Martin Sostre, interview with Vinny Sostre, 2012.

92. "The Open Road Interview with Martin Sostre," by David Spaner, *Open Road*, Summer 1976, 13.
93. Matt Delmont, *Half American: The Epic Story of African Americans Fighting World War II at Home and Abroad* (New York: Viking, 2022), 88.
94. Saturnino Sostre, then fifty-five, was required to register but likely would not have served.
95. This booming enlistment was part of a threefold increase since the US became an active participant in the war and was even greater among Black troops, rising from 98,000 in late 1941 to 470,000 in December 1942. See Induction Statistics, Selective Service System, January 17, 2023, https://www.sss.gov/history-and-records/induction-statistics; and Robert F. Jefferson, "Black Soldiers in World War II America," *Oxford Encyclopedia*, https://oxfordre.com/americanhistory/display/10.1093/acrefore/9780199329175.001.0001/acrefore-9780199329175-e-838.
96. Stuart Schrader, "Cops at War: How World War II Transformed U.S. Policing," *Modern American History* 4, no. 3 (July 2021): 164.
97. This figure was calculated using induction numbers from the Selective Service System's Induction Statistics. Thank you to Jesse Leo Kass for pointing this out. Overall figures from Military Police were compiled by Robert K. Wright, Jr. *Military Police* (Washington, DC: Center of Military History, 1992), 9–10, cited in Schrader, "Cops at War," 171.
98. For example, see James Whitman, *Hitler's American Model: The United States and the Making of Nazi Race Law* (Princeton, NJ: Princeton University Press, 2017).
99. J. R. Johnson (C.L.R. James frequently wrote under this pseudonym), "The Negro Question," September 11, 1939, *Socialist Appeal* 3, no. 68 (September 1939): 3.
100. Garrett Felber, *Those Who Know Don't Say: The Nation of Islam, the Black Freedom Movement, and the Carceral State* (Chapel Hill: University of North Carolina Press, 2020), 18.
101. "The Case of Martin Sostre," *The Oswegonian*, January 14, 1972.
102. Thomas Guglielmo, "A Martial Freedom Movement: Black G.I.s' Political Struggles during World War II," *Journal of American History* 104, no. 4 (March 2018): 879.
103. See Thomas Guglielmo, "'Red Cross, Double Cross': Race and America's World War II–Era Blood Donor Service, *Journal of American History* 97, no. 1 (June 2010): 63–90.
104. Jefferson, "Black Soldiers."
105. Ulysses Lee, *The Employment of Negro Troops* (Washington, DC: Center of Military History, 1963), 300.
106. Jefferson, "Black Soldiers."
107. Harvard Sitkoff, "Racial Militancy and Interracial Violence in the Second World War," *Journal of American History* 58, no. 3 (December 1971): 668.
108. Guglielmo, "Martial Freedom Movement," 880.

109. For a description of the fire and the records destroyed, see "The 1973 Fire, National Personnel Records Center," January 17, 2023, https://www.archives.gov/personnel-records-center/fire-1973.
110. Martin G. Sostre, testimony before Major George G. Gilbert. Jr., April 22, 1944, 1, Record of Trial by Court-Martial (256346), National Archives and Records Administration—St. Louis, Missouri (NARA—SL).
111. The MP headquarters was located at 587 ½ West Church Street.
112. Walter Howard, *Lynchings: Extralegal Violence in Florida during the 1930s* (Selinsgrove, PA: Susquehanna University Press, 1995), 17. I am grateful to Andy Eisen for pointing out this case to me.
113. For more on the case, see Gilbert King, *Devil in the Grove: Thurgood Marshall, the Groveland Boys, and the Dawn of a New America* (New York: Harper, 2012).
114. "Florida Terror," *Freedom Never Dies*, January 23, 2023, PBS, https://www.pbs.org/harrymoore/terror/k.html.
115. Lee, *Employment of Negro Troops.*
116. For more on the zoot suit riots, see Eduardo *Obregón Pagán, Murder at the Sleepy Lagoon: Zoot Suits, Race, and Riot in Wartime, L.A. (Chapel Hill: University of North Carolina Press, 2003); Catherine* Ramírez, *The Woman in the Zoot Suit: Gender, Nationalism, and the Cultural Politics of Memory* (Durham: Duke University Press, 2009); and Maricio *Mazón, The Zoot-Suit Riots: The Psychology of Symbolic Annihilation* (Austin: University of Texas Press, 1984).
117. Sitkoff, "Racial Militancy," 671.
118. Lee, *Employment of Negro Troops*, 355.
119. Lee wrote that MP units were not employed "until after local experiments with Negro military police detachments showed that their use in areas with large Negro troop populations paid dividends in better order, better relations between troops and the military police, and better relations with civilians in those communities which had learned to look upon Negro military policemen as something less than a threat to local customs." Lee, *Employment of Negro Troops*, 131.
120. I borrow this term from Micol Seigel, who defines policing as "violence work." See Seigel, *Violence Work: State Power and the Limits of Police* (Durham, NC: Duke University Press, 2018).
121. Lee, *Employment of Negro Troops*, 131–32.
122. Lee, *Employment of Negro Troops*, 348.
123. Delmont, *Half American*, xvii; Lee, *Employment of Negro Troops*, 348.
124. Martin G. Sostre, statement, September 30, 1943, Record of Trial by Court-Martial in the Case of United States of America vs. Martin Sostre (242653).
125. Pvt. Robert Weaver, testimony in *U.S.A v. Sostre,* 14, Record of Trial by Court-Martial (242653).
126. The testimony of the person who performed the autopsy noted that Turner had a "sharp incised laceration of the palm. . . . Evidently caused by some sort of sharp instrument; it could have been a knife." Schall, testimony in *U.S.A v. Sostre,* 8, Record of Trial by Court-Martial (242653). Turner's girlfriend also

cited a cut on his palm in her statement. See Alice Johnson, statement, October 1, 1943, Record of Trial by Court-Martial (242653).

127. Martin G. Sostre, statement, September 30, 1943.
128. Pretrial Investigating Officer's Report, October 7, 1943, Robert L. Bell to Captain Thomas L. Coleman, Record of Trial by Court-Martial, (242653).
129. Court findings, *U.S.A v. Sostre,* 71, Record of Trial by Court-Martial (242653).
130. By the time of his next court martial in April 1944, he claimed to have been a cop for ten months.
131. Excerpted from letter, July 21, 1944, in Airtel, St. Louis to Buffalo, November 24, 1965, Martin Sostre FBI File (100-NY-154100).
132. Statement of Master Sergeant Emmott B. Peter, Jr., April 24, 1944, Record of Trial by Court-Martial (256346).
133. Martin G. Sostre, testimony before Major George G. Gilbert., Jr. April 22, 1944, 1, Record of Trial by Court-Martial (256346).
134. Martin Sostre, testimony in *U.S.A v. Sostre,* 138, in Record of Trial by Court-Martial (256346).
135. Sostre, testimony before Major George G. Gilbert., Jr. April 22, 1944, 3.
136. Emmot B. Peter, Jr., memo, February 18, 1944, in Record of Trial by Court-Martial (256346).
137. Sostre, testimony in *U.S.A v. Sostre,* 139, in Record of Trial by Court-Martial (256346).
138. Sostre, testimony in *U.S.A v. Sostre,* 139, in Record of Trial by Court-Martial (256346).
139. Banks claimed he did not know if he had ever been arrested by Sostre before. Sostre said he had arrested him eight or nine times and that Banks would frequently fall asleep or not pay in a restaurant. According to Sostre, Banks had threatened him in the past, saying, "You won't be an MP all your life." See Sostre, testimony in *U.S.A v. Sostre,* 139, in Record of Trial by Court-Martial (256346).
140. Jeff Pinkston, testimony in *U.S.A. v. Sostre* 95, in Record of Trial by Court-Martial (256346). He variously described it as between four and seven inches long.
141. Edwin Banks, testimony in *U.S.A. v. Sostre*, 38, in Record of Trial by Court-Martial (256346).
142. Sostre, testimony in *U.S.A v. Sostre,* 143, in Record of Trial by Court-Martial (256346).
143. Sostre, testimony before Major George G. Gilbert., Jr. April 22, 1944, 9.
144. In a general court martial order no. 172 issued January 26, 1945, Sostre was one of several prisoners at Fort Hackson who were to be moved to Camp Gordon: Record of Trial by Court-Martial (256346). This aligns with the closing of Camp Gordon as a prisoner of war camp on January 29, 1945, as cited in Kathy Roe Coker, "World War II Prisoners of War in Georgia: German Memories of Camp Gordon, 1943–1945," *Georgia Historical Quarterly* 76, no. 4 (Winter 1992): 853.
145. A 1967 psychiatric evaluation, for example, noted that "he received a court martial for participating in a melee wherein various people were stabbed." In 1973,

he recalled "a fight between two companies in town." In a 1987 newspaper article, he said it "arose from a brawl." See Psychological evaluation by Dr. Howard C. Wilinsky and Michael J. Lynch; Martin Sostre, testimony, 52, in *Sostre v. Festa* (74-1520), NARA—KC; and "Radical Completes Another Building in Passaic," *The Record*, January 22, 1987.

146. Martin Sostre, interview with Vinny Sostre, 2002.
147. Martin Sostre, "Thoughts of a Black Political Prisoner in Solitary Confinement," *The Partisan* 5, no. 2 (April 1969), 14.
148. Mike Fabey, "Lessons of the Trade: Youth Project Under Fire," *Herald-News*, April 9, 1989.
149. Martin Sostre, "Pilots for Panthers: Assault on the Monster's Head," *Black News* 1, no. 1 (January 1970): 1.
150. "Radical Completes Another Building in Passaic," *The Record*, January 22, 1987. See Martin Sostre FBI File (100-NY-154100).
151. Martin Sostre, interview with Vinny Sostre, 2012.
152. Jessica Neptune, "The Making of the Carceral State: Street Crime, the War on Drugs, and Punitive Politics in New York, 1951–1973" (PhD diss., University of Chicago, 2012), 36, 49.
153. Psychological evaluation by Dr. Howard C. Wilinsky and Michael J. Lynch.
154. A full arrest record until 1964 is reproduced in Martin Sostre's FBI file. See Richard W. Dow, Summary Report, April 5, 1966, Buffalo, New York, 4–7, Martin Sostre FBI File (100-NY-154100).
155. Summary Report, Richard Dow, April 5, 1966, 6, Martin Sostre FBI File (100-NY-154100).
156. Neptune, "The Making of the Carceral State," 53–54. See also Nancy D. Campbell, "A New Deal for the Drug Addict: The Addiction Research Center," *Journal of the History of the Behavioral Sciences* 42, no. 2 (Spring 2006), 135–57.
157. Neptune, "Making of the Carceral State," 54.
158. Summary Report, Richard Dow, April 5, 1966, 6, Martin Sostre FBI File (100-NY-154100).
159. Damali Bashira, "Martin Sostre: What is Justice?," *Encore American and Worldwide News*, October 6, 1975, 9.
160. Arrastía, "From Prison, Sostre Urges More Struggle."
161. Rafael Cancel Miranda, "Julio Pinto Gandía," *Claridad en la Nación*, July 9, 2008; Margaret Power, "Friends and Comrades: Political and Personal Relationships between Members of the Communist Party USA and the Puerto Rican Nationalist Party, 1930s–1940s," 105–28, in Kevin Young, ed., *Making the Revolution: Histories of the Latin American Left* (Cambridge, UK: Cambridge University Press, 2019).
162. "Ex-Head of Puerto Rico Nationalist Party Held as Draft Evader," *New York Times*, June 6, 1945.
163. Evelyn Atwood, "Arrested Puerto Rican Nationalist Leader Opposes Wall St. Imperialism, *The Militant*, June 16, 1945, 6.

164. See Nelson Denis, *War against All Puerto Ricans: Revolution and Terror in America's Colony* (New York: Bold Type, 2015), 205–8, 208.
165. Joe Martin, "Puerto Ricans Nabbed Here in Truman Plot," *Daily News*, November 23, 1950.
166. Sostre, interview with D*í*az-Cotto.
167. Arrastía, "From Prison, Sostre Urges More Struggle."
168. As Miranda explained, "fifty years passed without revealing the role of Mr. Pinto Gandía in the attack on the United States Congress in 1954. In 2004, when the fiftieth anniversary of the armed action was celebrated, I finally revealed that the patriot Mr. Julio Pinto Gandía had been the main organizer of the action." See Miranda, "Julio Pinto Gandía."
169. "PR Nationalist Chief Here Gets 6 Months," *Daily News*, March 12, 1954.
170. Arrastía, "From Prison, Sostre Urges More Struggle."
171. Martin Sostre, interview with Vinny Sostre, 2002.
172. "Prisoner Who is Identified as Contact Man for Big Narcotics Ring Held in $50,000 Bail," *New York Times,* September 24, 1952; Edward Dillon, "Bring in Drug Seller Who Fled to Mexico," *Daily News*, September 24, 1952.
173. Memo, "Members of the Muslim Cult in State Prisons," June 9, 1960, 4, in Box 19, Items 147, Division of State Police, Non-Criminal Investigation Case Files, A0795-80, New York State Archives. See also *Luís* Astorga, "Drug Trafficking in Mexico: A First General Assessment," United Nations Educational, Scientific and Cultural Organization, 1999, available at https://unesdoc.unesco.org/ark:/48223/pf0000117644; George Grayson, *Mexico: Narco-Violence and a Failed State?* (Milton Park: Routledge, 2010); and George Grayson, "Mexican Cartels, Appendix 1," *Headline Series* 331 (Winter 2009), 68–69. Grayson writes that the Sinaloa Cartel began with the Herrera family in the 1940s, who later "cooperated with Ernesto 'Don Neto' Fonseca and Jorge Favela Escobar, who drew attention as key Sinaloan drug operatives in the 1950s and 1960s."
174. Benjamin Smith, *The Dope: The Real History of the Mexican Drug Trade* (New York: W. W. Norton, 2021), ePub version, 376, 522–23.
175. Neptune, "Making of the Carceral State," 57.
176. "Prisoner Who is Identified as Contact Man"; "Bring in Drug Seller Who Fled to Mexico." See also Sostre's medical history admission at Clinton prison, which listed him as a user of heroin, cocaine, and marijuana between 1943 and 1952. Clinton Prison, Medical History on Admission, March 5, 1953, Martin Sostre Prison File, NYSA_B0123-77_31828, New York State Archives.
177. Arrastía, "From Prison, Sostre Urges More Struggle."
178. Sing Sing Prison Receiving Blotter, December 12, 1952, Martin Sostre Prison File, NYSA_B0143-80_113153, New York State Archives.
179. Martin Sostre, interview with Vinny Sostre, 2002. This may have been true given that the Boggs Act mandated ten years as a maximum sentence for repeat offenses.
180. He later testified that he had accumulated as much good time as he possibly could ("over two years") prior to being placed in solitary confinement. See

Martin Sostre, testimony in *Pierce v. LaVallee,* 101, NARA—Kansas City, Missouri.

181. Rosenbaum and Kossy, "A Question of Justice," 3.

3. The Politicized Prisoner

1. "Michael Shields His Little Brother from the Sad News," *Daily Worker*, June 22, 1953.
2. Both sons, Michael and Robert, later took the surname of their adoptive parents, Anne and Abel Meeropol.
3. Michael Meeropol, interview with author, June 28, 2021.
4. "Hear Martin Sostre at the Teach-In on Dissent Activism and Frame-Up in America: Sacco-Vanzetti to Kent State," Flyer, Box 13, Folder 12, Elwin H. Powell Papers, University Archives, State University of New York at Buffalo.
5. Michael Powell, "Radical's Progress: Another Building," *The Record*, January 22, 1987.
6. "Twenty Years in Prison," *Pat Collins Show*, ep. 445, February 26, 1976, in author's possession, courtesy of Vinny Sostre.
7. Lorrin Rosenbaum and Judith Kossy, "A Question of Justice: The Case of Martin Sostre," *Index on Censorship* 5, no. 3 (1976): 3.
8. I am grateful to my comrade Alvamore Alexis Irizarry Jr. for this framing.
9. Angela Davis, ed., *If They Come in the Morning: Voices of Resistance* (London: Verso, 2016), 35.
10. Robert Bright, "The Self-Proclaimed Political Prisoner," 111, in *Proceedings of the 102nd Annual Congress of Correction of the American Correctional Association*, August 20–26, 1972 (College Park, MD: American Correctional Association, 1972).
11. *Attica: The Official Report of the New York State Special Commission on Attica* (New York: Bantam, 1972), 120n8.
12. The Boggses were writing under the auspices of the Committee for Political Development, a small organization they formed in the 1970s that combined local organizing and political education. See Committee for Political Development, "Attica and the Movement," September 1971, in author's possession, courtesy of Stephen Ward. See Garrett Felber and Stephen Ward, " 'This Argument is Far from Over': Martin Sostre, James and Grace Lee Boggs, and the Political Prisoner in Revolutionary Struggles," *Radical History Review* 146 (May 2023): 105–19. Others, such as law professor Stuart Brody, used this phrase later. See Stuart Brody, "The Political Prisoner Syndrome: Latest Problem of the American Penal System," *Crime and Delinquency* 20, no. 2 (April 1974): 97–106.
13. Martin Sostre, "The New Prisoner," *North Carolina Central Law Journal* 4, no. 2 (Spring 1973): 244–45.
14. See *Frame-Up! The Imprisonment of Martin Sostre*, dir. Joel Sucher, Steven Fischler, and Howard Blatt (Pacific Street Films, 1974). Elsewhere, Sostre wrote that "people in jail are political prisoners in the sense that they're there because this

country is so structured, in terms of lack of availability of jobs and of institutional racism, that for one portion of the population, most options are closed." See *Free Martin Sostre* (Northampton, MA: Mother Jones Press, 1975), 7.

15. Martin Sostre, "What Is to Be Done?," March 9, 1976, Black Mass Communications Project Collection, Robert S. Cox Special Collections and University Archives Research Center, UMass-Amherst.
16. Sostre, "The New Prisoner," 251.
17. His petition for executive clemency in 1975 claimed that the "Parole Board never gave written reasons . . . as to why parole was denied him. However, Mr. Sostre believes that the denial of parole occurred in part because he had sued the Parole Board under the Civil Rights Act of 1866, challenging its all-white racial composition. . . . Mr. Sostre also believes that he may have been denied parole because of his affiliation with the then relative new and unknown Black Muslim religion and because of litigation he initiated during the term of his incarceration, seeking to establish the right of all religious groups to free exercise of religion while in prison." Petition for Executive Clemency to the Honorable Hugh Carey, Governor of the State of New York, 4–5, in Executive Clemency Files, New York State Archives.
18. I am grateful to Stevie Wilson for this observation. For more on this point, see Wilson, "Political Prisoner or Politicized Prisoner: Does the Label Matter?," *Radical History Review* 146 (May 2023): 120–22. Sostre made a similar observation himself when he said that the "the box is the real barometer of who is a threat to the state." See Marlene Nadle, "The Convictions of a Man of Conviction," *Village Voice*, March 24, 1975.
19. Martin Sostre, interview with Vinny Sostre, 2012. In author's possession, courtesy of Liz and Vinny Sostre.
20. Arthur Dobrin, "An American Prisoner of Conscience," *The Progressive* 44, no. 5 (May 1980): 37.
21. Toussaint Losier and Dan Berger point out that "by refining and then spreading the legal arguments at the heart of these complaints, jailhouse lawyers like Sostre played a key role in building the movement that emerged in the late 1950s and 1960s." Dan Berger and Toussaint Losier, *Rethinking the American Prison Movement* (New York: Routledge, 2018), 63.
22. Mariame Kaba, quoted in Micah Herskind, "Some Reflections on Prison Abolition," *Medium*, December 7, 2019, https://micahherskind.medium.com/some-reflections-on-prison-abolition-after-mumi-5197a4c3cf98.
23. Quoted from a letter by Martin Sostre, February 23, 1975, in Kathie Streem, "Martin Sostre's Odyssey," *Berkeley Barb*, March 14–20, 1975, 7.
24. Garrett Felber, *Those Who Know Don't Say: The Nation of Islam, the Black Freedom Movement, and the Carceral State* (Chapel Hill: University of North Carolina Press, 2020), 16–18.
25. Felber, *Those Who Know Don't Say*, 18–27.
26. Malcolm X Little to Commissioner MacDowell, June 6, 1950, Malcolm X Prison File (no. 22843).

27. "Local Criminals, in Prison, Claim Moslem Faith Now," *Springfield Union*, April 21, 1950.
28. Martin Sostre, interview with Juanita Díaz-Cotto, May 25, 1993, in author's possession, courtesy of Juanita Díaz-Cotto.
29. See Manning Marable, *Malcolm X: A Life of Reinvention* (New York: Viking, 2011), 132.
30. Malcolm to Philbert, March 26, 1950, Box 3, Folder 1, Malcolm X Collection (MXC), Schomburg Center for Research in Black Culture, Manuscripts, Archives and Rare Books Division, New York Public Library.
31. Martin Sostre to Stokely Carmichael, March 16, 1968, Folder 252253-054-0001, Subgroup C, Washington Office, Series I, Administrative Files, Student Nonviolent Coordinating Committee Correspondence, SNCC Papers, ProQuest History Vault.
32. Quoted in notes by journalist Joe Shapiro from Martin Sostre's press conference upon his release, February 10, 1976, 3, in author's possession, courtesy of Joe Shapiro.
33. Sing Sing Prison Receiving Blotter.
34. Martin Sostre, testimony in *Pierce v. LaVallee*, 33-35, NARA—KC.
35. Martin Sostre to Governor Nelson Rockefeller, July 6, 1959, in Hugh Carey Papers, Executive Clemency, Governor's Records Guide, New York State Archives.
36. *Thirty-Third Annual Report of the State Commission of Correction*, 1959 (Ossining, NY: Sing Sing Prison, 1960), 9.
37. *Thirty-Third Annual Report*, 96–97.
38. *Thirty-Fourth Annual Report of the State Commission of Correction*, 1960 (Ossining, NY: Sing Sing Prison, 1961), 9, 100. I am borrowing "reproductive labor" here from a discussion between Craig Gilmore and James Kilgore. See Gilmore, "An Interview with James Kilgore," *Abolitionist* 23 (Fall 2014): 6.
39. *Thirty-Fourth Annual Report*, 1960, 8.
40. Sostre, testimony in *Pierce v. LaVallee,* testimony, 55, NARA—KC.
41. *Thirty-Third Annual Report*, 96.
42. Psychological evaluation by Dr. Howard C. Wilinsky and Michael J. Lynch, 1, in *People v. Sostre*, General Case Material, February 19, 1968, Folder 100243-029-0498, Supplement to Part 23: Legal Department Case Files, Series B: The Northeast, Section II: New York, Papers of the NAACP, ProQuest History Vault; Dobrin, "American Prisoner of Conscience," 36.
43. "Sostre: The Fight Goes On," interview with Martin Sostre by Abe Weisburd, December 27, 1975, *Guardian,* January 7, 1976, 4.
44. Martin Sostre to Office of the Adjutant General, April 19, 1954, in Record of Trial by Court-Martial (256346), NARA—St. Louis, Missouri.
45. Robert L. Carter to Martin Sostre, May 14, 1958, Folder 001475-005-0200, Part 22: Legal Department Administrative Files, 1956-1965, Series B, Administrative File, General Office File: Carter, Robert L., General Correspondence, Papers of the NAACP, ProQuest History Vault.

46. Martin Sostre to Jacob Hyman, April 16, 1963, Box 4, Folder 5, Jacob D. Hyman Papers, University Archives, State University of New York at Buffalo.
47. Martin Sostre to Dean Jacob Hyman, May 1, 1963, Box 4, Folder 5, Hyman Papers.
48. Nadle, "Convictions of a Man of Conviction."
49. See Crescencia Sostre to Governor Averell Harriman, July 16, 1957, in Hugh Carey Papers, Executive Clemency, Governor's Records Guide, New York State Archives and *Sostre v. Mailler*, 192 N.Y.S. 2d 777.
50. Opinion, *Sostre v. Mailler*, 192 N.Y.S. 2d 777.
51. Crescencia Sostre to Governor Averell Harriman.
52. *Sostre v. Mailler*, 192 N.Y.S. 2d 777.
53. Martin Sostre to Governor Rockefeller, July 6, in Hugh Carey Papers, Executive Clemency, Governor's Records Guide, New York State Archives.
54. Judge Constance Baker Motley removed Rockefeller from the state officials listed as defendants.
55. Martin Sostre to Governor Rockefeller, July 6, 1959, in Hugh Carey Papers, Executive Clemency, Governor's Records Guide, New York State Archives.
56. Thomas Bratcher, testimony in *SaMarion v. McGinnis*, 629, National Archives and Records Administration—New York, NY (NARA—NYC).
57. Sostre, "Report From Prison," *Undercurrent*, undated, 3, Box 28, Folder 9, Papers of Florynce Kennedy, Schlesinger Library, Radcliffe Institute.
58. Richard E. Woodward, "History of Muslims Presented to Uniformed Supervisors Association of the New York State Department of Correction," February 5, 1964, 7, Box 24, Items 831–839, Division of State Police, Non-Criminal Investigation Case Files, A0795-80, New York State Archives (NCICF-NYSA).
59. According to Sostre, the first petition may actually have been submitted in 1958. He later wrote: "The struggle commenced in Clinton Prison during 1958 when we first sued in Plattsburgh Supreme Court via writ of *mandamus* seeking the exercise of religious freedom." See Sostre, "The New Prisoner," 251.
60. Zaheer Ali, "Islamophobia Did Not Start at Ground Zero," *Root*, September 7, 2010.
61. Woodward, "History of Muslims," 8. The formation of this apparatus is documented in "Muslim Cult - State Prisons," Lieutenant G. W. Craig to Superintendent Arthur Cornelius Jr., April 28, 1961, Box 19, Item 145, NCICF-NYSA.
62. For 1961 estimate, see Richard E. Woodward, Bulletin, March 1961, Box 21, Items 336–339, NCICF-NYSA; for 1964, see Woodward, "History of Muslims," 7.
63. Dobrin, "American Prisoner of Conscience," 36.
64. Sostre, interview with Juanita Díaz-Cotto.
65. Sostre, interview with Vinny Sostre, 2012.
66. Martin Sostre, testimony in *Pierce v. LaVallee,* 33–35, NARA—KC.
67. William Worthy, "The Anguish of Martin Sostre," *Ebony*, October 1970, 122–24, 126, 128, 132.

68. James Pierce testified, "You have no direct access to the library." *Pierce v. LaVallee*, 65, US District Court, NY, Civil Case Files, Boxes 12–13, Case 7813.
69. Sostre, testimony in *Pierce v. LaVallee,* 67 and 87, NARA—KC.
70. Sostre, testimony in *Pierce v. LaVallee,* 59–60, NARA—KC.
71. Sostre, testimony in *Pierce v. LaVallee,* 66–67, NARA—KC.
72. William Bresinhan, reading document into trial transcript, *Pierce v. LaVallee,* 263, NARA—KC.
73. James Walker, testimony in *SaMarion v. McGinnis,* 480, NARA—NYC.
74. Sostre, testimony in *Pierce v. LaVallee,* 87, NARA—KC.
75. Joseph Magette, testimony in *SaMarion v. McGinnis,* NARA—NYC.
76. Attica prison report, March 1, 1961, quoted in *SaMarion v. McGinnis,* 1195, NARA—NYC. Reverend Theodore Rogers, whose brother-in-law was a Muslim incarcerated in New York, wrote that the "policy of the prison is to force Negroes to eat pork to prove they are not Muslims. Most Negroes are automatically suspect when they refuse to eat pork." See "Religious Persecution in New York Prisons," press release, n.d., Box 11, Folder 19, MXC.
77. Attica Prison Liberation Faction. Manifesto of Demands, available at https://libcom.org/article/attica-prison-liberation-faction-manifesto-demands-1971.
78. The Arabic instructor was likely Wallace D. Mohammed, not to be confused with Elijah Muhammad's son by the same name. Masia Mugmuk recalled that Mohammed "spoke Arabic very fluently. He had Arabic in his head. He memorized the whole Qur'an." See Masia Mugmuk, interview with author, March 18, 2021; Sostre, testimony in *Pierce v. LaVallee,* 95, NARA—KC; and Magette, testimony in *SaMarion v. McGinnis,* 708, NARA—NYC. Martin Sostre, Psychiatric Report at Clinton Prison, February 1, 1960, Department of Mental Hygiene, in author's possession. Special gratitude is due to Liz and Vinny Sostre, as well as Brad Thomson and Wally Hilke, for helping navigate the labyrinthian bureaucracy of the state to secure these files.
79. Sostre, testimony in *Pierce v. LaVallee,* 95, NARA—KC.
80. "Material was handed in such a form as to be lessons," William X SaMarion explained. "These lessons were to have been learned by heart, to be able to speak about." William SaMarion, testimony in *SaMarion v. McGinnis,* 376, NARA—NYC.
81. Mugmuk, interview with author, March 18, 2021.
82. Mugmuk recalled that "sometimes Malcolm X would come up as a Christian minister and he would feed them information on what's going on, and that's how we found out what was going on." Masia Mugmuk, interview with author, March 18, 2021. See also Orisanmi Burton, *Tip of the Spear: Black Radicalism, Prison Repression, and the Long Attica Revolt* (Berkeley: University of California Press, 2023), 190. In Mugmuk's original interview, he remembered that Malcolm met with James X Pierce, but it was confirmed later that this was Ned X Hines.
83. Mugmuk, interview with author.

84. Hekima, meaning "Wisdom" or "Man of Wisdom" in Kiswahili, referred to Ned X Hines.
85. Mugmuk, interview with author.
86. Bureau of Criminal Investigation, Memo, to Inspector W.F. Driscoll, February 4, 1960, Box 19, Items 11–20, NCICF-NYSA.
87. Quoted in *SaMarion v. McGinnis,* 1237, NARA—NYC.
88. Sostre wrote James X Ritchie from solitary confinement with specific instructions on how to order a subscription, noting, "We would send you the newspapers and a magazine that Aki Omar is getting but they won't allow it." See *Shaw v. McGinnis*, 14 N.Y. 2d 864 (1962), Respondent's Appendix, Appendix F, A120, Appellate Division Law Library, Rochester, New York.
89. Sostre, testimony in *Pierce v. LaVallee*, 45 and 69, NARA—KC.
90. Bureau of Criminal Investigation, Memo, to Inspector W. F. Driscoll, February 4, 1960, Box 19, Items 11–20, NCICF-NYSA.
91. Sostre, testimony in *Pierce v. LaVallee,* 271–72, NARA—KC.
92. Sostre testified that he "helped to phrase it." See *Pierce v. LaVallee,* 238–239 and 254, NARA—KC.
93. Sarah Gordon, *Spirit of the Law: Religious Voices and the Constitution in Modern America* (Cambridge, MA: Harvard University Press, 2010), 118.
94. Sostre testified that it was composed around April 1959. See *Pierce v. LaVallee,* 239, NARA—KC.
95. For a full copy of the constitution, see Box 11, Folder 19, MXC.
96. William Bresinhan, reading document into trial transcript, *Pierce v. LaVallee*, 256, NARA—KC.
97. William Bresinhan, reading document into trial transcript, *Pierce v. LaVallee*, 254, NARA—KC.
98. See Gregory Lewis, "Lifting the Ban on Gays in the Civil Service: Federal Policy Toward Gay and Lesbian Employees since the Cold War," *Public Administration Review* 57, no. 5 (September-October 1997): 387–95.
99. *Thirty-Fourth Annual Report*, 1960, 105. In 1963, Attica also reported having fifty-two inmates in segregation for mental reasons, protection, or those "suspected of having homosexual tendencies." See *Thirty-Seventh Annual Report of the State Commission of Correction*, 1963 (Albany: State Commission of Correction, 1964), 85.
100. Sostre, testimony in *Pierce v. LaVallee*, 250, NARA—KC.
101. Sostre, testimony in *Pierce v. LaVallee*, 70 and 75, NARA—KC.
102. William Bresinhan, questioning at trial in *Pierce v. LaVallee,* 197, NARA—KC.
103. Bresinhan, questioning at trial in *Pierce v. LaVallee,* 203 and 207, NARA—KC.

4. The Political Prisoner

1. Martin Sostre, testimony in *Pierce v. LaVallee*, 72–73, National Archives and Records Administration—Kansas City, Missouri (NARA—KC), 72–73;

SaMarion v. McGinnis, 347, National Archives and Records Administration—New York, New York (NARA—NYC).

2. Sostre, testimony in *Pierce v. LaVallee*, 72–73, NARA—KC.
3. Leon Haywood, Theodore Collins, Joseph Magette, James Walpole, Samuel Williams, John Earle, and Clayton Warren were all put in solitary. Sostre, testimony in *Pierce v. LaVallee*, 234–35, NARA—KC.
4. "Prisoners were generally understood to have little or no claim to their civil rights during their incarceration," note Toussaint Losier and Dan Berger. "State courts were often hostile to prisoners' claims, while federal courts often deferred petitions by state prisoners to state courts on the basis of federalism." See Dan Berger and Toussaint Losier, *Rethinking the American Prison Movement* (New York: Routledge, 2018), 58.
5. Pierce's correspondence with the commissioner regarding his suit was written in Sostre's unmistakable block handwriting and signed "Pierce." Other pages signed by Pierce are written in different handwriting. See James Pierce to Commissioner Paul McGinnis, August 18, 1960; William E. Leonard to James Pierce, August 24, 1960; and Notice of Motion, *Pierce V. La Vallee*, all in *Pierce v. La Vallee,* NARA—KC.
6. Garrett Felber, *Those Who Know Don't Say: The Nation of Islam, the Black Freedom Movement, and the Carceral State* (Chapel Hill: University of North Carolina Press, 2020), 58.
7. Lawrence O'Kane, "Muslim Negroes Suing the State," *New York Times*, March 19, 1961.
8. Michael Noon McCarty, "Limitation of State Prisoners' Civil Rights Suits in the Federal Courts," *Catholic University Law Review* 27, no. 1 (Fall 1977), 115n4.
9. James Jacobs, "The Prisoners' Rights Movement and Its Impacts, 1960–1980," *Crime and Justice* 2 (1980): 440. For more on *Pate* and the organizing that led to the decision, see Toussaint Losier, " ' . . . For Strictly Religious Reason[s]': Cooper v. Pate and the Origins of the Prisoners' Rights Movement," *Souls* 15, nos. 1–2 (2013): 19–38.
10. Derek L. Gaubatz, "RLUIPA at Four: Evaluating the Success and Constitutionality of RLUIPA's Prisoner Provisions," *Harvard Journal of Law and Public Policy* 28, no. 2 (2005): 507.
11. As Christopher Smith points out, "Because Section 1983 lawsuits provided the vehicle for judicial decisions that developed constitutional law affecting prisoners' rights, the *Cooper v. Pate* decision served as the foundational precedent essential to the later protection of all constitutional rights for prisoners. See Smith, *The Supreme Court and the Development of Law: Through the Prism of Prisoners' Rights* (New York: Palgrave Macmillan, 2016), 21–22.
12. See Berger and Losier, *Rethinking the American Prison Movement*, 64.
13. Sostre, testimony in *Pierce v. La Vallee*, 80, NARA—KC.
14. Sostre, testimony in *Pierce v. La Vallee*, 80–81, NARA—KC.
15. Sostre, testimony in *Pierce v. La Vallee*, 48 and 81, NARA—KC.

16. Thomas Bratcher, testimony in *SaMarion v. McGinnis*, 579, NARA—NYC and Sostre, testimony in *Pierce v. La Vallee,* 92, NARA—KC.
17. Bratcher, testimony in *SaMarion v. McGinnis*, 613, NARA—NYC.
18. William SaMarion, testimony in *SaMarion v. McGinnis*, 346-366, NARA—NYC.
19. Bratcher, testimony in *SaMarion v. McGinnis*, 585, NARA—NYC.
20. James Walker, testimony in *SaMarion v. McGinnis*, 440, NARA—NYC.
21. Martin Sostre, "The New Prisoner," *North Carolina Central Law Journal* 4, no. 2 (Spring 1973): 251.
22. "Complaint of Conditions at Attica State Prison," in Box 45, Folder 48, Congress of Racial Equality Papers, Part 3: Scholarship, Educational and Defense Fund for Racial Equality, 1960-1976, Series C: Legal Department Files, ProQuest History Vault.
23. Martin Sostre, speech delivered on June 24, 1976, reprinted in *The Militant*, September 3, 1976, 22.
24. Quoted in Affidavit on Motion to Proceed in Forma Pauperis, October 5, 1959, 4, *Pierce v. La Vallee,* NARA—KC.
25. Exhibit in *Sostre v. La Vallee,* dated September 22, 1959, in Reply, September 26, 1960, *Pierce v. La Vallee,* 293, NARA—KC.
26. A copy of Judge Brennan's letter to Attorney General Louis Lefkowitz dated October 7, 1959, *Pierce v. LaVallee*, NARA—KC.
27. Joseph Magette, testimony *SaMarion v. McGinnis,* 713, NARA—NYC.
28. In 1958, the reported total number of days of earned time lost for disciplinary reasons was 14,262, and in 1960 it had returned to similar levels at 14, 515. See *Thirty-Third Annual Report of the State Commission of Correction*, 1959 (Ossining, NY: Sing Sing Prison, 1960), 101; and *Thirty-Fifth Annual Report of the State Commission of Correction*, 1961 (Ossining, NY: Sing Sing Prison, 1962), 108.
29. For a more comprehensive overview of these practices, see Felber, *Those Who Know Don't Say*, 63-64.
30. Sostre, testimony in *Pierce v. La Vallee,* 199-203, NARA—KC.
31. Martin Sostre, Psychiatric Report, Clinton Prison, February 1, 1960, Department of Mental Hygiene. In author's possession.
32. Psychiatric Report, February 12, 1960.
33. Psychiatric Report, February 1, 1960.
34. Psychologist's Examination Report, January 30, 1960.
35. Fifteen Muslims at Green Haven in Stormville, New York also petitioned the court that spring. G. W. Craig to Martin F. Dillon, Members of the Muslim Cult in State Prisons Petitions to the Appellant Division, Second Department, April 27, 1960, Items 107-120, Division of State Police, Non-Criminal Investigation Case Files, A0795-80, New York State Archives (NCICF-NYSA).
36. Richard E. Woodward, "History of Muslims Presented to Uniformed Supervisors Association of the New York State Department of Correction," February 5, 1964, 8, Box 24, Items 831-839, NCICF-NYSA.

37. Memo to Chief Inspector, Bureau of Criminal Investigation, February 1, 1960, Box 19, Items 1–10, NCICF-NYSA.
38. Supplemental Report from Lieutenant G. W. Craig Martin F. Dillon, January 29, 1960, Box 19, Items 1–10; Martin F. Dillon to Lieutenant R. E. Sweeney, April 26, 1960, Box 19, Items 107–120, both in NCICF-NYSA.
39. Sostre, testimony in *Pierce v. La Vallee*, 85, NARA—KC.
40. Sostre, testimony in *Pierce v. La Vallee*, 144, NARA—KC.
41. Sostre, testimony in *Pierce v. La Vallee*, 142, NARA—KC.
42. Sostre, testimony in *Pierce v. La Vallee*, 141, NARA—KC.
43. Magette, testimony in *SaMarion v. McGinnis*, 718, NARA—NYC.
44. Warren Schaich and Diane Hope, "The Prison Letters of Martin Sostre: Documents of Resistance," *Journal of Black Studies* 7, no. 3 (March 1977): 291. They are excerpting from a letter from Sostre dated August 30, 1972.
45. Arthur Dobrin, "An American Prisoner of Conscience," *Progressive* 44, no. 5 (May 1980): 37.
46. "The Open Road Interview with Martin Sostre," by David Spaner, *Open Road*, Summer 1976, 13.
47. "Radical Self Care," Afropunk interview with Angela Davis, *Self Practice*, 2018, https://www.selfpractice.com.au/self-practice/angela-davis-on-radical-self-care.
48. Stephanie Evans, "Black Women's Historical Wellness: History as a Tool in Culturally Competent Mental Health Services, June 21, 2019, Association of Black Women Historians, http://abwh.org/2019/06/21/black-womens-historical-wellness-history-as-a-tool-in-culturally-competent-mental-health-services.
49. Monica Cadena, "The Story Behind Rosa Parks and Yoga," *Yoga Journal*, September 2, 2021, https://www.yogajournal.com/yoga-101/history-of-yoga/rosa-parks-yoga-images/.
50. Schaich and Hope, "The Prison Letters of Martin Sostre, 291–93.
51. Judge Brennan, in *Pierce v. La Vallee*, 100–101 and 225, US District Court, NY, Civil Case Files, Boxes 12–13, Case 7813.
52. *Pierce v. LaVallee,* Brief for Appellee, June 15, 1961, 5.
53. William SaMarion explained that he rejected it because it would "jeopardize [his] case in court." Elsewhere, Sostre claimed it was "not the book of my faith" and suggested a Catholic would raise the same objection about a Protestant book. SaMarion, testimony in *Pierce v. La Vallee*, 182, 188, and 213, US District Court, NY, Civil Case Files, Boxes 12–13, Case 7813.
54. Brennan, in *Pierce v. La Vallee*, 55, US District Court, NY, Civil Case Files, Boxes 12–13, Case 7813.
55. Sostre, testimony in *Pierce v. La Vallee*, 140, US District Court, NY, Civil Case Files, Boxes 12–13, Case 7813.
56. For full exchange, see *Pierce v. La Vallee*, 138–140, US District Court, NY, Civil Case Files, Boxes 12–13, Case 7813.
57. Brennan, in *Pierce v. La Vallee*, 117 and 225, US District Court, NY, Civil Case Files, Boxes 12–13, Case 7813.

58. Brennan, in *Pierce v. La Vallee*, 47, US District Court, NY, Civil Case Files, Boxes 12-13, Case 7813.
59. Brennan, in *Pierce v. La Vallee*, 254-255, US District Court, NY, Civil Case Files, Boxes 12-13, Case 7813.
60. See Memorandum Decision, Judge Brennan, 10 in Box 22, Items 536-45, NCICF-NYSA.
61. Brennan, in *Pierce v. La Vallee*, 255 and 53, US District Court, NY, Civil Case Files, Boxes 12-13, Case 7813.
62. Complaint by Edward Jacko on behalf of Pierce, Sostre, and SaMarion, October 18, 1961, in *Pierce v. La Vallee,* 293 F. 2d 233 (2. Cir. 1961) (Civil No. 7813), NARA—KC.
63. Bratcher, testimony in *SaMarion v. McGinnis,* 627 and 629-631, NARA—NYC.
64. Albert Meyer, testimony in *SaMarion v. McGinnis,* 1,202-1,203, NARA—NYC.
65. *Shaw v. McGinnis*, 14 N.Y. 2d 864 (1962), Respondent's Appendix, Appendix F, A120, Appellate Division Law Library, Rochester, New York.
66. *Shaw v. McGinnis*, 14 N.Y. 2d 864 (1962), A121.
67. See *Shaw v. McGinnis*, 14 N.Y. 2d 864 (1962), A122.
68. Magette, testimony in *SaMarion v. McGinnis*, 757 and 771-72, NARA—NYC.
69. *Shaw v. McGinnis*, 14 N.Y. 2d 864 (1962), A121.
70. See fuller discussion in Felber, *Those Who Know Don't Say*, 68-70.
71. Amended Complaint, 4, in *SaMarion v. McGinnis,* NARA—NYC.

Shaw v. McGinnis, 14 N.Y. 2d 864 (1962), A116.

72. *Shaw v. McGinnis*, 14 N.Y. 2d 864 (1962), A121.
73. Bresinhan, in *Pierce v. La Vallee*, 226, NARA—KC.
74. Brennan, in *Pierce v. La Vallee*, 19, NARA—KC. In fact, Sostre had just written to Brennan a little more than a week before the trial to ensure that the issue of accessing religious literature would be adjudicated. See Martin Sostre to Judge Brennan, November 5, 1961, in *Pierce v. La Vallee,* NARA—KC.
75. *Pierce v. La Vallee*, 340, NARA—KC.
76. Brennan, in *Pierce v. La Vallee,* 228, NARA—KC.
77. Sostre and Brennan, in *Pierce v. La Vallee*, 311, 313-14, 326, NARA—KC.
78. Damali Bashira, "Martin Sostre: What is Justice?," *Encore American and Worldwide News*, October 6, 1975.
79. Ruth Kinna, *Government of No One: The Theory and Practice of Anarchism* (London: Pelican, 2019), 66.
80. Brennan, in *Pierce v. La Vallee,* 329-30.
81. Kinna, *Government of No One*, 52.
82. "Muslims Win Right to Practice Islam in Jail: Muslims' Victory is Far Reaching," *Amsterdam News*, February 3, 1962.
83. Lawrence O'Kane, "Muslim Negroes Suing the State," *New York Times*, March 16, 1961.
84. Berger and Losier, *Rethinking the American Prison Movement*, 63.
85. Bresinhan, in *SaMarion v. McGinnis*, 28, NARA—NYC.
86. Bresinhan, in *SaMarion v. McGinnis*, 190-91, NARA—NYC.

87. Malcolm X, testimony in *SaMarion v. McGinnis*, 192; "N.Y. Court Studies Muslims' Rights Case," *Chicago Daily Defender*, October 16, 1963.
88. "Muslims Reveal 'Raw' Details of 'Solitary,'" *Muhammad Speaks*, November 15, 1962, 3.
89. Sostre, "The New Prisoner," 251.
90. Appellant's Brief, 18, in *Sostre v. McGinnis*, 28785 (Blue Side), NARA—NYC.
91. Martin Sostre to Thurgood Marshall, March 29, 1964, in *Sostre v. McGinnis* (no. 28785), NARA—NYC.
92. Margo Schlanger, "The Constitutional Law of Incarceration, Reconfigured," *Cornell Law Review* 103, no. 2 (January 2018): 368.
93. Martin Sostre to unknown (likely Sharon Fischer), July 5, 1972, Box 13, Folder 13, Elwin H. Powell Papers, University Archives, State University of New York at Buffalo.
94. Memo, Lieutenant W. C. Lovelock to Central Files, January 25, 1965, 3, Box 24, Items 970–79, NCICF-NYSA.
95. Martin Sostre, "Report from Jail to My Revolutionary Friends," in *Letters from Prison* (Buffalo, NY: Philosophical Society / Martin Sostre Defense Committee, July 1968), 24.

5. "A Power Base of Revolutionary Political Philosophy"

1. The complaint was later described along with another as "identical to and companion cases of *Sostre v. Wilkins and McGinnis*." See Appellants' Brief, *Bryant v. Wilkins*, 9–10, Appellate Division Law Library, Rochester, New York. In *Sostre v. Rockefeller*, Sostre said: "I helped make our briefs for him in that case." Martin Sostre, testimony in *Sostre v. Rockefeller,* 910, in author's possession, courtesy of Tomiko Brown-Nagin.
2. Lieutenant Supervisor John W. Monahan to Captain J. P. Nohlen, Assistance to Sherriff, Wyoming County, November 4, 1964, 5, Box 24, Items 910–19, Division of State Police, Non-criminal Investigation Case Files, A0795-80, New York State Archives (NCICF-NYSA).
3. Investigator H. L. Eichorst to Troop Commander, Troop "A," November 12, 1964; William Bresinhan, on behalf of Louis Lefkowitz, to Arthur Cornelius Jr., October 20, 1964, Box 24, Items 910–19, NCICF-NYSA.
4. Although the Wyoming County sheriff's department had seven uniformed officers equipped with a machine gun, tear gas, shotguns, and ammunition, he told the judge they lacked "sufficient manpower to control such a potentially explosive situation." J. P. Nohlen to John A. Roche, October 19, 1964; Monahan to Nohlen, November 4, 1964, 3, Box 24, Items 910–19, NCICF-NYSA.
5. Eichorst to Troop Commander, November 12, 1964. This language describing Muslims in the Nation as a "hate group" was popularized by the 1959 television documentary *The Hate That Hate Produced* (see Chapter 3).
6. The commissioner's rules and regulations were "drafted on the unconstitutional assumption" that he alone has authority to deem the Muslims a "sham,"

the judge determined. William B. Lawless, Memorandum, March 29, 1965, in Box 24, Items 910–19, NCICF-NYSA.

7. The other bookstores were located at 767 Jefferson Avenue and 289 High Street.
8. The name Sostre used for his bookstore fluctuated between "Afro-Asian Bookshop," "Afro-Asian Bookstore," and "Afro-Asian Book Shop," over the course of its two-and-a-half-year existence. Except in direct quotes, I have used "Afro-Asian Bookshop" throughout.
9. Martin Sostre, "Report from Jail to My Revolutionary Friends," in *Letters from Prison* (Buffalo, NY: Philosophical Society / Martin Sostre Defense Committee, July 1968), 20.
10. "To the Black Community: Message from Jail, an Interview with Martin Sostre," August 1, 1967, Folder 2, Subject Vertical Files, Civil Liberties—Blacks—Black Nationalism—Sostre, Martin, Labadie Collection, University of Michigan, Special Collections. See also Hearings Before the Committee on Un-American Activities, House of Representatives, 90th Congress, 2nd Session (Washington: US Government Printing Office, 1968), 2000; Martin Sostre, interview with Vinny Sostre, 2012. In author's possession, courtesy of Liz and Vinny Sostre.
11. Jerry Ross, interview with author, July 24, 2020.
12. Karima Amin, interview with author, November 30, 2021.
13. Sostre, "Report from Jail," 26.
14. The university, now known as the University at Buffalo, was referred to as the State University of New York at Buffalo (SUNY Buffalo) after it was turned into a research-oriented institution in 1962.
15. A 1969 article subtitled "the story of how the struggle to free political prisoners and expose political frame-ups led to a mass movement on the University Buffalo campus" said that "the consciousness of the radical students deepened as a result" of Sostre's trial; "The Buffalo Nine Ignite a Campus," *Partisan* 5, no. 2 (April 2, 1969): 8–9.
16. Dan Bentivogli, interview with author, February 24, 2021.
17. According to Domonique Griffin, "What urban renewal did manage to do was take federal monies that were intended for the benefit of the city as a whole and instead direct energy toward downtown development—making the city more attractive and accessible to largely white and increasingly middle-income suburbanites." Dominique Griffin, "They Were Never Silent, You Just Weren't Listening: Buffalo's Black Activists in the Age of Urban Renewal" (senior thesis, Trinity College, CT, 2017), 39–40, available at https://digitalrepository.trincoll.edu/theses/641/.
18. Malcolm McLaughlin, "Storefront Revolutionary: Martin Sostre's Afro-Asian Bookshop, Black Liberation Culture, and the New Left, 1965–1975," *The Sixties* 7, no. 1 (2014): 11.
19. Dan Berger, "Why Has COVID-19 Not Led to More Humanitarian Releases?," *Boston Review*, June 10, 2020.

20. The $135 figure comes from Sostre's "Report from Jail" and the $146 from "Black Freedom Fighter Turns His Back on Judge," *Workers World*, March 15, 1968.
21. Memo, Buffalo to New York, October 27, 1965, Martin Sostre FBI File (100-NY-154100).
22. Memo, New York to Buffalo, December 1, 1965, Martin Sostre FBI File (100-NY-154100).
23. Airtel, St. Louis to Buffalo, November 24, 1965, 5, Martin Sostre FBI File (100-NY-154100).
24. Sostre had been released to the home of Dora Bryant, the mother of the plaintiff Willis X Bryant. Investigator H. L. Eichorst, Memo, December 1, 1964, 3–4, in Box 24, Items 910–19, Division of State Police, NCICF-NYSA.
25. Henry Louis Taylor Jr., ed., *African Americans and the Rise of Buffalo's Post-Industrial City, 1940–Present*, vol. 2 (Buffalo: Buffalo Urban League, 1990), 4. As Gabriel Winant points out, Buffalo is among the numerous cities similar to Pittsburgh where "hospitals account for the majority of the largest employers"; Gabriel Winant, *The Next Shift: The Fall of Industry and the Rise of Health Care in Rust Belt America* (Cambridge, MA: Harvard University Press, 2021), 5.
26. Taylor, *African Americans*, 69.
27. See Table 2 in Brenda L. Moore, "Employment, Economic Opportunity and Class among Blacks in Buffalo," in *African Americans and the Rise of Buffalo's Post-Industrial City.*
28. Neil Kraus, *Race, Neighborhoods, and Community Power: Buffalo Politics, 1934–1997* (Albany: State University of New York Press), 115, 123–24. For excellent documentation of the experiences of these Black migrants, see can Griffin, "They Were Never Silent."
29. According to Henry-Louis Taylor Jr., "Like most big industrial cities," Buffalo "experienced a large influx of African Americans at the very moment that its economy was radically changing"; Taylor, *African Americans*, 4.
30. Kraus, *Race, Neighborhoods, and Community Power*, 98–100, 114–15. For more on the origins of racial segregation in Buffalo, see James Coughlin, *City of Distant Neighbors: The Proliferation and Entrenchment of Residential Segregation in Buffalo, New York (1934–1961)* (Buffalo: Burning Books, 2023).
31. According to surveillance by state police, Sostre lived at 421 High Street. Eichorst to Troop Commander, November 12, 1964, Box 24, Items 910–19, NCICF-NYSA.
32. Jaan Laaman, interview with author, July 27, 2021.
33. Bentivogli, interview with author.
34. Eichorst, Memo, December 1, 1964, 4, NCICF-NYSA.
35. Kenneth Warren, *Bethlehem Steel: Builder and Arsenal of America* (Pittsburgh: University of Pittsburgh Press, 2009), 186–88.
36. Thomas E. Leary and Elizabeth C. Sholes, *From Fire to Rust: Business, Technology,*

and Work at the Lackawanna Steel Plant, 1899–1983 (Buffalo: Buffalo and Erie County Historical Society, 1987), 55, 79.

37. Leary and Sholes, *From Fire to Rust*, 79.
38. Jaan Laaman's family emigrated from Estonia when he was a child, and he was raised in the predominantly Black neighborhood of Roxbury, Massachusetts, before settling in Buffalo; Jaan Laaman, interview with author.
39. Sixteen thousand workers walked out to protest Copeland's termination. Bruce Lambert, "Vincent Copeland, 77, Is Dead; Led Anti-War Protests in 1960's," *New York Times*, June 10, 1993; Vincent Copeland, *The Crime of Martin Sostre* (New York: McGraw-Hill, 1970), 37–38.
40. Martin Sostre to Roy Wilkins, August 22, 1970, *People v. Sostre*, General Case Material, July–October 1970, Folder 100243-030-0600, Part 23: Legal Department Case Files, Series B: The Northeast, Section II: New York, Papers of the NAACP, ProQuest History Vault.
41. Copeland, *Crime of Martin Sostre*, 43.
42. Sostre's father Saturnino died in 1966, while Martin was in Buffalo.
43. Sostre, "Report from Jail to My Revolutionary Friends," *Letters from Prison* (Buffalo, NY: Philosophical Society / Martin Sostre Defense Committee, May 1969, 2nd printing), 24.
44. William Worthy, "The Anguish of Martin Sostre," *Ebony*, October 1970, 123.
45. State surveillance reported that "Melvin Sims, has been corresponding with Martin Sostre. His letters are addressed to Martin Sostre at 240 Southampton Street, Buffalo, New York." Eichorst, Memo, December 1, 1964, 3. In December 1964, Buffalo Professor of Law J. D. Hyman wrote Martin's longtime comrade William SaMarion at Attica that he regretted he could not represent him in his "effort to obtain the books which Mr. Sostre wanted to leave you." Hyman to SaMarion, December 17, 1964, Box 4, Folder 4, Jacob D. Hyman Papers, University Archives, State University of New York at Buffalo.
46. New York State Department of Health; Albany, NY, USA; New York State Marriage Index, certificate number 6673, NYSA. Inv. H.L. Eichorst, Memo, Martin Gonzalez Sostre, March 5, 1965, 1, in Box 24, Items 1000-1006, NCICF-NYSA. The wedding was officiated at the South Park Missionary Baptist Church by Reverend Twilus V. Davis, the first Black chaplain of the Erie County Penitentiary. In his 1967 psychiatric evaluation, Sostre said he and Alberta Richardson had known each other for five months, lived together for several months and then separated. See psychological evaluation by Dr. Howard C. Wilinsky and Michael J. Lynch, *People v. Sostre*, General Case Material, February 19, 1968, Folder 100243-029-0498, Supplement to Part 23: Legal Department Case Files, Series B: The Northeast, Section II: New York, Papers of the NAACP, ProQuest History Vault.
47. Summary Report, Richard Dow, April 5, 1966, 9 and 12, Martin Sostre FBI File (100-NY-154100).
48. Sostre, "Report from Jail," *Letters from Prison*, 26. This partner may have been Wayman Diggs, whose name appears on a business card for a second store in

Frame-Up! The Imprisonment of Martin Sostre, dir. Joel Sucher, Steven Fischler, and Howard Blatt (Pacific Street Films, 1974).

49. Summary Report, Richard Dow, April 5, 1966, 2; Sandy Shevack, email to author, September 19, 2021.
50. Martin Sostre to Stokely Carmichael, March 16, 1968, Folder 252253-054-0001, Subgroup C, Washington Office, Series I, Administrative Files, Student Nonviolent Coordinating Committee (SNCC) Correspondence, SNCC Papers, ProQuest History Vault.
51. Sostre, "Report from Jail," 23.
52. Joshua Clark Davis, *From Head Shops to Whole Foods: The Rise and Fall of Activist Entrepreneurs* (New York: Columbia University Press, 2017), 38–39.
53. Colin Beckles, "Black Bookstores, Black Power, and the F.B.I.: The Case of Drum and Spear," *Western Journal of Black Studies* 20, no. 2 (Summer 1996): 64; Davis, *From Head Shops to Whole Foods*, 37–38. These two authors disagree about whether these Black-owned bookstores were anticapitalist; Beckles described most as economic ventures.
54. Joshua Clark Davis, "Black-Owned Bookstores: Anchors of the Black Power Movement," *Black Perspectives* (blog), January 28, 2017, https://www.aaihs.org/black-owned-bookstores-anchors-of-the-black-power-movement.
55. "The Smell of Fascism and the Sound of Courage in Buffalo, New York," *Workers World*, September 14, 1967.
56. Martin Sostre, testimony in *Sostre v. Festa* (74–1520), 44, NARA—KC.
57. Ross, interview with author.
58. Bentivogli, interview with author.
59. Dawud Hakim's small bookstore in West Philadelphia and Ed Vaughn's Book Store in Detroit were among the others in this period. Davis, *From Head Shops to Whole Foods*, 50, 55.
60. Jean Adams, interviewed in Griffin, "They Were Never Silent," 20.
61. Arthur Dobrin, "An American Prisoner of Conscience," *Progressive* 44, no. 5 (May 1980): 37–38.
62. Arto Williams, testimony in *People v. Robinson*, May 20, 1969, 210, Erie County Clerk's Office.
63. Geraldine (Robinson) Pointer, interview with William C. Anderson, October 5, 2023, in author's possession, courtesy of Pointer and Anderson.
64. Police inquired with Bethlehem Steel and found that Sostre worked there until August 3, 1966. Alvin Gristmacher to Michael Amico, Conversation with Informant, July 11, 1967, Carton 27, Herman Schwartz Papers, University Archives, State University of New York at Buffalo.
65. "Afro-Asian Bookstore," *Buffalo Criterion*, June 22, 1966, Buffalo Public Library, Grosvernor Room.
66. Sostre, "Report from Jail," 25.
67. Joseph Clore remembered him giving a speech about Black empowerment and businesses at a bar called the Humboldt Inn. Joseph Clore, interview with author, August 6, 2021.

68. Sostre, "Report from Jail."
69. Geraldine Robinson, testimony in *People v. Robinson*, 183, Erie County Clerk's Office.
70. Pointer, interview with Anderson.
71. Sostre, "Report from Jail," 27.
72. Grove Press reported that the book sold two hundred thousand copies in 1967 and four hundred thousand the following year. The Negro Book Club listed the autobiography as its bestseller. *Malcolm X Speaks* sold fifty thousand copies in 1967. Mel Watkins, "Black is Marketable," *New York Times*, February 16, 1969.
73. Sostre, "Report from Jail," 27.
74. Amin, interview with author.
75. Clore, interview with author.
76. Martin Sostre, "Letter from Jail to my Student Supporters and Friends," August 1, 1967, *Letters from Prison*, 31.
77. Felicetta testified to HUAC that these visits revealed "Communist, revolutionary, and black nationalist literature with a strong and inflammatory racial content." Hearings before the Committee on Un-American Activities, House of Representatives, 90th Congress, 2nd Session (Washington, US Government Printing Office, 1968), 1999.
78. Clore, interview with author. Sostre may have even received a letter from the FBI in May 1967, just months before the raid. A notation in Joan Franklin's legal materials reads "letter from Field office to Sostre," dated May 21, 1967. Franklin to Martin Sostre, August 18, 1970, *People v. Sostre*, General Case Material, July–October 1970, Folder 100243-030-0600.
79. Bob McCubbin, interview with author, January 13, 2021.
80. "*Memorandum on the Unfolding War*," October 29, 1950, Internal Bulletin Vol. XII, No. 4. https://www.marxists.org/history/etol/writers/marcy/gclass-war/1953_Global_Class_War.html.
81. Communist Cadre, "Global Class War," Workers and Oppressed Unite, 1979.
82. McCubbin, interview with author.
83. Ellie Dorritie, "Jeanette Merrill ¡Presente! – 'You Have to Be a Partisan in the Class Struggle,' " *Workers World*, September 29, 2022.
84. Mallory Merrill-Siljegovic, interview with author, September 29, 2022; obituaries of both Ed and Jeanette Merrill in *Workers World*.
85. For example, see photographs from September 28, 1961, meeting at Kleinhans Music Hall, Box 19, Items 146, NCICF-NYSA.
86. Leslie Feinberg, "Ed Merrill: Steelworker and Marxist educator," *Workers World*, February 13, 2005.
87. Feinberg, "Ed Merrill." Jerry Gross later changed his surname to Ross. In a letter to Sharon Fischer, he said that "even though to you and close friends I will always be 'Gross,' " his official documents are all Ross. "It is also symbolic of something important: a spiritual transformation from the time of leaving Buffalo." Jerry Ross to Sharon Fischer, undated, in author's possession, courtesy

of Jerry Ross. I have used Gross throughout the Buffalo period since that is the name he went by at that time.

88. Kenneth Heineman, *Campus Wars: The Peace Movement at American State Universities in the Vietnam Era* (New York: NYU Press, 1994), 107.
89. Frank Buell, "Rain-Soaked Pickets' Chants Echo Outside HCUA Session," April 29, 1964.
90. Heineman, *Campus Wars*, 108.
91. Dorritie, "Jeanette Merrill ¡Presente!"
92. Heineman, *Campus Wars*, 112–14.
93. Jerry Ross, interview with author, July 24, 2020.
94. Heineman, *Campus Wars*, 162.
95. As Bob McCubbin recounted, "You see the difference between the cultural change, beginning in the early 60s, and then getting more political—in Buffalo—and then by 65, it was political enough that we could entertain the possibility of a teach-in and actually have a turnout." McCubbin, interview with author.
96. Bob McCubbin, email message to author, December 15, 2020.
97. Ross, interview with author. He recalled that after Marcy and Copeland moved WWP to NYC, these leaders "left behind a skeleton crew in Buffalo that are the people that recruited me. . . . They tapped me to be the chairperson of Youth Against War and Fascism, so I kind of dropped the philosophical activities, except to use it as a front for YAWF to have meetings on campus."
98. Jerry Ross, interview with author, July 24, 2020.
99. Raymond Kruger, Summary Report, July 21, 1967, 3–5, Martin Sostre FBI File (100-NY-154100).
100. "Socialist Club Activities Will Include Speakers," *Spectrum*, January 27, 1967.
101. McCubbin, interview with author.
102. Sostre, *Letters from Prison*, 53.
103. Kraus, *Race, Neighborhoods, and Community Power*, 126.
104. Elizabeth Hinton, *America on Fire: The Untold History of Police Violence and Black Rebellion since the 1960s* (New York: Liveright, 2021), 8–15; Elizabeth Hinton, "On Violence and Nonviolence," *Boston Review*, September 10, 2018.
105. *Buffalo Challenger*, front page, July 6, 1967.
106. Sostre, "Report from Jail," 21.
107. Joe Shapiro, "In and Out of Prison: Revolutionary Politics in the 70s," *Introspect* 2, no. 1 (Spring 1976): 4.
108. Ed Vaughn, interview with author, October 4, 2021. See also Ed Vaughn, interview, June 6, 1989, No. 309, Henry Hampton Collection, *Washington University Library Film and Media Archive*; and Joshua Clark Davis, interview, June 5–6, 2013, P-0050, Southern Oral History Program, Southern Journalism: Media and the Movement, University of North Carolina Chapel Hill.
109. Sostre, "Report from Jail," 21.
110. Jerry Ross, interview with author; Sostre, "Report from Jail," 22.
111. Sostre, "Report from Jail," 22.
112. Sostre, "Report from Jail," 22.

113. "The Open Road Interview with Martin Sostre," by David Spaner, *Open Road*, Summer 1976, 13.
114. Sostre, "Report from Jail," 22.
115. Felicetta testified that they began their investigation into Sostre "just a little before the middle of July of 1967." Committee on Un-American Activities, House of Representatives, 90th Congress, 2nd Session (Washington, US Government Printing Office, 1968), 2017. State trooper John Alan Wilcox testified that he "took movies of the people going in and out of 1412 Jefferson" for several days leading up to the raid. Wilcox, testimony in *People v. Sostre*, 55, Erie County Clerk's Office.
116. Beverly's first name is spelled "Francis" by police but varies between "Francis" and "Frances" in Sostre's letters.
117. Gristmacher to Amico, "Activity Report," July 7, 1967.
118. Gristmacher to Amico, Conversation with Informant, July 11, 1967.
119. Sostre, "Report from Jail," 22.
120. Frank Besag and Philip Cook, *The Anatomy of a Riot: Buffalo, 1967* (Buffalo: University Press, 1970), 43–44.
121. Michael Amico to Frank Felicetta, "Intelligence Information in Regard to Recent Disorders in the City of Buffalo, New York," 5, August 3, 1967, Carton 27, Schwartz Papers.
122. "Lawyer Requests Disqualification of Grand Jurors," *Buffalo News*, August 4, 1967.
123. Committee on Un-American Activities, House of Representatives, 90th Congress, 2nd Session (Washington, US Government Printing Office, 1968), 2006.
124. Martin Sostre, "Some Comments on Anarchism," July 1973, Folder 2, Subject Vertical Files, Civil Liberties—Blacks—Black Nationalism—Sostre, Martin, Labadie Collection, University of Michigan, Special Collections.
125. Sostre, "Some Comments on Anarchism."
126. McLaughlin, "Storefront Revolutionary," 13.
127. For example, Sostre wrote that he "trained the young brothers who . . . took care of mucho business." Letter to Joan Franklin, June 5, 1970, *People v. Sostre*, General Case Material, January-June 1970, Folder 100243-030-0492. In 1970, Sostre publicly apologized from prison that he could not be "confronting the pig . . . as I did in the summer of 1967" and that his sentence was "put on me by the pigs for my revolutionary activity during the 1967 rebellion." "The Voice of Black Liberation," *Black News* 1, no. 2 (March 1970): 4. In another letter to Franklin, he wrote that there "are more Black businesses in Buffalo today because a group of dedicated brothers and sisters of which I was a part, took to the streets. At least 12 persons who participated can verify this." Sostre to Franklin, July 27, 1970, *People v. Sostre*, General Case Material, July-October 1970, Folder 100243-030-0600.
128. In it, Sostre is identified only as a "44 year old Negro Black Nationalist." But his age, as well as other key parts of the interview such as him "keeping my shop

open" and being asked about whether he wanted to "talk about [his] own case" all indicate that the interviewee was Sostre.

129. Although Sostre's interview is mysteriously missing from Besag's archival papers, a transcript was published in the book's appendix. Not all 138 interviews are present in Besag's papers. The folders jump from interviews 21–49 to 51–60, indicating that Sostre's interview (no. 50) was already missing when the materials were processed at the archive. Professor Besag donated the materials over multiple accessions between September/October 1967 and June/July 1968, when Sostre was arrested, incarcerated, and sentenced. The description of this collection notes: "All of the files that were not lost, were donated to the Archives—some were lost in Dr. Besag's office."
130. Besag, *Anatomy of a Riot*, Appendix, 136–38.
131. Martin Sostre to Richard Lipsitz, August 8, 1967, Martin's Letters, Martin Sostre Defense Committee Papers, in author's possession, courtesy of Ellie Dorritie and the Buffalo Workers World Party.
132. "Open Road Interview with Martin Sostre," 29.
133. Sostre, "Some Comments on Anarchism."
134. John Wilcox, testimony in *People v. Sostre*, 54–57, Erie County Clerk's Office.
135. Martin Sostre, testimony in *Sostre v. Festa*, 48–49, NARA—KC.
136. Arto Williams, testimony in *Sostre v. Festa*, 101–102, NARA—KC.
137. Arto Williams, testimony in *Sostre v. Festa*, 34–36, NARA—KC.
138. New York State Police, Arrest Report, September 3, 1967, Carton 27, Schwartz Papers.
139. Arto Williams, testimony in *Sostre v. Festa*, 28, NARA—KC.
140. When asked by filmmaker Steve Fischler whether he was told he would be released from jail in return, he answered: "Oh definitely so, guaranteed." See *Frame-Up! The Imprisonment of Martin Sostre*.
141. Arto Williams, testimony in *Sostre v. Festa*, 124–145, NARA—KC.
142. When asked if he was high when he met them, he responded, "Very much so." Arto Williams, testimony in *Sostre v. Festa*, 33, NARA—KC.
143. Alvin Gristmacher, Deposition in Application for Search Warrant, Carton 27, Schwartz Papers.
144. Martin Sostre, testimony in *Sostre v. Festa*, 50–51, NARA—KC.
145. Quoted in Orisanmi Burton, "Organized Disorder: The New York City Jail Rebellion of 1970," *Black Scholar* 48, no. 4 (2018): 29.
146. Joshua Clark Davis, "The FBI's War on Black-Owned Bookstores," *Atlantic*, February 19, 2018.
147. "Message from Jail: An Interview with Martin Sostre," August 1, 1967, Folder 2, Civil Liberties—Blacks—Black Nationalism—Sostre, Martin, Labadie Collection, University of Michigan, Special Collections.
148. "Letter from Jail to My Student Supporters and Friends," August 1, 1967, "Martin's Ltrs," MSDCP.

6. "The Court Is an Arena"

1. Manuel Bernstein, "Police Tie Sostre to Dope Sales: Suspect Linked to Disorders," *Buffalo Courier-Express*, July 16, 1967.
2. Lucian Warren, "Fanatics are Tied to June Violence," *Buffalo Courier-Express*, August 5, 1967; "Lawyer Requests Disqualification of Grand Jurors," *Buffalo News*, August 4, 1967.
3. "Sostre Defense Committee Answers HUAC and Felicetta," *Workers World*, July 5, 1968, 4; Bernstein, "Police Tie Sostre to Dope Sales.
4. "Court Permits Jury to Continue Sostre Probe," *Buffalo News*, August 8, 1967.
5. Bernstein, "Police Tie Sostre to Dope Sales."
6. Arthur Dobrin, "An American Prisoner of Conscience," *Progressive* 44, no. 5 (May 1980): 35.
7. See Steven Barkan, "Political Trials and the *Pro Se* Defendant in the Adversary System," *Social Problems* 24 (1976–1977); Emily Thuma, *All Our Trials: Prisons, Policing, and the Feminist Fight to End Violence* (Urbana: University of Illinois Press, 2019).
8. Bob McCubbin, editor, *Martin Sostre in Court* (Buffalo: Martin Sostre Defense Committee, July 1969), 13.
9. "A Message to the Buffalo Nine from Martin Sostre," September 19, 1969, *People v. Sostre*, General Case Material, August–December 1969, Folder 100243-030-0418, Supplement to Part 23: Legal Department Case Files, Series B: The Northeast, Section II: New York, Papers of the NAACP, ProQuest History Vault.
10. "A Message to the Buffalo Nine from Martin Sostre," September 19, 1969.
11. "The Case of Martin Sostre," *Oswegonian*, January 14, 1972, 1.
12. Martin Sostre, *Letters from Prison* (Buffalo, NY: Philosophical Society / Martin Sostre Defense Committee, July 1968), 65.
13. Confirmation of Psychiatric Report Proceedings, *People v. Sostre*, February 19, 1968, 27, Erie County Clerk's Office.
14. McCubbin, *Martin Sostre in Court*, 15.
15. The trial transcript, which is likely incorrect, reads: "If we don't exist, none of these tactics will be uncovered." Martin Sostre, testimony in *People v. Sostre*, 416, Erie County Clerk's Office.
16. Sostre, testimony in *People v. Sostre*, 379.
17. Brief of Defendant—Appellant, Introduction, *People v. Sostre*, 31, Erie County Clerk's Office.
18. Sostre, testimony in *People v. Sostre*, 379.
19. In December 1967, Sostre wrote his supporters that he had been "relatively passive and cooperative insofar as the jail is concerned, confining my attacks to the police and courts, with the exception of the jail strike of last summer." See Sostre, *Letters from Prison*, 43.
20. Denied access to the local press and uncensored communication with supporters outside, Sostre sued the Erie County Sheriff and filed formal complaints against the Postal Inspector. *Letters from Prison*, 40 and 44–47, includes a copy

of his writ of habeas corpus in the case of *Sostre v. Tutuska* and correspondence about the mail.

21. For media coverage of the strike, see "Erie Prisoners Still 'Sit In,'" *Ithaca Journal*, July 26, 1967; "Erie Prisoners Stay Out of Cells," *Democrat and Chronicle* (Rochester), July 26, 1967; and "Prisoners' 3-Day 'Sit Out' Ends after Sheriff Acts," *New York Times*, July 27, 1967. Several weeks later, an assemblyman from Brooklyn visiting the jail described it as "completely neglected . . . [with] no recognition of the current needs of prisoners": "Erie County Jail Called Criminals' Breeding Ground," *New York Times*, August 16, 1967. See also "22 Prisoners Stage Revolt in County Jail," clipping without date or newspaper indicated, "Work to Be Done" folder, Martin Sostre Defense Committee Papers (MSDCP), in author's possession, courtesy of Ellie Dorritie and the Buffalo Workers World Party.
22. See "Martin's Ltrs" folder, MSDCP.
23. Martin Sostre, "Letter from Jail to My Student Supporters and Friends," August 1, 1967, *Letters from Prison*, 31–32.
24. Sostre, *Letters from Prison*, 29.
25. Martin Sostre, "Report From Jail to My Revolutionary Friends," in *Letters from Prison*, 19–28, 28. The reprinted letter differs from Sostre's handwritten original in certain places. Notable is the title, which was originally "Letter to My Marxist Friends." Who changed the title and why they did so for *Letters from Prison* is unclear. Original letter in "Martin's Ltrs" folder, MSDCP.
26. In late July, *The Spectrum* reported that two groups were "vieing [*sic*] for the right to defend Mr. Sostre"—the Friends of the Martin Sostre Defense Committee and the American Coordinating Committee of the Left. "Martin Sostre Arrested; Charged with Inciting Riot," *Spectrum*, July 28, 1967. By August 8, a Martin Sostre Defense Committee had formed and listed the East-West Bookshop as its address. See "Buffalo Frame-Up of Black Militant," *Workers World*, August 3, 1967, 4.
27. McCubbin, *Martin Sostre in Court*, 57.
28. Bob McCubbin, interview with author, January 13, 2021.
29. Sharon Fischer became the chairperson of Sostre's Buffalo committee following his break with the WWP in 1970.
30. Court proceedings, *People v. Sostre and Robinson*, August 8, 1967, 6–7, Erie County Clerk's Office.
31. Jerry Gross, interview with author, July 24, 2020.
32. Martin Sostre to Roy Wilkins, August 22, 1970, *People v. Sostre*, General Case Material, July–October 1970, Folder 100243-030-0600, Part 23: Legal Department Case Files, Series B: The Northeast, Section II: New York, Papers of the NAACP, ProQuest History Vault.
33. "Fight to Free Martin Sostre, Framed Black Leader, Continues," *Workers World*, November 16, 1967, 6.
34. Undated notes by Jeanette Merrill titled "Re: Afro-Asian Bookstore-in-Exile," "Green Haven, re: Martin" folder, MSDCP.

35. Martin Sostre to Jerry Gross, October 26, 1967, Martin's Ltrs, MSDCP. H. Rap Brown (later Jamil al-Amin), then the national chair of the Student Nonviolent Coordinating Committee, had been jailed a month after Sostre and held initially on $25,000 bail. SNCC quickly raised $10,000 for Brown, although he was released when his bail was reduced to $10,000 the following month. See "H. Rap Brown Jailed; Bail Put at $25,000," *Courier-Journal and Times* (Louisville, KY), August 20, 1967; and "Rap Brown Is Released under Bond," *Winston-Salem Journal*, September 19, 1967.
36. McCubbin, *Martin Sostre in Court*, 57–58.
37. Sostre, *Letters from Prison*, 28, 53; Sostre to Richard Lipsitz, Chairman of the American Civil Liberties Union, August 8, 1967, "Martin's Ltrs" folder, MSDCP.
38. Sostre, *Letters from Prison*, 27, 53.
39. Martin Sostre to Gerald Gross, November 24, 1967, "Martin's Ltrs" folder, MSDCP. Sostre filed a complaint with the Erie County Bar Association, which ruled in favor of the firm.
40. For example, see Martin Sostre to Mr. Gage of the Bar Association of Erie County, October 24, 1967, "Martin's Ltrs" folder, MSDC Papers.
41. Martin Sostre to Richard Lipsitz, October 3, 1967 and Sostre to Jerry Gross, October 28, 1967, "Martin's Ltrs" folder, MSDCP.
42. Martin Sostre to Jerry Gross, October 5, 1967, "Martin's Ltrs" folder, MSDCP.
43. Sostre wrote of public defenders: "One should be very wary of putting one's life in the hands of a professional who has agreed to be, as lawyers have, an 'officer of the court.'" Sostre, *Letters from Prison*, 35.
44. For full hearing, see court proceedings, *People v. Sostre*, October 6, 1967, Erie County Clerk's Office.
45. Melanie Newport, *This Is My Jail: Local Politics and the Rise of Mass Incarceration* (Philadelphia: University of Pennsylvania Press, 2023), 95.
46. Newport, *This Is My Jail*, 94.
47. Martin Sostre, testimony in *People ex rel Sostre v. John Tutuska*, court proceedings, November 15, 1967, 12–13, Erie County Clerk's Office.
48. See "Buffalo Black Leader Defies Racist Court," *Workers World*, October 20, 1967, 8.
49. *People ex rel Sostre v. John Tutuska*, court proceedings, November 15, 1967, 17.
50. Martin Sostre and Judge Carlton Fisher, comments in *People ex rel Sostre v. John Tutuska*, court proceedings, November 15, 1967, 17.
51. Application for Reduction of Bail, court proceedings, *People v. Sostre*, October 9, 1967, 6–7, Erie County Clerk's Office. See also Sostre, *Letters from Prison*, 37.
52. Application for Reduction of Bail, 10. The DA also argued that this was necessary based on his previous conviction for bail-jumping, which Sostre argued was not true. See *People ex rel Sostre v. John Tutuska*, court proceedings, November 15, 1967, 9.
53. Martin Sostre to Jerry Ross, October 14, 1967, "Martin's Ltrs" folder, MSDCP.

54. Martin Sostre to Leticia Sostre c/o E. Merrill, June 24, 1968, "Green Haven, re: Martin" folder, MSDCP.
55. Martin Sostre to Gerald Gross, November 19, 1967, "Martin's Ltrs" folder, MSDCP. He refused to sell the mimeograph machine, however, considering it "an asset of the Defense Fund."
56. Gerald Gross FBI File (30-88-44-705), Memo, Buffalo Field Office, January 29, 1968, 4–6, in author's possession, courtesy of Jerry Ross.
57. *Letters from Prison*, 63. For arrests and protests in New York, see "Stop the Draft' Demonstrations Held across Country," and Madeline Levine and Peter Simon, "51 Turn in Draft Cards, Letters as Part of Stop the Draft Week," *Spectrum*, December 8, 1967.
58. Sostre to Jeanette, December 11, 1967, "Martin's Ltrs" folder, MSDCP.
59. Sostre to Jeanette, December 11, 1967, "Martin's Ltrs" folder, MSDCP. See also Sostre, *Letters from Prison*, 61.
60. For more on the history of community bail funds, see Jocelyn Simonson, *Radical Acts of Justice*: How Ordinary People are Dismantling Mass Incarceration (New York: The New Press, 2023), 28–31.
61. Robin Steinberg, Lillian Kalisch, and Ezra Ritchin, "Freedom Should Be Free: A Brief History of Bail Funds in the United States," *UCLA Criminal Justice Law Review* 2, no. 1 (2018): 82–85.
62. For examples of both, see Steinberg, Kalisch, and Ritchin, "Freedom Should be Free," 86–92.
63. Angela Davis et al., *Abolition. Feminism. Now* (Chicago: Haymarket, 2022), 31–32. See Sostre, *Letters from Prison*, 61.
64. As of 2021, the National Bail Fund Network (NBFN) consisted of ninety-five standalone bail funds. As NBFN director Pilar Weiss emphasized, these bail funds took inspiration from "Black liberation bail funds and queer bail funds that were started by people in those movements who were resisting the state and resisting state repression." Simonson, *Radical Acts of Justice*, 28, 31.
65. Sostre, *Letters from Prison*, 42.
66. Howard Wilinsky, interview with author, May 2, 2023.
67. Psychological evaluation by Dr. Howard C. Wilinsky and Michael J. Lynch, 3, *People v. Sostre*, General Case Material, February 19, 1968, Folder 100243-029-0498, Supplement to Part 23: Legal Department Case Files, Series B: The Northeast, Section II: New York, Papers of the NAACP, ProQuest History Vault.
68. Jonathan Metzl, *The Protest Psychosis: How Schizophrenia Became a Black Disease* (Boston: Beacon Press, 2009), xiii, xix.
69. Vincent Copeland, *The Crime of Martin Sostre* (New York: McGraw-Hill, 1970), 90.
70. Psychological evaluation, 5.
71. Sostre, *Letters from Prison*, 43.
72. Psychological evaluation, 5.
73. Gerald Gross, "Martin Sostre in Court," *Buffalo Challenger*, February 22, 1968.

74. At one point, he told the judge that he planned to appeal to the State Supreme Court and wanted to have a "nice, pretty record for everybody to see." See Confirmation of Psychiatric Report Proceedings, *People v. Sostre*, February 19, 1968, 48, Erie County Clerk's Office.
75. Martin Sostre, testimony in *People v. Sostre*, Confirmation of Psychiatric Report Proceedings, 43.
76. Horace R. Cayton, "The Psychology of the Negro under Discrimination," in *Mental Health and Mental Disorder: A Sociological Approach* (New York: W. W. Norton, 1955), 377–92, 377, 380.
77. Martin Sostre, cross-examination in *People v. Sostre*, Confirmation of Psychiatric Report Proceedings, 36–37.
78. Martin Sostre, testimony and cross-examination in *People v. Sostre*, Confirmation of Psychiatric Report Proceedings, 46, 102, and 114.
79. Days later, the prosecution's motion to sever Geraldine Robinson's trial from Sostre's was granted. Brief of Defendant—Appellant, Introduction, *People v. Sostre*, 8.
80. Martin Sostre, testimony and cross-examination in *People v. Sostre*, Confirmation of Psychiatric Report Proceedings, 127–28.
81. Elwin Powell, "Promoting the Decline of the Rising State," *Catalyst* 9 (1977): 13; Committee on Un-American Activities, House of Representatives, 90th Congress, 2nd Session (Washington, US Government Printing Office, 1968), 2021.
82. Jeanette Merrill to Richard Lipsitz, March 5, 1968, "William Worthy" folder, MSDCP.
83. "Solidarity!!" flyer, "William Worthy" folder, MSDCP.
84. Committee on Un-American Activities, House of Representatives, 90th Congress, 2024.
85. Marshall, comment in *People v. Sostre*, 136, Folder 100243-032-0601, Supplement to Part 23: Legal Department Case Files, Series B: The Northeast, Section II: New York, Papers of the NAACP, ProQuest History Vault.
86. Marshall, comment in *People v. Sostre*, 82, Folder 100243-032-0601, Supplement to Part 23: Legal Department Case Files, Series B: The Northeast, Section II: New York, Papers of the NAACP, ProQuest History Vault.
87. McCubbin, *Martin Sostre in Court*, 15; McCubbin, interview with author, January 13, 2021.
88. Martin Sostre, testimony in *People v. Sostre*, 180 and 155, Erie County Clerk's Office.
89. Martin Sostre, comment in *People v. Sostre,* 43, court proceedings, March 4, 1968, Erie County Clerk's Office.
90. Marshall, comment in *People v. Sostre,* 90, court proceedings, March 4, 1968, Erie County Clerk's Office.
91. Steverson's original affidavit from July 17, 1967, described Sostre getting money from Williams, handing it to Robinson, and going to the rear of the store. "He then extended his hand to the informant and the informant extended his hand

to meet Sostre's." Although he never described anything passing between them, he later testified at Sostre's appeal trial that he saw a "very small portion of a white glassine type object" pass between them. See Lewis Steverson, affidavit, July 17, 1967, Carton 27, Schwartz Papers and Lewis Steverson testimony in *Sostre v. Festa* (74-1520), 221–23, National Archives and Records Administration—Kansas City, Missouri (NARA—KC).

92. I am grateful to attorney Marc Cannan for noting this inconsistency between chronologies and drawing out these arguments about its implications.
93. *People v. Sostre*, 53, court proceedings, March 4, 1968, Erie County Clerk's Office.
94. Brief of Defendant—Appellant, Introduction, 11, *People v. Sostre.*
95. Of the fifty pages of *Martin Sostre in Court* covering all three trials, the final trial comprised thirty pages, more than the other two combined.
96. Marshall, comment in *People v. Sostre*, 380, sentencing proceedings, March 1, 1968, Erie County Clerk's Office.
97. McCubbin, *Martin Sostre in Court*, 36.
98. Marshall and Sostre, comments in *People v. Sostre*, 238 and 417, sentencing proceedings, March 14 and 18, 1968, Erie County Clerk's Office.
99. Copeland, *The Crime of Martin Sostre*, 142.
100. The examination of the jury was omitted from the trial transcript, so these quotations are taken from McCubbin, *Martin Sostre in Court*. In the transcript, only a parenthetical exists: "A jury of twelve was selected and examined by the Assistant District Attorney and Mr. Sostre." See Sentencing proceedings, *People v. Sostre*, 244, March 14, 1968, Erie County Clerk's Office.
101. McCubbin, *Martin Sostre in Court*, 29.
102. McCubbin, *Martin Sostre in Court*, 35, 37.
103. A few months earlier, a different judge had rejected his claims that his first trial was political: "There is nothing political about resisting a police officer. Nothing political about possession and sale of narcotics." See Court proceedings, January 31, 1968, 21, *People v. Sostre*, Erie County Clerk's Office.
104. Copeland, *The Crime of Martin Sostre*, 148.
105. Marshall, comments in *People v. Sostre*, sentencing proceedings, March 18, 1968, 419-420, Erie County Clerk's Office.

7. A Single-Minded Struggle for Prisoners' Rights

1. Martin Sostre, testimony in *Sostre v. Rockefeller*, October 29, 1969, 158, in author's possession, courtesy of Tomiko Brown-Nagin.
2. "I thought it was best for the interests of the inmate and for the state that this man be transferred to another institution," Attica's deputy warden explained. See Constance Baker Motley, Opinion: Findings of Fact, Conclusions of Law, in *Sostre v. Rockefeller* 68 Civ. 4058, May 14, 1970, in Jessica Mitford Papers, Box 39, Folder 1, Harry Ransom Center, University of Texas at Austin. As an example of how this distance put a strain on their organizing, Jeanette Merrill wrote

in her notes that Jerry Gross needed to pick up Sostre's attorney in Buffalo at 2:45 a.m. for a trip to Green Haven. Handwritten notes by Jeanette Merrill, "Late Thurs. night," April 18, 1968, "Green Haven, re: Martin" folder, Martin Sostre Defense Committee Papers (MSDCP), in author's possession, courtesy of Ellie Dorritie and the Buffalo Workers World Party.

3. When it was formed, the Republic of New Africa spelled Africa with a "c," later switching to "Afrika."
4. Martin Sostre, testimony in *Sostre v. Rockefeller*, October 29, 1969, 61–67.
5. David Gelman, "Martin Sostre: Up from Attica," *Newsday*, September 20, 1971, 11. See also *Oswald v. Sostre*, US Supreme Court Transcript of Record with Supporting Pleadings, Appendix A, 6A–9A; and *Free Martin Sostre*, pamphlet (West Somerville, MA: Martin Sostre Defense Committee), Folder 1, Subject Vertical Files, Civil Liberties—Blacks—Black Nationalism—Sostre, Martin, Labadie Collection, University of Michigan, Special Collections.
6. Martin Sostre to Joan Franklin, July 9, 1968; Franklin to Sostre, July 9, 1968, both in *People v. Sostre*, General Case Material, March–July 1968, Folder 100243-029-0711, Supplement to Part 23: Legal Department Case Files, Series B: The Northeast, Section II: New York, Papers of the NAACP, ProQuest History Vault.
7. See *Frame-Up! The Imprisonment of Martin Sostre*, dir. Joel Sucher, Steven Fischler, and Howard Blatt (Pacific Street Films, 1974).
8. Martin Sostre to Miss Leticia Sostre c/o E. Merrill, May 22, 1968, "Green Haven, re: Martin" folder, MSDCP.
9. Victor Rabinowitz, "The Expansion of Prisoners' Rights, *Villanova Law Review* 16, no. 6 (August 1971): 1050.
10. FBI surveillance of WWP NYC branch meeting, June 20, 1969, Martin Sostre FBI File (100-NY-154100).
11. Sostre is quoted in a letter from Jeanette Merrill to Kristin Booth Glen, June 3, 1969, "N.E.C.L.C." folder, MSDCP.
12. Martin Sostre to unknown (likely Sharon Fischer), July 5, 1972, Box 13, Folder 13, Elwin H. Powell Papers, University Archives, State University of New York at Buffalo.
13. "In Court with Sostre," *Workers World*, November 13, 1969, 9. I am grateful to Ted Kelly for sending the copies of *Workers World* cited in this chapter.
14. Bill Vaccaro, "Rally Coincides with Sostre's Trial," *Spectrum*, October 31, 1969.
15. "For the Prosecution . . . Sostre," *Great Speckled Bird*, November 10, 1969, 8.
16. Martin Sostre, testimony in *People v.* Sostre, Confirmation of Psychiatric Report Proceedings, February 19, 1968, 146, Erie County Clerk's Office.
17. Martin Sostre to unknown (likely Sharon Fischer), April 17, 1972, Box 13, Folder 13, Powell Papers.
18. MSDC newsletter, April 15, 1968, Exhibit No. 17-A by Frank Felicetta, Committee on Un-American Activities, House of Representatives, 90th Congress, 2nd Session (Washington, US Government Printing Office, 1968), 2029–30.

19. "Afro-Asian Bookstore in Exile Aids Jailed Liberation Fight," *Workers World*, May 23, 1968, 2.
20. Martin Sostre, *Letters from Prison* (Buffalo, NY: Philosophical Society / Martin Sostre Defense Committee, July 1968), 69.
21. He also envisioned an AABE book club, capitalizing on the committee's extensive mailing list by sending a catalog of books and pamphlets with an order form at the end. See Martin Sostre to Jeanette Merrill, June 24, 1968, "Green Haven, re: Martin" folder, MSDCP.
22. Jerry Ross, interview with author, July 24, 2020.
23. Claudia Dreifus, "The Crime of Martin Sostre, by Vincent Copeland," *East Village Other* 5, no. 34 (July 21, 1970): 16.
24. Bob McCubbin, email to author, December 15, 2020. Both received small stipends for a time, Gross from WWP and McCubbin from a professor at the university.
25. Joshua Clark Davis, *From Head Shops to Whole Foods: The Rise and Fall of Activist Entrepreneurs* (New York: Columbia University Press, 2017), 41. Lewis Michaux "took us down in the basement where the really rare stuff was. We'd buy what we could afford, and I think we probably used defense fund money to buy the books, but I'm not sure about that." McCubbin, interview with author, January 13, 2021. In a letter from a MSDC committee member to Michaux, they note that "in the past we have received a 30% discount." See Mrs. Joan Bentivogli to L. H. Michaux, January 14, 1970, "BFLO-1967" folder, MSDCP.
26. McCubbin, interview with author, January 13, 2021.
27. "Sostre Aid Faces Trial," *Spectrum*, November 1, 1968, 2; William Worthy, "Sostre in Solitary," *Boston Globe*, September 8, 1968.
28. Geraldine (Robinson) Pointer, interview with William C. Anderson, October 5, 2023, in author's possession, courtesy of Pointer and Anderson.
29. Martin Sostre to Jeanette Merrill, May 31, 1968, "Green Haven, re: Martin" folder, MSDCP. A few weeks earlier, he wrote, "I hope Geraldine is still reading and studying militant literature. I used to supply her with such literature for her education." Sostre to Merrill, May 12, 1968, "Green Haven, re: Martin" folder, MSDCP. Sostre particularly objected to the warden's refusal to add Geraldine Robinson to his list of correspondents because she was subject to the same trumped-up charges.
30. Martin Sostre to Jeanette Merrill, May 28, 1968, "Green Haven, re: Martin" folder, MSDCP.
31. Summons, Family Court of the State of New York, September 5, 1968, *People v. Robinson*, General Case Material, 1967–1969, Folder 100243-027-0279, Supplement to Part 23: Legal Department Case Files, Series B: The Northeast, Section II: New York, Papers of the NAACP, ProQuest History Vault. Although her legal husband, Eugene Robinson, was also named on the summons, his address was listed as unknown.
32. Neglect Petition, Family Court of the State of New York, September 5, 1968, *People v. Robinson*.

33. Martin Sostre to Joan Franklin, June 11, 1970, *People v. Sostre*, General Case Material, February 19, 1968, Folder 100243-030-0492, Supplement to Part 23: Legal Department Case Files, Series B: The Northeast, Section II: New York, Papers of the NAACP, ProQuest History Vault.
34. Sostre to Leticia Sostre c/o E. Merrill, May 4, 1968, "Green Haven, re: Martin" folder, MSDCP.
35. Martin Sostre to Mr. Clarence M. Maloney, April 1, 1968, "Green Haven, re: Martin" folder, MSDCP.
36. Jeanette Merrill, handwritten notes, "Late Thurs. night."
37. Paula Marie Seniors, *Mae Mallory, the Monroe Defense Committee, and World Revolutions: African American Women Radical Activists* (Athens: University of Georgia Press, 2024), 71–77.
38. Timothy Tyson, *Radio Free Dixie: Robert F. Williams and the Roots of Black Power* (Chapel Hill: University of North Carolina Press, 1999), 190.
39. Tyson, *Radio Free Dixie*, 204–5.
40. Tyson, *Radio Free Dixie*, 237; Ashley Farmer, *Remaking Black Power: How Black Women Transformed an Era* (Chapel Hill: University of North Carolina Press, 2019), 41–43.
41. Seniors, *Mae Mallory*, 10, 16.
42. Seniors, *Mae Mallory*, 26.
43. Seniors, *Mae Mallory*, 28–29. For more on the rift between Williams and Mallory and his reluctant support after she was arrested, see 185–89.
44. Farmer, *Remaking Black Power*, 45; Seniors, *Mae Mallory*, 60, 137, 170.
45. Farmer, *Remaking Black Power*, 43.
46. Farmer, *Remaking Black Power*, 48.
47. Bob McCubbin, email to author, October 25, 2021.
48. Merrill, handwritten notes.
49. "NAACP to Hear New York Lawyer," *Gazette News-Current*, June 15, 1967, 10.
50. See "Joan Franklin, Peace Corps Aide in Nigeria," *Detroit Tribune*, March 24, 1962; and "Internship Given for Rights Task," *Detroit Free Press*, April 20, 1964.
51. "Republic of New Afrika," in Molefi Kete Asante and Ama Mazama, eds., *Encyclopedia of Black Studies*, 418, (Thousand Oaks, CA: SAGE Publications, 2005).
52. Edward Onaci, *Free the Land: The Republic of New Afrika and the Pursuit of a Black Nation-State* (Chapel Hill: University of North Carolina Press, 2020), 1.
53. Robert Sherrill, ". . . We Also Want Four Hundred Billion Dollars Back Pay," *Esquire*, January 1, 1969, 74.
54. Onaci, *Free the Land*, 27. Franklin and Mallory were set to have dinner with Shabazz the night after the April 18, 1968, phone call with Merrill. SeeMerrill, handwritten notes.
55. Martin Sostre to Joan Franklin, May 14, 1968, *People v. Sostre*, General Case Material, March-July 1968, Folder 100243-029-0711.
56. Martin Sostre to Joan Franklin, September 8, 1969, *People v. Sostre*, General Case Material, August-December 1969, Folder 100243-030-0418,

Supplement to Part 23: Legal Department Case Files, Series B: The Northeast, Section II: New York, Papers of the NAACP, ProQuest History Vault.

57. Martin Sostre to Joan Franklin, May 22, 1968, *People v. Sostre*, General Case Material, March-July 1968, Folder 100243-029-0711.
58. Mae Mallory is listed as Joan Franklin's assistant. Like Sostre writing the Merrills under the auspices of his sister, this was likely a way to legitimize Mallory's involvement in the eyes of the state.
59. Mae Mallory to Martin Sostre, May 31, 1968, and Martin Sostre to Joan Franklin, June 10, 1968, *People v. Sostre*, General Case Material, March-July 1968, Folder 100243-029-0711.
60. Martin Sostre to Joan Franklin, June 24, 1968, *People v. Sostre*, General Case Material, March-July 1968, Folder 100243-029-0711.
61. Franklin reported being turned away and was eventually barred on the grounds that she needed a NY state law license. She also reported that William Worthy had been turned away. Copeland, *The Crime of Martin Sostre*, 165–66.
62. Excerpts from *Sostre v. Rockefeller* complaint, reproduced in "The Case of Martin Sostre," *Workers World*, December 27, 1968.
63. Joan Franklin to Martin Sostre and Martin Sostre to Joan Franklin, July 11, 1968, *People v. Sostre*, General Case Material, March-July 1968, Folder 100243-029-0711.
64. See Agenda re: Visit to Martin Sostre, *People v. Sostre,* General Case Material, Undated Fragments, Folder 100243-030-0846; and Joan Franklin to Jeanette Merrill, July 23, 1968, General Case Material, March-July 1968, Folder 100243-029-0711.
65. For more on Kochiyama and the OAAU, see Garrett Felber, "Harlem Is the Black World": The Organization of Afro-American Unity at the Grassroots," *Journal of African American History* 100, no. 2 (2015): 199–225. A photograph of Kochiyama next to Malcolm X minutes after he was killed at the Audubon Ballroom was published in "The Violent End of the Man Called Malcolm," *Life*, March 5, 1965, 6. For a comprehensive study of Kochiyama, see Diane Fujino's wonderful biography, *Heartbeat of Struggle: The Revolutionary Life of Yuri Kochiyama* (Minneapolis: University of Minnesota Press, 2005).
66. Mary Kochiyama to Brother Martin Sostre, March 11, 1969, Martin Sostre FBI File (100-NY-154100).
67. Harold Follette to Heinz H. Eisele, FBI, Poughkeepsie, New York, March 20, 1969, Martin Sostre FBI File (100-NY-154100).
68. Worthy wrote, "It was my own confrontation (on a journalistic passport prosecution) with the prospect of a prison term that leads me now to spend considerable time on the Sostre case." William Worthy to Dr. Wyatt Tee Walker, October 22, 1966, William Worthy Papers (unprocessed), Johns Hopkins University (WWP-JHU).
69. Robeson Taj Frazier, *The East Is Black: Cold War China and the Black Radical Imagination* (Durham, NC: Duke University Press, 2014), 75.
70. Frazier, *The East Is Black*, 95.

71. H. Timothy Lovelace Jr., "William Worthy's Passport: Travel Restrictions and the Cold War Struggle for Civil and Human Rights," *Journal of American History* 103, no. 1 (June 2016): 7, 14; Frazier, *The East Is Black*, 102. Original quote is from "U.S. Passport Policy Faces New Assault in Worthy Case," *Chicago Defender*, April 19, 1958.
72. Lovelace, "William Worthy's Passport," 2, 12.
73. Frazier, *The East Is Black*, 107; Lovelace, "William Worthy's Passport," 11.
74. William Worthy to James Hicks, September 8, 1968, WWP-JHU.
75. William Worthy to Paul O'Dwyer, August 29, 1968, WWP-JHU.
76. See Martin Sostre to Barbara Morris and Joan Franklin, October 26, 1969, *People v. Sostre*, General Case Material, August-December 1969, Folder 100243-030-0418; Sostre to Franklin, August 26, 1968, *People v. Sostre*, General Case Material, August–September 1968, Folder 100243-029-0790. See also Jeanette Merrill to Robert Williams, August 26, 1968, Black Power Movement: Robert F. Williams Papers, Series 1: Correspondence, July-August 1968, ProQuest Black Studies database.
77. William Worthy to Thomas A. Johnson, October 23, 1968, WWP-JHU.
78. William Worthy to Gil Austin, September 8, 1968, WWP-JHU.
79. Worthy, "Sostre in Solitary."
80. Joan Franklin to Martin Sostre, September 25, 1968, *People v. Sostre*, General Case Material, August–September 1968, Folder 100243-029-0790; "The Case of Martin Sostre," *Workers World*, December 27, 1968.
81. William Worthy to Burton Benjamin, September 6, 1968, WWP-JHU.
82. Jeanette Merrill to William Worthy, November 6, 1968, WWP-JHU.
83. In late 1968, Worthy wrote: "I've passed on numerous publicity suggestions to the Defense Committee, based on my own experiences on my own passport prosecution." William Worthy to Norman Wilson, November 10, 1968, WWP-JHU.
84. Like Sostre, Philip Brooks was held in jail without bail for six months. See Gerald Horne, *The Fire This Time: The Watts Uprising and the 1960s* (New York: Da Capo, 1997), 273–74.
85. See William Worthy Papers, JHU.
86. Merrill to Williams, August 26, 1968. See also "Books Destroyed, Representative of Afro-Asian Bookstore Calls Act Intentional," *Spectrum*, August 9, 1968; and Worthy, "Sostre in Solitary," *Boston Sunday Globe*, September 8, 1968.
87. "Books Destroyed"; "Black-Oriented Bookstore Opposes Norton Restriction," *Spectrum*, January 29, 1969.
88. Merrill wrote that "a number of Black instructors at the University of Buffalo send their students to the Afro-Asian Bookstore instead of patronizing the University of Buffalo Bookstore for Malcolm's works" and that "2 Black instructors at the University have placed 'Letters from Prison' on the required reading list for their courses." Jeanette Merrill to Kristin Booth Glen, August 17, 1969, "N.E.C.L.C." folder, MSDCP; Jeanette Merrill to Joan Franklin, September 15, 1968, WWP-JHU

89. "Black-Oriented Bookstore."
90. "The Demands—and the Reply," *Spectrum*, March 3, 1969.
91. Rod Gere, "Polity Endorses Hayes Occupation," *Spectrum*, March 24, 1969; Sostre, *Letters from Prison*, 72.
92. Matthews's extensive papers, the bulk of which are vertical files on activists and radical organizations, are held at the David M. Rubenstein Rare Book and Manuscript Library at Duke University.
93. Nelson L. Dawson, "From Fellow Traveler to Anticommunist: The Odyssey of J. B. Matthews," *Register of the Kentucky Historical Society* 84, no. 3 (Summer 1986): 285–88.
94. Dawson, "From Fellow Traveler," 293.
95. J. B. Matthews, *Odyssey of a Fellow Traveler* (New York: Mount Vernon Publishers, 1938).
96. Katherine Baker to Martin Sostre Defense Committee, March 5, 1969, Box 333, Folder 5, J. B. Matthews Papers.
97. Jeanette Merrill to Katherine Baker, March 16, 1969, Box 333, Folder 5, J. B. Matthews Papers.
98. Seniors, *Mae Mallory*, 92, 189.
99. Dawson, "From Fellow Traveler," 299.
100. "Newsletters: Subversives Revisited," *Time*, September 13, 1968.
101. Bob McCubbin, email message to author, January 16, 2023; Memo, October 2, 1968, Martin Sostre FBI File (100-NY-154100).
102. Jeanette Merrill to William Worthy, July 9, 1968, "William Worthy" folder, MSDCP.
103. See threatening letter, postmarked July 5, 1968, "William Worthy" folder, MSDCP.
104. Jeanette Merrill to William Worthy, July 9, 1968, "William Worthy" folder, MSDCP.
105. Summary Report, Buffalo Office, September 1968 (date redacted), 2, Gerald Gross FBI File (30-88-44-705), Memo, Buffalo Field Office, January 29, 1968, 4–6, in author's possession, courtesy of Jerry Ross; Linda Hanley, "Buffalo Nine: On Trial Today," *Spectrum*, February 17, 1969; Kenneth Heineman, *Campus Wars: The Peace Movement at American State Universities in the Vietnam Era* (New York: New York University Press, 1994), 210–11.
106. Merrill to Worthy, July 9, 1968, "William Worthy" folder, MSDCP.
107. The dates were from August 14, 1968, until December 1968. See *Oswald v. Sostre,* Appendix B, 66A.
108. Copeland, *The Crime of Martin Sostre*, 167.
109. Copeland, *The Crime of Martin Sostre*, 168.
110. Martin Sostre to Joan Franklin, July 27, 1970, *People v. Sostre*, General Case Material, July-October 1970, Folder 100243-030-0600. For example, his notation on the day Ray Broderick was beaten by guards read: "Ray Rogers, No. 13—it is either a '461' or '961' came up. Was beaten and placed in cell 13. Threatened to make him sign accident papers. John Carothers, 9988, was

moved from gallery to Cell 21." When Sostre originally asked Ray Broderick's name, he heard him say "Ray Rogers," so some letters refer to him by this name. See Martin Sostre, testimony in *Sostre v. Rockefeller*, 650.

111. Martin Sostre to Joan Franklin, September 19, 1968, *People v. Sostre*, General Case Material, August-September 1968, Folder 100243-029-0790.
112. The original letter was Martin Sostre to Joan Franklin, August 23, 1968, and his report on what was included was Martin Sostre to Joan Franklin, August 17, 1968, *People v. Sostre*, General Case Material, August-September 1968, Folder 100243-029-0790.
113. Martin Sostre to Joan Franklin, August 27, 1968; Martin Sostre to Joan Franklin, September 3, 1968, *People v. Sostre*, General Case Material, August-September 1968, Folder 100243-029-0790.
114. Martin Sostre, "Thoughts of a Black Political Prisoner in Solitary Confinement," *Partisan* 5, no. 2 (April 1969): 13-16, 15. The original essay before publication can be found in *People v. Sostre*, General Case Material, October-December 1968, Folder 100243-029-0858.
115. At Columbia, the organizing was rooted in a local, interracial coalition that opposed the displacement of Black residents and institutions for the expansion of this exclusionary and predominantly white university.
116. Sostre, "Thoughts of a Black Political Prisoner," 13-15.
117. Sostre, "Thoughts of a Black Political Prisoner," 15.
118. See Amy Sonnie and James Tracy, *Hillbilly Nationalists, Urban Race Rebels, and Black Power: Interracial Solidarity in 1960s-1970s New Left Organizing*, rev. ed. (New York: Melville House, 2011).
119. Sostre, "Thoughts of a Black Political Prisoner," 15.
120. Sostre, "Thoughts of a Black Political Prisoner," 15.
121. For example, see Lorenzo Kom'boa Ervin, *Anarchism and the Black Revolution* (1979; repr., London: Pluto Press, 2021).
122. The article was slated to be included in *Ramparts* magazine, but it is unclear why it was never published there. Sostre later mentioned that they asked for another article the following year. See Martin Sostre to Joan Franklin, December 4, 1969, *People v. Sostre*, General Case Material, August-December 1969, Folder 100243-030-0418.
123. Notice of Motion for Order of Show Cause, Show Cause Order, and Affidavit in the Matter of Martin Sostre v. Harold W. Follette, *People v. Sostre*, General Case Material, October-December 1968, Folder 100243-029-0858.
124. Sostre, "Thoughts of a Black Political Prisoner."
125. Toussaint Losier, "Against 'Law and Order' Lockup: The 1970 NYC Jail Rebellions," *Race and Class* 59, no. 1 (July-September 2017): 10.
126. See Juanita Díaz-Cotto, *Gender, Ethnicity, and the State: Latina and Latino Prison Politics* (Albany: State University of New York Press, 1996), 28; and Patrick Langan, "Race of Prisoners Admitted to State and Federal Institutions, 1926-1986," Bureau of Justice, May 1991. These figures are disproportionately high. In 1960, there were 2,297 white people and 1,906 Black people admitted to

state and federal institutions in New York. In 1970, only 879 white people, but 2,561 Black people were admitted. A similar trend occurred earlier in jails.

127. John Suiter, "Interview: Seale in S.F. County Jail," *Berkeley Barb*, November 14–20, 3. See also Kathleen Neal Cleaver, "Back to Africa: The Evolution of the International Section of the Black Panther Party (1969–1972), in *The Black Panther Party (Reconsidered)*, ed. Charles E. Jones (Baltimore: Black Classic Press, 1998), 233–34.
128. For example, see "Bobby Kidnapped, under the Fugitive Slave Law, *Black Panther*, November 8, 1969, 4; and "Panther Political Prisoners for U.S. Prisoners of War," *Black Panther*, November 22, 1969, 3.
129. For example, see NYPD surveillance of Panther Twenty-One rally, November 17, 1969; New York Police Department surveillance films, 1960–1980; REC 0063; NYPD_F_0693; Municipal Archives, City of New York.
130. See Martin Sostre to Joan Franklin, December 4, 1969, *People v. Sostre*, General Case Material, August–December 1969, Folder 100243-030-0418. The essay was eventually published in Sostre's own newspaper, *Black News*. Jeanette Merrill assured the BPP that "it is Martin's wish that the Black Panther Party have the very first issue to come off the press." Jeanette Merrill to Black Panther Party, attn: Big Man, January 20, 1970, "Related Corres." folder, MSDCP.
131. Martin Sostre, "Pilots for Panthers: Assault on the Monster's Head," *Black News* 1, no. 1 (January 1970).
132. Sostre to Franklin, August 13, 1969, *People v. Sostre*, General Case Material, August–December 1969, Folder 100243-030-0418.
133. Martin Sostre, interview with Doloris Costello, November 6, 1972, at Auburn Prison, WBAI radio, in author's possession, courtesy of Steven Fischler.
134. Don Knorr, "The Soft Approach Pays Solid Dividends with Tough Cons," *Daily News*, December 12, 1969.
135. Martin Sostre to Eddie Merrill, August 9, 1969, "Subscriptions," MSDCP.
136. Statement by Charles McKendrick, March 24, 1970, 8, in *Sostre v. Rockefeller*. "Punk," "gorilla," and "wolf" are all homophobic prison slang to describe exploitative sexual relationships.
137. Sostre to Franklin, August 13, 1969; Sostre to Eddie Merrill, August 9, 1969, "Subscriptions," MSDCP.
138. Martin Sostre, testimony in *Sostre v. Rockefeller*, 142–43. In late October 1969, he described the library as containing "pocket-books mostly that I have been receiving from my defense committee, dealing with Black problems."
139. Martin Sostre, testimony in *Sostre v. Rockefeller*, 1309. See also Jeanette Merrill to Jim Engel, January 27, 1970, "Related Corres." folder, MSDCP. After he returned from testifying in New York City in November, his committee sent another two dozen books. These included many he had carried in the original Afro-Asian Bookshop on Jefferson Avenue by authors such as E. Franklin Frazier, Langston Hughes, Richard Wright, Herbert Aptheker, and Lerone Bennett. List of purchased books, November 19, 1969, "Subscriptions," MSDCP.

140. The petitions and signatures can be found in "June 1969" folder, MSDCP.
141. Jeanette Merrill to Kris Booth Glen, August 17, 1969, "N.E.C.L.C." folder, MSDCP.
142. Merrill to Franklin, August 26, 1969.
143. Sostre to Franklin, August 13, 1969.
144. Sharon Fischer recalled that each issue of *Workers World* was reviewed "article by article" by the Media Review Committee in Albany before anyone inside could receive it. She also said that all three of Sostre's publications (presumably *Sostre in Court*, *Letters from Prison*, and *The Crime of Martin Sostre*) were banned in the prisons. See Sam Melville, *Letters from Attica*, annotated ed. (Chicago: Chicago Review Press, 2022), 199.
145. *Sostre v. Otis*, 330 F. Supp. 941 (S.D.N.Y. 1971).
146. "Listen, Rockefeller!," *Black News* 1, no. 1 (January 1970): 2. The warden's flimsy excuse for destroying the issues was that Sostre had denounced the Nation of Islam when approached about his religion being listed as Muslim. "In view of Sostre's remarks to me," McKendrick explained, "I believed that he would be insulted if these papers were given to him." Statement by Charles McKendrick, March 24, 1970, 2, in *Sostre v. Rockefeller*.
147. Quoted in letter from Jeanette Merrill to Libby at World View Publishers, October 4, 1969, "Subscriptions," MSDCP.
148. "Listen, Rockefeller!"
149. *Sostre v. Otis,* 330 F. Supp 941.
150. The BPP likely arrived in New York prisons around the fall of 1969, which aligns with Sostre starting a chapter at Green Haven before his August 1969 transfer and then another at Wallkill by October. The state had begun its surveillance of BPP inside by October 1970. See Muslim-BPP surveillance reports at Green Haven and elsewhere in Box 47, Division of State Police, Non-Criminal Investigation Case Files, A0795-80, New York State Archives (NCICF-NYSA). "*The Voice of Black Liberation,*" *Black News* 1, no. 2 (March 1970). *Martin* Sostre to Barbara Morris, October 26, 1969, *People v. Sostre*, General Case Material, August–December 1969, Folder 100243-030-0418.
151. Joan Franklin to Martin Sostre, November 10, 1969; Martin Sostre to Joan Franklin, December 4, 1969, *People v. Sostre*, General Case Material, August–December 1969, Folder 100243-030-0418.
152. Matthew D. Lassiter and the Policing and Social Justice HistoryLab, "New Bethel Incident," *Detroit under Fire: Police Violence, Crime Politics, and the Struggle for Racial Justice in the Civil Rights Era* (University of Michigan Carceral State Project, 2021), https://policing.umhistorylabs.lsa.umich.edu/s/detroitunderfire/page/home; Onaci, *Free the Land*, 33–34.
153. Onaci, *Free the Land*, 35.
154. Paraphrased in letter from Franklin to Sostre, November 10, 1969.
155. Statement by Charles McKendrick, March 24, 1970, 10, in *Sostre v. Rockefeller*.
156. Notes, Martin Sostre interview with Joe Shapiro, January 13, 1976, in author's possession, courtesy of Joe Shapiro.

157. See Ervin, *Anarchism and the Black Revolution*, 2; Joy James, *Imprisoned Intellectuals: America's Political Prisoners Write on Life, Liberation, and Rebellion* (Lanham, MD: Rowman & Littlefield, 2003), 165; and Lorenzo Kom'boa Ervin, interview with author, July 18, 2020.
158. Ervin, *Anarchism and the Black Revolution*, 2.
159. Nik Heynen and Jason Rhodes, "Organizing for Survival: From the Civil Rights Movement to Black Anarchism through the Life of Lorenzo Kom'boa Ervin," *ACME* 11, no. 3 (2012): 395.
160. Heynen and Rhodes, "Organizing for Survival," 400–402; Ervin, *Anarchism and the Black Revolution*, 3.
161. Heynen and Rhodes, "Organizing for Survival," 402–4.
162. Ervin, interview with author.
163. Ervin, *Anarchism and the Black Revolution*, 6.
164. Ervin, interview with author.
165. Ervin, *Anarchism and the Black Revolution*, 6.
166. Ervin, interview with author.
167. Although Ervin recalled that Sostre also gave him *Sabate: Guerilla Extraordinary* by Antonio Téllez, this was not published in Spanish until 1972 and English in 1974. See "Organizing for Survival," 406.
168. Heynen and Rhodes, "Organizing for Survival," 406.
169. Heynen and Rhodes, "Organizing for Survival," 402–4.
170. "We're Not Distinct from the People as Revolutionaries," interview with Lorenzo Kom'boa Ervin on *Millennials are Killing Capitalism*, December 16, 2021. https://millennialsarekillingcapitalism.libsyn.com/were-not-distinct-from-the-people-as-revolutionaries-lorenzo-komboa-ervin-on-anarchism-and-the-black-revolution.
171. Ervin, interview with author; Ervin, *Anarchism and the Black Revolution*, 6.
172. Ervin, interview with author.
173. "Martin Sostre Week—Oct. 26," *Black Panther*, November 1, 1969, 8.
174. "Rally Coincides with Sostre's Trial," *Spectrum*, October 31, 1969. Ortiz seems to have replaced Dixie Bayo, who is listed on the flyer.
175. "For the Prosecution . . . Sostre"; "Martin Sostre: A Political Prisoner Fights Back," *Liberation News Service*, October 23, 1969; "Rally Coincides with Sostre's Trial," *Spectrum*, October 31, 1969; "Martin Sostre Launches His Attack on the Ruling Class," *Liberation News Service*, October 30, 1969.
176. "Martin Sostre: A Political Prisoner Fights Back," *Liberation News Service*, October 23, 1969, 15.
177. "Free Martin Sostre Week" flyer, Box 17, Elizabeth Olmsted Smith Papers, University Archives, State University of New York at Buffalo.
178. "For the Prosecution . . . Sostre"; Copeland, *The Crime of Martin Sostre*, 175.
179. Copeland, *The Crime of Martin Sostre*, 175.
180. "For the Prosecution . . . Sostre"; "In Court With Sostre," *Workers World*, November 13, 1969.
181. Joshua Bloom and Waldo Martin, *Black against Empire: The History and Politics*

of the Black Panther Party (Berkeley, CA: University of California Press, 2016), 218–20; Tomiko Brown-Nagin, *Civil Rights Queen: Constance Baker Motley and the Struggle for Equality* (New York: Pantheon, 2022), 272–79.

182. Brown-Nagin, *Civil Rights Queen*, 227.
183. Brown-Nagin, *Civil Rights Queen*, 282.
184. Kristin Booth Glen, interview with author, July 27, 2021.
185. Kristin Booth Glen to Martin Sostre, June 16, 1969, "N.E.C.L.C." folder, MSDCP. William Worthy was also connected to Motley, as Jeanette Merrill relayed that Worthy "said that word had come from Judge Constance Baker Motley's office that she was extremely impressed by the affidavit and complaint prepared by Martin." Jeanette Merrill to Henry M. di Suvero, March 4, 1969, "N.E.C.L.C." folder, MSDCP.
186. "For the Prosecution . . . Sostre."
187. Warden Harold Folette, testimony in *Sostre v. Rockefeller*, 701.
188. Folette, testimony in *Sostre v. Rockefeller*, 689.
189. Rabinowitz, comment in *Sostre v. Rockefeller*, 1271–97.
190. Martin Sostre, testimony in *Sostre v. Rockefeller*, 85.
191. "The Crime of Solitary Described," *Workers World*, November 13, 1969.
192. Carruthers testified to losing forty pounds. See Copeland, *The Crime of Martin Sostre*, 168.
193. Sostre, testimony in *Sostre v. Rockefeller*, 1318.
194. Carothers, testimony in *Sostre v. Rockefeller*, 391.
195. Copeland, *The Crime of Martin Sostre*, 184. For details, see Sostre's testimony in *Sostre v. Rockefeller*, 117–27.
196. Copeland, *The Crime of Martin Sostre*, 183.
197. See *Sostre v. Rockefeller*, 719–21.
198. The phrase "inflammatory racist literature" is cited in *Sostre v. McGinnis* on appeal, 1651, in *Sostre v. Rockefeller*.
199. Victor Rabinowitz and Henry Sawner, exchange in *Sostre v. Rockefeller*, 1116–21.
200. Mark Walsh, comment in *Sostre v. Rockefeller*, 670.
201. Mark Walsh, comment in *Sostre v. Rockefeller*, 708.
202. Judge Constance Baker Motley, comment in *Sostre v. Rockefeller*, 705, emphasis added. As Rabinowitz pointed out, if 75 percent of prisoners were Black and Latinx, then, at the very least, "they bore 75 per cent of this brutality."
203. Mark Walsh, comment in *Sostre v. Rockefeller*, 707.
204. Judge Stephen Brennan, comments in *Pierce v. LaVallee*, 53 and 176, US District Court, NY, Civil Case Files, Boxes 12–13, Case 7813.
205. Martin Sostre to Joan Franklin, July 27, 1970.
206. Martin Sostre to Ed Merrill, May 29, 1970, related through letter to Joan Franklin, June 3, 1970, *People v. Sostre*, General Case Material, February 19, 1968, Folder 100243-030-0492.
207. Sam Melville to Bill Crain, July 26, 1970, in Melville, *Letters from Attica*, 134–35.

8. The New Prisoner

1. Dan Berger and Toussaint Losier, *Rethinking the American Prison Movement* (New York: Routledge, 2018), 74.
2. Orisanmi Burton, *Tip of the Spear: Black Radicalism, Prison Repression, and the Long Attica Revolt* (Berkeley: University of California Press, 2023), 32–33, 54.
3. Martin Sostre, “Report From Prison,” *Undercurrent*, undated, 3, Box 28, Folder 9, Papers of Florynce Kennedy, Schlesinger Library, Radcliffe Institute.
4. Burton, *Tip of the Spear*, 8–9.
5. Donald Newman, testimony before New York State Special Commission on Attica, Minutes of Meeting of November 15, 1971, 21, Box 86, Commission Meetings: Agenda and Minutes, *Attica Commission Investigation Files, New York State Archives.*
6. Statement by Charles McKendrick, March 24, 1970, 10, in *Sostre v. Rockefeller*, in author’s possession, courtesy of Tomiko Brown-Nagin.
7. Vincent Copeland, *The Crime of Martin Sostre* (New York: McGraw-Hill, 1970).
8. Martin Sostre, “The New Prisoner,” *North Carolina Central Law Journal* 4, no. 2 (Spring 1973): 251.
9. Sostre, “The New Prisoner,” 243–44.
10. Sostre to unknown (likely Sharon Fischer), July 5, 1972, Box 13, Folder 13, Elwin H. Powell Papers, University Archives, State University of New York at Buffalo.
11. Martin Sostre to Joan Franklin, December 4, 1969, *People v. Sostre*, General Case Material, August–December 1969, Folder 100243-030-0418, Supplement to Part 23: Legal Department Case Files, Series B: The Northeast, Section II: New York, Papers of the NAACP, ProQuest History Vault.
12. Martin Sostre, “Pilots for Panthers: Assault on the Monster’s Head,” *Black News* 1, no. 1 (January 1970).
13. Jeanette Merrill to “Big Man” (Elbert Howard), January 20, 1970, “Related Corres.” folder, Martin Sostre Defense Committee Papers (MSDCP), in author’s possession, courtesy of Ellie Dorritie and the Buffalo Workers World Party.
14. Martin Sostre to Joan Franklin, May 20, 1970, *People v. Sostre*, General Case Material, January–June 1970, Folder 100243-030-0492.
15. Martin Sostre, “Editorial: The Voices of Black Liberation,” *Black News* 1, no. 2 (March 1970): 4.
16. Jeanette Merrill to Joann Rabinowitz, January 21, 1970, “Related Corres.” folder, MSDCP.
17. Dan Berger, *Captive Nation: Black Prison Organizing in the Civil Rights Era* (Chapel Hill: University of North Carolina Press, 2014), 236.
18. Emily Thuma, *All Our Trials: Prisons, Policing, and the Feminist Fight to End Violence* (Urbana: University of Illinois Press, 2019), 9.
19. Berger, *Captive Nation*, 226.
20. Martin Sostre, “Martin Luther King Jr. Was a Lawbreaker: A Tribute to His Memory on the Second Anniversary of His Murder,” *Black News*, special supplement (April 1970).

21. Martin Sostre, "Message to the Young Lords," *Black News* 1, no. 1 (January 1970): 2. For more on the takeover, see Johanna Fernandez, *The Young Lords: A Radical History* (Chapel Hill: University of North Carolina Press, 2020), 155–91.
22. "Young Lords to Sostre," *Black News* 1, no. 2 (March 1970): 3.
23. Martin Sostre to Lolita *Lebrón, April 20, 1973, Mixed Materials 1, Folder 5,* Martin Sostre Collection (MSC), University of Michigan Library (Special Collections Research Center).
24. Jeanette Merrill to Mae Mallory, February 23, 1970, "Related Corres." folder, MSDCP.
25. For example, the same state police unit that was surveilling Martin Sostre took photos of Ed and Jeanette Merrill and other members of the WWP at an event at Kleinhans Music Hall in 1961. See photographic surveillance, September 28, 1961, Box 19, Item 146, Division of State Police, Noncriminal Investigation Case Files, A0795-80, New York State Archives (NCICF-NYSA). Merrill also explained to journalist William Worthy that she did not want to relay certain things over the phone. Jeanette Merrill to William Worthy, July 4, 1968, "William Worthy" folder, MSDCP.
26. See threatening letter, postmarked July 5, 1968, "William Worthy" folder, MSDCP.
27. Unfortunately, we have no direct record of the Merrills' side, but Martin narrated their conversation several times to Joan Franklin, at times quoting from it. For example, see Sostre to Franklin, May 20, 1970.
28. Martin Sostre to Ed Merrill, May 29, 1970, sent through Joan Franklin on June 3, 1970, *People v. Sostre*, General Case Material, January-June 1970, Folder 100243-030-0492.
29. As Merrill wrote: "*Black News* is Martin's own idea and is put out (lay-out work, etc.) by the defense committee at his request." Merrill to Rabinowitz, January 21, 1970.
30. Sostre to Merrill, May 29, 1970, via Franklin, June 3, 1970.
31. Sostre to Franklin, May 20, 1970.
32. Martin Sostre, "Thoughts of a Black Political Prisoner in Solitary Confinement," *Partisan* 5, no. 2 (April 1969): 15.
33. Sostre to Merrill, May 29, 1970, sent through Joan Franklin on June 5, 1970, *People v. Sostre*, General Case Material, January-June 1970, Folder 100243-030-0492.
34. Sostre to Merrill, May 29, 1970.
35. Jeanette Merrill to Joan Franklin, May 18, 1970, *People v. Sostre*, General Case Material, January-June 1970, Folder 100243-030-0492.
36. Sostre to Merrill, May 29, 1970.
37. Sostre to Franklin, May 20, 1970.
38. Workers World Party National Conference, Final Session, September 1, 1969, in Martin Sostre FBI File (100-NY-154100).
39. Jerry Ross, interview with author, July 24, 2020.

40. Martin Sostre to unknown (likely to Sharon Fischer), March 13, 1972, Elwin Powell Papers, Box 13, Folder 13.
41. "The Open Road Interview with Martin Sostre," by David Spaner, *Open Road*, Summer 1976, 28.
42. William Worthy, "The Anguish of Martin Sostre," *Ebony*, October 1970, 128.
43. Martin Sostre Defense Committee Press Release, September 4, 1969, *People v. Sostre*, General Case Material, August-December 1969, Folder 100243-030-0418. See also "1-Year Term Given to Mrs. Robinson in Interference Case," *Buffalo News*, September 5, 1969. She was paroled from Bedford Hills in September 1971.
44. In December 1969, *Daily World* published the addresses of hundreds of political prisoners, almost all of them men. Alongside a handful of women political prisoners such as Afeni Shakur, Joan Bird, and Ericka Huggins, who were incarcerated with their codefendants, Robinson was listed alone at Albion prison. See "Remember the Political Prisoners!," *Daily World*, December 23, 1969.
45. "Geraldine Robinson Must Be Set Free!," *The Activist* 1, no. 3 (October 5, 1969).
46. Corydon Ireland, "And Now It's You, Mrs. Robinson . . . ," *Spectrum*, July 18, 1969. A reader responded critically to this essay, calling it a "masterpiece of condescension." See "Condescension Robs the Meaning from Suffering," *Spectrum*, July 25, 1969, 3.
47. Geraldine (Robinson) Pointer, interview with William C. Anderson, October 5, 2023. In author's possession, with generous permission from Pointer and Anderson.
48. MSDC Press Release, September 4, 1969.
49. Proceedings regarding Motion to Sever, February 16, 1968, Erie County Clerk's Office. For Robinson's opposition, see page 41.
50. Martin Sostre, testimony in Proceedings regarding Motion to Sever, 33.
51. For example, when Sostre tried to draw up legal papers for Robinson at Green Haven, prison regulations against working a case that was not one's own were deployed as justification for his solitary confinement. Robinson wrote Joan Franklin shortly after Sostre's break with the WWP: "You mentioned in your letter about Martin's defense committee censoring the paper. I really don't understand them doing this. And I know Martin knows what's best." Jerry to Miss Franklin, June 2, 1970, *People v. Sostre*, General Case Material, January-June 1970, Folder 100243-030-0492.
52. Martin Sostre to unknown (likely Sharon Fischer), January 19, 1972, Elwin Powell Papers, Box 13, Folder 13.
53. This quotation from Otis Madison was often used by Cedric Robinson, including in the epigraph a chapter in *Forgeries of Memory and Meaning. See Robin D. G. Kelley, "Births of a Nation, Redux," Boston Review, November 5, 2020.*
54. Sostre to Franklin, May 20, 1970.
55. Judge Constance Baker Motley, Opinion, *Sostre v. Rockefeller*, 312 F. Supp. 863 (1970), May 14, 1970.

56. The total compensation came from the following calculations: twenty-five dollars a day in compensatory damages and ten dollars a day in punitive damages from Warden Follette and Commissioner McGinnis for each of Sostre's 372 days in solitary confinement. See Opinion, *Sostre v. Rockefeller* and Tom Wicker, "In the Nation: Due Process for Prisoners," *New York Times*, June 18, 1970.
57. See Timothy Ferris, "Court Loosens Prison Bars," undated, in MSDCP.
58. Sostre to Franklin, June 3, 1970.
59. Sostre to Franklin, May 20, 1970.
60. General counsel Nathaniel Jones wrote Franklin in April asking for a status report on the case. Jones to Franklin, April 14, 1970, *People v. Sostre*, General Case Material, January-June 1970, Folder 100243-030-0492.
61. Jones to Franklin, May 26, 1970, *People v. Sostre*, General Case Material, January-June 1970, Folder 100243-030-0492.
62. Franklin to Jones, May 26, 1970, *People v. Sostre*, General Case Material, January-June 1970, Folder 100243-030-0492.
63. Randy Tennen, "Martin Sostre: One Man's Drive for Prisoners' Rights," *Commentator*, November 17, 1971; "Warden Follette of Green Haven Dies," *Poughkeepsie Journal*, April 21, 1970.
64. See Martin Sostre to Joan Franklin, May 7, 1970; Martin Sostre to Barbara Morris, May 8, 1970; and Joan Franklin to Martin Sostre, May 20, 1970, all in *People v. Sostre*, General Case Material, January-June 1970, Folder 100243-030-0492.
65. Franklin to Sostre, May 20, 1970.
66. Martin Sostre to Joan Franklin, May 25, 1970, *People v. Sostre*, General Case Material, January-June 1970, Folder 100243-030-0492.
67. Martin Sostre to Joan Franklin, June 2, 1970, *People v. Sostre*, General Case Material, January-June 1970, Folder 100243-030-0492.
68. Martin Sostre to Joan Franklin, July 27, 1970, *People v. Sostre*, General Case Material, July-October 1970, Folder 100243-030-0600.
69. Martin Sostre to Roy Wilkins, August 22, 1970, *People v. Sostre*, General Case Material, July-October 1970, Folder 100243-030-0600.
70. Nathaniel Jones to Roy Wilkins and John Morsell, with handwritten reply from Wilkins, September 11, 1970, *People v. Sostre*, General Case Material, July-October 1970, Folder 100243-030-0600.
71. George Jackson, *Soledad Brother* (Chicago: Lawrence Hill, 1994), xi.
72. C. L. R. James, *The Future in the Present: Selected Writings* (UK: Lawrence Hill, 1977), 267.
73. Lee Bernstein, *America Is the Prison: Arts and Politics in Prison in the 1970s* (Chapel Hill: University of North Carolina Press, 2010), 54.
74. Copeland, *The Crime of Martin Sostre*, v, 173.
75. Copeland, *The Crime of Martin Sostre*, 198–99. One review of the book, by a white student from Buffalo, suggested that most white readers would diverge with Sostre on the issue of Black nationalism. "But, as Copeland (a white) so convincingly argues, that is for the Black people to decide for themselves." John

Liss, "Frame Up: The Crime of Martin Sostre," *American Expatriate in Canada*, November 1973, 55.

76. Sharon Fischer noted that the "Media Review Committee in Albany banned all three Sostre books from every inmate in the State, even Sostre himself." See explanatory note in Sam Melville, *Letters from Attica*, annotated ed. (Chicago: Chicago Review Press, 2022), 199.
77. In 1973, for example, he informed Dan Georgakas of a "smoking book I intend to publish this year or in early 1974." Martin Sostre to Dan Georgakas, June 27, 1973, in author's possession, courtesy of Dan Georgakas. In 1976, he also said that he planned to write a book "putting forth my politics of revolutionary anarchism, and using my own experience as an example." See Kathie Streem, "Martin Sostre: Out of Jail but Still a Freedom Fighter," *Berkeley Barb*, February 27 – March 4, 1976, 7.
78. Orisanmi Burton, "Revolution Is Illegal: Revisiting the Panther 21 at 50," *Spectre*, April 21, 2021.
79. Berger and Losier, *Rethinking the American Prison Movement*, 88.
80. Burton, *Tip of the Spear*, 31.
81. Burton, *Tip of the Spear*, 32–33.
82. Berger and Losier, *Rethinking the American Prison Movement*, 90; Kaysha Corinealdi, "Dr. Carlos E. Russell and the Origins of Black Solidarity Day," *Black Perspectives*, September 14, 2021, https://www.aaihs.org/dr-carlos-e-russell-and-the-origins-of-black-solidarity-day/.
83. Sostre, "The New Prisoner," 248; Burton, *Tip of the Spear*, 54.
84. Berger, *Captive Nation*, 84–85. Sostre ordered *Martin Sostre in Court* from Wallkill on August 30, 1969, and it was withheld. See *Sostre v. Otis*, 330 F. Supp. 941 (S.D.N.Y. 1971).
85. Berger and Losier, *Rethinking the American Prison Movement*, 90.
86. Burton, *Tip of the Spear*, 64–65.
87. Quoted in Burton, *Tip of the Spear*, 52.
88. "Revolutionary Brothers in Prison"; "Black Vanguard's 1971 'Tet' Offensive," *Vanguard* 1, no. 1 (February 8, 1971).
89. He wrote that the "red surrounding the star is the blood shed by Black people since their enslavement. In solitary confinement, I was never able to get a blood red marker." Martin Sostre to author, July 2013, in author's possession.
90. "Program of Black Vanguard for Liberation," *Vanguard* 1, no. 1 (February 8, 1971).
91. Martin Sostre to author, July 2013.
92. Berger and Losier, *Rethinking the American Prison Movement*, 92–93.
93. Burton, *Tip of the Spear*, 79–80.
94. Burton, *Tip of the Spear*, 83.
95. Burton, *Tip of the Spear*, 92.
96. Burton, *Tip of the Spear*, 88–94. Burton is careful to caution that the "D yard commune was not a utopian zone free of contradiction, conflict, or coercion." See 94–95.

97. Dan Georgakas, "Martin Sostre, Forgotten Revolutionary," *Fifth Estate*, August 12–25, 1972.
98. Sandy Shevack, interview with author, August 7, 2020.
99. Mariano Dalou Gonzalez to Sharon Fischer, May 8 (n.d., likely 1973), Mixed Materials 1, Folder 5, MSC, emphasis in original.
100. Jomo Sekou Omowale to Martin Sostre, May 8, 1974, Mixed Materials 1, Folder 5, MSC.
101. "Written Materials Seized in D-Yard After Assault," Fischer - Inventory of Seized Material, Box 86, *Attica Commission Investigation Files, New York State Archives.*
102. Sostre, "The New Prisoner," 251.
103. "Foco" theory posited that small groups engaging in guerilla warfare and carrying out revolutionary deeds would prompt a wider rebellion.
104. Martin Sostre, "Report from Prison," 3.
105. Sostre, "The New Prisoner," 251.
106. A few notable exceptions include Garrett Felber, *Those Who Know Don't Say: The Nation of Islam, the Black Freedom Movement, and the Carceral State* (Chapel Hill: University of North Carolina Press, 2020) and Orisanmi Burton, *Tip of the Spear: Black Radicalism, Prison Repression, and the Long Attica Revolt* (Oakland: University of California Press, 2023).
107. Burton, *Tip of the Spear*, 16.
108. Sostre, "The New Prisoner," 243–44.
109. Martin Sostre to unknown (likely Sharon Fischer), March 13, 1972, Box 13, Folder 13, Powell Papers.
110. Martin Sostre to unknown (likely Sharon Fischer, January 19, 1972, Box 13, Folder 13, Powell Papers.
111. Joseph Shapiro, "Martin Sostre Is Out of Prison but His Struggle Continues" (master's thesis, Columba University, 1976), 16.
112. Joe Shapiro, "In and Out of Prison: Revolutionary Politics in the '70s," *Introspect: The Carleton Journal of American Culture* 2, no. 1 (Spring 1976): 1–6.
113. Press Release, Martin Sostre Defense Committee, November 7, 1972, in *Courier-Express* Photograph Collection, Archives and Special Collections Department, E. H. Butler Library, SUNY Buffalo State.
114. Sostre, interview with Costello.
115. Berger and Losier, *Rethinking the American Prison Movement*, 113–14.
116. "N.Y. Convicts Form Union in State Prison," *Chicago Tribune*, February 8, 1972.
117. See *Goodwin v. Oswald* 462 F.2d 1237 (2d Cir. 1972).
118. For example, as historian Elizabeth Hinton notes, by 1977, it had "funneled a total of nearly $6 billion ($25 billion in today's dollars)" into new law enforcement initiatives. See Hinton, *From the War on Poverty to the War on Crime: The Making of Mass Incarceration in America* (Cambridge, MA: Harvard University Press, 2016), 281.
119. Emanuel Perlmutter, "Prisoners' Union Formed Upstate," *New York Times*, February 8, 1972; "Inmates at NY Prison Sign to Join Labor Union," *Boston Globe*,

February 8, 1972; "N.Y. Convicts Form Union in State Prison," *Chicago Tribune*, February 8, 1972.

120. Lynn Walker, interview with Joe Shapiro, 1976, in author's possession, courtesy of Joe Shapiro.
121. Berger, *Captive Nation*, 187.
122. Similarly, the second and final issue of *Black News* noted that prisoners worked "Slave Labor—1970 style," receiving only five cents a day for six hours of work. "Prison Notes," *Black News* 1, no. 2 (March 1970): 4.
123. Sostre, "The New Prisoner," 248, 250.
124. *Newkirk v. Butler* 499 F.2d 1214 (2d Cir. 1974).
125. Burton, *Tip of the Spear*, 179.
126. Berger and Losier, *Rethinking the American Prison Movement*, 113.
127. At Walla Walla, for example, members of the Black United Front and the BPP formed a Resident Governing Council (RGC) that lasted nearly four years. In 1972, it outlined a proposal to construct a one-hundred-person prison in Seattle to keep people closer to their communities. The RGC even designed the building and requested $1 million from the state for construction. As Berger and Losier note, the council also acted as an "ad hoc police force" that assaulted other prisoners with impunity. Berger and Losier, *Rethinking the American Prison Movement*, 112.
128. Warden Harold Butler testified, "We had requested the transfer of Martin Sostre on numerous occasions for disciplinary actions, for numerous reasons, and the department decided not to transfer him because they felt that he could create less problems in Wallkill than in any other institution." See Butler, testimony in *Newkirk v. Butler*, 560, National Archives and Records Administration—Kansas City, Missouri (NARA—KC).
129. Lynn Walker, interview with Joe Shapiro.
130. Judge Robert Ward, comment in *Newkirk v. Butler*, 647.
131. Martin Sostre to unknown (likely Sharon Fischer), June 29, 1972, Box 13, Folder 13, Powell Papers.
132. William Worthy, "The Anguish of Martin Sostre," *Ebony*, October 1970, 122–24, 126, 128–29, 132.
133. "Williams Swears He, Amico, Gristmacher Framed Sostre," *Column Left*, April 1, 1972, 4.
134. "Missing Heroin Perils Buffalo Narcotics Case," *Buffalo Evening News*, October 19, 1971; "Fires Policeman," *Ithaca Journal*, March 16, 1972.
135. Martin Sostre to unknown (likely Sharon Fischer), July 5, 1972, Box 13, Folder 13, Powell Papers.
136. He added, "Of course Shulamith does not go into spirituality, nor does she extend her theories to their logical conclusions, but the implications and myriad of facets are clear for those with awareness." Sostre to unknown (likely Sharon Fischer), date unknown, Box 13, Folder 13, Powell Papers.
137. Even his language of "bursting through" recalled the first page of *Dialectic:* "Radical feminism bursts through [traditional categories of thought]."

Shulamith Firestone, *The Dialectic of Sex: The Case for Feminist Revolution* (New York: William Morrow, 1970), 1. Firestone's Jewish parents' direct encounters with Nazism meant that she had an acute awareness of the linkage between white supremacy and genocide.

138. Martin Sostre to Sharon Fischer, January 28, 1972, Box 13, Folder 13, Powell Papers.
139. Andrew Cornell, *Unruly Equality: U.S. Anarchism in the Twentieth Century* (Oakland: University of California Press, 2016), 240.
140. Corinne Jacker, *Black Flag of Anarchy: Antistatism in the United States* (New York: Charles Scribner's Sons, 1968), 197.
141. Cornell, *Unruly Equality,* 240. For example, Dover Publications republished Bakunin's *God and the State*, Emma Goldman's autobiography, and a collection of Peter Kropotkin's writings, all in 1970.
142. Martin Sostre to Sharon Fischer, March 13, 1972, Box 13, Folder 13, Powell Papers.
143. Sostre to unknown (likely Sharon Fischer), December 11, 1972, Box 13, Folder 13, Powell Papers.
144. Sostre to unknown (likely Sharon Fischer), December 14, 1972, Box 13, Folder 13, Powell Papers.
145. Sostre to unknown (likely Sharon Fischer), March 4, 1972, Box 13, Folder 13, Powell Papers.
146. Sostre to unknown (likely Sharon Fischer), March 4, 1972, Box 13, Folder 13, Powell Papers.
147. Sostre, "The New Prisoner," 254.
148. Michael Kaufman, "Oswald Seeking Facility to House Hostile Convicts," *New York Times*, September 29, 1971.
149. According to one article, only three of thirty-five prisoners in the Rx Program were white. Les Payne, "A Prison Prescription That Was Not Renewed," *Newsday*, August 30, 1973.

9. "My Spirit Unbroken"

1. Martin Sostre, interview with Doloris Costello, November 6, 1972, at Auburn Prison, WBAI radio, in author's possession, courtesy of Steven Fischler. According to a press release by the MSDC, Sostre was one of fifty prisoners "keep-locked for refusing to shave facial hair." See "For Immediate Release," November 7, 1972, in author's possession, courtesy of Dan Georgakas.
2. Del Martin, "Attica Means All of Us," *The Activist: A Student Journal of Politics and Opinion*, 13, no. 2 (Spring 1972): 26–28. The brutality of January 30, 1973, is documented at length by Sostre in "Martin Sostre: A Classic Case of Repression," July 4, 1973, *The Rag*, 9.
3. Walt Shepperd, "Jimmy Sullivan Tells Some Chilling Stories," *Syracuse New Times*, September 29, 1974, in Box 13, Folder 12, Elwin H. Powell Papers, University Archives, State University of New York at Buffalo.

4. "Martin Sostre Brutalized; Facing Life Sentence for Opposing Rockefeller's Dehumanizing Policies," reproduction of letter from Martin Sostre to Judge Kaufman, Folder 2, Subject Vertical Files, Civil Liberties—Blacks—Black Nationalism—Sostre, Martin, Labadie Collection, University of Michigan, Special Collections.
5. Orisanmi Burton, *Tip of the Spear: Black Radicalism, Prison Repression, and the Long Attica Revolt* (Oakland: University of California Press, 2023), 149–52
6. For a fuller discussion of "The New Prisoner," see Burton, *Tip of the Spear*, 157.
7. As Burton points out, the Black Solidarity Day of 1970, which had been held "in defiance of administrative prohibitions" and prompted a prison rebellion, was proposed in 1973 as an institutional holiday. See Burton, *Tip of the Spear*, 179.
8. Burton, *Tip of the Spear*, 163.
9. Sostre, interview with Costello.
10. James Clarity, "Rockefeller Asks More Prison Aid," *New York Times*, April 17, 1972.
11. Martin Sostre, "The New Prisoner," *North Carolina Central Law Journal* 4, no. 2 (Spring 1973): 243.
12. "Martin Sostre: A Classic Case of Repression," *The Rag* 7, no. 29 (July 4, 1973): 9.
13. Les Payne, "A Prison Prescription That Was Not Renewed," *Newsday*, August 30, 1973.
14. As he wrote in an address from prison to a gathering in Boulder, Colorado, led by Ram Dass and *Chögyam Trungpa, "Beware of those who seek to subdue the person by dichotomizing the spiritual and physical. . . .* Only by seeking harmony and unity with the forces of nature which entails active opposition to all negative forces of oppression, can we develop to its full potential the heightened spiritual awareness and infinite love we claim is our goal." Martin Sostre, message to spiritual gathering in Boulder, Colorado, April 23, 1974, in author's possession, courtesy of Liz and Vinny Sostre.
15. Martin Sostre to Ed Dubinsky, n.d. (missing first page), in author's possession, courtesy of Hania Dubinsky.
16. Martin Sostre, "Spirituality in the Political Struggle for Liberation," Box 13, Folder 13, Powell Papers.
17. "The Open Road Interview with Martin Sostre," by David Spaner, *Open Road*, Summer 1976, 13.
18. Martin Sostre to unknown (likely Sharon Fischer), n.d., Box 13, Folder 13, Powell Papers.
19. Martin Sostre, reel-to-reel tape recording with Ed Dubinsky and Jackie Sharpe (now Sauter), May 1975, in author's possession, courtesy of Andrzeja Axt.
20. "Open Road Interview with Martin Sostre," 28.
21. Martin Sostre to Ed Dubinsky, April 23, 1975, in author's possession, courtesy of Hania Dubinsky.
22. Kathie Streem, "Martin Sostre: Out of Jail but Still a Freedom Fighter," *Berkeley Barb*, February 27 - March 4, 1976.

23. Martin Sostre, interview with Juanita Díaz-Cotto, May 25, 1993, in author's possession, courtesy of Juanita Díaz-Cotto.
24. The photographer was Eddie Adams, a photojournalist who won a Pulitzer Prize for the image. He later expressed his moral qualms about being valorized for the photo. "I was getting money for showing one man killing another," he reflected. "Eddie Adams' Iconic Vietnam War Photo: What Happened Next," *BBC*, January 29, 2018, https://www.bbc.com/news/world-us-canada-42864421.
25. Sostre to Dubinsky, April 23, 1975.
26. Quoted in Robert Graham, *We Do Not Fear Anarchy, We Invoke It: The First International and the Origins of the Anarchist Movement* (Oakland, CA: AK Press, 2015), 217.
27. Martin Sostre, "Some Comments on Anarchism," July 1973, Folder 2, Subject Vertical Files.
28. Sostre to Dubinsky, April 23, 1975.
29. Martin Sostre to Ed Dubinsky, April 23, 1975.
30. See title of chapter 6, Burton, *Tip of the Spear*, 183.
31. "Open Road Interview with Martin Sostre," 12.
32. Sostre, interview with Costello.
33. Lolita Lebrón to Martin Sostre, March 15, 1973, Mixed Materials 1, Folder 5, Martin Sostre Collection (MSC), University of Michigan Library (Special Collections Research Center).
34. Emily Thuma, *All Our Trials: Prisons, Policing, and the Feminist Fight to End Violence* (Urbana: University of Illinois Press, 2019), 56.
35. Lisa Guenther, *Solitary Confinement: Social Death and Its Afterlives* (Minneapolis: University of Minnesota Press, 2013), 67.
36. Marsha Weissman and Alan Rosenthal, "The Psychological Prison: Neither Freedom Nor Dignity," Maxwell Review 10, no. 2 (1974): 22. See also Jessica Mitford, *Kind and Usual Punishment: The Prison Business* (New York: Vintage, 1974), 108–9.
37. Mitford, *Kind and Usual Punishment*, 111–12.
38. Alan Eladio Gómez, "Resisting Living Death and Marion Federal Penitentiary, 1972," *Radical History Review* 96 (Fall 2006): 59.
39. Guenther, *Solitary Confinement*, 91–92. For more on supermax prisons, see Keramet Reiter, *23/7: Pelican Bay Prison and the Rise of Long-Term Solitary Confinement* (New Haven: Yale University Press, 2016).
40. Gómez, "Resisting Living Death," 60.
41. Mitford, *Kind and Usual Punishment*, 133.
42. "Power to Change Behavior: A Symposium Presented by the United States Bureau of Prisons," *Corrective Psychiatry and the Journal of Social Therapy* 8, nos. 1–4 (1962): 98.
43. "Power to Change Behavior," 103. One respondent was Dr. James Lowry, the medical officer in charge of the US Public Health Service hospital in Lexington, Kentucky, around the time Sostre was imprisoned there during the late

1940s. In the years that followed, the prison became the chief site for the notorious CIA torture and brainwashing program MK-Ultra.

44. Quoted in Burton, *Tip of the Spear*, 186–87.
45. Bob McCubbin, editor, *Martin Sostre in Court* (Buffalo: Martin Sostre Defense Committee, July 1969), 6–10.
46. See Complaint, 5, filed October 15, 1968, *Sostre v. Rockefeller*, in author's possession, courtesy of Tomiko Brown-Nagin.
47. "Martin Sostre: A Classic Case of Repression."
48. Burton, *Tip of the Spear*, 192; "Martin Sostre: A Classic Case of Repression."
49. "Martin Sostre: A Classic Case of Repression."
50. Burton, *Tip of the Spear*, 169.
51. Burton, *Tip of the Spear*, 195.
52. Burton, *Tip of the Spear*, 170.
53. Burton, *Tip of the Spear*, 184.
54. Burton, *Tip of the Spear*, 185, 201.
55. Gómez, "Resisting Living Death," 59.
56. Dan Georgakas, interview with author, June 18, 2021.
57. This seems to have been at least partially at Sostre's suggestion. In one letter, someone who is likely Ernest Nassar acknowledged his recommendation that they not send "everything we do to her anyhow" and assured him that their intent was to "soothe troubled waters and not stir them." Unknown (likely Nassar) to Martin Sostre, October 26, 1972, in author's possession, courtesy of Dan Georgakas.
58. Ernest Nassar to Sostre, November 19, 1972, in author's possession, courtesy of Dan Georgakas. Although no year is given in the letter, Nassar references Richard Nixon's victory weeks earlier.
59. Unknown (likely Nassar) to Sostre, October 26, 1972; Nassar to Sostre, November 19, 1973. See Dan Georgakas to Terben Krogh, Georgakas to Frede Jacoefen, Georgakas to Domman Smith, all November 19, 1972, in author's possession, courtesy of Dan Georgakas.
60. "Lobotomies for Radicals," *The Rag*, May 14, 1973, 10.
61. "Martin Ramirez-Sostre," *Palante*, March 15, 1973.
62. Speech by Eli Messinger, June 16, 1973, "A Conference on Behavior Modification," Box 9, Folder 175, Paul Lowinger Papers, University of Pennsylvania.
63. Walter Dunbar, Memo, June 20, 1973, reproduced in "End to ACTEC?," *Midnight Special* 3, no. 9 (September 1973): 10.
64. "End to ACTEC?," 10.
65. See *People v. Sostre*, Confirmation of Psychiatric Report Proceedings, February 19, 1968, 127–28, Erie County Clerk's Office.
66. Lower Gallery Rx Collective, "Intensified Struggle," *Midnight Special* 3, no. 8 (August 1973): 6–7.
67. See Jimmy Sullivan affidavit, July 1974 (day illegible), in author's possession, courtesy of Liz and Vinny Sostre.
68. Memo, S. Dobbs to W. Gard, May 19, 1973, *People v. Sostre*, Clinton County Clerk's Office.

69. Sullivan affidavit, July 1974.
70. Shepperd, "Jimmy Sullivan Tells Some Chilling Stories."
71. Walter Johnson, *Soul by Soul: Life Inside the Antebellum Slave Market* (Cambridge, MA: Harvard University Press, 1999), 144–45.
72. Johnson, *Soul by Soul*, 146–47.
73. David Oshinsky, *"Worse than Slavery": Parchman Farm and the Ordeal of Jim Crow Justice* (New York: Free Press, 1997), 2.
74. Hugh Ryan, *The Women's Houe of Detention: A Queer History of a Forgotten Prison* (New York: Bold Type Books, 2022), 262. The League was founded the year before as a consumer advocacy group that organized actions such as "buyers' strikes" to fight for the rights of laborers and improve working conditions. They were labeled a "Communist front" and targeted by J. B. Matthews, the same anticommunist whose partner likely spied on the Martin Sostre Defense Committee decades later.
75. Davis recounts being booked in her autobiography: "I learned that we were about to be searched internally. Each time prisoners left the jail for a court appearance, and upon their return, they had to submit to a vaginal and rectal exam." See Angela Davis, *Angela Davis: An Autobiography* (1972; repr., Chicago: Haymarket, 2021), 19.
76. Ryan, *Women's House of Detention*, 261–62. For a full account of Dworkin's experience and its impact, see 256–68. See also Jeremy Lybarger, "Finally Seeing Andrea," *Boston Review*, February 23, 2019.
77. Ryan, *Women's House of Detention*, 263–64.
78. Judge Constance Baker Motley, Opinion, *Sostre v. Rockefeller*, 312 F. Supp. 863 (1970), May 14, 1970.
79. Jalil Abdul Alim, "The Struggle at Auburn Prison," *Black Scholar* 2, no. 10 (June 1971): 53.
80. "Statement by James Dunn," quoted and reprinted in Michael Kaufman, "Troubles Persist in Prison at Auburn," *New York Times*, May 17, 1971.
81. The richest theorizing of the role of sexual assault in the state's siege at Attica can be found in Burton, "Gender War," in *Tip of the Spear*, 119–49. Other details can be found in Heather Ann Thompson, *Blood in the Water: The Attica Prison Uprising of 1971 and Its Legacy* (New York: Pantheon, 2016), 178–219.
82. Burton, *Tip of the Spear*, 130.
83. Johnson, *Soul by Soul*, 149–50.
84. Burton, *Tip of the Spear*, 137.
85. Burton, *Tip of the Spear*, 120.
86. I borrow the phrase "gender war" from Burton's chapter by the same name.
87. Martin Sostre to US Representative Bella Abzug, Reel 23, Folder 3, November 29, 1974, Hugh Carey Sub Series, 1975–1978, in author's possession, courtesy of Ori Burton.
88. "Open Road Interview with Martin Sostre," 12. Abner Louima was later assaulted by the NYPD in this way in 1997. Louima, a US citizen of Haitian origin was arrested, strip-searched, and sexually assaulted in the Seventieth

Precinct station house. His main assailant, Justin Volpe, was eventually convicted and sentenced to thirty years in federal prison; after twenty-four years, he was released on parole in April 2023. Two other NYPD officers were convicted of covering up the assault, and another pleaded guilty to perjury. Louima, who had three surgeries to repair the damage done to his body, received a civil settlement after he sued the NYPD.

89. Daniel Geary, *Beyond Civil Rights: The Moynihan Report and Its Legacy* (Philadelphia: University of Pennsylvania Press, 2015).
90. This was something Dworkin, herself a queer woman, later regretted doing in the aftermath of her experiences at the House of Detention a decade earlier.
91. Burton, *Tip of the Spear*, 125.
92. "Open Road Interview with Martin Sostre," 12
93. Dennis Cunningham, Affidavit of Attorney, January 1974, *People v. Sostre*, Clinton County Clerk's Office.
94. Martin Sostre, testimony in *Sostre v. Festa* (74-1520), 45–47, National Archives and Records Administration—Kansas City, Missouri (NARA—KC).
95. Arthur Dobrin, "An American Prisoner of Conscience," *Progressive* 44, no. 5 (May 1980): 37.
96. See "The Trial of Brother Clarence Torry [*sic*]," Box 13, Folder 15, Powell Papers. Torry had no recollection of ever meeting Williams, and the informant admitted in court years later that Sergeant Gristmacher had introduced him to a cop in Niagara Falls who orchestrated the arrest.
97. Arto Williams, testimony in *Sostre v. Festa*, 129–34.
98. John Steinmetz and John Wilcox, testimony in *People v. Sostre,* 50–57, Erie County Clerk's Office.
99. "The Agony and the Ecstasy of Radical Film Production," *Cineaste* 6, no. 4 (1974): 43–45.
100. Joel Sucher, testimony in *Sostre v. Festa,* 54–64, 149–152.
101. Peter Notaro, testimony in *Sostre v. Festa*, 161; "Perjury Indictment Looms Against '68 Sostre Witness," *Buffalo Courier-Express*, May 31, 1973, *Courier-Express* Clippings, Buffalo State Archives.
102. "Martin Sostre Denied New Trial," *The Militant*, March 27, 1974, 2.
103. "We feel that through confrontation with the realities of capitalist society, reality will be forced to strip away façade." See "Radical American Film Questionnaire," *Cineaste* 6, no. 1 (1973): 19.
104. Claudia Dreifus, "The Crime of Martin Sostre," *East Village Other* 5, no. 34 (July 21, 1970): 16.
105. "Radical American Film Questionnaire"; "The Agony and the Ecstasy of Radical Film Production."
106. Joel Sucher was born in a displaced persons camp in Germany, and his parents were both survivors of Auschwitz. Fischler remembered that the "Holocaust was ever present" in the Jewish neighborhoods of Brooklyn where they had grown up in during the 1950s. "There were survivors everywhere. That was

the sense of the community." See Joel Sucher, interview with author, August 21, 2020; and Steven Fischler, interview with author, July 29, 2020.

107. Sucher and Fischler, interviews with author.
108. The film was named *I Am Curious, Harold* in a spoof on the Swedish classic *I am Curious (Yellow)*.
109. Sucher, interview with author.
110. Fischler, interview with author.
111. Nearly fifty years later, Fischler proudly keeps a souvenir on his desk that the sheriff gave him during the interview: an analog "Sheriff Amico" drunk-driving calculator. See Fischler, interview with author.
112. For example, see Manuel Bernstein, "Police Tie Sostre to Dope Sales: Suspect Linked to Disorders," July 16, 1967, *Buffalo Courier-Express*.
113. "The Agony and the Ecstasy."
114. Quoted in *Frame-Up! The Imprisonment of Martin Sostre*, dir. Joel Sucher, Steven Fischler, and Howard Blatt (Pacific Street Films, 1974).
115. Joel Sucher, email to author, May 13, 2024.
116. Dan Georgakas, "Prison Films," *Cineaste* 6, no. 3 (1974): 34. Georgakas called this sequence the "highlight of the film" in his review of the documentary.
117. "The Agony and the Ecstasy."
118. "Martin Sostre Brutalized; Facing Life Sentence for Opposing Rockefeller's Dehumanizing Policies."
119. "For Immediate Release," July 6, 1973, Martin Sostre Defense Committee, Defense Committees Fund Left, Gordon Hall and Grace Hoah Collection of Dissenting and Extremist Printed Propaganda, Brown University.
120. This was likely written by poet Zoë Best. "Sostre Denied Federal Protection," August 15, 1974, Amherst, MA, MSDC, in author's possession, courtesy of Liz and Vinny Sostre.
121. Martin Sostre, testimony in *Davis v. McGinnis* 69 Civ. 303-306, NARA—KC.
122. "Open Road Interview with Martin Sostre," 13.
123. Sostre to Abzug, November 29, 1974.
124. Martin Sostre to Lolita *Lebrón, April 20, 1973, Mixed Materials 1, Folder 5,* Martin Sostre Collection (MSC), University of Michigan Library (Special Collections Research Center).
125. Maritza Arrastía, "From Prison, Sostre Urges More Struggle," *Claridad*, January 27, 1974. See also Alan Rosenthal, interview with author, June 2, 2022.
126. Sostre, quoting Tavares, in William Boardman, "At Dartmouth, Black Militant Sostre Relates His Fight," *Sunday Rutland Herald and the Sunday Times Argus*, June 5, 1977, 5.
127. Alan Rosenthal, interview with author, June 2, 2022.
128. "KO Smitty" to author, August 21, 2023, in author's possession.
129. Arthur Dobrin, "An American Prisoner of Conscience," *Progressive* 44, no. 5 (May 1980): 38.
130. Nassar to Sostre, November 19, 1972.
131. "For Immediate Release," July 6, 1973.

10. A Structure for the Future

1. Kay Branagan recalled making a concerted effort to get Antonio and Marjorie involved. See Branagan, interview with author, July 28, 2022.
2. Antonio Rodríguez, interview with author, July 16, 2022; Marjorie Miller, interview with author, July 27, 2022.
3. Miller, interview with author and email to author, July 18, 2023.
4. Several were concentrated in New York's North Country, where Sostre was held captive for most of these years. Between 1972 and 1975, there were defense committees in Amherst and West Somerville, Massachusetts; Buffalo, Brooklyn, New York City, Plattsburgh, Potsdam, and Woodstock, New York; Ann Arbor and Detroit, Michigan; Tucson, Arizona; and Eugene, Oregon. By the end of his incarceration, Sostre estimated eight active committees. Martin Sostre, speech delivered on June 24, 1976, reprinted in the *Militant*, September 3, 1976, 22.
5. Martin Sostre to Dan Georgakas, June 27, 1973, in author's possession, courtesy of Dan Georgakas.
6. Quoted in Luke Yakes, "Rethinking Prefiguration: Alternatives, Micropolitics and Goals in Social Movements," *Social Movement Studies* 14, no. 1 (2015): 2.
7. Martin Sostre to Ed Dubinsky, May 15, 1975, in author's possession, courtesy of Hania Dubinsky.
8. Yates, "Rethinking Prefiguration," 2–3.
9. Sostre to Dubinsky, May 15, 1975.
10. Martin Sostre to Karen St. Hilaire, June 28, 1975, in author's possession, courtesy of Anne Heidenreich.
11. William Boardman, "At Dartmouth, Black Militant Sostre Relates His Fight," *Sunday Rutland Herald and the Sunday Times Argus*, June 5, 1977, 5.
12. Martin Sostre, reel-to-reel tape recording with Ed Dubinsky and Jackie Sharpe (now Sauter), in author's possession, courtesy of Andrzeja Axt.
13. Andy Cornell, *Unruly Equality: U.S. Anarchism in the Twentieth Century* (Oakland: University of California Press, 2016), 284.
14. "The Open Road Interview with Martin Sostre," by David Spaner, *Open Road*, Summer 1976, 28.
15. Sostre, reel-to-reel tape recording with Dubinsky and Sharpe.
16. Cornell, *Unruly Equality*, 284.
17. Sostre, testimony in *Davis v. McGinnis*, 295.
18. Judge Constance Baker Motley, Opinion, May 14, 1970, *Sostre v. Rockefeller*, 312 F. Supp. 863 (S.D.N.Y. 1970).
19. Sostre, testimony in *Davis v. McGinnis*, 285, 301.
20. Martin Sostre to Judge Feinberg, November 4, 1974, *People v. Sostre*, Clinton County Clerk's Office.
21. Martin Sostre to Ernest Nassar, November 2, 1973, in author's possession, courtesy of Dan Georgakas.
22. "New York City Martin Sostre Defense Committee Formed," *Internationalist Newsletter* 1, no. 9 (May 1974): 1, in author's possession, courtesy of Dan Georgakas.

23. Martin Sostre Defense Committee bulletin, "East Coast Region," n.d., in author's possession, courtesy of Liz and Vinny Sostre.
24. Martin Sostre, "Some Comments on Anarchism," July 1973, Folder 2, Subject Vertical Files, Civil Liberties—Blacks—Black Nationalism—Sostre, Martin, Labadie Collection, University of Michigan, Special Collections.
25. Martin Sostre to Ed Dubinsky, April 23, 1975, in author's possession, courtesy of Hania Dubinsky.
26. "Open Road Interview with Martin Sostre," 28.
27. Martin Sostre Defense Committee bulletin, "East Coast Region."
28. "East Side to Hold Block Party for Opening of Sostre 'Bookstore in Exile,'" For Immediate Release, n.d., Mixed Materials 1, Folder 15, MSC.
29. A listing of the event called for people with artistic and musical talent, as well as a truck to transport a band called Chinchilla. See "Grand Opening," typed message, n.d., Mixed Materials 1, Folder 23, MSC.
30. "A letter from Sostre's Committee," August 11, 1974, *Claridad,* Mixed Materials 1, Folder 23, MSC. "We are in need of translators, typists, photo mechanics, electricians, writers, and general workers," they wrote. They also put out a call for places to show the film *Frame-Up.*
31. Statement from Martin Sostre, May 16, 1974, Box 178, Folder 11, Allen Ginsberg Papers, Special Collections, Stanford University. While the details for the break are not entirely clear, Georgakas wrote in a letter that June that the Sostre committee in New York City "called me up and accused me of stealing funds and with-holding materials and yak yak yak. They want me to 'come before them.' Well, fuck that. I told them we are going out of business the end of this quarter. Let's cut this as quickly as we can. It is becoming a sordid and depressing business." Georgakas, June 16, 1974, in author's possession, courtesy of Dan Georgakas. He also sent a final report on all materials related to the committee that were forwarded on MSDC letterhead and declared that the "Michigan and New Jersey Sostre Committees ceased to function in June 1974." See Georgakas, "Final Report on Resources Other Than Cash," Georgakas Papers, in author's possession, courtesy of Dan Georgakas.
32. Lennox Hinds, "A Decade in Struggle, 1968–1978," Report by the National Conference of Black Lawyers, 16.
33. Cornell, *Unruly Equality*, 240–41.
34. Cornell, *Unruly Equality*, 133–37, 133.
35. Andy Chruschiel, "Report Anarchist Meeting," June 1973, 3; Dorothy Day, "On Pilgrimage," *Catholic Worker*, June 1973, 2.
36. That July 1973, Sharon Fischer wrote an appeal to readers urging them to support Sostre. See "Martin Sostre," *Catholic Worker*, July–August 1973, 6.
37. Cornell, *Unruly Equality*, 169.
38. Daniel Berrigan newsletter, November 1973, Collection on Peace Activism (CPA), Box 19, Folder 2, Correspondence Daniel Berrigan, 1973–1976, Special Collections and Archives, DePaul University Library. Berrigan sent monthly

newsletters to friends and comrades with personalized messages hand-scrawled at the bottom.

39. Daniel Lewis, "Daniel J. Berrigan, Defiant Priest Who Preached Pacifism, Dies at 94," *New York Times*, April 30, 2016.
40. See Phil Berrigan to Martin Sostre, May 16, 1974, *Mixed Materials 1, Folder 5,* MSC.
41. Jim Forest, *At Play in the Lion's Den: A Biography and Memoir of Daniel Berrigan* (Maryknoll, NY: Orbis, 2017), 153.
42. Forest, *At Play in the Lion's Den*, 152.
43. That said, Dan Berrigan almost died while in prison after suffering a severe allergic reaction to a Novocain injection. Forest, *At Play in the Lion's Den*, 156.
44. Luca Falciola, *Up against the Law: Radical Lawyers and Social Movements, 1960s–1970s* (Chapel Hill: University of North Carolina Press, 2022), 157.
45. Forest, *At Play in the Lion's Den*, 150.
46. Dan Berrigan to Dennis Jacobsen, November 15, 1973, Box 19, Folder 2, CPA.
47. Berrigan to Jacobsen, postmarked November 29, 1974, Box 19, Folder 2, CPA. He sent a check for $2,000 from Ping and Carol Ferry, noting that he "had gotten a like am't for the Buffalo committee a few weeks ago."
48. Ping Ferry to Grace and Jim, November 30, 1974, Box 19, Folder 9, James and Grace Lee Boggs Papers (JGLBP), Walter P. Reuther Library, Wayne State University. The initial masking of Grace's role is evident in Dan Berrigan's reply to Ferry that "these may be small potatoes to you or me or our Black friend you quote."
49. See Grace Lee and Jimmy Boggs to Carol and Ping, December 4, 1974. The Boggses were not disconnected from prisoners' struggles, despite what their response might suggest. For example, in April 1973 James Boggs gave a lecture entitled "Socialism, Communism and Capitalism: The Dynamics of Revolution" at Milan Federal Prison as part of a nearly four-hour program with several question-and-discussion periods. He was also in contact with incarcerated people at the prison. See Box 19, Folder 9, JGLBP.
50. Garrett Felber and Stephen Ward, "The Argument Is Far from Over," *Radical History Review* no. 146 (May 2023): 109.
51. Berrigan response to Boggses, December 12, 1974, Box 19, Folder 9, JGLBP
52. Berrigan response to Boggses, December 12, 1974, Box 19, Folder 9, JGLBP. See copy of Boggses letter to Berrigan, sent to Dennis Jacobsen with handwritten note at the top by Daniel Berrigan: "I answered this which I thought pretty disgraceful." See Box 19, Folder 2, CPA
53. The quotation marks around humane are not a direct quotation, but the author's air quotes emphasize the fallacy of this formulation.
54. See Burton, *Tip of the Spear*, 79–149.
55. Martin Sostre, "The New Prisoner," *North Carolina Central Law Journal* 4, no. 2 (Spring 1973): 243–44.
56. Kathie Streem, "Martin Sostre: Out of Jail but Still a Freedom Fighter," *Berkeley Barb*, February 27 - March 4, 1976, 7.

57. *Free Martin Sostre: Letters and Quotations by Martin Sostre* (Northampton, MA: Mother Jones Press, 1975), 13.
58. Ping Ferry wrote Berrigan: "C. and I have been reading the debate with the Boggses. And feel as I always felt after reading S. Court decisions: agreed with both minority and majority opinions more often than not. Anyway here's something for Sostre." A check for $2,000 was attached. Ferry to Berrigan, December 20, 1974, Box 19, Carol Bernstein Ferry and W. H. Ferry Papers, Ruth Lilly Special Collections and Archives, Indiana University-Purdue University-Indianapolis. See also Berrigan to Jacobsen, n.d., Box 19, Folder 2, CPA.
59. Antonio Rodríguez, interview with author.
60. Dennis Jacobsen remembered, "I can't imagine there was anyone on the stand who didn't know a guard or had a relative who was a guard." Dennis Jacobsen, interview with author, May 31, 2022.
61. Jennifer Colver, "Issues Vital in Sostre Trial," *Press-Republican*, March 1, 1975.
62. Jenny recounted stories of segregated water fountains in San Juan, and Frank frequently derided the "capitalistas." Despite being excluded from the unions for his skin color, Frank valued organized labor and instilled a "very healthy disregard for rich people" in his children. Antonio and Sylvia Rodríguez, interviews with author, and Sylvia Rodríguez, July 16, 2022.
63. Marjorie remembered she and her siblings being the only Black students in their high school. Miller, interview with author.
64. Antonio Rodríguez, interview with author.
65. "Jail Mail Censorship Remarks Untrue, Sostre Panel Says," *Press Republican*, May 4, 1974.
66. According to Rodríguez, Sostre "covered up his initial surprise and said, 'Oh, brother, I see you have your collar on.' " Rodríguez, interview with author.
67. Branagan, interview with author.
68. *New World Notes*, vols. 1–6, in author's possession, courtesy of Janine Migden-Ostranger.
69. Marlene Nadle, "The Convictions of a Man of Conviction," *Village Voice*, March 24, 1975, 10.
70. Neal Browne, "Students, Apathy, and the Case of Martin Sostre," *Cardinal Points*, November 7, 1974.
71. Cornel Reinhart, "To the Editor," *Cardinal Points*, November 7, 1974.
72. Antonio Rodríguez, "Sostre Trial Starts Feb. 4," *Cardinal Points*, January 30, 1975.
73. Marjorie Miller remembered, "When it got real close to the trial and the lawyers came up, that was a real interesting and fun time, I've got to tell you, watching these radical people pour into Plattsburgh." Miller, interview with author.
74. Miller, interview with author.
75. Rodríguez, interview with author.
76. Bill Woods, "Father Berrigan Holds Press Mtg."; Christal LaBrie, "Justice for Martin Sostre," *Cardinal Points*, February 13, 1975.

77. One article mentioned at least nine jurors excluded for their relationship to prison staff. See Sue Botsford, "Feinberg Denies Dismiss Motion," *Press Republican*, February 6, 1975; and Sue Botsford, "9 Women, 3 Men on Sostre Jury," *Press-Republican*, February 14, 1975.
78. Others helping with legal support were associated with the Communist Workers Party. At least one of these was Dale Sampson, whose husband Bill was later murdered in the 1979 Greensboro Massacre in North Carolina. Jacobsen, interview with author.
79. Botsford, "Feinberg Denies"; "9 Women, 3 Men."
80. Joel Ray, "The (Latest) Trial of Martin Sostre," March 13, 1975, *WIN* magazine, 9, 22.
81. Nadle, "Convictions of a Man of Conviction," 12.
82. Botsford, "9 Women, 3 Men on Sostre Jury." For a full list of the 160 potential jurors with their name, age, occupation, education, residence, and experience as a juror, see "Trial Jurors," County Court—February 1975, in *People v. Sostre*, Clerk's Office, Clinton County Court.
83. Nadle, "Convictions of a Man of Conviction," 10, 12.
84. Sue Botsford, "Jury Finds Sostre Guilty; 12 Arrested in Outcry," *Press-Republican*, February 28, 1975. See also Louis Cafone, interview with author, May 10, 2022; and Joel Ray, interview with author, April 21, 2022. For quote, see Elizabeth Fink, Brief for Appellant, Argument, 4, *People v. Sostre*, Clinton County Clerk's Office.
85. Nadle, "Convictions of a Man of Conviction," 10. Mr. Magoo was a fictional character who originated in a cartoon in 1949 and was featured in an animated film in 1995. He is depicted as an elderly, wealthy, nearsighted man and characterized by his stubbornness and frustrations stemming from his difficulty seeing.
86. Nadle, "Convictions of a Man of Conviction," 10.
87. Jacobsen, interview with author.
88. Partial Proceedings, February 27, 1975, *People v. Sostre*, Clinton County Clerk's Office.
89. Antonio Rodríguez, email message to author, September 18, 2022.
90. Cafone, interview with author.
91. Gordon Stewart, "Sostre Convicted in Plattsburgh," *Hill News* (St. Lawrence University), March 6, 1975, 1, 6. In a conversation from jail, Wielopolski reportedly said that the conviction outraged him more than his own, which was a five-year sentence for a joint.
92. Partial transcript, Exhibit B, *People v. Sostre,* Clinton County Clerk's Office. In Stewart's account, Wielopolski said "you mother f . . . g pig." See Stewart, "Sostre Convicted in Plattsburgh." As Elizabeth Fink pointed out, the partial transcript of the trial was "sketchy, wholly incomplete, and grossly inaccurate in the parts that it attempts to report. It was evidently reconstructed in some part from the court reporter's memory, since he was not taking notes, but was standing and watching the events in the courtroom." See Brief for Appellant,

Statement of Facts, 1, *People v. Sostre*, Clinton County Clerk's Office. I tried to locate the remainder of the transcript beyond this final portion, but according to the chief county clerk, the court stenographer used an idiosyncratic shorthand and later was imprisoned and died in prison. Therefore, this transcript and others by the stenographer are unable to be reconstructed.

93. Stewart, "Sostre Convicted in Plattsburgh."
94. Cafone, interview with author.
95. Clinton county courthouse materials, 46.
96. Botsford, "Jury Finds Sostre Guilty"; Stewart, "Sostre Convicted in Plattsburgh." The full transcript is reconstructed in Partial Proceedings, February 27, 1975, 20–27.
97. Sylvia Rodríguez, interview with author.
98. Elizabeth Lapenne, interview with author, November 4, 2022.
99. Antonio Rodríguez, interview with author.
100. Nadle, "Convictions of a Man of Conviction," 12.
101. "Martin Sostre Beaten," *White Lightning* 27 (November–December 1974): 3. The story he recounted to Dennis Jacobsen was that his back door was smashed in with an ax and his legal file destroyed. "They were looking for the key affidavits." Jimmy Sullivan to Dennis Jacobsen, November 16, 1974, Box 19, Folder 9, JGLBP.
102. Sullivan to Jacobsen, November 16, 1974.
103. Another student wrote, "I saw injustice on February 27, 1975 in the Clinton County Courtroom, and if I must I will testify in court on that statement." Dorothy LaRose, "Fellow Students," *Cardinal Points*, March 6, 1975.
104. "Martin is Free!," *New World Notes* 1, no. 5.
105. Joel Ray, "Martin Sostre and the Lawlessness of the Law," *Courier and Freeman*, April 8, 1975.
106. Reel-to-reel tape recording of WTSC FM Potsdam, "Speakout" radio broadcast, April 15, 1975, with Ed Dubinsky, Joel Ray, Karen St. Hilaire, and Joan Lomba, in author's possession, courtesy of Andrzeja Axt.
107. WTSC FM Potsdam, "Speakout."
108. WTSC FM Potsdam, "Speakout."
109. Sostre to Dubinsky, April 23, 1975.
110. Sostre to Dubinsky, May 8, 1975, in author's possession, courtesy of Hania Dubinsky.
111. Sostre to Dubinsky, likely August 27, 1975 (this date is mentioned as the most recent letter in Dubinsky's response on September 12, 1975), and the first page is missing. In author's possession, courtesy of Hania Dubinsky.
112. WTSC FM Potsdam, "Speakout."
113. Clarence Mohr and Joseph Gordon, *Tulane: The Emergence of a Modern University, 1945–1980* (Baton Rouge: Louisiana State University Press, 2001), 363.
114. Mohr and Gordon, *Tulane*, 364; Ed Dubinsky to Martin Sostre, March 21, 1975, in author's possession, courtesy of Anne Heidenreich.
115. Dubinsky to Sostre, March 21, 1975.

116. Clarence Doucet, "Dubinsky Considers Himself to Be an SDS Revolutionary," undated interview in Doucet, *Shapes of Protest* (New Orleans: Times-Picayune Publishing, 1969). These were unpaginated reproductions of articles which originally appeared in the *Times-Picayune* between May 23 and June 1, 1969.
117. Most of this is recounted in Dubinsky to Sostre, March 21, 1975.
118. Ewa Dubinsky, email to author, October 7, 2024.
119. Undated (ca. early 1970s) autobiographical essay by Axt that she included with her application to a correspondence college to study psychology, in author's possession, courtesy of Hania Dubinsky.
120. Andrzeja Axt, message to author, with assistance from Murray Hirsch, May 3, 2022; autobiographical essay by Axt (n.d., ca. early 1970s).
121. Dubinsky to Sostre, March 21, 1975.
122. Ed Dubinsky to Martin Sostre, April 10, 1975, in author's possession, courtesy of Anne Heidenreich.
123. Sostre to Dubinsky, May 15, 1975.
124. Even this was debated within the groups, and exceptions were made. See Ed Dubinsky to Martin Sostre, July 10, 1975, in author's possession, courtesy of Anne Heidenreich.
125. "Establishing speedy and efficient communications is one of the main problems I am trying to get the Plattsburgh Defense Committee to solve," Sostre wrote Joel Ray in March 1975. See Sostre to Ray, March 18, 1975, in author's possession, courtesy of Joel Ray.
126. Sostre to Dubinsky, May 2, 1975, in author's possession, courtesy of Hania Dubinsky.
127. Dubinsky was struck by the rapidity with which the committees were able to change the date of the demonstration and how enthusiastic the various committees were about the rally. See Dubinsky to Sostre, April 10, 1975.
128. Sostre urged that the "demo should zero in on the sole issue of demanding a pardon or commutation of sentence." Sostre to Dubinsky, March 27, 1975, in author's possession, courtesy of Hania Dubinsky.
129. Franz Leichter, interview with author, August 8, 2022.
130. That April 1975, Leichter wrote Ramsey Clark, Basil Patterson, and Charlie Rangel to says that he was holding off on his letter for Sostre, which they had agreed to sign together. He was discussing it with Judah Gribetz, counsel to Carey, and Gribetz "promised to consider how best to handle this matter and to bring it before the Governor and let me know promptly." Franz Leichter to Clark, Patterson, and Rangel, April 23, 1975, in author's possession, courtesy of Liz and Vinny Sostre.
131. Ed Dubinsky to Martin Sostre, April 25, 1975, in author's possession, courtesy of Anne Heidenreich.
132. Ed Dubinsky to Martin Sostre, May 6, 1975, in author's possession, courtesy of Anne Heidenreich.
133. Andrzeje Dubinsky to Martin Sostre, June 6, 1975, in author's possession, courtesy of Hania Dubinsky. Axt did not yet have her US citizenship; to avoid being

deported, she kept a low profile and did not write him. In the letter, she wrote: "I have written thousands of letters to you in my head since you entered into my—our—life. This one will probably be one of the unsent ones. . . . Maybe when I will finally be able to officially write to you I will send all these notes."

134. Dubinsky to Sostre, July 10, 1975.
135. Dubinsky to Sostre, April 10, 1975.
136. Dubinsky to Sostre, May 6, 1975.
137. Sostre to Dubinsky, May 8, 1975.
138. Martin Sostre to Ed Dubinsky, May 25, 26, and 28, 1975, courtesy of Hania Dubinsky.
139. Damali Bashira, "Martin Sostre: What Is Justice?," *Encore American and Worldwide News*, October 6, 1975, 13; "Sostre Sentenced," *Journal* (Ogdensburg, NY), June 4, 1975; "4 More Years in Prison," *Ithaca Journal*, June 4, 1975; Sharon Fischer, "Sostre Sentenced Again," *Militant*, July 18, 1975; Joel Ray, "Sostre Draws 0–4 Years," *Courier and Freeman*, June 10, 1975.
140. Axt to Sostre, June 6, 1975. Dubinsky reported to Sostre that the Potsdam group returned from Plattsburgh with "renewed and strengthened dedication to the cause." Ed Dubinsky to Martin Sostre, June 10, 1975, in author's possession, courtesy of Anne Heidenreich.
141. Sostre to St. Hilaire, June 28, 1975.
142. Joe Shapiro, "Revolutionary Politics in the '70s," *Introspect: The Carleton Journal of American Culture* 2, no. 1 (Spring 1976): 6. Although Judge Feinberg originally ordered Sostre to be returned to Clinton, he was overruled by Judge James Oakes, who returned Sostre to federal custody in New York City. See "Demonstrators at Carey Talk, *Courier and Freeman*, June 17, 1975.
143. "Demonstrators at Carey Talk."
144. "Albany Sit-In," *Ithaca Journal*, June 20, 1975; Rev. Berrigan Sits in Protest," *Daily News*, June 20, 1975. See also Martin Sostre to Ed Dubinsky, June 14, 1975, in author's possession, courtesy of Hania Dubinsky. Assemblywoman Marie Runyon recalled that it was the "first and only time that [Carey's] office had been sat in, in Albany" and that "everybody, of course, was pretty mad." See Marie Runyon, interview with Joe Shapiro, 1976 (date unknown), in author's possession, courtesy of Joe Shapiro.
145. "Berrigan, Carey Discuss Clemency," *Democrat and Chronicle*, June 24, 1975.
146. Press Release for the Committee to Free Martin Sostre, n.d., in author's possession, courtesy of Kree Arvanitas.
147. "Martin Sostre," *Out Front*, September 8, 1975, 7.
148. For example, Tesi Kohlenberg, another part-time staff person of the committee, wrote the other committees offering to put together a newsletter on all defense committee activities to keep them up to date on what the others were doing. "That could be done quite easily out of this office." Undated letter from Tesi Kohlenberg, Kree Papers, 7303.
149. For example, see the partial list of supporters on letterhead from the Canton-Potsdam defense committee, enclosed with a letter from June 26,

1975, in author's possession, courtesy of Kree Arvanitas. See also list on letter to friends of the Committee to Free Martin Sostre from Joan Baez, Dick Gregory, and Ramsey Clark, in author's possession, courtesy of Kree Arvanitas

150. Letter to friends of the Committee to Free Martin Sostre from Joan Baez, Dick Gregory, and Ramsey Clark.
151. Jerry Ross to Sharon Fischer, October 10 (n.d., likely 1972), in author's possession, courtesy of Jerry Ross.
152. Derrick Morrison, "Amnesty Int'l Backs Sostre," *Militant*, October 12, 1973, 15.
153. *Amnesty International Annual Report, 1974–1975* (London: Amnesty International Publications, 1975), 78–79.
154. Paul Browne, "Carey to Consider Sostre Clemency," *Watertown Daily Times*, June 24, 1975. Many of these letters can be found in the Executive Clemency file of the Hugh Carey Papers at the New York State Archives. Religious and academic communities were the most common, along with several messages from sections of Amnesty International and its members both inside and outside the United States.
155. Letter to Friends of the Committee to Free Martin Sostre from Tesi Kohlenberg, n.d., in author's possession, courtesy of Kree Arvanitas. Quote is from Press Release for the Committee to Free Martin Sostre, undated.
156. Daniel Berrigan to Dennis Jacobsen, November 1975, Box 19, Folder 2, CPA.
157. Dubinsky to Sostre, June 10, 1975.
158. Ed Dubinsky to Martin Sostre, July 24, 1975, in author's possession, courtesy of Anne Heidenreich.
159. Dubinsky to Sostre, June 10, 1975.
160. Ed Dubinsky to Martin Sostre, June 29, 1975; Dubinsky to Sostre, June 10, 1975, in author's possession, courtesy of Anne Heidenreich.
161. Dubinsky to Sostre, July 24, 1975.
162. Ed Dubinsky to Martin Sostre, July 25, 1975, in author's possession, courtesy of Anne Heidenreich.
163. Ed Dubinsky to Martin Sostre, October 7, 1975, in author's possession, courtesy of Anne Heidenreich.
164. Emily Thuma, *All Our Trials: Prisons, Policing, and the Feminist Fight to End Violence* (Urbana: University of Illinois Press, 2019), 15–17.
165. Thuma, *All Our Trials*, 16. See also Christina Greene, *Free Joan Little: The Politics of Race, Sexual Violence, and Imprisonment* (Chapel Hill: University of North Carolina Press, 2022).
166. Dubinsky to Sostre, July 24, 1975 and "Action for Forgotten Women," *New World Notes* 1, no. 1 (Fall 1975): 5.
167. Thuma, *All Our Trials*, 19, 22.
168. Dubinsky to Sostre, October 7, 1975.
169. "New Developments in Case of Reformer Martin Sostre," *Courier and Freeman*, October 7, 1975.

170. See "Martin Sostre Week: Dec. 1–8" flyer, in *New World Notes* 1, no. 4.
171. Betsy Boehner and Tesi Kohlenberg, letter to supporters, December 19, 1975, in author's possession, courtesy of Joe Shapiro. The support from Sakharov was arranged through Paul Mayer, who met him at the 1973 World Peace Congress in Moscow. See James Wechsler, "For Martin Sostre," Committee to Free Martin Sostre, in author's possession, courtesy of Joe Shapiro.
172. Wechsler, "For Martin Sostre."
173. "Christmas Vigil to Free Martin Sostre at Carey's Office," Press Release, December 17, 1975, in author's possession, courtesy of Joe Shapiro.
174. Boehner and Kohlenberg, letter to supporters, December 19, 1975.
175. David Vidal, "The Prison Attorney," *New York Times*, December 25, 1975.
176. Martin Sostre, interview with *Abraham Aig*, WBAI radio, December 24, 1974, in author's possession, courtesy of Steven Fischler.

11. Minimum Security

1. Causewell Vaughan, "Freed by Gov, Sostre Quits Green Haven," *Daily News*, February 10, 1976.
2. Quoted in notes by journalist Joe Shapiro from Martin Sostre's press conference upon his release, February 10, 1976; and in Paul Mayer, "Martin Sostre Speaks to the Press," *WIN* magazine, February 26, 1976, 18. As Daniel Berrigan wrote Dennis Jacobsen, "A virtual miracle has occurred, given the world." Berrigan to Jacobsen, January 12, 1976, Collection on Peace Activism (CPA), Box 19, Folder 2, Correspondence Daniel Berrigan, 1973–1976, Special Collections and Archives, DePaul University Library.
3. Claude Marks, "Ruchell Cinque Magee Was Just Released from Prison after 67 Years Caged!," *San Francisco Bay View*, August 4, 2023; Judy Greenspan, "Ruchell Magee Wins His Freedom After 67 Years in Prison," *Workers World*, August 2, 2023.
4. Joseph Shapiro, "Martin Sostre Is Out of Prison but His Struggle Continues" (master's thesis, Columba University, 1976), 30. The *New York Times* quoted him slightly differently: "I am not going to say I am not bitter, although that may be fashionable." David Vidal, "A Freed Activist Sees No Change," *New York Times*, February 15, 1976.
5. Shapiro notes, February 10, 1976.
6. Vidal, "The Prison Attorney."
7. Martin Sostre, "What Is to Be Done?," March 9, 1976, Black Mass Communications Project Collection, Robert S. Cox Special Collections and University Archives Research Center, UMass-Amherst.
8. As Ruthie Wilson Gilmore explains: "The problem, in other words, is prison—and therefore the entire society." Ruth Wilson Gilmore and James Kilgore, "Some Reflections on Prison Labor," *Brooklyn Rail*, June 2019, https://brooklynrail.org/2019/06/field-notes/Some-Reflections-on-Prison-Labor.
9. Shapiro, "Martin Sostre Is Out," 33.

10. Shapiro notes, February 10, 1976. This is quoted slightly differently in Causewell Vaughn, "Freed Prisoner Vows," February 15, 1976 and Vidal, "A Freed Activist Sees No Change," *New York Times*, February 15, 1976.
11. Shapiro notes, February 17, 1976, in author's possession, courtesy of Joe Shapiro.
12. Carlito Rovira, interview with author, June 2, 2021.
13. "The Open Road Interview with Martin Sostre," by David Spaner, *Open Road*, Summer 1976, 13.
14. Martin Sostre, "Armed Struggle Natural Response to Fascist Rule," Folder 2, Subject Vertical Files, Civil Liberties—Blacks—Black Nationalism—Sostre, Martin, Labadie Collection, University of Michigan, Special Collections.
15. Michael Katz notes that "by 1970, more Americans lived in suburbs than in cities or rural areas." See Katz, *Why Don't American Cities Burn?* (Philadelphia: University of Pennsylvania Press, 2012), 31. Between 1967 and 1974, the number of Fortune 500 companies headquartered in New York City declined by 30 percent, relocating to suburbs. Such disinvestment was framed as resulting from the failures of liberal governance. See Benjamin Holtzman, *The Long Crisis: New York City and the Path to Neoliberalism* (New York: Oxford University Press, 2021), 12.
16. Kim Phillips-Fein, *Fear City: New York's Fiscal Crisis and the Rise of Austerity Politics* (New York: Metropolitan, 2017), 1–2.
17. Shapiro notes, February 20, 1976, in author's possession, courtesy of Joe Shapiro.
18. Joe Shapiro, "Activist Sostre Paroled; Now Pleads Others' Cases," *Columbia Press*, February 20, 1976.
19. Shapiro notes, February 17, 1976.
20. Paul Hofmann, "State Office Site Picked in Harlem; Complex Planned," *New York Times*, December 7, 1966.
21. As Michaux recalled, Governor Rockefeller told him, "We can't lose this collection." Sybil Baker, "Cover Promised for His Books," *Daily News* (New York), January 8, 1974.
22. The president of the Harlem Urban Development Corporation affirmed, "We take very seriously the governor's assurance to Mr. Michaux, and I have no question that it will be honored by Gov. Wilson." Sybil Baker, "Cover Promised for His Books," *Daily News* (New York), January 8, 1974.
23. "Eviction Fought in Harlem," January 6, 1974, *Daily News* (New York).
24. "Harlem Bookseller Michaux Dies," *Daily News* (New York), August 27, 1976. In a nearly full-circle moment, Runyon even suggested that Sostre open his new bookstore in the space vacated by Michaux's. See Marie Runyon, interview with Joe Shapiro, 1976 (exact date unknown), in author's possession, courtesy of Joe Shapiro.
25. "I came down from Buffalo just before I was framed," he told Joe Shapiro later. Shapiro notes, February 17, 1976.
26. James Baldwin interview, *Esquire*, July 1, 1968. I am grateful to Derecka Purnell for pointing me to this interview.

27. Marie Runyon, interview with Shapiro.
28. Shapiro notes, February 17, 1976.
29. Sostre, "What Is to Be Done?"
30. "Press Release from Black and Puerto Rican Student Community," *CUNY Digital History Archive*, https://cdha.cuny.edu/items/show/6932. See also Conor Tomás Reed, *New York Liberation School: Study and Movement for the People's University* (Brooklyn: Common Notions, 2023), 54–55.
31. Stephen Brier and Michael Fabricant, *Austerity Blues: Fighting for the Soul of Public Higher Education* (Baltimore: Johns Hopkins University Press, 2016), 84.
32. Conor Tomás Reed, "Hot City: Realizing the Dream of a Liberation University," *Verso Blog*, September 8, 2020. https://www.versobooks.com/blogs/news/4848-hot-city-realizing-the-dream-of-a-liberation-university.
33. Reed, *New York Liberation School*, 54.
34. Newspaper clipping (title unknown), *City PM*, May 17, 1976, Mixed Materials 1, Folder 24, Martin Sostre Collection (MSC), University of Michigan Library (Special Collections Research Center).
35. Dale Brichta, "200 Attend Anti-Cutback Rally; Retrenchment Proposal Debated," *Campus*, April 30, 1976, Materials 1, Folder 24, MSC.
36. Advertisement for "Tribute to Ethel and Julius Rosenberg," *Daily World*, June 5, 1976.
37. Michael Meeropol, interview with author, June 28, 2021.
38. José Pérez, "1,000 at U.N. Demand: 'Free the Five!,'" *Militant*, November 26, 1976, 20, 30; José Pérez, "Prisoner's Daughter Tours U.S. Cities," *Militant*, December 16, 1977. See also Shapiro notes, April 8, 1976, in author's possession, courtesy of Joe Shapiro.
39. Sostre, "What Is to Be Done?"
40. "Angela Davis, Martin Sostre to Speak at Rally," *Amsterdam News*, July 31, 1976.
41. "Angela Davis Here to Gain Support for Rally," *Amsterdam News*, August 14, 1976.
42. "Open Road Interview with Martin Sostre," 28.
43. Mayer, "Martin Sostre Speaks to the Press."
44. Kathie Streem, "Martin Sostre: Out of Jail but Still a Freedom Fighter," *Berkeley Barb*, February 27 - March 4, 1976, 7.
45. Sostre, "What Is to Be Done?"
46. "Open Road Interview with Martin Sostre," 28
47. It is significant that his other longtime supporter, Sharon Fischer, was not present. As Dan Berrigan said of Fischer that evening: "She's the hero of this whole deal and she's not here. Ten years of work she put in." Shapiro notes that he saw Best at the conference. Shapiro notes, February 10, 1976, and April 8, 1976.
48. "Militant speech," *Massachusetts Daily Collegian*, March 9, 1976.
49. Penny Schwartz, "Che Lumumba School," *Out Front*, May 1976, 8.
50. Sostre, "What Is to Be Done?," March 9, 1976.
51. Schwartz, "Che Lumumba School."
52. Sostre, "What Is to Be Done?," March 9, 1976.

53. For more on this struggle, see the 765 kV Line Protest Collection, MSS Coll. No. 130, Special Collections, St. Lawrence University Library.
54. Joel Ray, interview with author, April 21, 2022.
55. Jim Detjen, "Zap! Concern Grows over Possible Damage Produced by High Power Electric Lines," *Poughkeepsie Journal*, January 19, 1975.
56. It was later recommended this be extended to 550 feet due to the possible biological effects to humans chronically exposed to the lines. "What the North Country Needs to Know about Nuclear Power Plants," pamphlet, 11, 765 kV Line Protest Collection, MSS Coll. No. 130, Box 1, Special Collections, St. Lawrence University Library. See also materials and Joel Ray, "Hazards of High Wires," *Nation*, February 18, 1978, 179.
57. Ray, interview with author.
58. Joann Palmer Frear, "Though Out of Prison, Sostre Still 'Confined' by Society's Ills," *Watertown Daily Times*, March 31, 1976.
59. "Sostre Committee to Seek More Supporters," *Courier and Freeman*, September 16, 1975; flyer for talk at SUCP Union, in Mixed Materials 1, Folder 19, MSC.
60. "North Country Defense Committee: Who We Are. What We Do," pamphlet, 3, 765 kV Line Protest Collection, Box 1.
61. Ray, "Hazards of High Wires."
62. Ray, interview with author.
63. "I only have 10 months to wait . . . to become an American. I never thought I would be counting the days to that moment. Now it became a moment when I will be allowed to do what I feel want to. That's stupid. I won't really be allowed to. But they will be able to put me in jail instead of deporting me." Andrzeje Dubinsky to Martin Sostre, June 6, 1975, in author's possession, courtesy of Hania Dubinsky.
64. "Dear Women Together," Andrzeje Dubinsky, *Women Together* 2, no. 2 (June–July 1977): 12.
65. Dubinsky, "Dear Women Together."
66. "Open Road Interview with Martin Sostre," 28.
67. For the original 1974 manifesto, see the website Ganienkeh Territory, http://www.ganienkeh.net. For more on Ganienkeh, see Gail H. Landsman, *Sovereignty and Symbol: Indian-White Conflict at Ganienkeh* (Albuquerque: University of New Mexico Press, 1988).
68. Ewa Dubinsky, email to author, October 21, 2022.
69. "Sostre Vows Extremism in New Store," *Buffalo Evening News*, May 1, 1976.
70. Advertisement for Human Rights Seminar with Martin Sostre and Don Luce, *Spectrum*, April 28, 1976.
71. Ed Powell, "An Open Letter to Martin Sostre on His Return to Buffalo, Mayday 1976," Box 13, Folder 12, Elwin H. Powell Papers, University Archives, State University of New York at Buffalo.
72. "Sostre Decries Government Terror and Repression," *Spectrum*, May 3, 1976.
73. Best passed away in 2003. See "Deaths: Anglesey, Zoe," *New York Times*, February 14, 2003.

74. Melanie Best, interview with author, September 8, 2022.
75. Best, interview with author.
76. Liz Sostre, interview with author, March 30, 2022.
77. Liz Sostre, interview with author, March 30, 2022.
78. Liz Sostre, interview with author, March 30, 2022.
79. Liz Sostre, interview with author, March 30, 2022.
80. "It All Started With Attica . . . ," History of Prisoners' Legal Services of New York, https://plsny.org/pls-history.
81. Claudia Angelos, interview with author, October 20, 2022.
82. Lynn Barclay, interview with author, November 1, 2022.
83. Angelos, interview with author.
84. Liz Sostre, interview with author, March 30, 2022.
85. Ed Dubinsky to Martin Sostre, September 12, 1975, in author's possession, courtesy of Anne Heidenreich.
86. Roberta Gold, *When Tenants Claimed the City: The Struggle for Citizenship in New York City Housing* (Urbana: University of Illinois Press, 2014), 242.
87. Gold, *When Tenants Claimed the City*, 244.
88. As Gold writes, "The most distinctive development in housing rights during this period was a hybrid of radical and insider strategies: the establishment of legalized tenant control over deteriorated buildings. This innovation, created by tenant advocates and sympathetic officials, build on precedents set by tenants direct-action community campaigns of the 1960s and 1970s." Gold, *When Tenants Claimed the City*, 251.
89. Annemarie Sammartino, *Freedomland: Co-op City and the Story of New York* (Ithaca: Cornell University Press, 2022), 3–5. Sammartino points out elsewhere, "It was not actually a rent strike . . . [as] Co-op City's over 50,000 residents were technically cooperators, or co-owners of the development." See "After the Rent Strike: Neoliberalism and Co-op City," *Gotham Center for New York City History blog*, April 3, 2018, https://www.gothamcenter.org/blog/after-the-rent-strike-neoliberalism-and-co-op-city. Sostre told Joe Shapiro, "I'm for tenants taking over like Co-op City." See Shapiro notes, February 17, 1976. Marie Runyon also said that Sostre supported the strike even before he got out of prison. See Runyon, interview with Shapiro.
90. Gold, *When Tenants Claimed the City*, 254–55.
91. Gold, *When Tenants Claimed the City*, 6.
92. Ed Sullivan, interview with author, October 17, 2022.
93. Gregory Watson, interview with author, February 5, 2024.
94. Ed Sullivan, interview with author, October 17, 2022.
95. The prison is now called East Jersey State Prison. The Rahway Prisoners Council was later referred to as the Rahway People's Council and emerged in the aftermath of the 1971 revolt. "Rahway Prisoners Stage Work Stoppage," *New York Times*, February 27, 1973; "Two Convicts Sue over Transfers," *New York Times*, July 10, 1974.
96. Sandy Shevack, interview with author, August 7, 2020.

12. Organizing the Community

1. Sandy Shevack, interview with author, August 7, 2020; Sandy Shevack, "A Revolutionary Life," panel discussion, March 22, 2023, available at https://www.martinsostre.com/sostreat100.
2. Shevack, interview with author, August 7, 2020.
3. Shevack, "A Revolutionary Life."
4. Shevack, interview with author, August 7, 2020; Shevack, "A Revolutionary Life."
5. Sandy Shevack, conversation with author, September 21, 2023.
6. "We're Not Distinct from the People as Revolutionaries," interview with Lorenzo Kom'boa Ervin, *Millennials are Killing Capitalism*, December 16, 2021, https://millennialsarekillingcapitalism.libsyn.com/were-not-distinct-from-the-people-as-revolutionaries-lorenzo-komboa-ervin-on-anarchism-and-the-black-revolution.
7. Peter Kirchheimer, interview with author, November 14, 2022.
8. "We're Not Distinct from the People as Revolutionaries."
9. Malcolm X, "Message to the Grassroots," in *Malcolm X Speaks*, ed. George Breitman (1966; repr., New York: Grove, 1990), 9.
10. William Boardman, "At Darthmouth, Black Militant Sostre Relates His Fight," *Rutland Herald*, June 5, 1977.
11. Vinny Sostre, interview with author, September 9, 2022.
12. Shevack, interview with author, August 7, 2020. Sostre agreed: "People dream. Sandy and I objectified our dream." See Linda Bakonyi, " 'These Babies Are Truly Our Future,' " *Record*, October 6, 1993.
13. David Leonard, "Day-Care Center Is Symbol of Progress," *Record*, December 11, 1991.
14. Diana Rojas, "A Pair of Grass-Roots Go-Getters," *Record*, April 3, 1995.
15. Patricia Alex, "Job Corps with a Leftist Slant," *Record*, August 8, 1989.
16. Sandy Shevack, interview with author, November 15, 2022.
17. Sandy Shevack, interview with author, November 15, 2022.
18. Sandy Shevack, email message to author, November 10, 2022.
19. Shevack, interview with author, August 7, 2020
20. A plaque of Chavis still hangs in the apartment building JEAP rehabilitated at 180 Third Street.
21. Douglas Martin, "Lucius Walker, Baptist Pastor for Peace, Dies at 80," *New York Times*, September 11, 2010.
22. Sandy Shevack, email to author, November 30, 2022. The Public Welfare Foundation was established in 1947 by Charles Edward Marsh, a millionaire newspaper publisher from Ohio and Oklahoma who moved to Texas, where he co-owned a big chain of local papers and invested in oil wells. Kressley had recently joined as a program officer and eventually became its executive director from 1991 to 2006.
23. Saturnino Sostre's baptism certificate lists his father as a carpenter. See baptism certificate in Mixed Materials 1, Folder 8, Martin Sostre Collection (MSC),

University of Michigan Library (Special Collections Research Center). I am grateful to Pamela Cappas-Toro, who generously translated this. See also Martin Sostre, interview with Vinny Sostre, 2002, exact date unknown. In author's possession, courtesy of Liz and Vinny Sostre.

24. Liz Sostre, comment in interview between Martin and Vinny Sostre, 2012, exact date unknown. In author's possession, courtesy of Liz and Vinny Sostre.
25. Sostre, interview with Vinny Sostre, 2012.
26. Michael Powell, "Radical's Progress: Another Building," *Record*, January 22, 1987; Shevack, interview with author, August 7, 2020.
27. Sharrieff Bugg, interview with author, July 22, 2020.
28. Shevack, interview with author, August 7, 2020.
29. Quahim Muhammad, interview with author, April 8, 2021.
30. Jerry Patterson, interview with author, March 9, 2022; Muhammad, interview with author.
31. Shevack, interview with author, August 7, 2020.
32. Muhammad, interview with author.
33. Shevack, interview with author, August 7, 2020.
34. Muhammad, interview with author.
35. Tim Sturdivant, interview with author, September 21, 2021.
36. Sturdivant, interview with author.
37. Pedro Pagan, interview with author, August 11, 2020.
38. Sturdivant, interview with author.
39. Robert McFadden, "Sostre, Inmate Activist, Is Seized as a Fugitive," *New York Times*, May 24, 1986.
40. Jill Jonnes, "Courts Are Naming Administrators Now to Better Buildings," *New York Times*, June 21, 1981.
41. Vinny Sostre, interview with author, September 9, 2022.
42. Sandy Shevack, interview with author, March 29, 2022.
43. Sandy Shevack, email to author, November 10, 2022. See also Linda Bakonyi, "Putting His Politics into Action," *Record*, May 19, 1993.
44. Shevack, interviews with author, August 7, 2020, and November 21, 2022.
45. Liz Sostre, interview with author, March 30, 2022.
46. *The Bomb* masthead, Mixed Materials 1, Folder 4, MSC.
47. Anderson Lee, interview with author, July 27, 2020.
48. Linda Bakonyi, "Warm-Hearted Man in a Cold World," *Record*, April 28, 1993.
49. Pat Wilks, "Booked: Famed Fugitive Seized in Law School Library," *New York Post*, May 23, 1986.
50. John Randazzo and James Harney, "He's in the Phone Book," *Daily News*, May 24, 1986.
51. "Rights Activist Cleared of Attempted Murder," *Newsday*, June 19, 1987.
52. Patterson, interview with author.
53. Shevack, conversation with author, March 29, 2022.
54. Judy Voccaola, "Group Rehabilitates Housing and Gives Youths a Skill," *News* (Paterson), October 24, 1986.

55. Judy Voccola, "Youth Job Program of Passaic Wins $1,000 from Foundation," *North Jersey Herald-News*, November 14, 1985.
56. Rojas, "Grass-Roots Go-Getters."
57. Shevack, email to author, November 10, 2022.
58. Shevack, interview with author, August 7, 2020; Shevack, email to author, November 11, 2022.
59. Osvaldo Moczo, interview with author, June 11, 2021.
60. Shevack, conversation with author, March 29, 2022.
61. "First Ward Republican Association," *Morning Call* (Paterson), September 30, 1902; "1st Ward GOP Women to Install," *Morning Call* (Paterson), February 2, 1902.
62. It is unclear if the preschool was located in the building at 103 North Main. See Barbara Nelson, "Paterson's Self-Help Unit," *New York Times*, April 30, 1972.
63. Joe Donnelly, "No Deal on Recreation Center," *Record*, November 22, 1987.
64. According to Shevack, the group wanted $20,000 on top of $18,000 in back taxes and outstanding debts. Representatives of Northside Forces claimed JEAP offered only $2,000 to repair the building and lease it back to them. See also Donnelly, "No Deal on Recreation Center."
65. Donnelly, "No Deal on Recreation Center."
66. Joe Donnelly, "Building a Base of Workers," *Record*, March 6, 1988.
67. For more, see Joan Kruckewitt, *The Death of Ben Linder: The Story of a North American in Sandinista Nicaragua* (New York: Seven Stories Press, 1999).
68. Shevack, interview with author, August 7, 2020.
69. Mike Fabey, "Lessons of the Trade: Youth Project Under Fire," *Herald-News*, April 9, 1989.
70. Fabey, "Lessons of the Trade: Youth Project Under Fire."
71. Patricia Alex, "Jobs Program Serves Up Politics: Under Fire for Leftist Proselytizing," *Record*, April 14, 1989.
72. Patricia Alex, "Job Corps with a Leftist Slant," *Record*, August 8, 1989.
73. Devin Leonard, "Day-Care Center Is Symbol of Progress," *Record*, December 11, 1991.
74. Sandy Shevack, conversation with author, September 21, 2023.
75. Leonard, "Day-Care Center Is Symbol of Progress," *Record*.
76. Bakonyi, " 'These Babies Are Truly Our Future.' "
77. Sandy Shevack, conversation with author, September 21, 2023.
78. Sandy Shevack, email message to author, September 26, 2023. Geronimo Pratt was a Black Vietnam veteran who joined the Black Panthers and was framed for murder by the FBI and held in solitary. He was exonerated because the prosecution knew he was elsewhere at the time and was eventually released in 1997. Black Panther Party members Wopashitwe Mondo Eyen we Langa and Ed Poindexter were convicted of murdering a police officer in Omaha, but the state withheld exculpatory evidence, and both were recommended for parole by the state board. Both died in prison, in 2016 and 2023 respectively.
79. Sandy Shevack, email to author, October 3, 2023. Berenson was an American

who was convicted of collaborating with the Túpac Amaru Revolutionary Movement (MRTA), a revolutionary organization in Peru.

80. Francisco Torres, interview with author, September 20, 2021.
81. A folder in Yuri Kochiyama's papers is called "The Collective, via Martin Sostre" and dated 1991–1992. It contains a list with the contact information for thirteen former political prisoners, presumably the "collective." Most of them are written in Sostre's distinctive handwriting with all capitalized letters. See Yuri Kochiyama Papers, Box 7, Rare Book and Manuscript Library, Columbia University Library.
82. Akinyele Umoja, "Maroon: Kuwasi Balagoon and the Evolution of Revolutionary New Afrikan Anarchism," *Science and Society* 79, vol. 2 (April 2015): 196–220.
83. Ashanti Alston, interview with author, August 11, 2020.
84. Torres, interview with author.
85. Alston, interview with author.
86. Memo, April 29, 1992, FBI File (100A-NY-225409).
87. Public Information Request Form, Redacted Special Agent to FBI Butte Information Technology Center, December 26, 1995, FBI File (100A-NY-225409).
88. An FBI Summary Report from January 1996 lists background checks on Sostre performed by the New York Joint Terrorist Task Force, FBI File (100-NY-154100).
89. Colleen Malleo, "The Impact of *Abbott v. Burke* on Community-Based Preschool Teachers' Education, Employability, and Pedagogical Competencies" (PhD diss., Seton Hall, 2007), 18. As Malleo explains, "High-quality programs were defined as those having a class size of no more than 15 students with a certified teacher and teacher assistant in each class."
90. Malleo, "The Impact of *Abbott v. Burke*," 6.
91. Malleo, "The Impact of *Abbott v. Burke*," 5.
92. For example, a teacher in an Abbott district was required to receive a bachelor of arts, specialized training in early childhood development, and a state certification in childhood education from preschool to third grade within four years (later extended to six years). Malleo, "The Impact of *Abbott v. Burke*," 6, 18.
93. For some examples, see Jennifer Nelson, *More than Medicine: A History of the Feminist Health Movement* (New York: New York University Press, 2015); Sandra Morgen, *Into Our Own Hands: The Women's Health Movement in the United States, 1969–1990* (New Brunswick, NJ: Rutgers University Press); Barbara Winslow, *Revolutionary Feminists: The Women's Liberation Movement in Seattle* (Durham, NC: Duke University Press, 2023); Judy Norsigian, "Our Bodies Ourselves and the Women's Health Movement in the United States: Some Reflections," *American Journal of Public Health* 109, no. 6 (June 2019): 844–46; Lisa Levenstein, *They Didn't See Us Coming: The Hidden History of Feminism in the Nineties* (New York: Basic Books, 2020); and Emily Thuma, *All Our Trials: Prisons, Policing, and the Feminist Fight to End Violence* (Urbana: University of Illinois Press, 2019).

94. In his interview with Vinny in 2012, he recounted that he had "saved enough money to get into business with someone in New Jersey," referring to Shevack and JEAP. In a manila envelope titled "Sandy's original letter to me re: greed," Sostre describes the "profit of the business" when referencing the day care. See Martin Sostre, interview with Vinny Sostre, 2012 and Mixed Materials 1, Folder 7, MSC.
95. Sandy Shevack, conversation with author, September 21, 2023.
96. Sandy Shevack, email to author, October 3, 2023.
97. Letter from Judge Susan Reisner, re: *JEAP, Inc. v Sostre*, Docket No. C-116-02, May 2, 2003, in author's possession, courtesy of Sandy Shevack.
98. Sandy Shevack, interview with author, August 7, 2020.
99. Shevack, interview with author, August 7, 2020.
100. Recorded conversation between Liz and Vinny Sostre, May 2021, in author's possession, courtesy of Liz and Vinny Sostre.
101. See Airtel, SAC, Buffalo to SAC, St. Louis, November 24, 1965, 2, in Martin Sostre FBI File (100-NY-154100).
102. Martin Sostre, interview with Vinny Sostre, 2012.
103. Leslie Pickering, interview with author, May 23, 2024.
104. "3 Arrested for Climbing Washington Monument," *El Paso Times*, September 6, 1999.
105. Pickering, interview with author.
106. Pickering, interview with author.
107. Pickering, interview with author and flyers for public forums, in author's possession, courtesy of Leslie Pickering.
108. "Frame-Up; The Imprisonment of Martin Sostre," flyer, March 28, 2005, in author's possession, courtesy of Leslie Pickering.
109. Pickering, interview with author.
110. Pickering, interview with author.
111. Vanessa Thomas, "Arson Has Devastating Effect on Community Food Programs," *Buffalo News*, August 12, 2005.
112. "Hours of Service, Staff Cut at Branches Staying Open," *Buffalo News*, October 30, 2005.
113. Pickering, interview with author.
114. Sandra Tan, "Arissa Taken Off Volunteer Project," *Buffalo News*, February 9, 2006; George Sax, "Precedence: Routine. Did the FBI Try to Crush a Leftist Group with the *Buffalo News*' Help?," *Artvoice*, September 10, 2015.
115. Pickering, interview with author.
116. Bruce Beyer, "FBI Trampling Rights of Bookstore Owners," *Buffalo News*, March 23, 2016
117. See advertisement for "Visual Liberation: A Summer Film/Talk Festival," in Brecht Forum Records, TAM 635; Box 15, Tamiment Library / Robert F. Wagner Labor Archives, New York University.
118. Kazembe Balagun, interview with author, December 6, 2022.
119. Balagun, interview with author.

120. Quoted in "A Tribune to Nuh Washington," The Jericho Movement, May 7, 2000, https://www.thejerichomovement.com/profile/albert-nuh-washington-1941-2000.
121. Martin Sostre to Sharon Fischer, n.d. (likely March 13, 1972), Box 13, Folder 13, Elwin H. Powell Papers, University Archives, State University of New York at Buffalo.

Printed in the USA
CPSIA information can be obtained
at www.ICGtesting.com
JSHW010832191124
73865JS00004B/11